Gender, Conflict and International Humanitarian Law

This book conducts a gendered critique of the 'principle of distinction' in international humanitarian law (IHL), with a focus on recent conflicts in Africa.

The 'principle of distinction' is core to IHL, and regulates who can and cannot be targeted in armed conflict. It states that *civilians* may not be targeted in attack, while *combatants* and those civilians *directly participating* in hostilities can be. The law defines what it means to be a combatant and a civilian, and sets out what behaviour constitutes direct participation. Close examination of the origins of the principle reveals that IHL was based on a gendered view of conflict, which envisages men as fighters and women as victims of war. Problematically, this view often does not accord with the reality in 'new wars' today in which women are playing increasingly active roles, often forming the backbone of fighting groups, and performing functions on which armed groups are highly reliant. Using women's participation in 'new wars' in Africa as a study, this volume critically examines the principle through a gendered lens, questioning the extent to which the principle serves to protect women in modern conflicts and how it fails them. By doing so, it questions whether the principle of distinction is suitable to effectively regulate the conduct of hostilities in new wars.

This book will be of much interest to students of international law, gender studies, African politics, war and conflict studies, and international relations.

Orly Maya Stern is a senior fellow with Harvard Humanitarian Initiative, USA. She is also a researcher, consultant and human rights lawyer, and holds a PhD in law from the London School of Economics, UK.

Routledge Studies in Humanitarian Action

Series editors:

Andrej Zwitter

University of Groningen

Joost Herman

University of Groningen

and

Hassan Bashir

Texas A&M University at Qatar

This book series offers an interdisciplinary platform for the study of issues pertaining to humanitarianism, such as humanitarian principles, humanitarian space, resilience, safety and security, international law of humanitarian action, to mention but a few. It aims to broaden understanding of these issues and their interconnection from different angles – such as politics, law, economics, philosophy, psychology, sociology – brought together under the heading of Humanitarian Studies.

Routledge Handbook of Human Rights and Disasters

Edited by Flavia Zorzi Giustiniani, Emanuele Sommario, Federico Casolari and Giulio Bartolini

Gender, Conflict and International Humanitarian Law

A Critique of the 'Principle of Distinction'

Orly Maya Stern

For more information about this series, please visit: www.routledge.com/Routledge-Studies-in-Humanitarian-Action/book-series/RSHA

Gender, Conflict and International Humanitarian Law

A Critique of the 'Principle of Distinction'

Orly Maya Stern

Routledge
Taylor & Francis Group
LONDON AND NEW YORK

First published 2019 by Routledge

2 Park Square, Milton Park, Abingdon, Oxfordshire OX14 4RN
52 Vanderbilt Avenue, New York, NY 10017

Routledge is an imprint of the Taylor & Francis Group, an informa business

First issued in paperback 2019

British Library Cataloguing-in-Publication Data
A catalogue record for this book is available from the British Library

Library of Congress Cataloging-in-Publication Data
A catalog record has been requested for this book

ISBN: 978-1-138-30770-4 (hbk)
ISBN: 978-0-367-48051-6 (pbk)

Typeset in Times New Roman
by Wearset Ltd, Boldon, Tyne and Wear

To the powerful women who raised me, guided me, cared for me, and fought for my right to do what I choose to do.

Contents

Acronyms

APs	Additional Protocols to the Geneva Conventions on the Laws of War
AP1	Additional Protocol 1 to the Geneva Conventions and relating to the Protection of Victims of International Armed Conflict
AP2	Additional Protocol 2 to the Geneva Conventions and relating to the Protection of Victims of Non-International Armed Conflict
AU	African Union
CA3	Common Article 3, common to the four Geneva Conventions
CAR	Central African Republic
CIL	Customary International Law
DDR	Disarmament, Demobilisation and Reintegration
DRC	Democratic Republic of Congo
ECOWAS	Economic Community of West African States
FRELIMO	The Mozambique Liberation Front (Frente de Libertação de Moçambique)
GCs	Geneva Conventions on the Laws of War
IAC	International Armed Conflict
ICC	International Criminal Court
ICJ	International Court of Justice
ICL	International Criminal Law
ICRC	International Committee of the Red Cross
ICTR	International Criminal Tribunal for Rwanda
ICTY	International Criminal Tribunal for the Former Yugoslavia
IDP	Internally Displaced Person
IHL	International Humanitarian Law
IHRL	International Human Rights Law
ISIS	Islamic State of Iraq and Syria, or Islamic State
LRA	Lord's Resistance Army, Uganda
MONUSCO	United Nations Organization Stabilization Mission in the Democratic Republic of the Congo
NIAC	Non-International Armed Conflict
POW	Prisoner of War
RUF	Revolutionary United Front, Sierra Leone

SCSL	Special Court for Sierra Leone
SPLM/A	South Sudan People's Liberation Movement/Army
UN	United Nations
UNAMIR	United Nations Assistance Mission for Rwanda

Introduction

When one pictures conflict in Africa, images come to mind of young men on the back of four-wheel drives, carrying machine guns, leering menacingly at those around them. In the background women run, shielding small children, fearful of approaching fighters. These images, repeated in the media, movies and literature, reinforce a pervasive and polarised view of men and women in conflict: men as ruthless fighters and women as their innocent victims.

While it is true that such scenes do take place – men *do* fight and innocent women *are* frequently terrorised in conflict – these pictures only tell a part of the story. Their uniform focus conceals an important narrative; that of the women who actively participate in war. Women today participate in armed struggles in a wide range of ways, with growing numbers of women serving in both state armed forces and non-state armed groups. Women also contribute to armed efforts from within civilian populations; from the women who live alongside army barracks selling goods and services, to the women who took to Twitter as a means of contributing to the Arab Spring, to those forced by rebel groups to carry looted goods on their backs, their means of participation vary widely. In some settings women take part in active combat; fighting on the frontlines with rebel bands, detonating explosives and participating in military offensives. However, more often women take on support roles for armed groups, serving as cooks, porters, trainers, intelligence operatives and medics. While some occupy roles that resemble the roles of men, women often contribute to conflicts in gender specific ways, with the tasks they undertake and the way they carry these out shaped by culturally determined notions about the roles that are appropriate for women to hold. Women's modes of participation in conflict are therefore diverse, taking differing forms to men – as well as to traditional notions of what it means to be a fighter in war.

Women's experiences in armed groups differ. Some women hold leadership positions, are empowered and respected. Others occupy the bottom rungs of fighting groups, systematically abused and exploited. Sometimes women's involvement is voluntary, spurred by the same ideology or motivations as their male counterparts. At other times their involvement is involuntary, with women abducted and forced to take part against their will. All of this creates a complex and little understood picture, which differs greatly from the prevailing picture of women in war.

International humanitarian law ("IHL" or the "laws of war")[1] is the body of law responsible for regulating armed conflict. One of the principal purposes of IHL is to provide protection from the worst excesses of violence. IHL contains a complex set of rules aimed at protecting both civilians and combatants. However, if these laws are based on incorrect or out-dated understandings of women's involvement in conflict – or on an outright failure to consider women altogether – this raises question about the extent to which they can hope to be successful in this role. It is therefore crucial to examine the laws, the underlying assumptions they are grounded on, and the effects these have for women in conflict.

Feminist scholars have begun to do just that, with a growing body of scholarship examining IHL from a gendered perspective. This body of scholarship, described in Chapter 4, demonstrates how the experiences of women in conflict are ignored and concealed by the laws of war, and points to the ways in which the laws favour the interests of men over women.

This book focuses on the gendered aspects of one part of IHL – the principle of distinction. The principle of distinction sets out the obligation on warring parties to distinguish between 'combatants' and 'civilians', and between civilians who are 'directly participating' in hostilities and those who are not. In terms of the principle, combatants and civilians directly participating in hostilities may be the lawful intended targets of attack, while civilians who are not directly participating may not be. A complex set of laws contained primarily in the 1949 Geneva Conventions[2] (GCs) and their 1979 Additional Protocols[3] (APs) delineate requirements and definitions aimed at distinguishing civilians and combatants, specifying the privileges and obligations that come with belonging to each category. Civilian status provides legal protection from being the intended target of attack. Combatancy, on the other hand, comes with a number of privileges, including 'prisoner of war' (POW) status on capture and the right to lawfully participate in hostilities, immune from prosecution for the – normally illegal – acts that constitute war fighting, in so long as these acts comply with IHL. In order to be eligible for such privileges, combatants need to abide by IHL and to visually distinguish themselves from civilians, with privileges therefore operating as incentive for compliance.

While mandating that fighters respect the distinction between civilians and combatants, the law also delineates the distinction, with demarcations that have been revisited and revised over the years. To function effectively the legal lines drawn need to correlate with realities on the ground, as dissonance may result in confusion and non-compliance – and the consequent deaths of more civilians.

IHL makes a distinction between international armed conflicts (IACs), those fought between states, and non-international armed conflicts (NIACs), those fought within states or between state and non-state actors. Different bodies of law apply to IACs and NIACs, discussed in Chapter 5. IACs are well regulated, covered by the four GCs and the First Additional Protocol (AP1). NIACs are regulated less, covered by only one Article of the GCs, Article 3, common to all four GCs, and by the Second Additional Protocol (AP2). In NIACs, less law and comparatively little analysis and consensus makes the legal situation incomprehensive, uncertain and, many would argue, wholly inadequate. However, this body of law is of particular practical importance given that today, the majority of the world's conflicts are NIAC in character, or at least partially so.

While in IACs the law provides for a distinction between combatants and civilians, in NIACs the legal situation is more complex. In these conflicts there is no combatant/civilian divide – the conventions do not provide for 'combatant' status in NIACs. State actors, who negotiated and drafted the IHL conventions, did not wish to grant privileged combatant status, as well as legal and political recognition, to armed groups fighting against them.[4] The treaties do not allow those in non-state groups 'combatant' status, thereby excluding them from this status and its privileges. However, despite not wanting to recognise them as privileged combatants, states still wanted the right to target those fighting against them. As such, the law stipulates that non-state fighters, while not qualifying as 'combatants', still lose their legal protection from attack as a result of their 'direct participation' in hostilities. During the time that civilians 'directly participate' they may be targeted.[5] Problematically, the law does not provide a clear definition of 'direct participation', the crucial threshold that renders individuals targetable. Adding to the problem is that excluding non-state actors from combatancy makes non state actor's participation in hostilities illegal, whether they abide by IHL or not – thereby removing a key incentive for compliance with IHL.[6]

The principle of distinction is one of the law's primary protection mechanisms. It is designed to provide guidance to fighters about who they can and cannot lawfully target. The principle seeks to strike a balance between military needs and humanitarian concerns; the idea is that if adhered to, fighters will be able to do what they need to do to win a war – targeting those who pose a threat to their military efforts – while preventing harm to those who pose no threat and are thereby deserving of protection.[7] The principle's clarity, workability and continued relevance are therefore of significant practical importance. A failure to distinguish between those who are and are not fighting – both in law and in fact – can lead to increased civilian deaths in conflict.

The problem is that in recent conflicts it has become harder to distinguish combatants and civilians. Certain groups operating in modern conflicts have pushed the definitional elements of the principle of distinction to the extreme, challenging the understood lines between fighters and non-fighters. Terrorists,[8] child soldiers[9] and private civilian contractors[10] are just some of the groups that blur the lines between civilian and combatant. Female combatants also challenge the understood distinction – and they form the primary focus of this work. At times legal categorisations look so different from the features of those fighting today's wars that they hardly provide meaningful classification at all.

The principle of distinction is failing in modern conflicts. Today the vast majority of casualties of conflict are civilians. Around the turn of the twentieth century, civilians made up 5 per cent of those killed in war. This rose to 15 per cent during World War One, up to 65 per cent in World War Two and up to 90 per cent in the conflicts of the 1990s.[11] This dramatic rise demonstrates the principle's failure to ensure that conflict deaths are restricted to combatants. Today many armed actors disregard the principle altogether – along with the rest of IHL – not using this to guide their actions and targeting decisions. While this is often for reasons that have little to do with the law, some of the problems lie with IHL itself – legal inconsistencies, ambiguities and contradictions abound, particularly in the laws pertaining to NIACs. What we are left with is a legal principle in crisis.

'New wars' is the term that has been coined for the wave of conflicts that have become prevalent in recent years.[12] New wars, described in Chapter 3, are complex, multifaceted conflicts marked by the asymmetrical distribution of resources, weaponry and technology. These conflicts blend international and internal elements, as well as political, economic and ideological motives. New wars present numerous challenges to the principle of distinction. In these conflicts, un-uniformed fighters disguise themselves within civilian populations, intentionally violating the law's requirement that fighters physically distinguish themselves. Rather than civilian deaths being a by-product of hostilities, in new wars the targeting of civilians forms a central strategy. The principle of distinction was designed to provide a compromise between the interests of warring parties in military victory and humanitarian aims, prohibiting killing seen as non-essential to military victory.[13] Yet, in new wars the principle stands directly in the way of a key strategy of conflict. IHL's traditional incentivising and balancing systems are therefore strained in their application in these conflicts.[14]

Further complicating the conflict landscape has been the rise of international terrorism. Actions taken by groups labelled as 'terrorist groups' – often scarcely discernible from rebel groups or traditional non-state armed groups – and military operations aimed at countering these, appear to be the most recent chapter in the development of armed conflict. How conflicts related to terrorism fall within new wars theory, is the subject of some discussion.[15] What is clear is that terrorism has also challenged IHL and its accepted definitions. Today, the label 'terrorism' appears to operate as justification for disregarding laws, restrictions and accepted practices. Here, gender gets lost even further, with talk of male Islamist fighters paused only occasionally to describe their female victims, or the women who join them as 'jihadists' wives'.

The laws of distinction purport to be gender-neutral, applying in a formally equal manner to men and women alike. IHL contains some specific protections for female combatants, revealing that the drafters acknowledged there could be female fighters. However, an examination of IHL reveals that these laws were based on a particular gendered view of conflict that envisaged men and women playing certain roles – men as combatants and women as civilians.[16] This book will show that these underlying notions do not correlate with conditions on the ground, in which the effects of conflict, while clearly gendered, are not necessarily gendered in the ways envisaged by those drafting the law. When the laws of distinction are applied to the many women whose experiences do not correspond with the gendered notions underlying the law, this has consequences – direct and indirect, beneficial and harmful – that are not clearly understood and to date have been given little attention.

Two separate yet interrelated problems are therefore at play: the first is that IHL and the principle of distinction in general do not function effectively in new wars; the second is that in particular, the laws do not adequately incorporate the positions undertaken by women in such wars or effectively ensure women's protection in these. These dual problems raise questions about the continued utility of the principle of distinction, both in general and in respect of women.

Overview of the research

This book examines the principle of distinction through a gender lens, questioning whether the principle is suitable to effectively regulate modern day armed conflict. It considers whether the principle of distinction contains provisions that effectively encompass the roles played by women in African conflicts, or, rather, whether the laws are based on incorrect or out-dated perceptions of women's involvement, failing to reflect the contemporary gendered reality and thereby failing to adequately regulate. The book considers whether the principle of distinction in its current formulation serves women in modern conflict, or whether it fails to do so, instead putting women at greater risk and disadvantage.

This focus of this book is on women actively participating in new wars in Africa, with the book seeking to demonstrate how the law applies to them; how they are classified and whether and how they are protected by the principle of distinction. Taking illustrative examples from a number of African conflicts, the book demonstrates that the principle of distinction is inherently gendered, that applications of the laws have gendered consequences and that these gendered consequences undermine the operation of the principle. By utilising provisions that fail to adequately incorporate the roles played by women, the law fails to reflect the ways that people actually participate in conflict. This reduces its effectiveness and its ability to do what it purports to do; namely to provide coherent regulation and protection of civilians in conflict.

The overarching question explored by this book is whether the principle of distinction is able to regulate modern conflicts. It considers this question by examining a few interwoven themes:

- One theme is women in armed conflict, with the research looking at women's differing forms of participation and protection needs in conflict and its aftermath, and the ways in which IHL affects women in particular ways. A feminist lens underpins this theme.
- Another theme relates to new wars and problems with the operation of IHL in these. The book illustrates how many of IHL's classifications are unworkable in new wars and how traditional incentives for compliance with IHL fall short in these conflicts.
- Another theme is the inadequacy of the laws pertaining to NIACs and the problems with the legal divide between IACs and NIACs – a precursory step to the application of the principle of distinction.

- A final theme is conflict in Africa, the chosen geographic focus of this work, with its conflicts that in many ways epitomise new wars and which demonstrate many of the problems with the application of IHL in modern conflicts.

An examination of these themes together sheds light on the gendered aspects of the principle of distinction and its functioning in new wars, as well as on the broader question of whether IHL in its current formulation is capable of effectively regulating modern conflicts. Through these themes, this work demonstrates how the gendered problems with IHL interrelate with its broader problems, with gender forming one part of a complex, multifaceted picture that ultimately leads to a failing principle of distinction.

Central arguments

An application of the principle of distinction to women actively participating in African conflicts, reveals that the laws were drafted narrowly, effectively excluding many women from being recognised as 'combatants' or 'direct participants' in hostilities. Even when women are actively engaged in armed movements, the types of roles they typically play seldom meet the law's narrow definitions, which have been framed in traditional military ways, centring on actions that cause kinetic physical harm to an enemy. Accepted understandings of the principle leave little room for those playing non-fighting roles in armed groups – roles that women frequently hold.

The principle's effective exclusion of women has mixed consequences for them. On the one hand, the narrow framing of the law provides many women with legal protection from attack. If women participating in conflict do not qualify as combatants or direct participants, then they cannot be lawfully targeted – clearly working in some women's interests.

However, there are also harmful effects. For one thing, narrow definitions that prohibit fighters from targeting those who they feel to be integral to the fight against them, might encourage non-compliance with the law. Restrictive definitions that exclude women from combatancy or direct participation also propagate the view that women are not actively participating in conflict. If women's contributions to war efforts are not recognised, then women are more likely to be denied places at peace negotiations or post-war political positions. A failure to recognise women's participation also leads to them being excluded from demobilisation and reintegration assistance conferred on former combatants, welfare programmes for former fighters and reparations programmes. Post-conflict societies are constructed in part in response to ideas about who took part in armed struggles. Where women's participation is disregarded, so too are women's concerns and agendas in the post-conflict period.

There are other indirect effects, too; a framing of the law that discourages recognition of women's participation entrenches stereotypes about women as victims of conflict. Conceptualisations that paint all women as victims tacitly allow for, or normalise, the further victimisation of women. Even within armed groups, the perception that women are not 'real' combatants contributes to them being discriminated against and mistreated by their male armed group peers. Of course, these indirect effects cannot be attributed solely to the framing of the law – victimisation and marginalisation of women is prevalent in society and would no doubt persist regardless of the framing of the legal provisions. However, it is important to acknowledge the role that the law plays in social construction, as well as the part it plays in perpetuating stereotypes about women's positions in conflict-ridden societies.

Methodology and approach

In this work, the principle of distinction is critically evaluated by applying it to women participating in a range of ways in conflicts across Africa. The work seeks to determine how such women would be classified; whether they would be understood as 'combatants' or as 'civilians' and if their actions would constitute 'direct participation'. The research considers the effects of such classifications, both for those women participating and for women in conflicts in general, and looks at some of the issues that such applications of the law raise.

This research occupies a space within and between several bodies of scholarship, aiming to contribute to and address gaps in each and to link them. This research furthers each of these discussions by honing in on a novel group (women participating actively in conflict) in an under-examined region (Africa), highlighting the issues that this grounded application raises.

A body of scholarship questions the extent to which the principle of distinction remains adequate to regulate modern conflict.[17] Much of this literature has focussed on IACs, but there has been less discussion on these issues as they pertain to NIACs. Much has focused on the conflicts that the United States and other Western powers have been involved in, including those in Iraq and Afghanistan, exploring the issues these conflicts have raised for the principle of distinction – such as terrorism, the use of civilian contractors and the challenges arising from remote warfare.[18] Other types of conflicts and those in different regions have been subject to less academic and legal analysis. In particular, there has been little academic focus on the principle of distinction as it applies in modern African conflicts.

Armed conflict plays out differently in Africa to elsewhere in the world – as well as varying across the continent itself. While conflicts the world over have changed, the changes in African wars have differed somewhat. While in other regions conflicts have become more technologically sophisticated, in Africa thousands are still killed by machetes and small arms. While in other places conflicts are commonly fought for ideological or political goals, with combatants wresting for control of key centres, in Africa long-term low-level conflicts prevail, frequently involving rebel groups operating from the bush, fighting for and sustained by resources, often with no clear political or ideological motives or command structures. Despite – or maybe because of – these differences, African conflicts can be said to be the quintessential new wars, making African conflicts a useful lens with which to examine the application of IHL in new wars. Today, a significant proportion of the world's conflicts are fought on the African continent, giving research that hones in on Africa significant practical importance. The differences apparent in African conflicts, coupled with the large-scale violations of IHL witnessed in these, raise pressing questions about the extent to which IHL, drafted with a vastly different context in mind, is suitable to regulate African warfare.

The book focuses on women. Women are not merely another sub-group of study – women make up around half of all people affected by conflict, giving the study of women in conflict tremendous practical importance. However, in addition to the reasons why focusing on women is important *for women*, considering the way IHL applies to women can also teach us broader lessons. Understanding the way the law fails such a significant portion of the population provides insight into how it fails everyone. The law's inability to adequately regulate women in conflict also provides insight into the law's inability to regulate other groups that veer from the underlying visions of the drafters of the law.

A rich body of work considers women, law and war. 'Gender and IHL' tends to be discussed in isolation from other debates in IHL. Sadat notes how female lawyers focus on gender issues, finding themselves in an "all female ghetto", excluding and excluded by male colleagues.[19] This problem is not unique to the legal arena – in studies of conflict across various disciplines, women are either excluded or their identity as women becomes the central focus of the work. What is missing is writing that proceeds "without being gender blind, nor being blinded by their gender".[20] In the field of IHL there is a need for scholarship that integrates discussions on gender within broader discussions on topical IHL concerns, eking out the gendered elements of broader issues.

This book examines the law using a feminist theory lens, building on understandings that feminist scholars have developed about women, conflict and international law. Like all feminist writing, this work is motivated by a belief in the equality of men and women – equality that is severely challenged in the arena of conflict. This work considers what a gender-equal application of IHL might look like. It highlights the implications of the ways in which IHL currently operates, providing a grounded basis for assessing the law's effectiveness and for considering the possibility of transformation.

Focusing on both women and Africa challenges the principle of distinction at a double level. By placing women and Africa at the centre of this enquiry, this work puts the margins at the centre, challenging numerous layers of assumptions underlying IHL. Historically, IHL has attempted to normalise conflict around a vision – a vision of state armies resembling European/Western armies, consisting of uniformed men fighting each other across sovereign borders. This work seeks to refute the notions underlying IHL – notions of what *normal* war or *typical* fighters look like. It challenges IHL's normative vision of what conflict should be like, revealing why this vision is problematic and not reflective of current conflicts, and illustrating the strain that 'atypical' subjects or contexts – in fact highly typical today – place on an already failing principle.

One may ask, why should it matter whether IHL is gender sensitive when so many fighters disregard the law anyway? In new wars – in Africa and beyond – fighters breach the law at will, little knowing nor caring whether their actions violate international treaties and customary international law. Many fighters in Africa are scarcely educated or trained – and certainly not trained in the nuances or even the centralities of IHL. What is more, non-state actors' actions fall outside of the bounds of legality anyway, by virtue of the fact that they are violating domestic law by fighting against governments, and as such conformity with international law is unlikely to be a large influencing factor. Challenges around compliance with IHL, particularly in NIACS, are discussed in Chapter 5. Given large-scale non-compliance, what difference do the gendered nuances of IHL actually make for the protection of women?

In answer to this question, a belief underpinning this work is that compliance will be promoted by ensuring that IHL is workable and reflective of real situations on the ground. Laws that are aimed at situations bearing little resemblance to real modern conflicts encourage non-compliance, if for no other reason than that the law is too impractical and confusing to actually adhere to. A second belief underlying this work is that it is important to have a body of law that incentivises *all* actors to comply. To promote compliance the state-centric nature of IHL and the many barriers to non-state actors' inclusion need to be addressed. These two themes will be revisited throughout this work, thereby continuously addressing two key causes of non-compliance. Beyond this, this book does not attempt to propose solutions to the problem of non-compliance with IHL. This is a critical issue, yet one that falls beyond the scope of this work. Still, it must be borne in mind that any approaches taken to improve the law from a gendered perspective will continue to be hampered by a lack of adherence. No matter how well crafted, how gender equitable and how protective a law may be for women, if it is not complied with, its protective effects will be limited.

This book aims to provide a greater understanding of the nature of a problem: the principle of distinction's failure to adequately regulate women's participation in hostilities. It does not aim to solve this problem nor to propose specific revisions to the law. That being said, the conclusion chapter will briefly consider some potential approaches that could be followed to improve the legal situation, noting how these might be approached and the challenges these might raise.

In this book, empirical material has been collated to provide the factual material about women in African conflict, to which the law is applied in later chapters. This research draws on material derived from academic writing, humanitarian organisations, non-governmental organisations, the media, as well as judgments of the international criminal tribunals. I have previously conducted fieldwork in a number of conflict-affected countries in Africa, including South Sudan, northern Nigeria, Central African Republic, Sierra Leone and northern Uganda. As such, the secondary material used in this book was understood in light of significant experience in these contexts. This research does not centre on specific case studies, but rather considers women across a number of conflicts in Africa. This approach allowed for a greater number of issues to be explored than a case study approach would have allowed, as different conflicts bring out distinct issues. Incorporating numerous examples more accurately illustrates the variations in women's roles and circumstances and more clearly portrays a sense of the difficulties involved in regulating in a way that suitably encompasses these variations. This approach also allows the results of this research to be more generalisable, ensuring that recommendations do not risk being suited to only one context or to a certain type of participation in conflict – arguably a problem with the existing law. Nevertheless, despite not using case studies, this book often draws on certain examples, with some conflicts coming up more frequently. These tend to be conflicts where women have played greater roles, or those that contain features that are particularly useful for this application of the law and which illustrate key points of value to the discussion. The countries that come up more often are also those where there is a greater volume of documented material on female involvement, as well as those countries where I have spent time researching, as I know and understand these better.

This study is informed by a feminist perspective and is guided by a conviction that equality between men and women is of paramount importance – even where equality of treatment might have negative effects for some women. This work is also written from a humanitarian perspective. The study of IHL has largely been split between those who prioritise the interests of military actors and those who are motivated by humanitarian ideals. This book belongs to the latter. Military necessity is discussed and considered as it is understood that only by adequately accommodating military concerns will military actors comply with IHL – which will in turn lead to greater humanitarian results.

My experiences have played a part in shaping the research approach. I am a South African woman who grew up during South Africa's state of emergency and the closing years of Apartheid. While I did not participate in South Africa's armed struggle, I lived through this and was affected by it. Over the past years, I have worked in conflict-affected countries across Africa and the Middle East, conducting research on a range of projects relating to women, combatants and law. I arrived at the topic of this book through my experience in the field, directly witnessing the ways in which the law fails the women who rely on its protection. My background is that of a researcher, humanitarian worker and lawyer. I have never served in the military and have never been involved in targeting decisions. I have studied the ways in which such decisions are made in battle and the factors affecting these decisions. However, I am conscious of the fact that my understandings of IHL are limited by the fact that I have never directly applied this in combat. No amount of research can match understandings gained by personal experience of war.

Breakdown of chapters

In this book, Chapters 2, 3, 4 and 5 each set out a central element of this research; the principle of distinction, women's participation in African conflicts, feminist theory and IACs/NIACs. Chapters 6, 7 and 8 bring this all together, conducting a practical application of the law to women participating in African conflicts, analysing the results and seeking to answer the central questions that this research poses.

Chapter 2 contains an in-depth exploration of the principle of distinction, setting out the content of the law that is critically analysed throughout this work. The chapter describes the laws of distinction in both IACs and NIACs, highlighting the areas of controversy and the places where the law is problematic. It does this so that the gendered problems with the principle, can be considered in light of its broader problems.

Chapter 3 describes Africa's conflicts and the varied ways in which women participate in these, providing the facts to which the law is applied in later chapters. The chapter also discusses new wars, locating African conflicts within this theoretical categorisation, considering the gendered aspects of new wars as well as their tricky relationship with IHL. Chapter 4 discusses feminism and IHL, allowing this book to build on insights from this body of theoretical thought. After highlighting the central concerns of feminist theory and examining how these relate to conflict and female combatancy, the chapter describes the critiques that feminist scholars have made about IHL and about the principle of distinction.

Chapter 5 considers the distinction between IACs and NIACs – a preliminary legal assessment that must be made in any given situation in order to know which version of the principle of distinction is to be applied. The chapter highlights the practical and legal difficulties in making such a classification in new wars, illustrating how this preliminary step is in fact a step that often cannot properly be made. The chapter pays particular attention to the regulation of NIACs, demonstrating the failings with this regulatory body and the problems this creates for a workable IHL system.

In Chapter 6 the law is applied to the facts. The principle of distinction is applied to women participating in a range of ways in African conflicts, seeking to see how different women would be classified, which women would be classified civilians or combatants, which types of actions would constitute direct participation and which women can therefore be the lawful targets of attack. The chapter highlights the difficulties in making such classifications and illustrates how few women actually fit within the law's narrow categorisations. Chapter 7 pulls it all together. The chapter explores the differing effects that the principle of distinction has for women – for both those participating and not participating in hostilities, and those that are positive and negative, direct and indirect, applicable during conflict and after conflict, questioning whether ultimately the principle serves and protects women in modern conflicts or the extent to which it fails to do so. Chapter 8 concludes the book, recapping the major themes and arguments. The chapter examines some approaches that could be taken to improve the legal situation, considering the problems and risks inherent in these.

The nature of warfare is constantly changing, with IHL developing alongside these changes. Among the many changes seen in recent years has been an increase in the numbers of women actively involved in the waging of war. If IHL is unable to adapt to shifts in conflict and to changing modes of participation, it will be rendered irrelevant. Revisiting the principle of distinction is an important step required to bring the law in line with the realities of modern conflict. It is hoped that this research will play a role in illuminating one facet of the failings of the principle – that relating to women – and that this may ultimately contribute to the development of a more realistic, more inclusive and ultimately better adhered to principle of distinction.

Notes

1 When referring to IHL, this book refers to the full body of law that makes up the laws of war, including treaty law – made up of the Hague Conventions (1899 and 1907), the four Geneva Conventions (1949) and the two Additional Protocols to the Geneva Conventions (1977) – as well as other peripherally relevant treaties, case law and customary international law.

2 Articles 3–4, Geneva Convention Relative to the Protection of Civilian Persons in Time of War (Fourth Geneva Convention), 12 August 1949, 75 UNTS 287.

3 Articles 43–48 and 50–52, Protocol 1 Additional to the Geneva Conventions of 12 August 1949, and relating to the Protection of Victims of International Armed Conflicts (Protocol I), 8 June 1977, 1125 UNTS 3 and Article 13, Protocol 2 Additional to the Geneva Conventions of 12 August 1949, and relating to the Protection of Victims of Non-International Armed Conflicts (Protocol II), 8 June 1977, 1125 UNTS 609.

4 Crawford, Emily. *The Treatment of Combatants and Insurgents Under the Law of Armed Conflict*. Oxford: Oxford University Press, 2010.

5 Article 13(3) Additional Protocol 2.

6 Lamp, Nicolas. 'Conceptions of War and Paradigms of Compliance: The "New War" Challenge to International Humanitarian Law'. *Journal of Conflict and Security Law* 16, no. 2 (1 July 2011): 225–262.

7 Schmitt, Michael. 'Military Necessity and Humanity in International Humanitarian Law: Preserving the Delicate Balance'. *Virginia Journal of International Law* 50 (2010): 795–839.

8 Hoffman, Michael. 'Rescuing the Law of War: A Way Forward in an Era of Global Terrorism'. *Parameters* 35, no. 2 (2005): 18–35. Quenivet, Noelle. 'The "War on Terror" and the Principle of Distinction in International Humanitarian Law'. *Colombian Yearbook of International Law* 3 (2010): 155–186.

9 Sinha, Alex. 'Child Soldiers as Super-Privileged Combatants'. *The International Journal of Human Rights* 17, no. 4 (2013): 584–603.

10 Cameron, Lindsey. 'Private Military Companies: Their Status under International Humanitarian Law and its Impact on their Regulation'. *International Review of the Red Cross* 88, no. 863 (2006): 573–598. Faite, Alexandre. 'Involvement of Private Contractors in Armed Conflict: Implications under International Humanitarian Law'. *Defence Studies* 4, no. 2 (2004): 166–183.

11 'Impact of Armed Conflict on Children'. UNICEF, www.unicef.org/graca/patterns.htm. This was based on the findings of Graça Machel's report on the impact of conflict on children: Machel, Graça. *Impact of Armed Conflict on Children: Report of Graça Machel*, United Nations Department of Public Information, 1996.

12 Kaldor, Mary. *New and Old Wars: Organised Violence in a Global Era*. 3rd edition. Redwood City, CA: Stanford University Press, 2013.

13 Schmitt, supra note 8.

14 Lamp, supra note 7.

15 Kaldor, supra note 13.

16 Kinsella, Helen. *Securing the Civilian: Sex and Gender in the Laws of War*. Boston, MA: Boston Consortium on Gender, Security and Human Rights, 2004.

17 Schmitt, Michael. 'The Principle of Discrimination in 21st Century Warfare'. *Yale Human Rights & Development Law Journal* 2 (1999): 143–182. Swiney, Gabriel. 'Saving Lives: The Principle of Distinction and the Realities of Modern War'. *International Lawyer (ABA)* 39 (2005): 733–758.

18 See, for example, Lewis, Michael and Crawford, Emily. 'Drones and Distinction: How IHL Encouraged the Rise of Drones'. *Georgetown Journal of International Law* 44 (2013): 1127–1166. Kidane, Won. 'The Status of Private Military Contractors under International Humanitarian Law'. *Denver Journal of International Law and Policy* 38 (2010): 361–419. Quenivet, supra note 9.

19 Sadat, Leila. 'Avoiding the Creation of a Gender Ghetto in International Criminal Law'. *International Criminal Law Review* 11 (2011): 655–662.

20 Felices-Luna, Maritza. 'The Involvement of Women in Anti-Establishment Armed Groups: Deviance in the Service of a Citizenship Enterprise'. *Champ Penal/Penal Field* 4 (2007), at 4.

Bibliography

Books and articles

Anghie, Antony. *Imperialism, Sovereignty, and the Making of International Law*. Cambridge: Cambridge University Press, 2007.

Cameron, Lindsey. 'Private Military Companies: Their Status under International Humanitarian Law and its Impact on their Regulation'. *International Review of the Red Cross* 88, no. 863 (2006): 573–598.

Crawford, Emily. *The Treatment of Combatants and Insurgents under the Law of Armed Conflict*. Oxford University Press, 2010.

Faite, Alexandre. 'Involvement of Private Contractors in Armed Conflict: Implications Under International Humanitarian Law'. *Defence Studies* 4, no. 2 (2004): 166–183.

Felices-Luna, Maritza. 'The Involvement of Women in Anti-Establishment Armed Groups: Deviance in the Service of a Citizenship Enterprise'. *Champ Penal/Penal Field* 4 (2007).

Hoffman, Michael. 'Rescuing the Law of War: A Way Forward in an Era of Global Terrorism'. *Parameters* 35, no. 2 (2005): 18–35.

Jalloh, Charles. 'Regionalizing International Criminal Law'. *International Criminal Law Review* 9 (2009): 445–500.

Kaldor, Mary. *New and Old Wars: Organised Violence in a Global Era*. 3rd edition. Redwood City, CA: Stanford University Press, 2013.

Kidane, Won. 'The Status of Private Military Contractors under International Humanitarian Law' *Denver Journal of International Law and Policy* 38 (2010): 361–419.

Kinsella, Helen. *Securing the Civilian: Sex and Gender in the Laws of War*. Boston, MA: Boston Consortium on Gender, Security and Human Rights, 2004.

Koskenniemi, Martti. *The Gentle Civilizer of Nations: The Rise and Fall of International Law, 1870–1960*. Cambridge: Cambridge University Press, 2002.

Koskenniemi, Martti. 'International Law in Europe: Between Tradition and Renewal'. *The European Journal of International Law* 16, no. 1 (2005): 113–124.

Lamp, Nicolas. 'Conceptions of War and Paradigms of Compliance: The "New War" Challenge to International Humanitarian Law'. *Journal of Conflict and Security Law* 16, no. 2 (1 July 2011): 225–262.

Lewis, Michael and Crawford, Emily. 'Drones and Distinction: How IHL Encouraged the Rise of Drones'. *Georgetown Journal of International Law* 44 (2013): 1127–1166.

Quenivet, Noelle. 'The "War on Terror" and the Principle of Distinction in International Humanitarian Law'. *Colombian Yearbook of International Law* 3 (2010): 155–186.

Sadat, Leila. 'Avoiding the Creation of a Gender Ghetto in International Criminal Law'. *International Criminal Law Review* 11 (2011): 655–662.

Schmitt, Michael. 'Military Necessity and Humanity in International Humanitarian Law: Preserving the Delicate Balance'. *Virginia Journal of International Law* 50 (2010): 795–839.

Schmitt, Michael. 'The Principle of Discrimination in 21st Century Warfare'. *Yale Human Rights & Development Law Journal* 2 (1999): 143–82.

Sinha, Alex. 'Child Soldiers as Super-Privileged Combatants'. *The International Journal of Human Rights* 17, no. 4 (2013): 584–603.

Swiney, Gabriel. 'Saving Lives: The Principle of Distinction and the Realities of Modern War'. *International Lawyer (ABA)* 39 (2005): 733–758.

Cases

Separate and Dissenting Opinion of Judge Odio Benito. *The Prosecutor* v. *Thomas Lubanga Dyilo*, ICC-01/04-01/06, 2012.

Treaties

Geneva Convention Relative to the Protection of Civilian Persons in Time of War (Fourth Geneva Convention), 12 August 1949, 75 UNTS 287.

Protocol 1 Additional to the Geneva Conventions of 12 August 1949, and relating to the Protection of Victims of International Armed Conflicts (Protocol I), 8 June 1977, 1125 UNTS 3.

Protocol 2 Additional to the Geneva Conventions of 12 August 1949, and relating to the Protection of Victims of Non-International Armed Conflicts (Protocol II), 8 June 1977, 1125 UNTS 609.

Other policy documents

International Criminal Court Policy Paper on Sexual and Gender-Based Crimes, 2014.

Website

'Impact of Armed Conflict on Children'. UNICEF, www.unicef.org/graca/patterns.htm. This was based on the findings of Graça Machel's report on the impact of conflict on children: Machel, Graça. *Impact of Armed Conflict on Children: Report of Graça Machel*, United Nations Department of Public Information, 1996.

2 The principle of distinction

The principle of distinction is one of the fundamental tenets of IHL. It provides that a distinction must be made between 'combatants' and 'civilians', and between those civilians 'directly participating' in hostilities and those who are not. The principle states that combatants and civilians directly participating in hostilities may be the lawful intended targets of attack, while civilians who are not directly participating may not be. The principle aims to regulate the conduct of participants in conflict, in order to provide protection to those not participating. It also operates to classify individuals, providing legal identities in times of conflict.

The principle of distinction is of critical importance to the protection of civilians. Confusion between civilians and combatants – both in law and in fact – can result in greater numbers of civilians being harmed. Where those fighting cannot tell the difference between those who pose a threat to their military efforts and those who do not, civilians are more likely to be killed. So too, where the law does not make it clear who fighters may or may not target, civilians bear the brunt. It is therefore crucial that this distinction be clearly demarcated in law and strictly adhered to in practice.

However, unlike in conflicts of the past when uniformed soldiers faced each other on demarcated battlefields, in new wars it is harder to distinguish civilians and combatants. Fighting often takes place in urban centres, with fighters carrying out attacks before blending into civilian backdrops. Civilians frequently take part in hostilities, providing ad hoc support and assistance to armed movements. Terrorists and a range of un-uniformed irregular fighting groups, participating in undeclared, geographically decentralised and complex struggles, have further complicated matters, leading many to question whether the principle of distinction is still suitable to regulate the rapidly shifting face of modern conflict. Among the many groups whose activities challenge the definitions in the law are women, the focus of this work, who provide an interesting illustration of the blurring lines between fighter and non-fighter.

This chapter begins with a brief history of the principle of distinction, tracing the ways this body of law has developed alongside changes in warfare. The chapter considers the laws of distinction in both IACs and NIACs. For IACs it describes the ways in which combatancy requirements have evolved through the

IHL treaties. It interrogates the accepted position of having two opposing categories, civilian and combatant, considering the status of other possibly emerging categorisations, such as 'unlawful combatant'. In the discussion on NIACs, the concept of 'direct participation' is discussed and the status of non-state armed groups is explored.

Broadly speaking, two central categories of critique are explored in this chapter. First, the chapter highlights the many controversies relating to the wording and substance of the law, arguing that the law is uncertain in its meaning, application and interpretation. The principle of distinction can only be successful if armed actors adhere to it, and this complex set of laws should be considered with its intended audience in mind; those who are supposed to apply it in conflict – in a context like Africa, often barely educated fighters. A second set of critiques, extrinsic to the law's complexity and wording, revolve around whom the principle is favouring in being framed in particular ways. The principle is not uniform in its application and divergent rules apply to different actors in different contexts. There are divergent rules for state and non-state actors, in IACs and NIACs, and even for men and women. The constructed laws, the chosen wording and even the ambiguities benefit certain parties and prejudice others. This state-created system prioritises the interests of states. It also prioritises military interests, despite the humanitarian façade the law employs – with some arguing that the principle ultimately legitimises violence by allowing the targeting of those who meet certain definitions.[1] Among the many layers of privileging is a gendered one, explored throughout this book.

A brief historical overview

The distinction between combatant and civilian has had a long and fluid history, shifting alongside changes in warfare, politics and the views and beliefs of society. The laws of distinction developed gradually, progressing in response to key historical events. Tracking these changes demonstrates how this body of law can develop to keep pace with changing circumstances – suggesting it can continue to develop should new changes in warfare provide the need.

This section provides a brief history of the distinction between combatant and civilian. Not purporting to be a comprehensive chronicle,[2] this account rather points to key events that have influenced the development of these concepts. This history below is for the most part European-focused – as is much of the history and discourse on the formation of international law.[3] Largely absent from this historical account are shifts in conflict that took place in Africa, as these played little direct part in shaping IHL.[4] While the history below is focused largely on men, who have always been the dominant players in conflict, it will demonstrate that women have also actively taken part in conflicts throughout the years, albeit in ways that differed to those in which men participated.

Since the early years of written history, combatants have been distinguished from civilians. However, the group of people perceived to belong to each category has continuously changed. Historically, a dichotomy has existed between those who wanted to limit permission to fight to privileged members of organised armies, and those – often those being occupied or attacked – who preferred to enable all citizens to join in fighting, supporting a less restricted fighting class. Over the years, participation in conflict has broadened and narrowed, reflecting these positions. Once IHL began to define requirements for 'combatancy', a related tension became evident between those who wished to include only a restricted group under this legally privileged category and those who argued the value of incorporating a wider group of fighters within the fold of combatancy as a means to promote broader compliance with IHL. This history and the descriptions of the laws that follow illustrate the continual tensions between these positions.

Although wars were fought in earlier periods, this historic overview begins in medieval times. Then fighters came from a privileged class, with wars fought by knights. Knights' actions were constrained by ideas of chivalry, rather than by law.[5] While the majority of knights were men, instances of women being given knighthoods were also recorded. For example, the *Order of the Hatchet* in Catalonia was an order of knighthood founded in 1149 purely for women, to honour the women who had fought to defend the Spanish town of Tortosa from Moor attack.

Participation in the Crusades, the religious military campaigns of the eleventh, twelfth and thirteenth centuries, was open to all Christian men. Those who went on Crusade were awarded the 'Crusade Indulgence' of remission of sin. To join, Crusaders took a vow before receiving a cross from the Pope or his representatives, becoming 'soldiers of the church'.[6] Men from all classes of feudal society went on Crusade – although many peasants had no choice but to accompany their lords or employers. In the earlier years many non-fighters went along on Crusade, including many Crusaders' wives, but this began to be seen as a drain on resources, leading the Pope to encourage non-fighters to remain at home and instead donate money to fund the journeys of other Crusaders, in exchange for which they would receive the Crusade Indulgence themselves.[7] This was an early example of recognition of the alternative contributions that women could make while not actually fighting.

The idea of privileged participation was challenged by the formation of nation-states, beginning around the time of the Hundred Years War (1337–1453). States began to garner loyalty, and a willingness arose from the population to fight for their nations – rather than for feudal lords. The series of dynastic wars that brought about this change created the need for larger armies, resulting in armies being opened up to all men, greatly expanding the pool of those involved in war fighting.[8] It was during these wars that Joan of Arc famously led the French army to a number of victories, after alleging she heard the voice of God telling her to lead the army.[9]

Following from this great expansion in armies, states began to experience problems with demobilised soldiers, who fought for pay and continuously changed allegiances. To bring forces under increased national control, military ranks and administrative structures were created, military discipline was introduced and permanent pay began to be provided to soldiers. This led to the gradual development of stable, permanent national armed forces. Over the years that followed, advances in weaponry created the need for increased training and discipline, leading to armies that by the 1600s had the shape and form of modern militaries.[10] This once again entrenched a stark distinction between soldiers and the general population, with armies now consisting mostly of trained armed men.

Around 1800, with the onset of the revolutions of the Napoleonic era, populations began to revolt against the feudal government system. Peasants took up arms en masse, again expanding the legions of those fighting.[11] Although it was primarily men who fought these wars, women travelled alongside military groups and were often present at the fronts. In French regiments, women wearing clothes of partially military design cared for the wounded and sold tobacco and refreshments at the front. So too, some British soldiers' wives accompanied their husbands on service and many other unofficial camp followers also attached to British regiments.[12]

Up until this point all of the mechanisms aimed at regulating conflict – including national laws, bilateral treaties, customary rules, the rules of the church and those of chivalry – had been utilitarian in nature, aimed largely at facilitating those who were fighting. This became known as the Hague Tradition, a term referring to the nineteenth century peace conferences in The Hague. In 1863 a new movement emerged with the founding of the International Committee of the Red Cross (ICRC), concerned with the protection of victims of war. This movement became known as the Geneva Tradition.[13] These two movements remain evident today; Hague Laws are those concerned with regulating the means and methods of warfare, while Geneva Laws focus on the protection of specific classes of persons in conflict.[14] The principle of distinction is understood to be part of Hague Law, as it imposes limitations on the means and methods of combat.[15]

In the mid nineteenth century the formal codification of the laws of war began, bringing the first written manifestations of the principle of distinction. It was during an internal conflict that the written principle of distinction first appeared. During the American Civil War, President Lincoln commissioned Dr Francis Lieber to codify the laws of war based on the customs of nations. The resulting Lieber Code (1863) was issued to the Union Army, with Article 22, which hinted at an early formulation of the principle, stating:

> Nevertheless, as civilization has advanced during the last centuries, so has likewise steadily advanced, especially in war on land, the distinction between the private individual belonging to a hostile country and the hostile country itself, with its men in arms. The principle has been more and more acknowledged that the unarmed citizen is to be spared in person, property, and honor as much as the exigencies of war will admit.[16]

Of course, despite the presence of this clause in the Lieber Code, civilians were continuously targeted during the American Civil War. Women were subjected to specific forms of targeting, in the form of large-scale sexual violence, the invasion of their homes and the theft of their produce.[17] This was the first conflict in which Americans were conscripted, although most volunteered to enlist. While the Union and Confederate armies did not allow female enlistment, historians report that a few hundred women fought as combatants, disguised and pretending to be men. In addition, many thousands of women "... made bandages for the wounded and knit(ted) socks to keep the soldiers' feet warm and dry" and "worked to manufacture arms, ammunition, uniforms, and other supplies for the soldiers".[18]

The principle of distinction was formally introduced to international law five years after the Lieber Code, with the 1868 St Petersburg Declaration. While the Declaration's stated purpose was to ban small explosive bullets, its preamble noted that, "the only legitimate object which States should endeavor to accomplish during war is to weaken the military forces of the enemy".[19]

At the 1899 and 1907 Hague Peace Conferences, nations attempted to comprehensively codify the laws of war.[20] The ensuing Hague Conventions incorporated a weak form of the principle of distinction. The 1907 Hague Convention's section IV on respecting the laws and customs of war on land prohibited "the attack or bombardment, by whatever means, of towns, villages, dwellings, or buildings which are undefended",[21] while the section addressing war on the sea specifically distinguished undefended locations, which could not be targeted, from industries crucial to the enemy's war effort, which could be.[22]

It is ironic that as the principle of distinction began to properly emerge in international law, civilians started to be killed in far greater numbers in conflict. The budding principle was put to the test during World War One (1914–1918). Europe became embroiled in a 'total war' in which civilian-controlled industries were central to the war effort, leading to a profound temptation to attack them. Technically the distinction between 'civilian' and 'military' targets was respected during the war and for the most part 'civilian targets' were not specifically attacked. However, this was diminished by the wide meaning given to the concept of 'military targets', which included facilities where large numbers of civilians worked.[23] While not a targeted attack as such, the British navy tried to strangle the supply of food and raw material to Germany, in what was called the 'hunger blockade', causing the deaths of up to 763,000 German civilians,[24] a move clearly not in keeping with the spirit of the principle. In the German invasion of Belgium, dubbed by Allied wartime propaganda as 'the Rape of Belgium', civilians were targeted in a number of incidents; historians estimate that up to 6,000 Belgian civilians were killed.[25] All of this points to the principle's limited success in protecting civilians during the war. World War One had a significant impact on the women of Europe. With most young men away at war or killed, women began to work in greater numbers in industry and played crucial roles in keeping manufacturing and agricultural production alive. Large numbers of women also served as nurses in the war effort. An estimated 150,000 women served in World War One, with the largest contingents coming from Britain (80,000) and USA (30,000).[26]

World War One was the first conflict in which airplanes were used on a large scale and the first time that aerial bombardment of civilian centres took place. Responding to this, The Hague Rules of Air Warfare were drafted by jurists at The Hague in 1923. These Rules clearly affirmed the principle of distinction, prohibiting targeting of civilians and incorporating a comprehensive list of legitimate targets of attack. The Rules expressly prohibited attacks against enemy 'civilian morale' – attacks that would become a significant feature in World War Two. Sadly, not one country endorsed these rules, with analysts speculating that these would have restricted the use of aircrafts too much for governments to agree to[27] – a demonstration of the way that IHL has been shaped to prioritise state military interests.

World War Two dealt a significant blow to the ideals of the principle of distinction. On 1 September 1939, the day Germany invaded Poland, President Roosevelt sought the agreement of certain European governments that they would not bomb "civilian populations in unfortified cities", receiving agreement from France, England and Germany. Swiney notes that, "Perhaps never in the history of armed conflict has a promise been more thoroughly broken".[28] 'Total war' took place on an unprecedented scale, with all segments of society mobilised, widespread conscription and entire economies geared up for war. Despite parties to World War Two paying lip service to the international laws of war, which now included the weak distinction provisions described above, military actors became increasingly willing to attack targets that would undermine civilian morale. With the aim of affecting the enemy nation's resolve to continue fighting, such targets were considered legitimate military objectives. By 1943, parties had abandoned the principle of distinction altogether. In January 1943, Roosevelt and Churchill met to discuss their strategy for the war, creating the Casablanca Directive, which called for, "the progressive destruction and dislocation of the German military, industrial and economic system, and the undermining of the morale of the German people to a point where their capacity for armed resistance is fatally weakened".[29] Both sides to the war attacked opposition cities. Germany, in addition to attacking Allied civilian populations, also proceeded with the systematic killing of large segments of the European population, without distinction as to their nationalities or genders. This included European Jewry, of whom six million were killed. Women took part in large numbers during World War Two, working in war-related industries, providing logistic support to militaries and serving as nurses. Hundreds of thousands of women took on combat roles, particularly in anti-aircraft units. Large numbers also joined resistance movements. About 1.5 million women took part in the war effort – around 800,000 from USSR, 350,000 from USA and 300,000 from Britain.[30] Still, despite the increased numbers of women serving as soldiers, few women were obliged to enlist. The majority of adult women were exempt from conscription as they were married or had small children.[31] The two World Wars played a major role in women's military, political, economic and social emancipation.

Following the devastation of World War Two, the 1949 Geneva Conventions were drafted – and today these remain the basis of IHL, with 194 countries having ratified them in whole or with reservations. The four GCs outlined the principle of distinction in far greater detail. Until the GCs, the treaties regulating conflict dealt only with conflicts between states. With the GCs the legal distinction between IACs and NIACs was entrenched and divergent rules began to develop for each – including diverging versions of the principle of distinction.

During the Cold War 'proxy wars' were fought, in which armed groups or smaller countries acted on behalf of the opposing superpowers. Seemingly internal wars were fuelled and controlled by external powers, taking on (often insidious) international elements. Anti-colonial struggles also took place, like those in Kenya, Algeria, Angola and Eritrea, and religious and ethnic conflicts increased.[32] Rather than large armies with uniformed combatants being the dominant norm, there was a rise in smaller armed groups employing irregular fighters.[33] Conflicts moved further from having linear battlefields or 'fronts', to increased battles taking place within civilian centres. Mao Tse-Tung wrote that in guerrilla warfare, the general civilian population is the water in which the fish (the guerrilla) survives – an observation telling of the challenges guerrilla warfare presented for the principle of distinction.[34] The GCs with their IAC focus became inadequate to regulate such conflicts. Countries that relied on voluntary recruitment began finding it more difficult to find male volunteers, leading to some militaries opening up more roles to women, including USA (due mainly to the Vietnam War), Australia, Germany, Britain, Sweden, Greece and Belgium.[35]

In 1974, responding to these changes in warfare, the ICRC brought together a number of countries for the Diplomatic Conference on the Reaffirmation and Development of International Humanitarian Law Applicable in Armed Conflicts. The Conference deliberated for three years before producing two Additional Protocols to the GCs. AP1 dealt with IACs, while AP2 dealt exclusively with certain types of NIACs, the first treaty to comprehensively do so. The APs addressed both military and humanitarian concerns, finally bringing together the Hague and Geneva traditions.[36] As of today, 172 countries have ratified AP1 and 166 countries AP2. AP1 has been ratified by 45 African Union states and AP2 by 44.[37] Notably, a number of significant countries have not ratified these, including the USA, Japan, India, Pakistan and Israel. A number of countries have made significant reservations, indicating a lack of consensus on several aspects of the Protocols.[38] Despite this, the APs were a significant development in the law and to a large extent shape IHL today.

Conflicts continued to change in the years since the APs. Conflicts that one could characterise as 'new wars' began to be fought. Since September 11, 2001 there have been further shifts, both in the nature of conflict and with regard to the legal claims made in response to these. Responding to the attacks on the USA, America launched conflicts in Afghanistan and Iraq, as well as its global 'war on terror'. These conflicts, which feature distinct 'new' and 'old' elements,[39] have brought new challenges to accepted understandings of IHL. The US administration has proposed controversial interpretations of IHL, including relying on the categorisation 'unlawful combatant' to deny legal status and rights to terror suspects. While it remains to be seen what effect this will have on the evolution of IHL, what seems evident is that some level of legal shift is taking place.

Despite frequent violations of the principle of distinction, there is now consensus on the fact that the principle constitutes customary international law (CIL).[40] However, question still remains as to which specific parts of the principle are customary law.[41] In 2005 the ICRC published a study setting out what it believed to be the rules of customary IHL.[42] It included within this the principle of distinction, setting out the rules of distinction pertaining to both IACs and NIACs, which they see as forming part of customary law. Rule 1 states that, "The parties to the conflict must at all times distinguish between civilians and combatants. Attacks may only be directed against combatants. Attacks must not be directed against civilians". While this is applicable in both IACs and NIACs, the study clearly states that the term "combatant" here is explicitly used "in its generic meaning", to indicate persons who do not enjoy the civilian protection against attack, yet does not imply a right to combatant or prisoner of war status. Rules relating to combatancy and prisoner of war status are not CIL for NIACs.[43]

On a different legal track, there have been developments in weapons law, with certain laws passed that prohibit the use of weapons that violate the principles of distinction and proportionality by being too indiscriminate – including the 1997 Mine Ban Treaty and the 2010 Convention on Cluster Munitions.[44]

IHL has been shown to be responsive, both proactively and reactively, to the changing nature of conflict. However, the extent to which IHL provisions actually translate into the protection of individuals remains questionable. What follows is a description of the principle of distinction in its current formulation, setting out the laws that are applied to women in African new wars in a later chapter.

The principle of distinction

The principle of distinction in international armed conflict

In IACs, regulated primarily by the GCs and AP1, a distinction is made between 'civilians' and 'combatants'. Article 48 AP1 states:

> In order to ensure respect for and protection of the civilian population and civilian objects, the Parties to the conflict shall at all times distinguish between the civilian population and combatants and between civilian objects and military objectives and accordingly shall direct their operations only against military objectives.

The laws set out who qualifies as civilian and combatant. Combatancy requirements have changed with the various treaties. Article 1 of the 1907 Hague Regulations laid out the "qualifications of belligerents", stating that the armed forces of belligerent states, as well as militias and volunteer corps could be belligerents, so long as they met four conditions: they were subordinate to responsible command, they had a fixed distinctive emblem recognisable at a distance, they carried their arms openly and they acted in accordance with the laws of war.[45]

Article 4 GC3 set out requirements to qualify for prisoner of war (POW) status – requirements understood to be the GC's requirements for combatancy. Armed forces of state parties to a conflict, as well as "Members of other militias and members of other volunteer corps, including those of organized resistance movements, belonging to a Party to the conflict …"[46] can qualify, provided they fulfil certain requirements. GC3 incorporated the four Hague requirements and added two additional ones; having a level of organisation or discipline and belonging to or acting for a state party to a conflict.[47] Notably, in GC3 these requirements are prescribed for irregular forces, yet not for regular forces. Dinstein explains that there was a presumption that due to the nature of regular forces, they would automatically meet these conditions.[48] These requirements form an onerous burden for irregular forces to meet, particularly as secrecy and surprise are key features of guerrilla warfare.[49]

AP1 altered the law significantly. Article 43 AP1 reaffirmed four of the GC requirements (measure of organisation, responsible command, internal disciplinary system, aimed at ensuring compliance with IHL). AP1 made no distinction between the regular armed forces of a state and its irregular forces, imposing the requirements on both, making this the first time that regular armed forces were expressly required to comply with requirements to qualify as combatants.[50] Article 44 went on to change the law, stating that while combatants are obliged to comply with IHL, violations do not deprive them of the right to be combatants (or rather, of the right to POW status). Furthermore, Article 44(3) states that where owing to the nature of hostilities a combatant cannot distinguish himself, s/he is released from this obligation. Article 44(4) adds that although those who do not distinguish themselves are deprived of POW status, they must still be given every protection accorded to POWs.

Article 44 has been the subject of much criticism. Fleck explains that during drafting, those states who supported guerrilla independence movements, or who had themselves attained independence in this way, supported removing the obligations for fighters to distinguish themselves, while other states strongly opposed removing this requirement. This Article was the compromise reached after much debate.[51] Dinstein describes this Article as, "convoluted, not to say opaque", arguing that it renders the distinction between lawful and unlawful combatants to be of nominal value, thereby tilting the balance of protection in favour of irregular combatants. Whereas in the GCs the requirements were onerous, "The pendulum in the Article has swung from one extreme to the other, reducing *ad absurdum* the conditions of lawful combatancy".[52] This, he argues, will inevitably be bad for civilians as combatants will be more likely to target civilians if they believe that enemy fighters could be pretending to be civilians while still retaining the right to fight and benefitting from POW status.[53] Talbot Jensen adds that allowing fighters to operate without uniforms or distinguishing elements undermines the reciprocity elements that previously underpinned the principle.[54] There have been numerous reservations made on Article 44 by signatories to AP1,[55] and Article 44 was a key reason that many countries did not ratify the Protocol.[56]

Civilians are defined negatively in the law – any person who does not qualify as a combatant is a civilian. Article 50 AP1 states that a civilian is any person who does *not* fit into one of the categories of combatant set out in Article 4(A) (1), (2), (3) and (6) GC3 or Article 43 AP1.

Being either a civilian or a combatant comes with privileges, restrictions and obligations. Civilians do not have the right to participate in hostilities and have no international law immunity from prosecution for taking part in hostilities. For the most part, civilians do not receive POW status on capture (although a few categories of civilians do – set out in Article 4 GC3). Crucially, civilians may not be the lawful intended targets of attack. This does not mean that all civilian deaths in battle are unlawful. Distinction works together with the other IHL principles of 'proportionality'[57] and 'necessity'. While civilians may not be the direct intended targets of attack, if they are killed as an unintended or indirect consequence of an attack that is otherwise lawful, or as 'collateral damage', this might still be lawful – so long as the attacks were proportionate to the military goal and necessary to achieve the required military objective. Importantly, a civilian's legal protection from attack is suspended if and when a civilian 'directly participates' in hostilities[58] – a term discussed later in this chapter.

Combatants may be the intended targets of attack and may be attacked at all times, even when they are not actually fighting. They remain legitimate targets until they withdraw from hostilities by demobilising or becoming *hors de combat* – by laying down arms, becoming wounded or shipwrecked.[59] Combatant status comes with a number of privileges. Combatants have the right to participate in hostilities (Article 43(2) AP1) and may not be prosecuted for taking part in hostilities or for the many, normally illegal, acts that constitute war fighting (i.e. killing), in so far as these acts are in accordance with IHL.[60] On capture, combatants acquire POW status and are entitled to be detained and treated in a particular way, the details of which are set out in GC3. There are a number of protections for female POWs specifically.[61] Combatants have to fulfil various obligations. They are obligated to comply with IHL. They are also obliged to physically distinguish themselves as combatants by wearing distinctive signs and carrying their arms openly. It is a violation of the principle of distinction for combatants to purposefully disguise themselves as civilians.

Creating the categories: civilians and combatants

The framing of the law is indicative of an acceptance of the fact that combatants are the opposite and corollary of civilians and that the categories are co-determined, so that a civilian is that which a combatant is not.[62] However, even when the GCs were drafted, it was evident that there was not such a clear distinction between combatants and civilians – with the Judge Advocate General of the United States War Department noting in 1945 that the distinction is "more apparent than real".[63] To a great extent the two categories were manufactured, as it served a purpose to have a binary classification – a favoured regulatory approach. The question when drafting the GCs was not how to distinguish between combatants and civilians, but rather how to delineate the difference between them.[64]

When determining how widely or narrowly the definition of combatant was to be framed, a difficult calculation had to be made. If the law defined combatancy too widely, allowing un-uniformed fighters to qualify, this would result in the blurring of combatants and civilians and the potential erosion of the principle of distinction. However if combatancy were defined too narrowly, this would exclude fighters from the fold of the law, problematic as inclusion provides incentive for compliance with IHL. Over the years, states have shifted their positions on this point. AP1 marked the shift from promoting humanitarian protection by retaining a narrow category of privileged fighters to incentivising more irregular fighters to abide by humanitarian norms by offering them privileged status.[65]

Interrogating these categories raises question about whether the classification requirements – and in fact the categories themselves – were ever valid or still are today. The binary opposition of these categories should be questioned, probing whether having two distinct categories is a useful or even viable way to deal with the regulation of participation in conflict. Among others, feminist scholars have pointed to problems with the use of such binary distinctions.[66]

A related question is whether there should only be two categories, or whether there is a need for a possible additional category for those who do not fit neatly into one of the two. Most would agree that there is no category of quasi-combatant in IHL.[67] However, over the years, a number of terms have been proposed for those who fall between the two main categories, including 'non-combatant', 'illegal combatant', 'enemy combatant', 'unlawful combatant', 'belligerent', 'unprivileged belligerent' and 'unlawful belligerent'.[68] What is clear is that *civilians who fight* have been – and continue to be – the problematic piece of the puzzle.

The concept of 'unlawful combatant' has been around for years,[69] appearing in case law, military manuals and legal literature, although the term and its definition have never actually appeared in the IHL treaties. A person who sometimes engages in military operations, while at other times purports to be a civilian is said to be neither civilian nor lawful combatant but rather, an unlawful combatant. Such a person is a combatant, in that s/he can be targeted as such (and does not receive civilian protection from attack), yet does not receive the privileges conferred on lawful combatants, such as POW status and immunity from prosecution.[70] This 'status' therefore offers the least protection.[71] This categorisation has gained prominence in recent years, due largely to America using this classification as a means to deny POW status and other rights to terror suspects[72] – an approach that has been strongly criticised.[73] Crawford argues that,

> Given the almost uniform resistance to US attempts to proclaim a 'Geneva' status of 'unlawful enemy combatant', it is doubtful such a legal category

> exists. The term 'unlawful combatant' serves a descriptive function only. Arguably, the concept has no real international legal consequences that attach to its use, regardless of what the United States has asserted.[74]

The Israeli Supreme Court has also refused to accept that unlawful combatants are a distinct third category, reasoning that neither the treaties nor CIL provide a legal basis for recognising a third category.[75]

A complex body of law sets out who is a combatant. Classification is most clear for members of state armies, and less so for members of irregular state forces. There is even more confusion for civilians who fight for these forces. And as a result of AP1, there are now those classified in one way, yet treated as though they were classified in another. As the following section will illustrate, the situation becomes even more complex when applied to non-state armed groups in NIACs.

The principle of distinction in non-international armed conflict

Unlike in IACs, in NIACs the important divide is not between combatants and civilians, but rather between those who play a 'direct part' (or 'directly participate') in hostilities and those who do not. States, who created the IHL system, did not wish to grant privileged combatant status – as well as legal and political recognition – to those within their countries fighting against them.[76] Therefore, in the NIAC treaties there are no combatants granted the right to participate in hostilities.[77] Crawford explains that,

> By definition, any person who participates in an internal armed conflict who is not a member of the State's armed forces is an 'unlawful combatant' – that is, a person who is not immunized for their warlike acts under international law.[78]

Problematically, as their mere participation in hostilities is illegal whether they comply with IHL or not, non-state actors are left with less reason to comply with the law.[79]

Despite not wanting to recognise non-state fighters or to grant them combatant privileges, states wanted to retain the right to target those fighting against them. Therefore, Article 13(3) AP2 states: "Civilians shall enjoy the protection afforded by this part, unless and for such time as they take a direct part in hostilities". So in NIACs the key determinant of whether one may be targeted in attack is whether one 'directly participates' in hostilities. However, despite the fact that such significant consequences ride on this term, there has been little clarity and consensus on its meaning. The treaties provide no definition of direct participation and scholars have had greatly differing views about what direct participation entails.

The question of what *should* constitute direct participation is a difficult one. In many conflicts, particularly civil wars, large parts of populations become involved in war efforts, even if only indirectly. Demarcating a line between those directly participating and those merely contributing indirectly – or put differently, determining the point at which that contribution should negate one's legal immunity from attack – is a challenging task. Some argue that direct participation should be interpreted narrowly, so that fewer activities qualify, ensuring that more people retain protection from attack. Others contend that there is more protective value in interpreting the term liberally. Schmitt argues that,

> … narrowly interpreting direct participation in hostilities, although appearing to expand the protection of humanitarian law to greater numbers of individuals, actually increases the risk to the civilian population. Narrow interpretations both sow confusion, and, much more nefariously, encourage disrespect for the principle among those who suffer militarily from the actions of those said not to be directly participating. In particular, in modern combat it is illogical to tie participation to the direct release of kinetic forces. Not only may non-kinetic force be deadlier, but activities far from the 'battlefield' may be as important, perhaps more so, than actually 'pulling the trigger'.[80]

The Commentaries to the APs (Commentaries) provide some insight as to what actions the drafters intended to constitute direct participation. The Commentaries, published in 1987, were written mainly by people who had taken part in the Diplomatic Conference as members of the ICRC delegation, and aimed to explain the provisions of the Protocols. The Commentaries state that "Direct participation in hostilities implies a direct causal relationship between the activity engaged in and the harm done to the enemy at the time and the place where the activity takes place".[81] The Commentaries also explain that acts of direct participation are "acts which by their nature and purpose are intended to cause actual harm to the personnel and equipment of the armed forces".[82] They add that acts 'in preparation of' and 'returning from' an attack can be included as part of incidents of direct participation – however, this leads to the further questions about what these additional phrases mean. The Commentaries limit the term 'preparatory operation' by specifically referring to its military nature – meaning that preparatory acts would not encompass activities like recruiting, administration, training, propaganda, political work and law enforcement. Preparatory acts would include certain types of military-related logistic support for fighting groups, but would exclude non-military support tasks[83] – the types of tasks often performed by women.

The International Criminal Tribunal for the former Yugoslavia (ICTY) has weighed in on the discussion about direct participation. In *Prosecutor* v. *Stanislav Galic*, the ICTY Trial Chamber relied on the Commentaries' definition, stating that acts of direct participation were "acts of war which by their nature or purpose are likely to cause actual harm to the personnel or *matériel* of the enemy armed forces".[84] In *Prosecutor* v. *Strugar*, the Appeals Chamber held that conduct amounting to direct participation is not limited to combat activities.

However, it also noted that to consider all activities in support of military operations to be direct participation would render the principle of distinction meaningless in practice.[85] The ICTY Trial Chamber in *Prosecutor* v. *Dragomir Milosevic*, said that there is a need to distinguish between "direct participation in hostilities" and "participation in the war effort".[86] Although direct participation has been extensively discussed by the ICTY, the tribunal has added little clarity, alluding to the differences between direct and non-direct participation, yet refraining from actually defining the term. This has arguably contributed more confusion to an area already laden with differing opinions.

In 2009 responding to widespread concern about the lack of clarity on this term, the ICRC released its 'Interpretive Guidance on the Notion of Direct Participation in Hostilities under International Humanitarian Law' (Interpretive Guidance).[87] This was drafted following a long consultative process and set out the ICRC's view on how this law should be interpreted to best align with the realities of modern conflict.[88] The Interpretive Guidance establishes criteria for determining what behaviour qualifies as direct participation in hostilities. While not binding as law, the Interpretive Guidance has sought to develop the law, filling in gaps and opening the way to new interpretations and new potential avenues of development. The fact that this was done through guidelines, rather than through a process of legal amendment, speaks to some of the challenges around amending IHL, discussed in the conclusion chapter.

The Interpretive Guidance proposes that to qualify as direct participation an act must fulfil three requirements. First, the act must be likely to adversely affect the military operations or military capacity of a party to the conflict, or alternatively to inflict death, injury or destruction on persons or objects protected against direct attack (*threshold of harm*); second, there must be a direct causal link between the act and the harm likely to result from that act or a coordinated military operation of which that act constitutes an integral part (*direct causation*); and third, the act must be specifically designed to cause harm in support of one party to the conflict to the detriment of another (*belligerent nexus*).[89] The Interpretive Guidance restricts acts 'in preparation for' an attack by stating that in order to be part of the direct participation, the act must form an integral part of the attack in question. General acts that build the capacity of an armed group to launch attacks are not included in this.[90] The effects of an act, or rather its violent consequences, do not have to be felt immediately – activities that have delayed effects, such as laying explosives, can still constitute direct participation.[91]

The Interpretive Guidance's proposed interpretations veer somewhat from previously held understandings of the law and have received mixed responses.[92] Goodman and Jinks have summarised some of the central critiques the Interpretive Guidance received.[93] Those coming from the human rights school are concerned with the threats the Interpretive Guidance's broad definition of direct participation pose for people's rights, in that it allows many to become legitimate targets. In contrast, those coming from a military perspective contend that direct participation must accord with the practical realities of military operations, with discretion and freedom of action left to those planning attacks. They argue that the Interpretive Guidance unjustifiably restricts legitimate military targets.[94] For the purposes of this book, the Interpretive Guidance provides another example of gender-neutral regulation, which does not consider women and which fails to adequately encompass the roles played by women within its definitions. As with other IHL mechanisms, the Interpretive Guidance has no gender component and fails to recognise how participation plays out differently for women.

Article 13(3) AP2 states that a person who directly participates in hostilities loses immunity from attack, "for such time as they take a direct part in hostilities". Direct participation therefore results in a temporary loss of protection. Once the direct participation has ended, the person in question regains their civilian protection and can no longer be lawfully targeted. The temporary nature of the loss of protection is a key difference between civilians directly participating and combatants, who lose their immunity for the duration of hostilities or until they leave armed forces or lay down their arms. However, questions arise about the actual duration of an act of direct participation and, in turn, the duration of the resulting loss of protection. When exactly does an act of direct participation start and end? In each case, which particular acts in preparation for the main act are included, so that the loss of protection would last during those times too? This question is dealt with in some detail in the Interpretive Guidance, which discusses the duration and modalities of the loss of protection from attack.[95]

One of the key issues arising from the temporary loss of immunity is the potential 'revolving door' problem. The concern is that the temporary loss of immunity would allow civilians to participate in fighting and then to claim immunity as soon as they stop fighting, picking and choosing when they wish to be protected and when they wish to be participating. The example is often given of the 'farmer by day, fighter by night'.[96] Watkin adds that, "A 'revolving door' interpretation of direct participation could lead to allegations of perfidy and the misuse of civilian status".[97] This might be perceived as unacceptable to military opponents seeking to eliminate those who fight against them, encouraging non-compliance with IHL.

A final point to make about the principle of distinction in NIACs is that GC Common Article 3 provides a minimum level of protection in certain NIACs to those "persons taking no active part in the hostilities …" While the level of protection granted by this provision is very basic, CA3 applies more widely than AP2, which is only applicable to limited types of NIACs. This minimum set of protections is therefore important in situations where the more comprehensive AP2 does not apply.

Organised armed groups

The preceding section has examined the status of *individuals* participating in NIACs. However, it is also important to think about this at the *group* level.

While it is clear that members of non-state armed groups do not qualify as combatants, there is a lack of consensus in treaty law, state practice, military manuals, international jurisprudence and academic writing as to whether they are civilians.[98] There have been a number of approaches proposed to deal with this. One has been to classify members of armed groups as civilians who lose their protection due to their direct participation.[99] Some take this further and say that membership in armed groups is a continuous form of direct participation in which members, "owing to their continuous direct participation in hostilities, lose protection from attack for the entire duration of their membership".[100] Another view is that members of armed groups are not classified as civilians, but rather make up a separate category, which writers like Bartolini label as 'fighters' – although he admits that this is hard to infer from treaty provisions.[101] In the same vein, the San Remo Manual on the Law of Non International Armed Conflict uses the term 'fighters' rather than 'combatants' to avoid confusion with the use of the latter term in IACs. Its Article 1.1.2 (a) states: "For the purposes of this Manual, fighters are members of armed forces and dissident armed forces or other organized armed groups, or taking an active (direct) part in hostilities".[102]

The Interpretive Guidance proposes an altogether new approach to non-state armed groups. It suggests that one must distinguish a non-state *party* to a NIAC (like a secessionist movement, rebellion or insurgency) from its *armed wing* (which it calls an "organised armed group"). In the same way that state parties to a conflict consist of their armies and other supportive segments of the state, like political and administrative branches of government, so too do non-state parties to conflicts have both military and non-military facets. Those in the military wing make up the "organised armed group", as opposed to all others in the movement, who merely support or are in other ways affiliated with the non-state party.[103]

The Interpretive Guidance talks about how to determine who is a 'member' of an 'organised armed group', acknowledging that it may be difficult to distinguish a non-state party from its armed wing, as "there may be various degrees of affiliation with such groups that do not necessarily amount to 'membership' within the meaning of IHL".[104] The Interpretive Guidance proposes that membership of an organised armed group depends on having a "continuous combat function", meaning a person's continuous function involves directly participating in hostilities. This is a way to distinguish those who are members of organised armed groups from those who "… directly participate in hostilities on a merely spontaneous, sporadic, or unorganized basis, or who assume exclusively political, administrative or other non-combat functions".[105] The Interpretive Guidance emphasises that even where people accompany organised armed groups, if they themselves do not hold a continuous combat function, they will not be considered *members*.[106] This proviso is important when considering women who accompany Africa's armed groups. While civilians who directly participate only lose their protection for the duration of their participation, in terms of the Interpretive Guidance, those who have a continuous combat function lose their protection for the duration of their membership of the organised armed group.[107]

The ICRC's approach to armed groups has also been subject to criticism. Watkin argues that it provides non-state armed groups with a unique status, effectively creating a third category and producing membership criteria that are not founded in either treaty or customary law. He notes that this contradicts the ICRC's claim that the Interpretive Guidance was not purporting to change the law, but rather to provide interpretations of the law within existing parameters. Watkin also points out that those providing non-combat support to non-state armed groups are protected from attack, while those playing identical roles in state armed forces are considered combatants and subject to attack.[108] Consider the cook in an armed group and army.

As the above description makes clear, there are significant problems relating to the principle of distinction in NIACs. One concern is the uncertainty resulting from the lack of definitions and consensus on key terms. In addition, the way the laws were drafted exclude non-state actors from combatancy privileges and from being able to lawfully fight – and hence from incentive to comply with IHL. This model, designed by states with state interests in mind, fails to produce an inclusive system capable of motivating and regulating non-state actors. Given the increase in prevalence of NIACs today, this is becoming a growing source of concern.

This chapter has summarised the complex web of laws that make up the principle of distinction. Different rules apply in IACs and NIACs and to state and non-state actors. IHL was intended to create a level of reciprocity, providing rules and a level playing field to give some order during the chaos of conflict. The law has failed in achieving this. Its uneven application privileges certain parties in ways that promote non-compliance, arguably hindering the law's capacity to perform its intended task.

Although purporting to be gender neutral, the laws of distinction assume a certain type of combatant and civilian: male uniformed combatants and female civilians. However, as the following chapter will describe, new wars in Africa look little like this. Women participate, yet participate in different ways, ways that scarcely resemble the notions of participation and combatancy encompassed in this law above. The resulting disjuncture will form a key enquiry of this work.

Notes

1 Jochnick and Normand argue that the laws of war have tended to regulate areas of warfare only after these are no longer meaningful, like by banning those methods that no longer have utility, while allowing new destructive technology. Jochnick, Chris af and Normand, Roger. 'The Legitimation of Violence: A Critical History of the Laws of War'. *Harvard International Law Journal* 35 (1994): 49–95.

2 For a more comprehensive history of the principle of distinction, see Kinsella, Helen. *The Image before the Weapon: A Critical History of the Distinction between Combatant and Civilian*. Ithaca, NY: Cornell University Press, 2011.

3 Lorca, Arnulf Becker. 'Eurocentrism in the History of International Law'. In *The Oxford Handbook of the History of International Law*, 1034–1057. Oxford: Oxford Handbooks Online, 2012.

4 Writers have discussed IHL's relationship to non-European 'others' in the colonies and the role that Europe's colonisation project had in shaping the law. See Megret,

Frederic. 'From "Savages" to "Unlawful Combatants": A Postcolonial Look at International Humanitarian Law's "Other"', In *International Law and Its Others*. Cambridge: Cambridge University Press, 2006.

5 Watkin, Kenneth. 'Combatants, Unprivileged Belligerents and Conflicts in the 21st Century, Background Paper Prepared for the Informal High-Level Expert Meeting on the Reaffirmation and Development of International Humanitarian Law, Cambridge, 27–29 January 2003'. *Programme on Humanitarian Policy and Conflict Research at Harvard University* (2003).

6 Riley-Smith, Jonathan. *The Crusades, Christianity, and Islam*. New York: Columbia University Press, 2008.

7 Brady, Laura. 'Essential and Despised: Images of Women in the First and Second Crusades, 1095–1148'. New York: ProQuest Dissertations Publishing, 1992. Bom, Myra M. *Women in the Military Orders of the Crusades*. 1st edition. New Middle Ages. New York: Palgrave Macmillan, 2012.

8 Gabriel, Richard and Metz, Karen. 'A Short History of War, the Evolution of Warfare and Weapons'. Strategic Studies Institute, U.S. Army War College, www.au.af.mil/au/awc/awcgate/gabrmetz/gabr0019.htm.

9 Gies, Frances. *Joan of Arc: The Legend and the Reality*. 1st edn. New York: Harper & Row, 1981.

10 Ibid.

11 Talbot Jensen, Eric. 'The ICJ's Uganda Wall: A Barrier to the Principle of Distinction and an Entry Point for Lawfare'. *Denver Journal of International Law and Policy*, 35, no. 2 (2007): 241–274.

12 'Napoleonic Wars: Women at Waterloo'. Historynet.com, 2006. www.historynet.com/napoleonic-wars-women-at-waterloo.htm. Hagemann, Karen. '"Heroic Virgins" and "Bellicose Amazons": Armed Women, the Gender Order and the German Public during and after the Anti-Napoleonic Wars'. *European History Quarterly* 37, no. 4 (2007): 507–527.

13 Talbot Jensen, supra note 8.

14 Kalshoven, Frits and Zegveld, Liesbeth. *Constraints on the Waging of War, An Introduction to International Humanitarian Law, International Committee of the Red Cross*. 4 vols. Cambridge: Cambridge University Press, 2011.

15 It has also been incorporated into Geneva law and is also accepted as constituting a rule of customary international law. The principle of distinction is thus fully embedded into IHL.

16 Lieber, Francis, *Instructions for the Government of Armies of the United States in the Field*, Art. 22 (1863), in Swiney, Gabriel. 'Saving Lives: The Principle of Distinction and the Realities of Modern War'. *International Lawyer (ABA)* 39 (2005): 733–758, at 737.

17 Murphey, Kim. *I Had Rather Die: Rape in the Civil War*. Virginia: Coachlight Press, 2014.

18 Women of the American Civil War, Americancivilwar.com, http://Americancivilwar.com/women/women.html.

19 Preamble, *Declaration Renouncing the Use, In Times of War, of Explosive Projectiles Under 400 Grammes Weight* (1868). Saint Petersburg, 29 November–11 December 1868.

20 The 1899 conference had 26 state delegates taking part, while the 1907 conference had delegates from 43 states.

21 Article 25, Convention (IV) Respecting the Laws and Customs of War on Land, The Hague, 18 October 1907.

22 Articles 1 and 2, Convention (IX) Concerning Bombardment by Naval Forces in Time of War, The Hague, 18 October 1907.

23 Swiney, supra note 13.

24 Vincent, Paul. *The Politics of Hunger: The Allied Blockade of Germany, 1915–1919*. Athens, Ohio: Ohio University Press, 1985.
25 Lipkes, Jeff. *Rehearsals: The German Army in Belgium, August 1914*. Leuven: Leuven University Press, 2007.
26 Creveld, Martin van. 'The Great Illusion: Women in the Military'. *Millennium – Journal of International Studies* 29, no. 2 (2000): 429–442.
27 Hanke, Heinz. 'The 1923 Hague Rules of Air Warfare – A Contribution to the Development of International Law Protecting Civilians from Air Attack'. *International Review of the Red Cross* 33, no. 292 (1993): 12–44.
28 Swiney, supra note 13, at 740.
29 Resulting from this, approximately one million Germans were wounded or killed in bomber attacks and 7.5 million were made homeless. Ibid.
30 It is possibly because of the communist ideology, which emphasised gender equality, that so many women from Russia were used in the war effort. However, only about 2–3 per cent of them were military personnel. The rest served mainly in administrative or medical positions.
31 Creveld, supra note 23.
32 Neff, Stephen. *War and the Law of Nations: A General History*. Cambridge: Cambridge University Press, 2005, at 282–283.
33 Talbot Jensen, supra note 8.
34 Parks, Hays. 'Part IX of the ICRC "Direct Participation in Hostilities" Study: No Mandate, No Expertise, and Legally Incorrect'. *New York University Journal of International Law and Politics* 42 (2010): 769–830.
35 Creveld, supra note 23.
36 Talbot Jensen, supra note 8.
37 Ewumbue-Monono, Churchill. 'Respect for International Humanitarian Law by Armed Non-State Actors in Africa'. *International Review of the Red Cross* 88, no. 864 (2006): 905–924.
38 Gaudreau, Julie. 'The Reservations to the Protocols Additional to the Geneva Conventions for the Protection of War Victims'. *International Review of the Red Cross* 849 (2003): 143–84. An Article on which there have been significant reservations is Article 44, which relates to the principle of distinction (and specifically to combatant status for guerrilla fighters), discussed later in this chapter.
39 See Kaldor, Mary. *New and Old Wars: Organised Violence in a Global Era*. 3rd edn. Redwood City, CA: Stanford University Press, 2013.
40 Sassoli, Marco. 'Legitimate Targets of Attack under International Humanitarian Law'. *Programme on Humanitarian Policy and Conflict Research at Harvard University*. Background Paper Prepared for the Informal High-Level Expert Meeting on the Reaffirmation and Development of International Humanitarian Law, Cambridge (27 January 2003).
41 Dinstein, Yoram. 'The ICRC's Customary International Humanitarian Law Study'. In *The Law of War in the 21st Century: Weaponry and the Use of Force*, Vol. 82. International Law Studies, 2006. McCormack, Timothy. 'An Australian Perspective on the ICRC Customary International Humanitarian Law Study'. In *The Law of War in the 21st Century: Weaponry and the Use of Force*, Vol. 82. International Law Studies, 2006.
42 Henckaerts, Jean-Marie and Doswald-Beck, Louise. *Customary International Humanitarian Law, Volume 1: Rules, International Committee of the Red Cross*. Cambridge: Cambridge University Press, 2005. These rules have been subject to some criticism, most notably in terms of the methodology used. For a discussion, see Bellinger, John and Haynes, William. 'A US Government Response to the International Committee of the Red Cross Study Customary International Humanitarian Law'. *International Review of the Red Cross* 89, no. 866 (2007): 443–471, or Wilmshurst, Elizabeth and Breau, Susan. *Perspectives on the ICRC Study on*

Customary International Humanitarian Law. Cambridge: Cambridge University Press, 2007.

43 In terms of the study, other customary international law rules of the principle of distinction include Rule 2, stating that, "Acts or threats of violence the primary purpose of which is to spread terror among the civilian population are prohibited" (applicable in IACs and NIACs); Rule 3, that, "All members of the armed forces of a party to the conflict are combatants, except medical and religious personnel" (applicable only in IACs); Rule 4, stating that, "The armed forces of a party to the conflict consist of all organised armed forces, groups and units which are under a command responsible to that party for the conduct of its subordinates" (applicable only in IACs); and Rule 5, "Civilians are persons who are not members of the armed forces. The civilian population comprises all persons who are civilians" (applicable in IACs, and also in NIACs – although it states that practice is ambiguous as to whether members of armed opposition groups are considered members of armed forces or civilians). Rule 6 states that, "Civilians are protected against attack unless and for such time as they take a direct part in hostilities" (applicable in IACs and NIACs).

44 Convention on the Prohibition of the Use, Stockpiling, Production and Transfer of Anti-Personnel Mines and on Their Destruction, 18 September 1997 ATS 3/ 36 ILM 1507 and Convention on Cluster Munitions, 30 May 2008, C.N.776.

45 Kalshoven and Zegveld, supra note 11.

46 Article 4, GC3

47 Dinstein, Yoram. *The Conduct of Hostilities under the Law of International Armed Conflict*. Cambridge: Cambridge University Press, 2004.

48 The Privy Council in *Mohamed Ali et al.* v. *Public Prosecutor* (1969) AC 430, at 449, held that regular armed forces also have to meet these requirements.

49 Dinstein, supra note 42.

50 Kalshoven, Zegveld, supra note 11.

51 Fleck, Dieter. *The Handbook of Humanitarian Law in Armed Conflicts*. 2nd edition. Oxford: Oxford University Press, 2008.

52 Dinstein, supra note 42, at 47.

53 Ibid.

54 Talbot Jensen, supra note 8.

55 For example, a number of states declared that they understood the application of 44(3) to be limited to situations of occupations or conflicts of self-determination. See Gaudreau, supra note 35.

56 Parks, Hays, supra note 31.

57 Found in, Art 51(5)(b), Art 57(2), Art 85(3) AP1.

58 13(3) AP2

59 Solis, Gary. *The Law of Armed Conflict: International Humanitarian Law in War*. Cambridge: Cambridge University Press, 2010.

60 Gasser, Hans-Peter. *International Humanitarian Law: An Introduction*. Bern: Haupt, 1993.

61 For example, GC3 Art 25 and Art 88.

62 Kinsella, Helen. *Securing the Civilian: Sex and Gender in the Laws of War*. Boston, MA: Boston Consortium on Gender, Security and Human Rights, 2004.

63 Nurick, Lester. 'The Distinction between Combatant and Non-Combatant in the Law of War'. *American Journal of International Law* 39 (1945): 680–697.

64 Kinsella, supra note 54.

65 Watkin, supra note 4.

66 Charlesworth, Hilary and Chinkin, Christine. *The Boundaries of International Law: A Feminist Analysis*. Manchester: Manchester University Press, 2000.

67 Sassoli, supra note 37.

68 For a discussion of the term 'non-combatant' and the way its meaning has shifted over time, see Watkin, supra note 4, at 3–4.

69 See, Scheipers, Sibylle. *Unlawful Combatants: A Genealogy of the Irregular Fighter*. 1st edn. New York, NY: Oxford University Press, 2015.
70 Dinstein, supra note 47.
71 One should note that although unlawful combatants are denied POW status, they are still protected under Article 75 of AP1, which provides a minimum level of protection to those who fall into the hands of adversaries yet do not benefit from any more favourable protections. They would also remain protected by relevant provisions of human rights law. In *Al-Skeini and Others* v. *The United Kingdom, ECHR 1093–55721/07, 2011*, the European Court of Human Rights held that the United Kingdom's human rights obligations applied extraterritorially to its acts in fighting the Iraq war, opening up the way for the extraterritorial application of human rights obligations in conflict situations. In NIACs they would also be entitled to protection in terms of CA 3.
72 For a summary of arguments made by the United States Government in this regard, see, Bellinger, John. 'Legal Issues in the War on Terrorism – A Reply to Silja N. U. Voneky'. *German Law Journal* 8, no. 9 (2007): 871–878.
73 See for example, Voneky, Silja. 'Response – The Fight Against Terrorism and the Rules of International Law – Comment on Papers and Speeches of John B. Bellinger, Chief Legal Advisor to the United States State Department'. *German Law Journal* 8 (2007): 747–760.
74 Crawford, Emily. *The Treatment of Combatants and Insurgents under the Law of Armed Conflict*. Oxford: Oxford University Press, 2010, at 60.
75 *The Public Committee Against Torture in Israel et al.* v. *the Government of Israel*, HCJ 769/02, 14 December 2006, at para 28.
76 States argued that to grant protected status to rebels and insurgents would go against the system of sovereign states. They argued that if states were to grant combatant immunity to non-state actors, they would effectively be suspending their criminal and treason laws. See Crawford, supra note 66.
77 Sperroto, Federico. 'The Legal Status of Armed Opposition Groups in Afghanistan'. *openDemocracy*, 23 March 2010. [Online]
78 Crawford, supra note 66, at 68.
79 Lamp, Nicolas. 'Conceptions of War and Paradigms of Compliance: The 'New War' Challenge to International Humanitarian Law'. *Journal of Conflict and Security Law* 16, no. 2 (2011): 225–262.
80 Schmitt, Michael. ''Direct Participation in Hostilities' and 21st century Armed Conflict'. In Fischer, Horst (ed.), *Crisis Management and Humanitarian Protection: Festschrift Fur*, 505–529. Berlin: BWV, 2004, at 529.
81 Commentary on Additional Protocol 1, ICRC, Geneva, p. 516 (1679), in Queguiner, Francois Jean. 'Direct Participation in Hostilities under International Humanitarian Law'. *Program on Humanitarian Policy and Conflict Research at Harvard University* (2003), at 2–3.
82 Commentary on Additional Protocol 1, ICRC, (op. cit. footnote 2), para 1942, in Schmitt, supra note 72, at 508.
83 Queguiner, supra note 73.
84 *The Prosecutor* v. *Stanislav Galic*, ICTY Trial Judgment, IT-98-29-T, 2003, para 48.
85 *The Prosecutor* v. *Strugar*, ICTY Appeals Chamber Judgment, IT-01-42-A, 2008, para 176.
86 *The Prosecutor* v. *Dragomir Milosevic*, ICTY Trial Judgment, IT-98-29/1-T, 2007, para 947.
87 'Interpretive Guidance on the Notion of Direct Participation in Hostilities Under International Humanitarian Law'. *International Review of the Red Cross* 90, no. 872 (2009): 991–1047.
88 Ibid.

89 Part 2 V 1–3, Ibid.
90 Part 2 V 2 a, Ibid.
91 Queguiner, supra note 73.
92 For some of the discussion arising in response to the Interpretive Guidance, see the *Journal of International Law and Politics* issue 42:3 (Spring 2010), which hosted a forum, largely dedicated to discussing the Interpretive Guidance.
93 Goodman, Ryan and Jinks, Derek. 'The ICRC Interpretive Guidance on the Notion of Direct Participation in Hostilities under International Humanitarian Law: An Introduction to the Forum'. *New York University International Law and Politics* 42 (2010): 637–640.
94 Ibid.
95 Part 2 V1, Interpretive Guidance, supra note 79.
96 Interpretive Guidance, supra note 79.
97 Watkin, supra note 4, at 12.
98 Part 2 II 1 a, Interpretive Guidance, supra note 79.
99 Bartolini, Giulio, in Matheson, Michael and Momtaz, Djamchid (eds), *Rules and Institutions of International Humanitarian Law Put to the Test of Recent Armed Conflicts*. Leiden; Biggleswade: Martinus Nijhoff, 2011.
100 Part 2 II 1 a, Interpretive Guidance, supra note 79. The Interpretive Guidance criticises this approach, saying it undermines the conceptual integrity of the categories that underlie the principle of distinction in that it leads to a situation where parties to a conflict have entire armed forces that remain classified as civilians. In the expert meetings leading up to the Interpretive Guidance, this approach was also criticised as it blurred the distinction between a loss of protection based on conduct and a loss of protection based on status or function.
101 Bartolini, supra note 90.
102 Art 1.1.2(a), Schmitt, Michael, Garraway, Charles and Dinstein, Yoram. 'The Manual on the Law of Non-International Armed Conflict, San Remo'. International Institute of Humanitarian Law, 2006.
103 Part 2, II, 3 a, Interpretive Guidance, supra note 79.
104 Part 2, II, 3 b.
105 Part 2, II, 3 b.
106 Part 2, II, 3 a.
107 Part 1, VII.
108 Watkin, Kenneth. 'Opportunities Lost: Organised Armed Groups and the ICRC 'Direct Participation in Hostilities' Interpretive Guidance, International Law and Politics'. *International Law and Politics* 42, no. 3 (2010): 641–695.

Bibliography

Books and articles

Bartolini, Giulio, in Matheson, Michael and Momtaz, Djamchid (eds), *Rules and Institutions of International Humanitarian Law Put to the Test of Recent Armed Conflicts*. Leiden; Biggleswade: Martinus Nijhoff, 2011.

Bellinger, John. 'Legal Issues in the War on Terrorism – A Reply to Silja N. U. Voneky'. *German Law Journal* 8, no. 9 (2007): 871–878.

Bellinger, John, and Haynes, William. 'A US Government Response to the International Committee of the Red Cross Study Customary International Humanitarian Law'. *International Review of the Red Cross* 89, no. 866 (2007): 443–471.

Bom, Myra M. *Women in the Military Orders of the Crusades*. 1st edn. New Middle Ages. New York: Palgrave Macmillan, 2012.

Brady, Laura. 'Essential and Despised: Images of Women in the First and Second Crusades, 1095–1148'. ProQuest Dissertations Publishing, 1992.

Charlesworth, Hilary, and Chinkin, Christine. *The Boundaries of International Law: A Feminist Analysis*. Manchester: Manchester University Press, 2000.

Crawford, Emily. *The Treatment of Combatants and Insurgents Under the Law of Armed Conflict*. Oxford: Oxford University Press, 2010.

Creveld, Martin van. 'The Great Illusion: Women in the Military'. *Millennium – Journal of International Studies* 29, no. 2 (2000): 429–442.

Dinstein, Yoram. *The Conduct of Hostilities under the Law of International Armed Conflict*. Cambridge: Cambridge University Press, 2004.

Dinstein, Yoram. 'The ICRC's Customary International Humanitarian Law Study'. In *The Law of War in the 21st Century: Weaponry and the Use of Force*, Vol. 82. International Law Studies, 2006.

Ewumbue-Monono, Churchill. 'Respect for International Humanitarian Law by Armed Non-State Actors in Africa'. *International Review of the Red Cross* 88, no. 864 (2006): 905–924.

Fleck, Dieter. *The Handbook of Humanitarian Law in Armed Conflicts*. 2nd edition. Oxford: Oxford University Press, 2008.

Gabriel, Richard and Metz, Karen. *A Short History of War: The Evolution of Warfare and Weapons*. Strategic Studies Institute, U.S. Army War College, n.d. www.au.af.mil/au/awc/awcgate/gabrmetz/gabr0019.htm.

Gasser, Hans-Peter. *International Humanitarian Law: An Introduction*. Bern: Haupt, 1993.

Gaudreau, Julie. 'The Reservations to the Protocols Additional to the Geneva Conventions for the Protection of War Victims'. *International Review of the Red Cross* 849 (2003): 143–184.

Gies, Frances. *Joan of Arc: The Legend and the Reality*. 1st edn. New York: Harper & Row, 1981.

Goodman, Ryan and Jinks, Derek. 'The ICRC Interpretive Guidance on the Notion of Direct Participation in Hostilities Under International Humanitarian Law: An Introduction to the Forum'. *New York University International Law and Politics* 42 (2010): 637–640.

Hagemann, Karen. '"Heroic Virgins" and "Bellicose Amazons": Armed Women, the Gender Order and the German Public during and after the Anti-Napoleonic Wars'. *European History Quarterly* 37, no. 4 (2007): 507–527.

Hanke, Heinz. 'The 1923 Hague Rules of Air Warfare – A Contribution to the Development of International Law Protecting Civilians from Air Attack'. *International Review of the Red Cross* 33, no. 292 (1993): 12–44.

Henckaerts, Jean-Marie and Doswald-Beck, Louise. *Customary International Humanitarian Law, Volume 1: Rules, International Committee of the Red Cross*. Cambridge: Cambridge University Press, 2005.

Jochnick, Chris af and Normand, Roger. 'The Legitimation of Violence: A Critical History of the Laws of War'. *Harvard International Law Journal* 35 (1994): 49–95.

Kaldor, Mary. *New and Old Wars: Organised Violence in a Global Era*. 3rd edn. Redwood City, CA: Stanford University Press, 2013.

Kalshoven, Frits and Zegveld, Liesbeth. *Constraints on the Waging of War, an Introduction to International Humanitarian Law, International Committee of the Red Cross*. 4 vols. Cambridge: Cambridge University Press, 2011.

Kinsella, Helen. *The Image before the Weapon: A Critical History of the Distinction Between Combatant and Civilian*. Ithaca, NY: Cornell University Press, 2011.

Kinsella, Helen. *Securing the Civilian: Sex and Gender in the Laws of War*. Boston, MA: Boston Consortium on Gender, Security and Human Rights, 2004.

Lamp, Nicolas. 'Conceptions of War and Paradigms of Compliance: The "New War" Challenge to International Humanitarian Law'. *Journal of Conflict and Security Law* 16, no. 2 (2011): 225–262.

Lieber, Francis, *Instructions for the Government of Armies of the United States in the Field*, Art. 22 (1863), in Swiney, Gabriel. 'Saving Lives: The Principle of Distinction and the Realities of Modern War'. *International Lawyer (ABA)* 39 (2005): 733–758, at 737.

Lipkes, Jeff. *Rehearsals: The German Army in Belgium, August 1914*. Leuven: Leuven University Press, 2007.

Lorca, Arnulf Becker. 'Eurocentrism in the History of International Law'. In *The Oxford Handbook of the History of International Law*, 1034–1057. Oxford: Oxford Handbooks Online, 2012.

Megret, Frederic. 'From "Savages" to "Unlawful Combatants": A Postcolonial Look at International Humanitarian Law's "Other"'. In Orford, Anne (ed.), *International Law and Its Others*, 256–317. Cambridge: Cambridge University Press, 2006.

McCormack, Timothy. 'An Australian Perspective on the ICRC Customary International Humanitarian Law Study'. In *The Law of War in the 21st Century: Weaponry and the Use of Force*, Vol. 82. International Law Studies, 2006.

Murphey, Kim. *I Had Rather Die: Rape in the Civil War*. Virginia: Coachlight Press, 2014.

Neff, Stephen. *War and the Law of Nations: A General History*. Cambridge: Cambridge University Press, 2005, at 282–283.

Nurick, Lester. 'The Distinction between Combatant and Non-Combatant in the Law of War'. *American Journal of International Law* 39 (1945): 680–697.

Parks, Hays. 'Part IX of the ICRC "Direct Participation in Hostilities" Study: No Mandate, No Expertise, and Legally Incorrect'. *New York University Journal of International Law and Politics* 42 (2010): 769–830.

Queguiner, Francois Jean. 'Direct Participation in Hostilities under International Humanitarian Law'. *Program on Humanitarian Policy and Conflict Research at Harvard University* (2003), at 2–3.

Riley-Smith, Jonathan. *The Crusades, Christianity, and Islam*. New York: Columbia University Press, 2008.

Sassoli, Marco. 'Legitimate Targets of Attack under International Humanitarian Law'. *Programme on Humanitarian Policy and Conflict Research at Harvard University*. Background Paper Prepared for the Informal High-Level Expert Meeting on the Reaffirmation and Development of International Humanitarian Law, Cambridge (27 January 2003).

Scheipers, Sibylle. *Unlawful Combatants: A Genealogy of the Irregular Fighter*. 1st edn. New York, NY: Oxford University Press, 2015.

Schmitt, Michael. '"Direct Participation in Hostilities" and 21st century Armed Conflict'. In *Crisis Management and Humanitarian Protection: Festschrift Fur*, 505–529. Fischer, Horst Berlin: BWV, 2004, at 529.

Schmitt, Michael, Garraway, Charles and Dinstein, Yoram. *The Manual on the Law of Non-International Armed Conflict, San Remo*. International Institute of Humanitarian Law, 2006.

Solis, Gary. *The Law of Armed Conflict: International Humanitarian Law in War*. Cambridge: Cambridge University Press, 2010.

Sperroto, Federico. 'The Legal Status of Armed Opposition Groups in Afghanistan'. *openDemocracy*, 23 March 2010.

Talbot Jensen, Eric. 'The ICJ's Uganda Wall: A Barrier to the Principle of Distinction and an Entry Point for Lawfare'. *Denver Journal of International Law and Policy*, 35, no. 2 (2007): 241–274.

Vincent, Paul. *The Politics of Hunger: The Allied Blockade of Germany, 1915–1919*. Athens, Ohio: Ohio University Press, 1985.

Voneky, Silja. 'Response – The Fight Against Terrorism and the Rules of International Law – Comment on Papers and Speeches of John B. Bellinger, Chief Legal Advisor to the United States State Department'. *German Law Journal* 8 (2007): 747–760.

Watkin, Kenneth. 'Combatants, Unprivileged Belligerents and Conflicts in the 21st Century, Background Paper Prepared for the Informal High-Level Expert Meeting on the Reaffirmation and Development of International Humanitarian Law, Cambridge, 27–29 January 2003'. *Programme on Humanitarian Policy and Conflict Research at Harvard University* (2003).

Watkin, Kenneth. 'Opportunities Lost: Organised Armed Groups and the ICRC 'Direct Participation in Hostilities' Interpretive Guidance, International Law and Politics'. *International Law and Politics* 42, no. 3 (2010): 641–695.

Wilmshurst, Elizabeth and Breau, Susan. *Perspectives on the ICRC Study on Customary International Humanitarian Law*. Cambridge: Cambridge University Press, 2007.

Cases

Al-Skeini and Others v. *The United Kingdom, ECHR 1093-55721/07, 2011.*

The Privy Council in *Mohamed Ali et al.* v. *Public Prosecutor* (1969) AC 430.

The Prosecutor v. *Dragomir Milosevic*, ICTY Trial Judgment, IT-98-29/1-T, 2007.

The Prosecutor v. *Stanislav Galic*, ICTY Trial Judgment, IT-98-29-T, 2003.

The Prosecutor v. *Strugar*, ICTY Appeals Chamber Judgment, IT-01-42-A, 2008.

The Public Committee Against Torture in Israel et al. v. *the Government of Israel*, HCJ 769/02, 14 December 2006.

Treaties

Convention (IV) Respecting the Laws and Customs of War on Land, The Hague, 18 October 1907.

Convention (IX) Concerning Bombardment by Naval Forces in Time of War, The Hague, 18 October 1907.

Convention on the Prohibition of the Use, Stockpiling, Production and Transfer of Anti-Personnel Mines and on Their Destruction, 18 September 1997 ATS 3/ 36 ILM 1507.

Convention on Cluster Munitions, 30 May 2008, C.N.776.

Declaration Renouncing the Use, In Times of War, of Explosive Projectiles Under 400 Grammes Weight (1868).

Geneva Convention Relative to the Protection of Civilian Persons in Time of War (Fourth Geneva Convention), 12 August 1949, 75 UNTS 287.

Geneva Convention Relative to the Treatment of Prisoners of War (Third Geneva Convention), 12 August 1949, 75 UNTS 135.

Geneva Convention for the Amelioration of the Condition of Wounded, Sick and Shipwrecked Members of Armed Forces at Sea (Second Geneva Convention), 12 August 1949, 75 UNTS 85.

Geneva Convention for the Amelioration of the Condition of the Wounded and Sick in Armed Forces in the Field (First Geneva Convention), 12 August 1949, 75 UNTS 31.
Protocol Additional to the Geneva Conventions of 12 August 1949, and relating to the Protection of Victims of International Armed Conflicts (Protocol I), 8 June 1977, 1125 UNTS 3.
Protocol Additional to the Geneva Conventions of 12 August 1949, and relating to the Protection of Victims of Non-International Armed Conflicts (Protocol II), 8 June 1977, 1125 UNTS 609.

Other policy documents

Commentary on Additional Protocol 1, ICRC, Geneva, (1679).
'Interpretive Guidance on the Notion of Direct Participation in Hostilities Under International Humanitarian Law'. *International Review of the Red Cross* 90, no. 872 (2009): 991–1047.

Websites

The National Archives, www.nationalarchives.gov.uk/pathways/firstworldwar/spotlights/blockade.htm.
Women of the American Civil War, Americancivilwar.com, http://Americancivilwar.com/women/women.html.

3 Women in conflict in Africa

Across the African continent women have become embroiled in conflicts. Most are civilians; fleeing hostilities, searching for refuge, struggling to protect and feed their families. Others are actively involved in waging war. Some women live and move with armed groups, wearing uniforms, carrying weapons and taking part in armed activities. Some take care of armed groups' domestic needs – responsible for sustaining life and family on armed group bases. Some women participate voluntarily, out of conviction for an armed movement's aims. Others do what they can to avoid hostilities, yet are forcibly recruited and drawn in against their wills. From Muammar Gaddafi's band of female bodyguards, to the freedom fighters of South Sudan's People's Liberations Army (SPLM), to the abducted girls of the Lord's Resistance Army (LRA), fighting with their babies tied to their backs, Africa's female fighters have been a vastly diverse group.

Despite their many differences, there are some important commonalities between them; African women participate in conflict in gender-specific ways, which are often shaped by African norms and expectations about female-appropriate behaviour. Their experiences in armed groups are influenced by the status of women in their societies prior to hostilities. Holding a range of roles, often simultaneously, African women provide a striking illustration of the blurring lines between victim and perpetrator, empowered and exploited, voluntary and coerced, combatant and civilian.

This chapter will describe some of the women who actively participate in conflicts in Africa, providing the facts that will underpin the legal analysis later in this book. The chapter begins with a discussion on African conflicts, placing these within a historical context and looking at the differing types of conflicts and the diverse actors who participate in these. African conflicts are located within the theoretical categorisation of 'new wars', and the gendered aspects of new wars are explored, as are the challenges around the implementation of IHL in these wars. The chapter will briefly look at female combatancy worldwide, to locate Africa's female fighters among their international counterparts. It will then describe women who actively participate in African conflicts, discussing how and why women are recruited, the types of roles they play in armed groups and what these experiences are like. The chapter will conclude with a description of the challenges female former fighters face in the post-conflict period.

In this chapter 'Africa' refers to the African continent, including adjacent islands. The continent, as described, has 54 states,[1] nine territories and two states with limited recognition. Included on this enormous landmass are the 'Africanist' countries of sub-Saharan Africa, as well as the Arabic countries of the north and eastern parts of the continent. Some of the countries that have been part of the so-called Arab Spring, including Libya, Egypt and Tunisia, lie on the African continent, and as such some aspects of the Arab Spring have been included in this discussion on African conflict.

The diverse landscape of armed conflict in Africa

A brief history

To understand the nature of conflict in Africa, one needs to consider the recent political history of the continent. Africa's countries have had vastly differing histories. This section does not attempt to provide a comprehensive history of conflict on the continent, but rather to illustrate broad and general patterns of political change and turmoil, which provide a background against which current and recent African conflicts can be understood.

Prior to colonial times, Africa was made up of numerous kingdoms, often broken down along tribal lines. During the 1800s, European powers fought for colonial control of territory in Africa. African colonies were considered important for a number of reasons. They could be exploited, providing European powers with resources like crops, minerals and labour. They were important in the building of empires and were a key source of national prestige for European powers. The colonies were also a venue for those dispersing religious gospel and 'civilising' practices.[2] In 1884–1885, Germany's Chancellor Otto von Bismarck initiated the Berlin Conference, in which imperial boundaries in Africa were agreed upon by European powers and guidelines were created for the acquisition of African colonies. In the years that followed, in what became known as the 'scramble for Africa', European powers took control of vast portions of African territory, often through violent means.[3] By 1905 Africa was almost entirely colonised, the only exceptions being Liberia, which had been settled by African-American former slaves, and Ethiopia, which managed to resist colonisation by the Italians. Britain and France colonised the largest portions of the continent, with Germany, Spain, Italy, Portugal and Belgium also establishing African colonies.

Borders demarcated by colonialists were often arbitrary, cutting across ethnic population lines and grouping diverse people into newly formed countries.[4] Colonialism functioned differently in different colonies, leading to distinct dynamics and later, to differing forms of resistance in the anti-colonial conflicts. 'Settler colonialism', seen in former colonies like Zimbabwe, Kenya, South Africa and Algeria, saw large-scale colonialist immigration for political, economic or religious reasons. In 'exploitation colonialism', found in Egypt and central Africa, fewer colonialists immigrated to the territories, with the focus instead being on trade and extraction of resources. Colonial territories were governed in different ways. Largely, formal colonies were governed by colonial immigrants who formed the administrative and civil services of the colony. In protectorates, colonial powers ruled through local population groups, elevating certain ethnic or other groups to relative power – a practice that set the scene for later conflicts between local groupings. Colonial powers exploited their colonies, often failing to develop, educate or empower those within their realm.

Colonialism was central to the formation and expansion of international law, and in turn international law promoted European imperialism.[5] Anghie notes,

> This law legitimised conquest as legal, and decreed that lands inhabited by people regarded as inferior and backward were terra nullius. In other cases imperial powers claimed that native chiefs had entered into treaties which gave those powers sovereignty over non-European territories and peoples. The ability of natives to enter into such treaties was paradoxical, given that they were characterised as entirely lacking in legal status.[6]

Through European expansion, international law was spread around the world, working to make it a universal system.

Following World War One, questions arose as to what to do with the colonies of nations that had been conquered in the war. An arrangement was reached whereby Britain and France administered most of Germany's former African colonies as 'mandates', supervised by the League of Nations.[7] Mandates were different to colonies, at least in theory, in that they were less militarised, more equitable commercially and had more of a focus on furthering the interests of local populations. The mandate system aimed to supervise powers in colonial or postcolonial positions, based on a view that mandate countries were not yet developed enough to ensure their own political wellbeing.[8] Mandates began to shift the way that people perceived colonialism and European imperialism.[9]

During the twentieth century self-determination began increasingly to be recognised as important, and by the 1960s and 1970s it had started to be understood as a right.[10] The rights of colonised people to independence began to garner international support.[11] In the 1949 Geneva Conventions, wars of independence were understood to be 'non-international' and were largely excluded from the GC's ambit.[12] Twenty years later at the 1974–1977 Diplomatic Conference leading to the APs, wars of independence had become a controversial topic. Western states were resistant to conferring formal status onto such conflicts. However, owing to international pressure, AP1 included in its ambit "… armed conflicts in which peoples are fighting against colonial domination and alien occupation and against racist regimes in the exercise of their right of self-determination …" (Article 1.4). Independence struggles broke out across the continent mostly in the 1950s to 1970s. The decolonisation processes differed across countries. While in some countries the process was peaceful with colonial powers leaving of their own accord, in others it was cruelly resisted, with a series of often-brutal wars ensuing between departing colonial powers, local groups vying for control of territory and interested regional parties. The anti-colonial conflicts were often messy, involving numerous actors – national, regional and international – and spilling over borders across regions.

As colonial powers departed, former colonies were left with the task of building functioning states. Departing colonisers left colonies with varying levels of administrative capacity, and provided them with differing levels of continued support – or outright abandonment – depending on the nature of the colonial rule and the circumstances surrounding their departure. Many of the infant states lacked administrative, political, civil and other human capacity. On colonial departure, disparate and often hostile population groups began to fight for competing interests and power struggles emerged between those vying for power.

Opinions of the International Court of Justice (ICJ) framed many de-colonial transfers, forming a legal backdrop to the struggles taking place. As an example, in 1975 the ICJ provided an Advisory Opinion on the disputed territory of Western Sahara,[13] previously colonised by Spain, yet claimed by both Morocco and Mauritania, as well as by an internal movement demanding independence. The ICJ had to consider whether at the time of Spanish colonisation the territory was *terra nullius* (belonging to no one) and, if not, what legal claims Morocco and Mauritania had over the territory. The Court held that the territory had not been *terra nullius* at the time of colonisation, that Morocco and Mauritania's legal ties with the territory did not imply sovereignty, and that self-determination lay with the people of Western Sahara. The ICJ's decision was largely disregarded by interested parties and was interpreted differently by various parties to support their own views. In October 1975 Moroccan troops invaded Western Sahara. Today Western Sahara is still administered by Morocco, although the United Nations has never recognised Morocco's claim over the territory. The ICJ today continues to frame conflicts, as well as diverting other disputing countries from going to war.[14]

During the Cold War, Africa gained renewed importance for political, economic and strategic reasons, with colonisation giving way to competition over ideological influence. The superpowers sought to influence African states, with the USSR and the USA pouring economic aid and arms onto the continent and interfering politically as they fought to control the balance of world power. A number of African liberation leaders were killed or deposed – sometimes with the help of foreign powers seeking to control the leadership of the fledgling countries. Among these were Patrice Lumumba, Prime Minister of the newly independent Congo, killed in 1961; Félix-Roland Moumie of Cameroon, who was poisoned in 1960; and Sylvanus Olympio, the leader of Togo, killed in 1963. Mehdi Ben Barka, the opposition leader of Morocco, was kidnapped in France in 1965 and was never found. Eduardo Mondlane, the leader of Mozambique's FRELIMO, died from a parcel bomb in 1969. The superpowers fought each other through 'proxy wars', as the result of a direct clash between nuclear powers would have been disastrous. A *New York Times* journalist wrote that African countries were, "... turned into pawns, knights and rooks on a cold war chessboard by the superpowers ..."[15] Following the end of the Cold War, superpower interest in the region waned, with superpowers abandoning the states they had been involved in. This abandonment, too, laid the groundwork for conflicts that later arose.

In recent years, Africa has become significant in terms of international terrorism. In the late 1990s American embassies were bombed in Nairobi and Dar es Salaam. An Al-Qaeda cell was located in Nairobi in the 1990s and terror attacks took place against Israeli targets in Mombasa in 2002. In 2013 Somali group Al-Shabaab attacked Nairobi's Westgate Shopping Mall killing 67 people. Counter-terror actors talk of the risk created by "ungoverned spaces". Africa's zones of instability have provided a safe-haven and breeding ground for international and domestic terror groups alike, as well as for local chapters of international groups.[16] Links between various terror groups have been established on the continent; for example, there have been reports that Nigeria's Boko Haram has sent new recruits to Mali for training.[17] The 'horn of Africa' (in particular Kenya, Ethiopia, Djibouti, Somalia, Eritrea, Sudan) is a significant source-point for international terrorism.[18] Somalia, in particular, has been considered a safe-haven for terrorists; years of conflict and the decline of international engagement in Somalia led to there being hardly any Western presence in the country, allowing terrorists to operate there relatively freely. Still, Somalia has not been as significant a terror environment as feared. The United States Institute of Peace explains that,

> … Somalia's lawlessness creates conditions of insecurity – extortion, kidnapping, betrayal – that constitute a risky environment for terrorist operations. The paucity of Western targets inside Somalia makes it an unlikely site for attacks. The low number of non-Somali residents make it exceptionally difficult for a foreign terrorist to go unnoticed in the country.[19]

Somalia today plays a role as a short-term transit point, allowing persons and arms to cross the porous border into Kenya. The 'White Widow', British Samantha Lewthwaite, widow of one of the London 7/7 terrorist bombers, was allegedly a member of Somalia's Al-Shabaab. Global terrorism has created access points for international military involvement in Africa, with the presence of terrorists used as justification for military intervention – such as seen in Mali in 2012. Classifying armed behaviour as terrorism seems to operate as justification for military actions that would otherwise be unacceptable under international law. This problem does not only stem from Western states; there has been a growing problem of African governments using counter-terror measures to curtail legitimate political protest,[20] seen in recent years in Libya and Egypt.

A number of African countries remain unstable today. Some have experienced repeated attempts at overthrowing and replacing governments – with a few becoming so unstable that their governments have lost effective control, with them dubbed as 'failed states'.[21] Perhaps the best-known examples are Somalia and the Democratic Republic of Congo (DRC).

The north African revolutionary conflicts that formed part of the Arab Spring have been the latest development in a region of ever-shifting tensions. Rising militant Islamism has added further instability, with extremist Islamist groups responsible for rising insecurity in Nigeria, Libya, Somalia, Egypt and Sudan.

Africa's current conflicts vary from full-scale inter-state conflicts – like those fought between Ethiopia and Eritrea, and Libya and Chad – to struggles for liberation, fights for democracy, coups or political power struggles. Conflicts have been fought over ethnicity, religion, marginalisation and political beliefs. Some conflicts have even spilled over into genocide.[22] Some have been short and acute, while others have been longer term and lower level. Across the continent conflicts have operated as a barrier to development and economic advancement.[23] Many African conflicts have become 'internationalised'; even quintessential internal conflicts have attracted the attention of foreign troops, rebels, media and aid organisations. Fighters, arms and refugees move easily across Africa's porous borders, with conflicts frequently spilling over into neighbouring countries.

Actors in African conflict

A range of actors operate within these divergent conflicts, each with differing goals and motivations. Mateos explains that a "net of actors" in conflict is made up of "primary actors", those who engage directly in violence, including members of armed groups, guerrillas, militias, paramilitary forces, warlords, organised criminal gangs, police, mercenaries, fundamentalist groups and regional troops; "secondary actors", who, although not directly participating in hostilities, have an interest in their continuation, including criminal networks, regional governments, business interests, local and regional traders, international governments, private security companies and those in the arms trade; and "tertiary actors", who intervene to try to manage the confrontation, including those in the diaspora, civil society, media, regional and international governments, international organisations, diplomatic and humanitarian organisations and donor agencies.[24]

African conflicts are frequently 'asymmetrical', with parties diverging in terms of resources, weaponry, funds and support.[25] In liberation and civil wars, colonial or government armies, often highly resourced with modern arms and equipment, battle local fighters with fewer resources. However, these movements frequently have popular support, a different type of resource. Those fighting against states, who are unable to match their military power, often resort to guerrilla tactics. For example, the Lord's Resistance Army of northern Uganda developed the ability to fight and hide in certain terrains, enabling them to resist the immeasurably better resourced Ugandan government army for over 20 years. Lacking popular support, the group resorted to terrorising local populations in order to dissuade resistance, also abducting thousands of child soldiers to build their ranks.[26]

New wars, which many African conflicts typify, are characterised by a blurring between combatants and criminals. New wars' armed groups frequently finance themselves through what Peterson calls the "illicit international informal economy". He explains that,

> … the expansion of illicit activities – trafficking in drugs, sex workers, migrants, dirty money, black market goods – provides necessary financing for war resources. These markets defy territorial boundaries and state-based legal regimes; they are increasingly regional and even global; and deregulation amplifies opportunities for laundering 'dirty' money.[27]

Armed actors develop networks to further their goals, with partnerships created between armed groups, those in organised crime, arms suppliers, corporate suppliers and corrupt governments.[28] On the African continent, these activities are not restricted to African actors. As an example, Lebanese group Hezbollah runs illegal operations across Africa, particularly in West Africa, providing it the means with which to keep its Middle Eastern battle going. Hezbollah has had links to both legal and illegal trades, including money laundering, drug trafficking and dealing in 'blood diamonds'.[29] Criminal networks also work to keep conflicts going. For example, when a new government or leader emerges in Somalia, criminal networks finance those opposing the leader, regardless of who they are, as preventing a functioning government is crucial to maintaining their operations.[30]

Conflicts are frequently fought with the goal of controlling resources. In turn these resources provide the funding to keep fighting going, creating a dangerous cycle. In Sierra Leone the market for 'blood diamonds' fuelled the war and in turn funded it. Gettleman describes the thinness of motivations provided for conflict.

> Ethnic tensions are a real piece of the conflict, together with disputes over land, refugees, and meddling neighbour countries. But what I've come to understand is how quickly legitimate grievances in these failed or failing African states deteriorate into rapacious, profit-oriented bloodshed. Congo today is home to a resource rebellion in which vague anti-government feelings become an excuse to steal public property. Congo's embarrassment of riches belongs to the 70 million Congolese, but in the past 10 to 15 years, that treasure has been hijacked by a couple dozen rebel commanders who use it to buy even more guns and wreak more havoc.[31]

A similar logic applies to looting in conflict; people wage war in order to loot, and loot in order that they can continue to wage war.[32]

State armies in Africa range from well-organised armed forces, in which tightly disciplined uniformed soldiers adhere to structured systems of command, to poorly resourced, ill-disciplined forces, who frequently mutiny and change allegiances, lack lines of authority, are incapable of sustained military action and seem scarcely different from non-state armed groups. Non-state groups, too, range dramatically, from large-scale, well organised, disciplined, trained and funded groups, to small bands of fighters that are frequently difficult, if not impossible, to distinguish from criminal groups – not least of all because they participate in both activities.

As well as those who *fight* with armed groups, there are also many who merely travel or live with them, including those known in humanitarian circles as “women and children associated with fighting forces”.[33] These women and children are reliant on armed groups for survival, protection and support, and in turn, armed groups rely on them for the services they provide – including selling goods and providing domestic, sexual or other services – services that are critical to the continued functioning of armed groups, particularly in protracted conflicts.

People not living with or near to armed groups, but rather within civilian populations might also provide ad hoc support to armed groups, providing them with supplies, lodgings, labour, assistance and information. Recent conflicts have even seen support provided on the Internet, with civilians using social media to campaign for armed movements as part of the Arab Spring.[34] Sometimes civilian support is provided voluntarily by those supporting a movement's goals; sometimes it is given involuntarily, extorted by fear, intimidation or compulsion. Frequently, the line between voluntary and involuntary support is hard to distinguish – with civilians being aware that failure to ‘support’ a group may result in dire consequences.[35]

Peacekeepers are also important actors in African conflicts. Since 1948 there have been 54 United Nations (UN) peacekeeping missions in Africa.[36] There are currently eight ongoing UN operations on the continent.[37] Regional groups like the Economic Community of West Africa States (ECOWAS) and the African Union (AU) are also building their capacity to carry out peacekeeping and African peacekeeping contingents are increasingly being deployed.[38] Peacekeeping operations tend to have limited mandates. Formally, these operations are present at the invitation of host states, in order to enforce peace agreements or ceasefires between parties. Peacekeepers are not supposed to fight for either party to a conflict. In some situations peacekeeping operations are granted a mandate to intervene to protect civilians – although there tends to be a lack of clarity about what this means in practice, as mandates are not operationally defined.[39] There has been criticism about peacekeeping and its frequent failure to protect civilians, due to political reasons or limited mandates, personnel or resources.[40] The failure of UNAMIR (United Nations Assistance Mission for Rwanda) to protect civilians during Rwanda's genocide was one of the most highly criticised failures in peacekeeping history.[41] In recent years, alternative approaches have been suggested to address peacekeeping failures. For example, the Arab League has proposed the creation of a regional fighting force to combat militants. While this may have the authority and mandate to act more strongly, it could lead to other problems, particularly as this force will not be focused primarily on civilian protection – so could result in negative humanitarian consequences.

Although the actors mentioned above have been grouped for the purpose of description, in practice, the distinctions between them tend to be fluid. It is the unclear dividing lines between various modes of participation and different personnel in African conflicts that create such difficulties when applying IHL's principle of distinction in these contexts.

New wars

> There is a very simple reason why some of Africa's bloodiest, most brutal wars never seem to end: They are not really wars. Not in the traditional sense, at least. The combatants don't have much of an ideology; they don't have clear goals. They couldn't care less about taking over capitals or major cities – in fact, they prefer the deep bush, where it is far easier to commit crimes. Today's rebels seem especially uninterested in winning converts, content instead to steal other people's children, stick Kalashnikovs or axes in their hands, and make them do the killing. Look closely at some of the continent's most intractable conflicts, from the rebel-laden creeks of the Niger Delta to the inferno in the Democratic Republic of the Congo, and this is what you will find.[42]

'New wars' is the term coined for the wave of conflicts that have become prevalent since the end of the Cold War.[43] These complex, multifaceted conflicts blur numerous lines, including distinctions between public and private, internal and external, economic and political, civilian and military – even war and peace.[44] Proponents of the new wars doctrine argue that 'new wars' differ from 'old wars' in a number of important ways.

New wars tend to be largely internal in nature, although they blend international and internal elements. Kaldor explains that,

> … although most of these wars are localized, they involve a myriad of transnational connections so that the distinction between internal and external, between aggression (attacks from abroad) and repression (attacks from inside the country), or even between local and global, are difficult to sustain.[45]

New wars are intrinsically linked to globalisation – or as Kaldor puts it, to the "intensification of global connectedness – political, economic, military, cultural …"[46] As the world opens up due to globalisation, authoritarian states become weaker, creating a void that other actors can fill.[47]

Participation in new wars differs. A range of diverse actors operate in these – state and non-state, public and private, domestic and foreign.[48] Conflicts have moved from being 'vertically organised', or dominated by state-based groups, as old wars were, to being fought by decentralised private groups with a range of motives.[49] Akkerman notes that,

> State monopolies of violence are being eroded by privatization of violence. The main actors are no longer regular armies, but paramilitary groups, criminal gangs, brigades of volunteers, foreign mercenaries such as private security companies and regular foreign troops.[50]

A range of armed groups operate in cooperation with each other and against each other. These complex and changing forms of participation create challenges for IHL's notions of participation and combatancy, a central theme in this book.

Whereas old wars were financed by states, new wars tend to be financed through external resources, including diaspora, criminality, exploitation of natural resources and the informal economy.[51] New wars are characterised by collapsing formal economies and the resultant increase in and competition over illicit economic activities, which both maintain and incentivise these conflicts.[52] Newman explains that,

> Much of new wars literature has argued that economic motives and greed are the primary underlying driving forces of violent conflict. Indeed, the violence itself creates opportunities for entrepreneurship and profit; the continuation of violence rather than military 'victory' is primary.[53]

Importantly, the goals of new wars differ to those of old wars. In the past, conflicts focused on territorially based geopolitical goals, often framed in terms of political ideologies. New wars have shifted the focus towards identity politics, where claims to power are based on identity labels, be they ethnic, religious, clan or linguistic.[54] Political leaders use manufactured ideologies and crises to mobilise support, providing a frame over which people can fight collectively, thereby bolstering or justifying their economic motives. The identities relied on are part traditional and part constructed. They correspond with real feelings of belonging, while overemphasising differences between in and out-groups, in order to amass support.[55]

A different logic underlies new wars. Rather than these being a contest of wills between opposing parties, they are a mutual enterprise, allowing for mobilisation around extremist ideologies and economic gain, which take on greater importance than military victory or defeat. Winning the war is not the primary goal – keeping it going might holds more value for the actors involved. This causes these wars to be persistent rather than extreme. A war's 'enemies' might not be opposing armed groups – with who there may in fact be cooperation – but rather *other* ethnic or religious groups as a whole.

Civilian causalities and forced displacement are significant features in new wars, where harming civilians might be a key strategy or goal of conflict, rather than an unfortunate by-product.[56] As the goal of new wars is not defeat over an armed opponent, targeting is not restricted to military opponents – but instead, to the civilians who make up the ethnic or *other* groups. A later section will point to the challenges this introduces for IHL's principles such as military necessity as well as for the principle of distinction. Whereas in old wars, states could rely on or demand popular support, in new wars fighting groups cannot depend on this, instead opting to control populations by terrorising them. Fear and compliance is achieved by targeting civilians and committing brutal acts of violence, including sexual violence, abduction and child recruitment.

This distinction between 'old' and 'new wars' has been contested. Some claim that new wars theory is problematic as it is based on insufficient evidence or empirical support. Critics contend that recent data has emerged which reveals that conflicts labelled as new wars do not actually display *new* features and that phenomena credited to new wars actually existed beforehand.[57] Another perspective is that existing evidence has been interpreted incorrectly to reach this theory and that those who emphasise the differences between new and old wars have done so based on a mischaracterisation of the categories and labels of war.[58] An argument made is that efforts by new wars proponents to find common patterns between recent conflicts have resulted in them ignoring key differences between them.[59] Responding to these criticisms, Kaldor, who coined the term new wars, points to the functionality of this categorisation – rather than to its literal 'newness'. Rather than the 'new' having to do with any particular features, "The term 'new' is a way to exclude 'old' assumptions about the nature of war and to provide the basis for a novel research methodology".[60] She explains that new wars theory can have valuable policy implications; As traditional categorisations of conflict do not correlate with current realities of and motivations for conflict, policy prescriptions based on these tend to be confused and unhelpful.

As well as new wars as a whole being contested, component parts of new wars claims are also challenged. Scholars dispute the fact that new wars are more violent than old ones. Melander *et al.* argue that human impact, battle severity and conflict deaths have actually been lower in the post-Cold War period than during the Cold War, a proposition they substantiate with data on various indicators, including battle-deaths and numbers of civilians killed and displaced.[61] Kalyvas notes that the perception that *civil wars* are particularly cruel predates new wars, pertaining also to civil wars that took place before and during the Cold War period. He argues that the *means* of violence in new wars may appear more jarring, leading to a false perception that violence is worse. Kalyvas explains, "… our understanding of violence is culturally defined. Killings by knife and machete tend to horrify us more than the often incomparably more massive killings by aerial and field artillery bombings".[62] Kaldor responds to these critiques, arguing that the problem with the data her critics rely on, is that this has been analysed using 'old wars' assumptions. For example,

> … the emphasis on battle deaths has the counter-intuitive effect of leaving out major episodes of violence. As Milton Leitenberg puts it: "There were few 'battle deaths' in Cambodia between 1975 and 1978, comparatively few in Somalia in 1990 and 1991, or in Rwanda in 1994: but it would simply be bizarre if two million dead in Cambodia, 350,000 in Somalia and 800,000 or more in Rwanda were omitted from compilations".[63]

This points to a value of new wars theory: in helping incorporate non-traditional conflict situations into the mould – which might otherwise be overlooked or passed over – it allows for a more inclusive view of armed violence in the modern world.

While the new wars critiques raise important concerns, there does seem to be something important going on in recent conflicts that merits examination. Conflicts change continuously in nature, motives, weaponry and actors – in fact, when it comes to war, change seems to be the only constant. The new wars literature attempts to describe the latest shift. The specifics and characteristics of this change are open to discussion – and academic exchange over new wars will undoubtedly play a role in crystallising this. However, there is value in this categorisation as it provides a tool with which to explore recent shifts, with new wars literature allowing for targeted assessment into certain aspects of modern conflicts, as well as providing a lens through which new policy approaches, solutions and regulations might be developed.

Regardless of whether one accepts this categorisation, or the details thereof, this framework is useful for the analysis of modern African conflicts, which exhibit many of the features associated with new wars. Using this categorisation allows us to assess various factors seen in African wars – such as conflict motivations, collaboration amongst enemies, civilian targeting and economic pillaging – through a helpful conceptual lens, providing possible coherence and explanations for phenomenon witnessed. This book therefore treats new wars as a useful conceptual categorisation rather than a historical fact.

Women in new wars

The gendered aspects of new wars merit consideration, an area that has to date been given little attention in new wars literature.

Ethnic and nationalistic components of new wars work against women's interests. In times of war, drawing out differences between men and women becomes a means by which in-groups and out-groups are created and solidified. Women's identities and behaviour are framed as markers of ethnic consciousness. As a result, women are pushed towards more traditional roles, with these becoming symbols and depositories of culture.[64] Women are forced to conform to certain expectations regarding behaviour and appearance. Women who fail to do so put themselves at risk.[65] In Somalia, women's submission to the boundaries of Islam became a visible mark of victory for Al-Shabaab. Al-Shabaab has violently enforced strict Sharia law, forcing women to wear the hijab and even reportedly banning women from wearing bras, which they felt to be immodest and 'deceptive'. Media reports tell of Al-Shabaab rounding up women who appear to have firm busts, inspecting whether the firmness is 'natural' and if not, flogging them.[66] Where ethnic or cultural identities take on greater salience, there often grows a resistance to women asserting their differences or challenging cultural norms.

Caprioli argues that inherent in nationalism – a driving force in new wars – is an opposition towards feminist goals. As men are considered "guardians of culture and tradition", any changes to the balance of power between men and women are seen as threatening to nationalist efforts. When a community is under threat, leaders encourage women to support collective community objectives, regardless of whether these run contrary to gender equality goals. Female leaders in turn avoid addressing gender equality so that they will not be seen to be undermining national or group solidarity. Women often find themselves with competing interests – their own interests as women, and the interests of their group, as defined by men. They are expected to prioritise national and ethnic security over their personal security as women.[67]

Many features of new wars make women vulnerable (many of these features might also apply to NIACs more broadly). When conflicts reach civilian populations, as new wars frequently do, the proportion of female casualties tends to rise.[68] New wars are associated with large-scale displacement, with population groups fleeing as they are the objects of attack. Women figure more prominently in refugee and internally displaced person (IDP) populations, with displacement bearing a particular toll on women.[69]

Women are vulnerable to sexual violence in new wars. New wars are characterised by the presence of disorganised fighters in civilian centres, with less organisation and discipline within armed groups lending itself towards sexual violence. Greater levels of close-hand violence allow for high levels of rape, with proximity between fighters and civilians providing opportunities for this to occur. The increase of small arms within communities also puts women at greater risk of attack.[70] As the new wars' armed groups can rely less on popular support they are more likely to violently target civilians as a means for control, and one form this takes is sexual violence. Sexual violence is also used as a tool for ethnic cleansing in new wars, being an effective means of encouraging populations to flee.[71]

Reasons for sexual violence in new wars also relate to identity politics. As women take on the role of ethnic depiction, women are targeted as a means of attacking a people or culture. Handrahan explains that,

> If ethnicity is patriarchal, male honour and national identity are located within the female, as women's bodies are used as 'vehicles' for the symbolic depiction of political purpose.... Male ethnic violence, then, is directed inwards towards, 'their women' and outwards onto 'other's women', in order to restrict and control 'their' ethnicity and to intimidate and contaminate the ethnic 'other', respectively.[72]

There are other ethnically motivated reasons for rape; children born of rape might be seen to take on a rapist's ethnicity, with rape being a way to 'dilute' an ethnic group, further motivating rape in new wars.[73]

Weak states characterise new wars and state weakness negatively impacts women. Weak or collapsing states provide fewer mechanisms and facilities to protect or empower women, like judicial structures, police and protective legislation. State weakness also means fewer services for women, including health, reproductive health and social services.

New wars lead to failed formal economies, which in turn drive up the costs of goods and basic staples required by women to support their families. In times of economic trouble, more men travel as migrant workers, leaving women to care for their families. Men also leave to join fighting groups, or are killed. The absence of men can cause great challenges for women, particularly in countries with cultural, social and religious prohibitions on women accessing public spaces, transport, work and education. In many places, due to patriarchal norms, women are not given the education, skills or the access to resources that allow them to cope with the challenges brought about by conflict, making it even more difficult for them when their male family members are absent.[74] Women in such situations might be forced towards transactional sex, exploitation, prostitution or trafficking.

Women's gender therefore makes them vulnerable in new wars, a vulnerability that creates the need for explicit and targeted legal protections for women – quite the opposite of what the gender-neutral laws of IHL provide. The section that follows will consider some other reasons why IHL does not function to protect women in new wars.

IHL in new wars

> Even if you could coax these men out of their jungle lairs and get them to the negotiating table, there is very little to offer them. They don't want ministries or tracts of land to govern. Their armies are often traumatized children, with experience and skills (if you can call them that) totally unsuited for civilian life. All they want is cash, guns, and a license to rampage. And they've already got all three. How do you negotiate with that?[75]

Many of the key features that characterise new wars are in themselves violations of the principle of distinction and IHL. In new wars, un-uniformed fighters purposefully disguise themselves as civilians to blend into civilian backdrops – a violation of the duty of fighters to distinguish themselves. The targeting of civilians forms a key strategy or goal of these wars. Traditionally, the principle of distinction was understood to provide a compromise between humanitarian concerns and warring parties' interests, with the principle prohibiting those actions seen as non-essential to the goal of military victory. However, in new wars, the principle of distinction stands squarely in the way of key strategies or objectives of conflict.[76] Fundamental aspects of IHL are therefore at odds with certain realities of new wars, as compared to old wars.

Lamp argues that the problem has to do with the 'paradigm of compliance' – that which leads parties to comply with the law. IHL's enforcement system is based on assumptions about the nature of parties to a conflict, their motives and their interests. For IHL's paradigm of compliance to remain relevant and plausible, a conflict would need to conform to these assumptions. The problem is that the conception of conflict underlying IHL's paradigm of compliance is very different to what can be seen in new wars. For one thing, IHL contains assumptions about what parties to a conflict should look like; IHL was created to regulate states. Where it did allow non-state actors into its fold, their armed forces had to look quite similar to those of states to be included. Parties to new wars do not align with this assumption. In new wars, states are frequently not the principal actors. In fact, these conflicts often take place in the context of state failure. Even when state armies are involved, these have often disintegrated to badly organised, ill-disciplined, fragmented looting groups, which are not wholly different from non-state armed groups. Non-state groups in new wars seldom meet IHL's ideal of territory-controlling, law-abiding, responsible-command-led groups, to which the NIAC laws might apply.[77]

A second assumption that fails to hold true in new wars is that regardless of the aims of fighting, fighters seek to achieve those aims by defeating the military forces of an enemy. This assumption rests on the premise that their conflict aims *can* in fact be achieved by defeating enemy forces. However in new wars, parties often do not seek to achieve their aims by defeating enemy forces. Sometimes military victory is not possible – as a group does not have the military power, because the enemy they are fighting avoids confrontation, or because the goal they are fighting for is not one that can actually be achieved through battle victory.[78] Fighting might not be aimed at military victory, but rather at the *goal* of displacing or exterminating segments of the population – as seen in Burundi, Rwanda and Sudan. Lamp explains that,

> Instead of trying to defeat the enemy militarily and seeking a political solution in subsequent negotiations, the parties in these conflicts usually attempt to create 'facts on the ground' by expelling or killing civilians, burning villages and thus reshaping the ethnic composition of a region or country.... Ethnic cleansing will secure an area for an ethnic group much more firmly and lastingly than a military victory followed by negotiations.[79]

Military victory might be seen as less beneficial than keeping a conflict going, with actors profiting economically or socially from an enduring state of conflict[80] – seen in Sierra Leone and DRC.

The problem therefore is that in new wars, IHL is incompatible with warring parties' strategies and goals. It is no longer the case that actors can achieve their goals within the framework of these rules – the assumption underlying IHL. Rather, in new wars IHL stands squarely in the way of actors attaining their goals. Instead of IHL outlawing only those acts unnecessary to winning, in new wars the law has a prohibitive effect on parties' ability to achieve their aims.[81] This is likely to affect parties' willingness to comply with IHL.

Other structural factors also encourage non-compliance in new wars. One factor is the exclusionary effect of IHL's reach. In terms of the law, non-state actors cannot qualify as combatants who are legally entitled to fight, and they can always be prosecuted domestically for their actions in war. This means their actions are conducted from the space of illegality, regardless of whether they abide by IHL or not.[82] As combatancy privileges are supposed to provide incentive for compliance with IHL, denying privileges to non-state actors removes any such incentive. Simply put, non-state actors, the key actors in new wars, are less likely to support a law that is consistently disadvantageous to them.

Many factors therefore negatively affect compliance with IHL in new wars – a situation that can only be bad for women, who are then deprived of the law's protective reach. Of course, it is important to not blame IHL for more than its part. The reasons for violations of IHL and for the targeting of civilians are complex – pertaining to strategies of war, ethnic hatred, asymmetry of resources, fighting capabilities and many other factors. Problematic law might exacerbate these problems, but should not be seen as being the overarching cause. As Jakob Kellenberger, former President of the ICRC noted, "One should have no illusions that there are any legal tools or policy arguments that can avail in those instances when the law is being systematically flouted, if the political will to abide by it is lacking".[83]

In addition to the principle of distinction, other IHL principles are also challenged in new wars. Many wartime actions are justified by the principle of 'military necessity', which in essence justifies those actions required for parties to succeed in their military goals. This poses a real problem in new wars; if harming civilians *is* a goal of conflict, and if targeting civilians genuinely does facilitate military aims, should the killing of civilians be justified in terms of military necessity? If sexual violence as a 'weapon of war' is demonstrated to be an effective tool for achieving conflict aims, does military necessity justify its use? The problem with 'necessity' in new wars is returned to in Chapter 6.

Women in combat

The section that follows paints the picture of women in arms around the world, in order to locate African female fighters within a growing global trend.

The scope for female participation in different types of conflicts

Scholarship, supported by empirical data, suggests that different types of conflicts provide differing scope for female participation. Women feature less as participants in IACs than in NIACs, as the former are fought primarily by state armies, which tend to be more male dominated.[84] Armed movements working towards liberation goals, or working against state authority, tend to provide more practical and ideological space for female involvement. Liberation movements often strive for wide-ranging goals of societal transformation, often including in these goals improvements in the status of women, making them more receptive to female involvement. Sometimes the practical needs of liberation groups lead them to recruit women, and this in turn leads to groups adopting a woman's rights agenda.[85] Despite such goals, existing gender roles are often perpetuated in liberation groups. It is not always the case that liberation struggles bring increased space for gender equality and female participation. Moghadam explains that there are broadly speaking two modes of revolution – with variations within these. One mode is modernising, including in its aims the emancipation of women, with women's elevation seen as linked to progress. In the second, as groups fight for freedom, they cling back to traditional and patriarchal practices as these come to represent their identity.[86]

Other types of armed movements provide less space for women's involvement or for a women's empowerment agenda. Where armed groups are fighting for survival – against starvation, attack or other dangers – there tends to be little time and energy for women's rights, with these issues falling from a group's agenda.[87] At the other extreme, rebel groups that fight for control over resources with few political goals tend to have little in the way of women's rights objectives. Where women do form part of these groups, they tend to be exploited – much like the minerals and resources these groups exploit. During its war, Sierra Leone's RUF exploited the country's lucrative diamond fields, using abducted girls to guard the mines and weapons stockpiles, sexually abusing them en masse. Although many thousands of women were forced to join the RUF, women's liberation and advancement never entered their agenda.

In struggles where ethnic or cultural identity takes on a greater salience, common in new wars, there tends to be resistance to women asserting their differences or challenging cultural norms by taking part in hostilities.[88] The same is the case where struggles are linked to religion. Women's compliance with traditional roles becomes a marker for the strength of culture – with deviations seen as a threat.[89] As such, combatancy roles for women are discouraged and participating women tend to be victimised – by the enemy, by those in their own groups and even by fellow women in their communities. Islamist extremist groups generally exclude women from the public space in general and from any significant participation in their armed movements.

When militant Islamists take over an area, they often impose Sharia law, leading women to be subjugated and excluded from public life. Interestingly, Islamist groups have not consistently excluded women. There have been reports that hard-line Somali Islamists Al-Shabaab have trained a limited number of women[90] and have used women as operatives. Nigeria's Boko Haram has abducted many girls, some of whom have reportedly become fighters, being trained to shoot and lay bombs, and sent on operations, including suicide bombing missions.[91] Today, a large proportion of Boko Haram's suicide bombers are young women and girls. Paradoxically, Islamist encroachments can also open up space and provide incentive for women to stand up against this. In Somalia, hundreds of women have reportedly been recruited by the government army to join the fight against Al-Shabaab.[92] In Iraq, there has been much media attention garnered towards the Kurdish women taking part in the fight against the Islamic State group (ISIS). Paradoxically therefore, a movement's aim to suppress women can provide opportunity for them to speak up and fight against them, creating dramatic contrasts.

Women in combat: the international picture

In recent years there has been an increase in the numbers of women serving in both state armies and non-state armed groups the world-over. Care must be taken to not overstate women's involvement; despite the increases, women are still far less active in combat than their male counterparts.

As of 2008 (the most recent statistic that could be located), 5 per cent of *state* combatants around the world were female.[93] Today, most countries allow women into their armed forces in some capacity, yet this is a fairly recent development.[94] Women were only accepted into most armies from the mid twentieth century. In the United States women were permitted to enlist from 1948; in the United Kingdom, 1949; Canada, 1951; Germany, 1975; Netherlands, 1979; and Spain, 1988. In countries with compulsory draft, a separate question has been whether women should be drafted. Today, only China, Eritrea, Israel, Libya, Malaysia, North Korea, Peru and Taiwan have compulsory draft for women.[95] Many countries have resisted mandatory conscription for women, perceiving this as symbolic of military weakness or desperation. In 1989 a high-ranking woman in the South African National Defence Force commented that conscripting women "would have been bad from a morale point of view.... It would almost be acknowledging defeat to have to resort to using women".[96]

The fact that many state armies now enlist women does not necessarily mean that women are allowed to *fight*. Most countries still do not allow women into active combat, with female soldiers' roles often restricted to administration, logistics and medical services. Only a few countries allow women into combat, including Australia, New Zealand, Canada, Denmark, Finland, Italy, Germany, Norway, Israel, Serbia, Sweden, Switzerland and the USA (where the ban on women in combat was only overturned in 2013). Even in these countries, the combat roles available to women are restricted. Partly as a result of this exclusion, women are denied the opportunity to rise to top military ranks and are deprived of military promotions. A noteworthy example is Israel, which has a two-year compulsory draft for women (as opposed to three years for men), but with certain combat positions reserved only for men. Despite the fact that women make up 33 per cent of the Israeli Defence Force and 51 per cent of its officers, the top military positions are still held by men.[97]

Despite their increasing numbers, female soldiers are frequently mistreated by others in their ranks. Californian Congresswoman Jane Harman famously remarked that a female American soldier is more likely to be raped by a fellow soldier than killed by enemy fire in Iraq.[98] The sexual assault rate in the American military is twice the rate than in the American civilian population. Many women do not report these assaults out of a fear of being ostracised, a concern that reporting will affect their chances of military promotion and a belief that little would be done by the military structures anyway.[99] Sexual assault is therefore not unique to the African military experience – although forms of sexual violence do differ.

The proportion of women in non-state groups is higher than in state armies, although exact statistics are hard to come by. While the proportion of women in non-state groups varies across geographic regions and conflicts, on average it ranges from between 10 to 30 per cent of fighters.[100]

There has been an increase in the number of female suicide bombers used. As of 2007, of the 17 groups worldwide that used suicide bombing as a tactic, more than half employed female suicide bombers. Between 1985 and 2006, over 220 female suicide bombers conducted an estimated 15 per cent of all suicide bombings.[101] Female suicide attackers can be of particular value to terror groups. As a result of widely held assumptions that women are less violent, women can pass more easily through checkpoints, can blend into crowds arousing less attention and their clothing can more easily conceal explosives. Female suicide bombers also garner more media attention – with attacks by women receiving eight times as much media coverage than those by men, a fact that is invaluable to groups that aim for highly publicised attacks.[102] Bloom explains that,

> This tactic also makes the terrorists appear more threatening by erasing the imagined barriers between combatants and non-combatants, terrorists and innocent civilians. This is the underlying message conveyed by female bombers: terrorism has moved beyond a fringe phenomenon; insurgents are all around you.[103]

Women are also increasingly present in peacekeeping operations, though the percentages of women are still low. While in 1993 women made up only 1 per cent of military personnel deployed as United Nations (UN) peacekeepers, in 2012 women made up 3 per cent of military personnel and 10 per cent of police personnel in UN missions – out of an estimated 125,000 peacekeepers.[104] Three all-female UN police forces have been deployed; one made up of Indian women in Liberia and two forces of Bangladeshi women in Haiti and DRC. As of 2013 there were three women leading peacekeeping operations and one female acting head. Peacekeepers tend to be combatants of national armies, deployed abroad as part of national contingents in peacekeeping operations. South Africa deploys the largest numbers of female peacekeepers, however as a percentage of its overall deployments, women only make up 14–15 per cent of peacekeepers (as of 2011). Fifty-four per cent of Namibia's peacekeepers are female; however, as it deploys a relatively small number of peacekeepers, the actual number of women is low. Thirty-one per cent of Zimbabwean peacekeepers are female.[105] Increased participation by women in peacekeeping was mandated by a number of Security Council Resolutions, including by SC Res 1325, illustrating the value of regulation in promoting this.

Women also serve as private military contractors – groups that are increasing active in modern conflicts. One reason private security companies hire women is that they are cheaper and will work for lower wages than men. Female contractors are often put into administrative roles. Largely the more 'frontline' and dangerous the task a private group is sent into, the fewer women are sent.[106]

Women in war in Africa

The section that follows paints a picture of women who take part in African conflicts, setting out the facts to which the principle of distinction will be applied in later chapters. This description below spans numerous African countries and conflicts, and seeks to provide a sense of the variations in women's experiences – recognising that there is no such thing as the 'typical' African female fighter's journey. Women are used in different ways by different armed groups and have highly diverse experiences. While it is impossible for a chapter like this to describe all of these experiences, the chapter seeks to paint a picture of some, pointing to interesting gendered features evident in certain contexts.

First, the numbers. The exact proportions of women in African state armies is unknown, however it is thought to be no more than the world average for state armies (which in 2008 was 5 per cent). The southern African regional average is 10.5 per cent.[107] The most gender-integrated army on the continent is the South African army, in which women make up 27 per cent of forces. The Namibian army has 26 per cent women and Seychelles and Zimbabwe have 20 per cent each. DRC has approximately 7 per cent women, while Malawi and Mozambique have 5 per cent each.[108] African non-state armed groups range dramatically in the numbers of women they employ; however, at the top end, some groups have had 30–40 per cent women – such as groups in DRC,[109] Eritrea[110] and Sierra Leone. Much of what is described in the sections below pertains to women in non-state groups.

A large proportion of female fighters are recruited before they turn 18. Girls under 18 have been part of fighting forces in Angola, Burundi, DRC, Eritrea, Ethiopia, Liberia, Libya, Mozambique, Rwanda, Sierra Leone, South Africa, South Sudan, Sudan and Uganda.[111] In Sierra Leone, while adult women were estimated by some to have made up 25 per cent of fighters, girls were estimated at about 12 per cent of all fighters.[112] It is often harder to find numbers for women *over* 18, as many adult women do not go through formal disarmament, demobilisation and reintegration (DDR) processes, while girls (as with boy soldiers) are frequently assisted through tailored processes for child soldiers by dedicated organisations and agencies, allowing for better statistics.[113] Girls have been important actors in African conflicts and girl soldiers, like women, are often critical to the continued functioning of armed groups. McKay and Mazurana emphasise that girls "... are not, and never have been, simply 'camp followers'; they are essential to the economy of armed forces, troop morale, their survival and reproductive needs".[114]

Drawing a line between adult female fighters and girl fighters can be misleading. Coulter et al. note that,

> In many African societies a girl becomes a woman at marriage or after child birth, events that frequently take place before they turn 18 ... the clear-cut distinction between child and adult as defined by 'the straight 18' principle (18 as the minimum age for all forms of military recruitment) in an analysis of female fighters in Africa tends to obscure both their lived realities and their needs in relation to the context within which they are operating.[115]

Transition from girlhood to womanhood can be fluid.[116] Girls are subjected to certain experiences because they *will* be women, or are perceived to be women. This chapter describes women and girls together, as in practice their experiences tend to be similar and they are not differentiated by those on the ground. Put differently, women's experiences do not necessarily change when they reach the age of 18.

However, despite the fact that women and girls are described together in this work, it is important to acknowledge girls as a distinct category. Additional law applies to girl soldiers, over and above the rules of IHL that pertain to women. International law prohibits the use of child soldiers, including girls. Article 38 of the Convention on the Rights of the Child (1989) says that States must take all feasible measures to ensure that children who are not yet 15 do not take a direct part in hostilities.[117] In the Optional Protocol to the Convention on the Rights of the Child on the Involvement of Children in Armed Conflict (2000) this age was lifted to 18.[118] The African Charter on the Rights and Welfare of the Child (1990), which also prohibits the recruitment of children, defines a child as "every human being below the age of 18 years".[119]

An important point to consider in the context of child recruitment – and one that relates to this book's discussions on the principle of distinction – is the issue of 'direct' and 'indirect' participation. Article 38 of the Convention on the Rights of the Child[120] states that children cannot be recruited to play a *direct* part in hostilities. The Optional Protocol to the Convention on the Rights of the Child[121] states that children cannot "take a direct part in hostilities". So too, Article 22.2 of the African Charter on the Rights and Welfare of the Child[122] calls on States to ensure that children do not play a *direct* part in hostilities. Like these human rights conventions, in IHL Article 77(2) of AP1 also uses the word 'direct'. In contrast, AP2 prohibits *any* participation of children, with Article 4(3)(c) of AP2 stating that, "children who have not attained the age of fifteen years shall neither be recruited in the armed forces or groups nor allowed to take part in hostilities".[123] The Rome Statute of the ICC prohibits the use of children under 15 to "participate actively in hostilities" in both IACs and NIACs.[124] Therefore, AP2 aside, what is prohibited by international law is the recruitment of children into *direct* participation in hostilities.[125] However, as this chapter will describe, many women and girls are used by armed groups in *indirect* – or non-fighting support – roles, roles that can be equally detrimental to children's well-being. The laws' use of the word 'direct' excludes girls in indirect roles from their ambit.[126]

Armed groups in Africa recruit women for a range of reasons. Sometimes women are recruited as there are not enough men to fight, as men might have fled, been killed or captured, creating the need for additional labour.[127] At times women are recruited because they are believed to excel at certain tasks. In many African countries women carry items like water and firewood on their heads and are therefore used to moving swiftly with heavy loads. When the Ugandan army launched operation Iron Fist in 2002 to destroy LRA bases in South Sudan, the LRA needed to keep moving, so it required porters to carry its food and weapons. The LRA therefore began abducting more women, using them to carry these loads.[128] Women can carry out certain tasks that men are unable to, such as gaining access to civilian centres or crossing checkpoints without drawing the attention that men would. Women are frequently recruited to perform tasks that men do not wish to perform, or tasks that are not considered culturally appropriate for men, such as cooking and cleaning for armed groups.[129] Women as the more powerless in African societies are a cheap and easily exploitable labour source. They can be coerced into action as they have less power to assert themselves, and lower expectations of fair treatment. There are also symbolic reasons for recruiting women; women might be recruited to send a message to a population that a movement is inclusive and is campaigning for *all* the population's goals – as seen with Mozambique's FRELIMO and South Sudan's SPLM.

In turn, women join armed movements for a number of reasons. Some join voluntarily: out of belief in the cause; for financial gain; because they have no alternative means for survival or protection; in order to escape problems at home; or because their parents, siblings or spouses were part of a movement.[130] Women frequently join as they feel unsafe *as women* in times of conflict – fearing violence – including sexual violence – and hoping for the relative protection recruitment might offer.[131] In some armed groups, women are able to learn new skills and to improve their education and career options. Joining armed movements can allow women positions of power not otherwise available to them in the traditional patriarchal communities they come from.[132]

In several African conflicts women have been forced to join armed groups – as in Angola, Burundi, DRC, Ethiopia, Liberia, Mozambique, Sierra Leone, Somalia, Sudan and Uganda.[133] Abductions frequently take place as part of violent raids, where women and girls – often together with men and boys – are forcibly removed from their homes and taken to armed group bases. It is sometimes difficult to distinguish voluntary and involuntary recruitment, as women join out of a combination of choice, pressure and fear. Sometimes, while not actually abducted, women are threatened or fear the consequences of not joining groups. In Mozambique those who refused to assist FRELIMO were taken to be enemy collaborators, threatened and sometimes killed. While many may have felt sympathy for the group's objectives, their decisions to join may not have been entirely due to these sympathies.[134] West notes that FRELIMO portrayed female participants "… as volunteers committing 'acts of heroism' on behalf of the revolution, even if these young people might have felt that they had no option but to comply with FRELIMO 'requests' of them".[135]

The idea that girls under 18 can *voluntarily* enlist is contested. Radhika Coomaraswamy, United Nations Special Representative for Children and Armed Conflict, testified to the International Criminal Court in its Lubanga hearings about the difficulties in distinguishing voluntary and involuntary recruitment in children because of their lack of alternative options, survival mechanisms and role models[136] – an argument that can also be made for adult women. Another argument is that because of their age, children do not have the legal capacity to truly consent to recruitment, rendering any child recruitment non-consensual. As with children, it is clear that a voluntary/involuntary binary is too simplistic to describe women's participation – a theme revisited later on in this book.

Once they are part of armed groups, some women are trained and readied for war. The quality and content of training varies greatly between groups as well as within them. Sometimes men and women are trained together or in the same ways, and sometimes they are trained wholly differently. Training might include physical fitness, instruction on the use of weapons, ambush skills, pillaging techniques, defence, sabotage and other fighting methods. In some contexts training is designed to harden recruits to help them to kill without conscience. In Sierra Leone's Revolutionary United Front (RUF) women, like their male counterparts, were given someone to kill as part of their training and were threatened with death themselves if they refused to comply. Ideological indoctrination is sometimes also included, making women more willing to fight.[137] Like men, women might be taught to hate those in opposing groups or populations, being told how opposition fighters were responsible for the war, for the deaths of their family members, or for the troubles that they have faced. In some settings women have been given alcohol and drugs as part of their indoctrination – as once addicted, they are easier to control. A Sierra Leonean woman explained, "When they saw how nervous and uncomfortable we were [during the training], they gave us drugs.... Before the injection, I was nervous, afraid and unsure of myself. Later, after the injection, I felt more confident".[138]

Women play a range of roles within African armed groups. These roles vary greatly between groups, and can also shift and change within a group throughout the course of a conflict. The roles played by women are of particular importance for this work, as they determine whether women 'directly participate' or not, important for the application of the principle of distinction.

In some armed groups women serve in combat positions. They are given arms and fight in much the same ways as men would. Women have served in active combat in Angola, Burundi, DRC, Eritrea, Ethiopia, Liberia, Mozambique, Rwanda, Sierra Leone, Somalia, Sudan and Uganda. Women sometimes even lead combat units or battalions.[139] In some armed groups women serve in mixed gender battalions, while in others there are women-only wings or battalions. South Sudan's SPLA had an all-female battalion, Kateeba Banaat (translated as "the girls' battalion"), formed in 1984. Although trained in combat skills, the women of the group were only allowed into active combat on one occasion, an unsuccessful attack on the town of Njoko, before an SPLA ruling was made that women could no longer serve in active combat. Kateeba Banaat and subsequent female battalions were redirected to non-combat roles.[140] In 1967, FRELIMO in Mozambique formed the Destacamento Feminino (DF), an all-female detachment. Its members were sent to Tanzania for politico-military training, similar to that given to male recruits. The women of DF operated in a number of different capacities and in limited cases took part in active combat, however as with Kateeba Banaat, halfway through the war FRELIMO decreed that women could no longer serve in active combat.[141]

Women have shown themselves to be capable of committing highly violent acts. They have been complicit in perpetrating terrible crimes, often against civilians. At times these acts have been coerced; in Sierra Leone, at fear of death, women were forced to kill, beat, cut off limbs and torture others, including their own family or community members. Sometimes this was done to bind them to a group, making them doubt whether their families and communities would accept them back following these acts. At other times these acts have been voluntary.

There can be benefits to women in acting in violent and cruel manners. For example,

> … in the context of Sierra Leone, the more aggressive girls were seen to be and the more destruction and looting they undertook, the more valued they were within the ranks of the RUF. Girls became increasingly conscious of the fact that the more violent they were, the safer they became within the armed group … engaging in extreme forms of violence also brought privileges within Sierra Leone's RUF, such as better access to food and looted goods, and in some cases led to promotion within the ranks.[142]

Women who acquire fighting skills and carry guns can better ensure their own protection – including from those within their groups.[143]

Women serve in *military-related support* roles, acting as guards, spies, intelligence operatives, messengers, minesweepers, porters and medics, often at the frontlines. Some women act as military and political strategists and communications officers. They might train others on military tactics or on how to fight and use weapons.[144] Women can be highly effective in gathering intelligence and mobilising support, as they can move around attracting less attention than unfamiliar men. For example, some women in the SPLA, which fought for independence from Sudan, were tasked with gathering intelligence. To do this they would pose as traders, travelling into Sudan, gathering information on route. One woman explained:

> When you are a woman other women will make friends with you and be very open. In Khartoum I could make friends with the Ministers' wives and they would just open their mouths automatically, and talk with another woman. In the villages I would sit with my children, and there you could learn what the people thought, what was happening, and who was moving from here to there.… I am not fighting with a gun, but I am fighting with my mouth.[145]

In Algeria's War of Independence about 2,000 women joined the armed resistance, the *Maquis*, where they were tasked with jobs like informing the civilian population about the political situation and providing them with information on hygiene.[146] What is evident is that African female combatant's roles often looking nothing like the roles that IHL assumes for combatants.

Most women in armed groups hold domestic roles, acting as cooks, childcarers and providers of sexual or reproductive services. Women often play similar roles in armed groups to those they did at home before recruitment, namely cooking, cleaning and serving men.[147] The importance of these roles to the continued functioning of armed groups should not be understated. Denov explains that,

> Domestic work within the context of armed groups is often regarded as peripheral and insignificant. It is increasingly being recognized, however,

> that armed groups cannot function without such labour. Given an armed group's lack of resources, manpower, their need to keep moving, and their often-limited organizational structure, the domestic activities and loads carried by girls are invaluable to the very survival and success of a fighting force.[148]

Women often hold numerous roles concurrently, moving between them.[149] A female combatant might fight in battle, but then also be expected to cook, clean and be available for sex.[150] The ICC's Lubanga judgment describes how in DRC, in addition to cooking and domestic duties, girls held many of the same fighting, guarding and other roles that boys did.[151] The moment when combat duties end and support duties begin are neither clear nor defined. Rather, these are understood to be dual but continuing parts of female fighter's roles – much like women juggling work and family duties in a non-conflict setting. As such, trying to categorise women, deciding who is a fighter, who merely 'supports' armed groups, and if they do both, when each is happening, is often not possible – although this is what the principle of distinction seeks to do. Even the line between those who are *members* of armed groups and those who merely support groups peripherally can be fluid. Krosch's description of a female combatant in Eritrea illustrates this well:

> … when food stocks ran low, Rigbe moved her family to the Gash Barka Region to find work around the military camps at the front. Laundry, gardening, trench digging, cooking and companionship became her new occupations as she followed the EPLF for four years. Eventually she was trained to fire weapons, repair trucks and to care for the wounded and sick. When I asked Rigbe why she became a fighter in the Liberation Struggle she simply replied that they were her 'family'.[152]

African women have been involved in genocide. By 2006 almost 2,000 women had been incarcerated in Rwandan prisons for genocide offences – albeit less than 6 per cent of all genocide-related detainees. Women participated in various ways in the Rwandan genocide, though historic records and court testimonials show that for the most part they did not actually commit murders themselves – although in some cases they did. Hutu women were involved in looting Tutsi property, stealing from dead Tutsis and reporting on those who were hiding. They supported the men involved in killing, cooking for them, bringing them food at the roadblocks and encouraging them.[153] Following the genocide, 47 women were placed on the list of 'Category 1' suspects (out of a list of 2,202), which included planners, organisers and instigators of the genocide and those in leadership positions in politics, military and the church. The most famous was Pauline Nyiramasuhuko, the former Rwandan Minister for Family Welfare and the Advancement of Women, accused of ordering the deaths of thousands of Tutsis. Nyiramasuhuko was the first woman convicted by the International Criminal Tribunal for Rwanda (ICTR). Her conviction included, among other things, ordering Interhamwe to rape Tutsi women, and she was charged as responsible as a superior for rape.[154]

One of the 'roles' that women are expected to fill in armed groups are providers of sexual services. The sexual uses of female combatants have taken various forms. In Angola girls were expected to perform sexual acts on male fighters during military campaigns and following attacks, as rewards for victory. Girls would perform sexual dances to maintain the morale of male soldiers and to make sure they remained alert at times when attacks were imminent and expected.[155] In some groups women are deemed sexually available to all the group's men to use as they will. A study conducted about girls in armed groups in Uganda, Mozambique and Sierra Leone found that nearly all girls abducted by rebel groups were raped, and that gang rape and sexual torture were prevalent parts of the experiences of abducted girls – with girls in some groups being raped by numerous men, often on the same day.[156]

Sometimes women and girls are allocated as sexual partners to particular male members of armed groups. These arrangements have been called 'bush marriages' or 'AK-47 marriages' and the women known as 'wives'.[157] Many thousands of girls, mostly in their early teens, were abducted by Uganda's LRA and threatened with torture and death if they attempted to escape. Girls were allocated to male rebels as 'wives', with larger numbers of girls allocated to rebels with greater seniority in the group. Joseph Kony, leader of the LRA, was said to have had around 88 'wives' as of 2007. While the 'wives' needed to service their husbands sexually and to take care of their domestic needs, such as cooking, cleaning and child rearing, they were also trained to fight and were used in both combat and military support roles.[158] Being allocated as a 'wife' can provide some level of protection, as 'wives' are only expected to service their 'husbands', rather than being sexually available to all members of the group.[159] In Sierra Leone some 'wives' of commanders held considerable power and influence within RUF compounds. When commanders were on mission, their 'wives' would control their compounds. 'Wives' were involved in determining how looted items should be distributed, deciding who from the compounds should be sent on raiding, abduction and spying missions, and enforcing discipline in the camps. Some commanders' 'wives' had bodyguards and even advised their 'husbands' on military strategies.[160] In addition to women within armed groups providing sexual services, many militaries and armed groups support prostitution bases nearby or attached to military bases.[161]

In some armed groups women are responsible for child rearing and taking care of the reproductive needs of a group – particularly necessary in longer-term conflicts. The LRA had special 'breeder camps' set up for this purpose. A camp called Nsitu was created for mothers with babies and children, where there was a higher level of security and where the basic needs of mothers and their children were provided for. Once the children grew old enough they themselves were recruited into the LRA ranks.[162] Of course, not all armed groups operate in this way. When women in Burundi's CNDD-FDD gave birth, they were forced to hand over their children to families who were not in the area in which they were fighting. Congolese girls testified in the ICC's Lubanga case that if they fell pregnant, they might be thrown out of the armed group, landing up on the streets of Bunia.[163] In South Sudan, a decision was made by late SPLA leader John Garang that women should be kept away from active combat in order that they could "keep up the reproductive front" to maintain the population levels, replacing the many South Sudanese who were dying in the war.[164] There, giving birth was framed as women's contribution to the war effort. Women travelled to and from the frontlines to be impregnated, before returning to the bush to resume normal duties. When a South Sudanese man died in battle, his wife would be 'taken over' by another man, who would support her and her children and impregnate her again.[165]

The treatment of women in armed groups also varies greatly. For some women armed group experiences are wrought with violence and abuse, with breaches of the rules, mistakes and misbehaviour dealt with by beatings and punishments. In other groups women are treated well – they are respected for the roles they play and their contributions and presence are valued. Many women experience greater levels of gender equality within armed groups than they did in the societies in which these groups are found, with armed groups allowing them more opportunities and power than would have been possible had they not joined.[166] In some contexts, women have earned leadership positions in armed groups and have risen up the ranks of command. However, for the most part, top positions tend to be retained by men. In Algeria's *Maquis*, life was reported to be very similar for men and women, with women taking part in all aspects of the war effort. However, despite this, the command was all male and there were only a few women in key decision-making roles.[167] In some contexts, where women are promoted to positions of power, they face a lack of respect, with male troops refusing to follow their orders.[168]

An important source of labour and support for armed groups is that which is provided to them from civilian populations (as opposed to from their 'members'). Non-state groups are often reliant on community support, assistance and information, as well as being dependent on communities for food, resources and shelter. The ways that armed groups treat civilians is influenced by this need for support. Where possible, armed groups attain this support voluntarily, as might be possible in liberation struggles or where armed groups fight for popular causes. In South Sudan, popular support was critical to the SPLA's success, with most of the population contributing to the war effort in some way. A South Sudanese woman explained,

> Even if you are young you can do something. You can grind sorghum. Your father and brother and husband have gone to the war, so if you remain at home looking after the family you are also fighting. You are taking care of the children and the people who are suffering. You dig the garden and take some to the war and some for the children.[169]

Community support may be less readily available where groups are not driven by ideologies acceptable to those in the local population. In such cases, armed groups might gain 'support' by force, often by directing extreme levels of violence towards civilians, as is often seen in new wars. Armed groups in many countries have attacked communities, forcing community women to serve them while the groups loot and pillage. Coomaraswamy, then Special Rapporteur on Violence Against Women, reported that,

> When fighters took control of a village, sometimes a fighter would force a woman from the village to cook for him. When women crossed checkpoints, sometimes a fighter would take a woman from the checkpoint and force her to cook for him. Women reported that being forced to cook for a soldier meant that she was subjected to his control in a variety of ways: more than half of the women who were forced to cook experienced sexual violence.[170]

As with armed group membership, when dealing with civilians, the line between voluntary and coerced support is not always clear. In Mozambique's *zonas libertados* (the liberated zones), FRELIMO called on civilians to help the guerrillas by providing food, portering and providing information about the enemy's movements. West notes that,

> Sympathy for the insurgency was widespread in these areas, but fear and respect for FRELIMO guerrillas were inseparable: those who refused to aid FRELIMO were considered by the Front to be collaborators with the colonial regime and were threatened and sometimes executed.[171]

Support from civilian populations can take numerous forms. During the uprisings of the Arab Spring, many took to Twitter or social media to call people together, publicise news about protests and garner support for the movements.[172] In a more extreme form of participation, some women reportedly go on 'sexual Jihad' – offering themselves into sexual service for those fighting Islamic Jihads. From 2014 women travelled to Syria to serve the fighters of ISIS as wives. Similar reports have been made in Africa, with Tunisian authorities claiming that women have offered themselves sexually to Jihadists in Tunisia – although these claims have been disputed.[173]

A concern for the purposes of this research, is that while assisting armed groups *civilians* might not be discernible from *members* of the groups. They are therefore vulnerable to attack by the opposing side. This potential for confusion is not adequately mitigated or addressed by the principle of distinction. The challenges for the principle caused by the increased presence of and participation by civilians on the battlefield have been well documented.[174] However, these discussions have focused on male civilian participation (such as private civilian/security contractors), not considering the unique involvement of civilian women and the particular risks this brings them.

Women's participation in African conflicts must be considered against the backdrop of existing constructions of gender on the continent. Female combatants violate these gender constructions, often taking on roles that veer greatly from those accepted in their societies. However, simultaneously, traditional notions remain evident in the treatment, use and abuse of female combatants.

Women in African conflicts play roles that differ substantially to traditional understandings of combatancy. The complex, often abusive and involuntary circumstances surrounding women's membership of armed groups are incongruent with the picture of responsible combatancy on which IHL is premised. Yet, in research, rhetoric, demobilisation efforts and IHL, the experiences of men continue to be taken as 'normal'.[175]

Female fighters in the post-conflict period

The post-conflict period can be a difficult time for women. Peace treaties may officially end wars, yet insecurity lingers, albeit at lower levels. Former enemies return home to the same communities, and peace agreements do little to prevent the anger and violence that spills over.[176] Violence remains a constant feature in women's lives post-conflict.[177] This is not restricted to the public space – it enters the home too, with reported high levels of domestic violence in the periods following conflict. Levels of sexual violence often subsist at conflict-levels or even increase.

Gender-relations often shift during conflicts, with women taking on roles not otherwise available to them both in armed groups and in broader society.[178] However, increased spaces for women in conflict do not necessarily translate to greater space after war. Many men returning from war want things to return to 'normal' and for women to resume their former positions – leaving the public space and households to be once again headed by men. Some women find this reversal difficult, creating friction within households. Men whose positions in society and the family feel under threat sometimes resort to violence against women.[179]

In many contexts, women have been drawn to armed struggles by the fact that groups incorporate women's empowerment within their stated goals. However, gains made in terms of women's empowerment are quickly reversed post-conflict, with promises of women's rights slipping off the agenda as soon as peace is reached – as seen in Mozambique,[180] Eritrea[181] and South Sudan,[182] among others. In some places conditions for women arguably become worse than prior to hostilities. Some of the countries of the Arab Spring were relatively liberal before the uprisings yet became more conservative post-revolution. Tunisia was previously one of the most secular Islamic states and its women enjoyed full legal equality since the 1950s. Following its 2010–2011 revolution, the Islamic Ennahda was voted in, with a series of concerning developments following suit, including the creation of a new draft Constitution that referred to women as "complementary to men".[183]

In Egypt, the Muslim Brotherhood, which took over following the 2011 toppling of Hosni Mubarak's government, was also more conservative in terms of women's rights. Egypt has seen a dramatic increase in sexual assaults since the revolution, many of which were conducted by mobs of men on Tahrir Square while political protests took place.[184] One of the reasons given for these attacks is that men feel threatened by women's increased space – and sexual assaults are used to get women to go back inside.[185] The situation improved to some extent since Abdel Fattah el-Sisi, who has a better attitude towards women's rights, ousted the Brotherhood in a military coup. Post-conflict societies can move in various directions; reverting to traditionalism, moving towards democracy, or working with hybrid systems that mix these. Whichever the direction, the results for women tend not to be great, with women's concerns often similarly ignored.

In folklore about bravery and revolution, women's roles in conflicts are quickly forgotten, with the men of the struggles pedestalled and celebrated. While women may have played active roles in armed struggles, these are seldom given the recognition they deserve. As a result, women tend to be denied the rewards of participation, left out of peace negotiations and passed over for political positions post-conflict. Where women are included in political and peace processes, this is often done to meet internationally encouraged quotas and to please donors, yet women are often not given a proper place and are given little real opportunity to provide their input.[186] Of course, the fact that women's wartime roles are not acknowledged can also have beneficial effects for them. Rwandan lawyers have alleged that judges trying genocide cases have sympathy for women, causing them to acquit or to look for reasons to acquit them.[187] Hogg explains that,

> There is also some evidence that in the pursuit of justice following the genocide, women have benefited from the 'chivalry' of men … male witnesses, investigators, prosecutors and judges are so infected by gender stereotypes that they either cannot perceive of women as criminals or feel protective towards them in spite of their suspected or proven criminality.[188]

Female former combatants face numerous challenges post conflict. As well as experiencing many of the same obstacles that male former combatants face – including difficulties returning home and finding viable employment – female ex-combatants experience a host of problems particular to women. They are often stigmatised and marginalised and sometimes rejected altogether by their communities, as has been documented in Uganda,[189] Central African Republic (CAR)[190] and South Sudan.[191] Much of this stigma centres on sexual activity. They are stigmatised as they are assumed to have had sex in armed groups, because of the 'shame' of being raped, or for becoming pregnant while unmarried.[192] Women leaving armed groups with children have a particularly hard time, as children act as evidence of sex, rape and the violation of cultural taboos.[193]

Given the stigma and rejection, many female former combatants are left destitute. Lacking other viable options, some enter the sex trade. Female combatants frequently reintegrate by themselves rather than going through formal DDR processes aimed at assisting former combatants to reintegrate into civilian life. Sometimes they choose not to be formally demobilised as they wish to keep their involvement in armed groups secret or to downplay it, fearing the stigma they are likely to face on their return to their communities.[194] Some women choose to remain with their rebel 'husbands' post conflict, despite the fact that they may not have entered these unions voluntarily. In many African countries, having *a* husband, even such a husband, is seen as preferable to not having one. The fear of not finding a husband is a major concern for African women and women leaving armed groups have particular difficulties in this regard.[195]

Women who have served in armed groups often have difficulty returning to traditional gendered structures once they have been exposed to alternative models of interaction.[196] Community members often perceive female former combatants as troublesome, bad influences or undesirable. The problems do not stem entirely from community prejudices. McKay and Mazurana report that girls released from armed groups displayed, "Anti-social behaviour – such as being aggressive, quarrelsome, using abusive language, killing and eating others' animals, abusing drugs and smoking—violated gender norms and affected their ability to readjust to their community and the community's response to them".[197]

Women who participate in hostilities struggle to have their needs met post-conflict, in part because their experiences are different to those of men; misunderstood and not recognised as meaningful participation in hostilities. While male former combatants can readily have their war-wounds treated, many women cannot, as these injuries are sexual and stigma around sexual violence prevents women seeking help.[198] Some solutions proposed to assist female former fighters are wholly inappropriate. For example, some have suggested that women should marry their 'bush husbands' or captors, to assist in their reintegration and ensure continued maintenance or support. No one would ever suggest that boys or men formalise their relationships with their captors/rapists as a reintegration solution.[199]

The picture is not all bad. Despite the challenges, women have been shown to have tremendous agency in the post-conflict period. Across the continent, women have been involved in working towards peace, particularly at the local level. In West Africa, organisations like the Mano River Union's Women's Peace Network have been highly active, supported by broader regional women's networks like Femmes Africa Solidarite – collaborations that have allowed women to transmit ideas between conflict zones.[200] The Pro-Femmes/Twese Hamwe Collective in Rwanda, an association of 35 women's organisations, played a significant part in facilitating dialogue between Hutus and Tutsis in post-genocide Rwanda.[201] And one should not overlook the contribution of 'ordinary' women who work to rebuild their families and communities following conflict. This above all else is what allows societies to resurface and rebuild after war – although, like much other female participation, these contributions tend to be overlooked.

Ranging from empowering experiences where women fight for social change, to situations of kidnap, sexual slavery and abuse, one cannot neatly sum up the diverse experiences of female fighters and commit them to one category or to a neat legal definition. However, despite the variations there remains some value in thinking about these women as a group. African women participate in conflict against a backdrop of African norms and cultural practices, with patriarchy and high levels of gender violence informing and shaping their involvement. Women across the continent are held to similar expectations about acceptable female behaviour and suffer similarly when transgressing these norms, even when doing so involuntary. Stigma, fear of societal ostracisation and limited alternative opportunities shape their armed group experiences.

The women who participate in African conflicts have largely been neglected in academic legal literature. The laws of distinction, drafted with a different context and different participants in mind, strain at the seams when applied to them. However, as new wars become the norm and conflicts look increasingly different to the wars of the twentieth century, fighters like the women in Africa begin to resemble the norm, making an examination of the adequacy of the laws in dealing with such groups imperative.

Notes

1 This figure is contested. It varies depending on how one classifies certain disputed territories.
2 For more information on the history and causes of colonialism in Africa, see Duignan, Gann Peter, and Turner, Victor (eds), *Colonialism in Africa 1870–1960 Volume Three: Profiles of Change: African Society and Colonial Rule*. Cambridge: Cambridge University Press, 1971.
3 Ajala, Adekunle. 'The Nature of African Boundaries' 18, no. 2 (1983): 177–189.
4 Shah, Anup. 'Conflicts in Africa – Introduction'. *Global Issues*, 12 May 2010.
5 Anghie, Antony. *Imperialism, Sovereignty and the Making of International Law*. Cambridge: Cambridge University Press, 2005. Bowden, Brett. 'The Colonial Origins of International Law – European Expansion and the Classical Standard of Civilization'. *Journal of the History of International Law* 7 (2005): 1–23.
6 Anghie, Antony. 'The Evolution of International Law: Colonial and Postcolonial Realities'. *Third World Quarterly* 27, no. 5 (1 January 2006): 739–753, at 745.
7 Article 22 of the Covenant of the League of Nations 1919, provided for the mandates, giving particulars about the ways these should work in different areas.
8 Nele, Matz. 'Civilization and the Mandate System under the League of Nations as Origin of Trusteeship'. *Max Planck Yearbook of United Nations Law* 9, no. 1 (2005): 47–95.
9 Callahan, Michael. *A Sacred Trust: The League of Nations and Africa, 1929–1946*. Eastbourne: Sussex Academic Press, 2004.
10 Article 1(2) and 55 of the United Nations Charter referred to self-determination. Both the International Covenant on Economic, Social and Cultural Rights, 1966 (Article 1), and the International Covenant on Civil and Political Rights, 1966 (Article 1), affirm the right to self-determination. A number of other international resolutions and instruments further supported this – including the United Nations General Assembly's Resolution on Decolonisation 1514 (1960).
11 Higgins, Noelle. The Approach of International Law to Wars of National Liberation. *Martin Monograph Series. (Monograph 3).* Martin Institute, University of Idaho, Moscow, Idaho. (2004).
12 Article 2 of all four Geneva Conventions of 1949.
13 *Western Sahara*, Advisory Opinion, ICJ Reports, General List No. 61, 1975.

14 For example, in 1994 the ICJ delivered a judgment in the Case Concerning the Territorial Dispute, (*Libyan Arab Jamahiriya* v. *Chad*), ICJ 1994, affirming Chad's sovereignty over the Aouzou Strip. The ICJ also judged on the land and maritime boundary between Cameroon and Nigeria, in Land and Maritime Boundary between Cameroon and Nigeria (*Cameroon* v. *Nigeria: Equatorial Guinea intervening*), ICJ 2002. The countries were on the brink of war before the dispute was referred to the ICJ in 1994. In 2002 judgment was made that sovereignty over the Bakassi region rested with Cameroon. Similarly, the ICJ has ruled on a dispute between Botswana and Namibia over the Kasikili/Sedudu Island in Case concerning Kasikili/Sedudu Island (*Botswana* v. *Namibia*), ICJ, 1999.

15 Holmes, Steven. 'The World; Africa, From the Cold War to Cold Shoulders'. *New York Times*, 7 March 1993.

16 Piombo, Jessica. *Terrorism and U.S. Counter-Terrorism Programs in Africa: An Overview*. Centre for Contemporary Conflict, 2007.

17 Dreazen, Yochi. 'The New Terrorist Training Ground'. *The Atlantic*, October 2013.

18 *Terrorism in the Horn of Africa*. United States Institute of Peace, Special Report 113, 2004.

19 Ibid., at 9.

20 Ford, Jolyon. *Counter-Terrorism and the Rule of Law in Africa: The Second Decade after 2001*. Institute for Security Studies, 2013.

21 There is controversy about the definition of a failed state. While some factors have been suggested to indicate state failure, there is no consensus on these. Easterly, William and Freschi, Laura. 'Top 5 Reasons Why "Failed State" Is a Failed Concept'. Aidwatch, 13 January 2010. Available from: www.nyudri.org/aidwatch archive/2010/01/top-5-reasons-why-%E2%80%9Cfailed-state%E2%80%9D-is-a-failed-concept

22 Article 2 of the Genocide Convention defines when genocide occurs, in order to activate state's legal obligations with respect to genocide. UN General Assembly, *Convention on the Prevention and Punishment of the Crime of Genocide*, 9 December 1948, A/RES/260.

23 *World Development Report 2011: Conflict, Security, and Development*. Washington DC: World Bank, April 2011.

24 Mateos, Oscar. 'Beyond Greed and Grievance, Towards a Comprehensive Approach to African Armed Conflicts: Sierra Leone as a Case Study'. In *Understanding Africa's Contemporary Conflicts Origins, Challenges and Peacebuilding*. Institute for Security Studies, 2010.

25 Arreguín-Toft, Ivan. 'Contemporary Asymmetric Conflict Theory in Historical Perspective'. *Terrorism and Political Violence* 24, no. 4 (2012): 635–657. Arreguín-Toft, Ivan. *How the Weak Win Wars: A Theory of Asymmetric Conflict*. Cambridge: Cambridge Studies in International Relations; Cambridge University Press, 2005.

26 Butime, Herman. 'Examining the Relevance of the Theories of Guerrilla Warfare in Explaining the Lord's Resistance Army Insurgency in Northern Uganda'. *University of Wollongong Thesis Collection*, Wollongong: University of Wollongong Australia, 2012.

27 Peterson, Spike. '"New Wars" and Gendered Economies'. *Feminist Review* 88 (2008): 7–20, at 13–14.

28 Ibid.

29 'The Globalisation of Terror: Hezbollah in Africa'. *International Centre for the Study of Radicalisation, Department of War Studies, Kings College* http://icsr.info/2012/02/the-globalisation-of-terror-hezbollah-in-africa/. Karmon, Ely. *The Iran/Hezbollah Strategic and Terrorist Threat to Africa*. International Institute for Counter-Terrorism, 2012.

30 Gettleman, Jeffrey. 'Africa's Forever Wars'. *Foreign Policy*, April 2010.

31 Ibid.

32 Kalyvas, Stathis. '"New" and "Old" Civil Wars: A Valid Distinction?' *World Politics* 54, no. 01 (2001): 99–118.
33 Children and Women Associated with Armed Forces and Groups, Issue Paper, Second International Conference on DDR and Stability in Africa Kinshasa, Democratic Republic of Congo, 12–14 June 2007.
34 'The Role of Social Media in the Arab Uprisings – Past and Present'. *Westminster Papers in Communication and Culture* 9, no. 2 (2013).
35 West, Harry. 'Girls with Guns: Narrating the Experience of War of Frelimo's 'Female Detachment''. *Anthropological Quarterly* 73, no. 4 (2000): 180–194.
36 'African Peacekeeping Operations'. Council on Foreign Relations. www.cfr.org/africa/african-peacekeeping-operations/p9333.
37 These are in Western Sahara, Mali, DRC, Darfur (Sudan), Abyei (Sudan), South Sudan, Côte d'Ivoire and Liberia.
38 Holt, Victoria and Shanahan, Moira. *African Capacity-Building for Peace Operations: UN Collaboration with the African Union and ECOWAS*. Washington DC: The Henry L. Stimson Centre, 2005.
39 Holt, Victoria and Glyn, Taylor. *Protecting Civilians in the Context of UN Peacekeeping Operations: Successes, Setbacks and Remaining Challenges*. New York: Department of Peacekeeping Operations and the Office for the Coordination of Humanitarian Affairs of the United Nations, 2009.
40 For example, Boot, Max. 'Paving the Road to Hell: The Failure of U.N. Peacekeeping'. *Foreign Affairs*, April 2000.
41 Dallaire, Roméo. *Shake Hands with the Devil: The Failure of Humanity in Rwanda*. New York: Carroll & Graf, 2005. Brattberg, Erik. 'Revisiting UN Peacekeeping in Rwanda and Sierra Leone'. *Peace Review* 24, no. 2 (2012): 156–162.
42 Gettleman, supra note 30.
43 Others contend that these started from the end of World War Two. See Melander, Erik, Öberg, Magnus and Hall, Jonathan. 'Are "New Wars" More Atrocious? Battle Severity, Civilians Killed and Forced Migration Before and After the End of the Cold War'. *European Journal of International Relations* 15, no. 3 (2009): 505–536.
44 Ibid.
45 Kaldor, Mary. *New and Old Wars: Organized Violence in a Global Era*. 2nd edn. Cambridge: Polity, 2006, at 2.
46 Ibid., at 4.
47 Kaldor, Mary. 'In Defence of New Wars'. *Stability* 2, no. 1 (2013).
48 Malantowicz, Artur. 'Do 'New Wars' Theories Contribute to Our Understanding of the African Conflicts? Cases of Rwanda and Darfur'. *Africana Bulletin* 58 (2010).
49 Kaldor, supra note 45.
50 Akkerman, Tjitske. 'New Wars, New Morality?' *Acta Politica* 44, no. 1 (2009): 74–86, at 76.
51 Peterson, supra note 27.
52 Newman, Edward. 'The 'New Wars' Debate: A Historical Perspective Is Needed'. *Security Dialogue* 35, no. 2 (2004): 173–189.
53 Ibid., at 177.
54 Kaldor, supra note 45.
55 Schäfer, Heinrich. 'New Wars and Religious Identity Politics'. In: Julio de Santa Ana (ed.), *Religions Today. Their Challenge to the Ecumenical Movement*, 89–104. Geneva: WCC Publications, 2005.
56 See Kaldor, supra note 45.
57 Akkerman, supra note 50.
58 Kalyvas, supra note 32.
59 Newman, supra note 52.
60 Kaldor, supra note 45, at 3.
61 Melander et al., supra note 43.

62 Kalyvas, supra note 32, at 114.
63 Leitenberg, Milton. 'Deaths in Wars and Conflicts in the 20th Century'. Cornell University/Peace Study Programme, Occasional Paper, 2006 at 8.
64 Caprioli, Mary. *Gender Equality and Civil Wars*. CPR Working Papers, World Bank, Conflict Prevention and Reconstruction Unit, 2003.
65 Peterson, supra note 27.
66 'Somali Women Whipped for Wearing Bras'. *FoxNews.com*, 19 October 2009.
67 Caprioli, supra note 64.
68 Smith, Dan. 'Women, War and Peace'. *A Briefing Paper for the UNDP Human Development Report Office*. Oslo: International Peace Research Initiative, 1997.
69 For more information on the effects of displacement on women, see Beyani, Chaloka. *Improving the Protection of Internally Displaced Women: Assessment of Progress and Challenges*. Brookings Institution, 2014.
70 Farr, Vanessa, Myrttinen, Henri and Schnabel, Albrecht. *Sexed Pistols: The Gendered Impacts of Small Arms and Light Weapons – United Nations University*. Tokyo: United Nations University Press, 2009.
71 Wood, Elisabeth. 'Variation in Sexual Violence During War'. *Politics & Society* 34, no. 3 (2006): 307–342. Jones, Adam. 'Gender and Ethnic Conflict in ex-Yugoslavia'. *Ethnic and Racial Studies* 17, no. 1 (1994): 115–134.
72 Handrahan, Lori. 'Conflict, Gender, Ethnicity and Post-Conflict Reconstruction'. *Security Dialogue* 35, no. 4 (2004): 429–445, at 437.
73 Rajagopalan, Swarna. 'Gender Violence, Conflict, Internal Displacement and Peacebuilding'. *Peace Prints: South Asian Journal of Peacebuilding* 3, no. 1 (2010): 1–15.
74 Gardam, Judith. 'War, Law, Terror, Nothing New for Women'. *The Australian Feminist Law Journal* 32 (2010): 61–75.
75 Gettleman, supra note 30.
76 Bassiouni, Cherif. 'The New Wars and the Crisis of Compliance with the Law of Armed Conflict by Non-State Actors'. *The Journal of Criminal Law and Criminology (1973–)* 98, no. 3 (2008): 711–810. Lamp, Nicolas. 'Conceptions of War and Paradigms of Compliance: The 'New War' Challenge to International Humanitarian Law'. *Journal of Conflict and Security Law* 16, no. 2 (2011): 225–262.
77 Lamp, supra note 76.
78 Ibid.
79 Ibid., at 234–235.
80 Gettleman, supra note 30.
81 Lamp, supra note 76.
82 Ibid.
83 Kellenberger Jakob, foreword, in Mack, Michelle. *Increasing Respect for International Humanitarian Law in Non-International Armed Conflicts*. Geneva: International Committee of the Red Cross, 2008, at 2.
84 Alison, Miranda. 'Women as Agents of Political Violence: Gendering Security'. *Security Dialogue* 35, no. 4 (2004): 447–463.
85 Ibid.
86 Moghadam, Valentine. *Modernising Women: Gender and Social Change in the Middle East*. Boulder, CO: Lynne Rienner, 1993.
87 Mazurana, Dyan. *Women in Armed Opposition Groups in Africa and the Promotion of International Humanitarian Law and Human Rights: Report of a Workshop Organized in Geneva by Geneva Call and the Program for the Study of International Organization(s) August 26–29, 2004*.
88 Peterson, supra note 27, at 16.
89 Ibid.
90 'Somalia Al-Shabab Militants Training Women Fighters'. *Alshahid Network*, 2013.
91 *'Our Job is to Shoot, Slaughter and Kill': Boko Haram's Reign of Terror in North-East Nigeria*. London: Amnesty International, 2015.

92 Nuune, Rashid. 'Women on the Frontlines. Gender No Barrier to Carrying an AK47'. *Somalia Report*, 22 August 2011.
93 Juma, Monica, and Makina, Anesu. 'Africa: Women Not Afraid of the Frontline'. Africa Policy Institute, *The Monitor* (Kampala), 2008.
94 For a history of women in the military see Titunik, Regina. 'The Myth of the Macho Military', *Polity* 40, no. 2, (2007): 137–163. King, Anthony. 'Women in Combat'. *The RUSI Journal* 158, no. 1 (2013): 4–11. For information about women in American, British and Canadian state armies, state policies and the consequences of these, see, Barry, Ben. 'Women in Combat'. *Survival: Global Politics and Strategy* 55, no. 2 (2013): 19–30.
95 'Women in the Military'. CBC News Online, 30 May 2006.
96 Interview with SADF women colonel 1989, in Cock, Jacklyn. 'Women and the Military: Implications for Demilitarization in the 1990s in South Africa'. *Gender & Society* 8, no. 2 (1994): 152–169, at 156.
97 'More Female Soldiers in More Positions in the IDF'. *Website of the Israeli Defence Force*. 2013. www.idf.il/1086–14000-en/Dover.aspx.
98 Gibbs, Nancy. 'Sexual Assaults on Female Soldiers: Don't Ask, Don't Tell'. *Time*, 8 March 2010.
99 Ibid.
100 Denov, Myriam. *Girls in Fighting Forces: Moving Beyond Victimhood*. A Summary of the Research Findings on Girls and Armed Conflict from CIDA's Child Protection Research Fund, 2007.
101 Bloom, Mia. 'Female Suicide Bombers: A Global Trend'. *Daedalus* 136, no. Winter (2007): 94–102.
102 Schweitzer, Yoram. *Female Suicide Bombers: Dying for Equality?* Tel Aviv: Jaffee Centre for Strategic Studies, 2006.
103 Bloom supra note 101, at 101.
104 'Women in Peacekeeping'. United Nations Peacekeeping, www.un.org/en/peacekeeping/issues/women/womeninpk.shtml.
105 Southern African Women Making Inroads into the Peace and Security Sector, Institute for Security Studies, 2012.
106 Creveld, Martin van. 'The Great Illusion: Women in the Military'. *Millennium – Journal of International Studies* 29, no. 2 (2000): 429–442.
107 Juma, Makina, supra note 93.
108 Southern African Women, supra note 105.
109 Verhey, Beth. *Reaching the Girls Study on Girls Associated with Armed Forces and Groups in the Democratic Republic of Congo*. London: Save the Children, 2004.
110 Krosch, Sara. '"A New Race of Women": The Challenges of Reintegrating Eritrea's Demobilized Female Combatants'. (Masters Thesis, Clark University, Worcester, Massachusetts), 2005.
111 McKay, Susan, and Mazurana, Dyan. *Where Are the Girls? Girls in Fighting Forces in Northern Uganda, Sierra Leone and Mozambique: Their Lives During and After War*. Montreal: Rights & Democracy, 2004.
112 Coulter, Chris. 'Female Fighters in the Sierra Leone War: Challenging the Assumptions?' *Feminist Review* 88, no. 1 (2008): 54–73.
113 Ibid., at 58.
114 Jean-Louis Roy, in the preface of McKay and Mazurana, supra note 110.
115 Coulter, Chris, Persson, Mariam and Utas, Mats. 'Young Female Fighters in African Wars Conflict and its Consequences'. *Policy Dialogue, Nordiska Afrikainstitutet* 3. NAI Policy Dialogue (2008), 1–54, at 8, footnote 2.
116 Charlesworth, Hilary, and Chinkin, Christine. *The Boundaries of International Law: A Feminist Analysis*. Manchester University Press, 2000.
117 Article 38, Convention on the Rights of the Child, 20 November, 1989, A/RES/44/25. One should note an interesting anomaly in this Convention. For the

purposes of the Convention as a whole, a 'child' is defined as any person below the age of 18. However, Article 38, which deals with child soldiers, diverges from the rest of the Convention, making the relevant age 15 for the purposes of that clause only.

118 Optional Protocol to the Convention in the Rights of the Child on the Involvement of Children in Armed Conflict, 25 May, 2000, A/RES/54/263, Article 1.

119 Article 2, The African Charter on Rights and Welfare of the Child, OAU Doc. CAB/LEG/24.9/49, 1990.

120 Convention on the Rights of the Child, supra note 117.

121 Optional Protocol to the Convention on the Rights of the Child supra note 118.

122 African Charter on Rights and Welfare of the Child, supra note 119.

123 Articles 8(2)(b)(xxvi) and (e)(vii) of the Rome Statute make child recruitment a crime, 'Conscripting or enlisting children under the age of fifteen years into the national armed forces or using them to participate actively in hostilities'. Article 4 of the Statute for the Special Court for Sierra Leone gives the court power over 'Conscripting or enlisting children under the age of 15 years into armed forces or groups or using them to participate actively in hostilities'.

124 Arts 8(2)(b)(xxvi) and 8(2)(e)(vii).

125 The question of which actions fall within the prohibition on recruiting child soldiers has been considered by various tribunals, most notably in the ICC's Lubanga trial, where one of the questions raised was whether girls who had been used by armed groups in support and sexual roles were 'actively' participating in hostilities. The Lubanga trial judgements interpreted 'active participation' broadly to include both direct and indirect participation. Lubanga is appealing his conviction, with one of the bases of appeal being that 'active' participation should be limited to direct participation in hostilities.

126 Hardwood, Catherine. 'Guest Post: A Matter of Distinction: "Active" and "Direct" Participation in Hostilities and the War Crime of Using Child Soldiers'. *Spreading the Jam*, July 2014. https://dovjacobs.com/2014/07/14/guest-post-a-matter-of-distinction-active-and-direct-participation-in-hostilities-and-the-war-crime-of-using-child-soldiers/

127 Alison, supra note 84. Alison makes this point in relation to the LTTE in Sri Lanka, however this is applicable in other contexts too.

128 McKay, Mazurana, supra note 111.

129 Alison, supra note 84.

130 Ibid.

131 Mazurana, supra note 87.

132 McKay, Mazurana, supra note 111.

133 Ibid.

134 West, supra note 35.

135 Ibid., at 185.

136 *Situation in the Democratic Republic of the Congo in the case of the Prosecutor* v. *Thomas Lubanga Dyilo*, ICC-01/04–01/06, 2012, at 280.

137 Denov, supra note 100.

138 Ibid., at 6.

139 Mazurana, supra note 87.

140 Stone, Lydia, 'We were all soldiers': Female Combatants in South Sudan's Civil War, in Bubenzer, Friederike and Stern, Orly (eds), *Hope, Pain & Patience: The Lives of Women in South Sudan*. Johannesburg: Jacana Media, 2012.

141 West, supra note 35.

142 Denov, supra note 100, at 15.

143 Ibid.

144 Mazurana, supra note 87.

145 Stone, supra note 140.

146 Sajjad, Tazreena. 'Women Guerillas: Marching Toward True Freedom? An Analysis of Women's Experiences in the Frontlines of Guerilla Warfare and in the Post-War Period'. *Agenda: Empowering Women for Gender Equality* no. 59 (2004): 4–16, at 7–8.
147 McKay, Mazurana, supra note 111.
148 Denov, supra note 100, at 7–8.
149 Mazurana, supra note 87.
150 Verhey, supra note 109.
151 *Prosecutor* v. *Thomas Lubanga Dyilo*, supra note 136.
152 Krosch, supra note 110.
153 Hogg, Nicole. 'Women's Participation in the Rwandan Genocide: Mothers or Monsters?' *International Review of the Red Cross* 92, no. 877 (2010): 69–102.
154 *The Prosecutor* v. *Pauline Nyiramasuhuko*, ICTR-98-42-T, 2011.
155 Denov, supra note 100.
156 McKay, Mazurana, supra note 111.
157 The RUF trial in the Special Court for Sierra Leone found that forced marriage is distinct from sexual slavery. The Appeals Chamber in *Prosecutor* v. *Alex Tamba Brima, Ibrahim Bazzy Karmara and Santigie Borbor Kanu* held that forced marriage was an 'other inhumane act', meaning that it fell into the category of crimes against humanity. The court emphasised the psychological and mental elements to the harm caused by this crime, and the additional injury caused by the use of the term 'wife'. Mallesons, Stephen. 'Special Court for Sierra Leone – Forced Marriage as an "other Inhumane Act"'. *Humanitarian Law Perspectives*, Topic 6(a) (2010).
158 Ekiyor, Thelma, *Female Combatants in West Africa: Progress or Regress?* WANEP – From the Field. 5th edition (2002).
159 Lowiki, Jane, and Pilsbury, Allison, *Disarmament, Demobilisation and Reintegration, and Gender-based Violence in Sierra Leone*, excerpts from 'Precious Resources, Adolescents in the Reconstruction of Sierra Leone', Women's Commission for Refugee Women and Children, (2002).
160 McKay, Mazurana, supra note 111.
161 Turpin, Jennifer. 'Many Faces, Women Confronting War'. In *The Women and War Reader*. New York: New York University Press, 1998.
162 McKay, Mazurana, supra note 111.
163 *Prosecutor* v. *Thomas Lubanga Dyilo*, supra note 135, at para 891.
164 Stone, supra note 140.
165 Stone, Lydia. *No Standing, Few Prospects: How Peace Is Failing South Sudanese Female Combatants and WAAFG*. Human Security Baseline Assessment, Sudan Issue Brief. Small Arms Survey, 2008.
166 Mazurana, supra note 87.
167 Sajjad, supra note 146.
168 Mazurana, supra note 87.
169 Stone, supra note 140, at 33.
170 Coomaraswamy, Radhika. *Report of the Special Rapporteur on Violence Against Women, its Causes and Consequences*. United Nations, Commission on Human Rights, Fifty-fourth Session, 1998.
171 West, supra note 35, at 183.
172 'The Role of Social Media in the Arab Uprisings, supra note 35.
173 'Tunisia's "Sexual Jihad" – Extremist Fatwa or Propaganda?' BBC, 27 October 2013. www.bbc.com/news/world-africa-24448933
174 Cameron, Lindsey. 'Private Military Companies: Their Status under International Humanitarian Law and its Impact on their Regulation'. *International Review of the Red Cross* 88, no. 863 (2006): 573–598. Faite, Alexandre. 'Involvement of Private Contractors in Armed Conflict: Implications Under International Humanitarian Law'. *Defence Studies* 4, no. 2 (2004): 166–183.

175 Mazurana, supra note 87.
176 *Intrastate Conflict and Gender*. Information Bulletin. Office of Women in Development, USAID, 2000.
177 Manjoo, Rashida, and McRaith, Calleigh. 'Gender-Based Violence and Justice in Conflict and Post-Conflict Areas'. *Cornell International Law Journal* 44 (2011): 11–31. Ward, Jeanne. *If Not Now, When?: Addressing Gender-Based Violence in Refugee, Internally Displaced, and Post-Conflict Settings: A Global Overview*. Reproductive Health for Refugees Consortium, 2002.
178 Harders, Cilja. 'Gender Relations, Violence and Conflict Transformation'. In Austin, Beatrix, Fischer, Martina, and Giessmann, Hans J. (eds), *Advancing Conflict Transformation. The Berghof Handbook II*. Opladen/Farmington Hills: Barbara Budrich Publishers, 2011.
179 Stern, Orly. 'This Is How Marriage Happens Sometimes'. In Bubenzer, Friederike, and Stern, Orly (eds). *Hope, Pain and Patience: The Lives of Women in South Sudan*. Johannesburg: Jacana Media, 2012.
180 West, supra note 35.
181 Krosch, supra note 110.
182 Aldehaib, Amel. *Sudan's Comprehensive Peace Agreement Viewed Through the Eyes of the Women of South Sudan*. Fellows Programme Occasional Paper. Institute for Justice and Reconciliation, 2010.
183 'Arab Spring Revolutions Don't Reach Women'. *DW.DE*, 25 November 2012.
184 *Gender-Based Violence against Women around Tahrir Square*. London: Amnesty International, 2013. Kingsley, Patrick. '80 Sexual Assaults in One Day – The Other Story of Tahrir Square'. *Guardian*, 5 July 2013,
185 Auger, Bridgette. On Location Video: Assaulted in Tahrir, Global Post, 8 February 2013.
186 Mazurana, supra note 87.
187 Hogg, supra note 153.
188 Ibid., at 81.
189 'Uganda: Bleak Future for Former Female Fighters'. *IRINnews*, 8 March, 2011.
190 Lamb, Guy, and Stern, Orly. *Assessing the Reintegration of Ex-Combatants in the Context of Instability and Informal Economies, The Cases of the Central African Republic, the Democratic Republic of Congo and South Sudan*. Washington DC: World Bank, Transitional Demobilization and Reintegration Program, 2011.
191 Stone, supra note 140.
192 Hobson, Matt, *Forgotten Casualties of War: Girls in Armed Conflict*. London: Save the Children, (2005), at 1–27.
193 McKay, Mazurana, supra note 111.
194 Verhey, supra note 109.
195 McKay, Mazurana, supra note 111.
196 Alison, supra note 84.
197 McKay, Mazurana, supra note 111, at 36.
198 Jean Claude, Omba, Kittel, France and Piette, Dannielle. 'Stigma of Victims of Sexual Violence's in Armed Conflicts: Another Factor in the Spread of the HIV Epidemic?' *Epidemiology: Open Access* 03, no. 02 (2013): 1–3.
199 Mackenzie, Megan. 'Securitizing Sex?' *International Feminist Journal of Politics* 12, no. 2 (2010): 202–221.
200 Cockburn, Cynthia. 'Gender Relations as Causal in Militarization and War'. *International Feminist Journal of Politics* 12, no. 2 (2010): 139–157.
201 *Intrastate Conflict and Gender*, supra note 176.

Bibliography

Books and articles

'African Peacekeeping Operations'. *Council on Foreign Relations*. www.cfr.org/africa/african-peacekeeping-operations/p9333.

Aldehaib, Amel. *Sudan's Comprehensive Peace Agreement Viewed through the Eyes of the Women of South Sudan*. Fellows Programme Occasional Paper. Institute for Justice and Reconciliation, 2010.

Alison, Miranda. 'Women as Agents of Political Violence: Gendering Security'. *Security Dialogue* 35, no. 4 (2004): 447–463.

Anghie, Antony. *Imperialism, Sovereignty and the Making of International Law*. Cambridge: Cambridge University Press, 2005.

Anghie, Antony. 'The Evolution of International Law: Colonial and Postcolonial Realities'. *Third World Quarterly* 27, no. 5 (1 January 2006): 739–753.

Ajala, Adekunle. 'The Nature of African Boundaries' 18, no. 2 (1983): 177–189.

Akkerman, Tjitske. 'New Wars, New Morality?' *Acta Politica* 44, no. 1 (2009): 74–86

'Arab Spring Revolutions Don't Reach Women'. *DW.DE*, 25 November 2012.

Arreguín-Toft, Ivan. 'Contemporary Asymmetric Conflict Theory in Historical Perspective'. *Terrorism and Political Violence* 24, no. 4 (2012): 635–657.

Arreguín-Toft, Ivan. *How the Weak Win Wars: A Theory of Asymmetric Conflict*. Cambridge: Cambridge Studies in International Relations; Cambridge University Press, 2005.

Bassiouni. Cherif. 'The New Wars and the Crisis of Compliance with the Law of Armed Conflict by Non-State Actors'. *The Journal of Criminal Law and Criminology (1973–)* 98, no. 3 (2008): 711–810.

Barry, Ben. 'Women in Combat'. *Survival: Global Politics and Strategy* 55, no. 2 (2013): 19–30.

Beyani, Chaloka. *Improving the Protection of Internally Displaced Women: Assessment of Progress and Challenges*. Brookings Institution, 2014.

Bloom, Mia. 'Female Suicide Bombers: A Global Trend'. *Daedalus* 136, no. Winter (2007): 94–102.

Butime, Herman. 'Examining the Relevance of the Theories of Guerrilla Warfare in Explaining the Lord's Resistance Army Insurgency in Northern Uganda'. *University of Wollongong Thesis Collection* Wollongong: University of Wollongong, 2012.

Boot, Max. 'Paving the Road to Hell: The Failure of U.N. Peacekeeping'. *Foreign Affairs*, April 2000.

Bowden, Brett. 'The Colonial Origins of International Law – European Expansion and the Classical Standard of Civilization'. *Journal of the History of International Law* 7 (2005): 1–23.

Callahan, Michael. *A Sacred Trust: The League of Nations and Africa, 1929–1946*. Eastbourne: Sussex Academic Press, 2004.

Cameron, Lindsey. 'Private Military Companies: Their Status under International Humanitarian Law and its Impact on their Regulation'. *International Review of the Red Cross* 88, no. 863 (2006): 573–598.

Caprioli, Mary. *Gender Equality and Civil Wars*. CPR Working Papers, World Bank, Conflict Prevention and Reconstruction Unit, 2003.

Charlesworth, Hilary, and Chinkin, Christine. *The Boundaries of International Law: A Feminist Analysis*. Manchester: Manchester University Press, 2000.

Children and Women Associated with Armed Forces and Groups, Issue Paper, Second International Conference on DDR and Stability in Africa Kinshasa, Democratic Republic of Congo, 12–14 June 2007.

Cock, Jacklyn. 'Women and the Military: Implications for Demilitarization in the 1990s in South Africa'. *Gender & Society* 8, no. 2 (1994): 152–169.

Cockburn, Cynthia. 'Gender Relations as Causal in Militarization and War'. *International Feminist Journal of Politics* 12, no. 2 (2010): 139–157.

Coomaraswamy, Radhika. *Report of the Special Rapporteur on Violence Against Women, its Causes and Consequences*. United Nations, Commission on Human Rights, Fifty-fourth Session, 1998.

Coulter, Chris. 'Female Fighters in the Sierra Leone War: Challenging the Assumptions?' *Feminist Review* 88, no. 1 (2008): 54–73.

Coulter, Chris, Persson, Mariam, and Utas, Mats. 'Young Female Fighters in African Wars Conflict and its Consequences'. *Policy Dialogue, Nordiska Afrikainstitutet* 3. NAI Policy Dialogue (2008), 1–54.

Creveld, Martin van. 'The Great Illusion: Women in the Military'. *Millennium – Journal of International Studies* 29, no. 2 (2000): 429–442.

Dallaire, Roméo. *Shake Hands with the Devil: The Failure of Humanity in Rwanda*. Carroll and Graf, 2005. Brattberg, Erik. 'Revisiting UN Peacekeeping in Rwanda and Sierra Leone'. *Peace Review* 24, no. 2 (2012): 156–162.

Denov, Myriam. *Girls in Fighting Forces: Moving Beyond Victimhood*. A Summary of the Research Findings on Girls and Armed Conflict from CIDA's Child Protection Research Fund, 2007.

Dreazen, Yochi. 'The New Terrorist Training Ground'. *The Atlantic*, October 2013.

Duignan, Gann Peter, and Turner, Victor (eds), *Colonialism in Africa 1870–1960 Volume Three: Profiles of Change: African Society and Colonial Rule*. Cambridge: Cambridge University Press, 1971.

Easterly, William, and Freschi, Laura. 'Top 5 Reasons Why "Failed State" Is a Failed Concept'. Aidwatch, 13 January 2010. www.nyudri.org/aidwatcharchive/2010/01/top-5-reasons-why-%E2%80%9Cfailed-state%E2%80%9D-is-a-failed-concept

Ekiyor, Thelma, *Female Combatants in West Africa: Progress or Regress?* Accra: WANEP – From the Field. 5th edition, 2002.

Faite, Alexandre. 'Involvement of Private Contractors in Armed Conflict: Implications Under International Humanitarian Law'. *Defence Studies* 4, no. 2 (2004): 166–183.

Farr, Vanessa, Myrttinen Henri, and Albrecht Schnabel. *Sexed Pistols: The Gendered Impacts of Small Arms and Light Weapons – United Nations University*. Tokyo: United Nations University Press, 2009.

Ford, Jolyon. *Counter-Terrorism and the Rule of Law in Africa: The Second Decade After 2001*. Institute for Security Studies, 2013.

Gardam, Judith. 'War, Law, Terror, Nothing New for Women'. *The Australian Feminist Law Journal* 32 (2010): 61–75.

Gender-Based Violence against Women around Tahrir Square. London: Amnesty International, 2013.

Gettleman, Jeffrey. 'Africa's Forever Wars'. *Foreign Policy*, April 2010.

Gibbs, Nancy. 'Sexual Assaults on Female Soldiers: Don't Ask, Don't Tell'. *Time*, 8 March 2010.

Handrahan, Lori. 'Conflict, Gender, Ethnicity and Post-Conflict Reconstruction'. *Security Dialogue* 35, no. 4 (2004): 429–445.

Harders, Cilja. 'Gender Relations, Violence and Conflict Transformation'. In Austin, Beatrix, Fischer, Martina, and Giessmann, Hans J. (eds) *Advancing Conflict Transformation. The Berghof Handbook II*, 132–55. Opladen/Farmington Hills: Barbara Budrich Publishers, 2011.

Hardwood, Catherine. 'Guest Post: A Matter of Distinction: "Active" and "Direct" Participation in Hostilities and the War Crime of Using Child Soldiers'. *Spreading the Jam*, July 2014.

Higgins, Noelle. The Approach of International Law to Wars of National Liberation. *Martin Monograph Series. (Monograph 3). Martin Institute, University of Idaho* (2004).

Hogg, Nicole. 'Women's Participation in the Rwandan Genocide: Mothers or Monsters?' *International Review of the Red Cross* 92, no. 877 (2010): 69–102.

Hobson, Matt, *Forgotten Casualties of War: Girls in Armed Conflict*. London: Save the Children 2005, at 1–27.

Holmes, Steven. 'The World; Africa, From the Cold War to Cold Shoulders'. *New York Times*, 7 March 1993.

Holt, Victoria, and Shanahan, Moira. 'African Capacity-Building for Peace Operations: UN Collaboration with the African Union and ECOWAS'. The Henry L. Stimson Centre, 2005.

Holt, Victoria, and Taylor, Glyn. *Protecting Civilians in the Context of UN Peacekeeping Operations: Successes, Setbacks and Remaining Challenges*. Department of Peacekeeping Operations and the Office for the Coordination of Humanitarian Affairs of the United Nations, 2009.

Intrastate Conflict and Gender. Information Bulletin. Office of Women in Development, USAID, 2000.

Jean Claude, Omba, Kittel, France and Piette, Dannielle. 'Stigma of Victims of Sexual Violence's in Armed Conflicts: Another Factor in the Spread of the HIV Epidemic?' *Epidemiology: Open Access* 03, no. 02 (2013): 1–3.

Jones, Adam. 'Gender and Ethnic Conflict in ex-Yugoslavia'. *Ethnic and Racial Studies* 17, no. 1 (1994): 115–134.

Juma, Monica, and Makina, Anesu. 'Africa: Women Not Afraid of the Frontline'. Africa Policy Institute, *The Monitor* (Kampala), 2008.

Kaldor, Mary. 'In Defence of New Wars'. *Stability* 2, no. 1 (2013).

Kaldor, Mary. *New and Old Wars: Organized Violence in a Global Era*. 2nd edn. Cambridge: Polity, 2006.

Kaldor, Mary. 'New Wars. Counter-Insurgency or Human'. *The Broker – Connecting Worlds of Knowledge*, 28 May 2009. [Online]

Kalyvas, Stathis. '"New" and "Old" Civil Wars: A Valid Distinction?' *World Politics* 54, no. 01 (2001): 99–118.

Karmon, Ely. *The Iran/Hezbollah Strategic and Terrorist Threat to Africa*. Herzliya: International Institute for Counter-Terrorism, 2012.

Kellenberger Jakob, Foreword, in Mack, Michelle. *Increasing Respect for International Humanitarian Law in Non-International Armed Conflicts*. Geneva: International Committee of the Red Cross, 2008.

Krosch, Sara. '"A New Race of Women": The Challenges of Reintegrating Eritrea's Demobilized Female Combatants'. (Master's Thesis, Clark University, Worcester, Massachusetts), 2005.

Lamb, Guy and Stern, Orly. *Assessing the Reintegration of Ex-Combatants in the Context of Instability and Informal Economies, the Cases of the Central African Republic, the*

Democratic Republic of Congo and South Sudan. Washington DC: World Bank, Transitional Demobilization and Reintegration Program, 2011.

Lamp, Nicolas. 'Conceptions of War and Paradigms of Compliance: The "New War" Challenge to International Humanitarian Law'. *Journal of Conflict and Security Law* 16, no. 2 (2011): 225–262.

Leitenberg, Milton. 'Deaths in Wars and Conflicts in the 20th Century'. Cornell University/Peace Study Programme, Occasional Paper, 2006.

Lowiki, Jane, and Pilsbury, Allison, *Disarmament, Demobilisation and Reintegration, and Gender-based Violence in Sierra Leone*, excerpts from *Precious Resources, Adolescents in the Reconstruction of Sierra Leone*, Women's Commission for Refugee Women and Children, (2002).

Malantowicz, Artur. 'Do "New Wars" Theories Contribute to Our Understanding of the African Conflicts? Cases of Rwanda and Darfur'. *Africana Bulletin* 58 (2010): 159–172.

Mackenzie, Megan. 'Securitizing Sex?' *International Feminist Journal of Politics* 12, no. 2 (2010): 202–221.

Mallesons, Stephen. 'Special Court for Sierra Leone – Forced Marriage as an "other Inhumane Act" '. *Humanitarian Law Perspectives*, Topic 6(a) (2010).

Manjoo, Rashida and McRaith, Calleigh. 'Gender-Based Violence and Justice in Conflict and Post-Conflict Areas'. *Cornell International Law Journal* 44 (2011): 11–31.

Mateos, Oscar. 'Beyond Greed and Grievance, Towards a Comprehensive Approach to African Armed Conflicts: Sierra Leone as a Case Study'. In Bowd, Dr Richard and Chikwanha, Dr Annie Barbara (eds), *Understanding Africa's Contemporary Conflicts Origins, Challenges and Peacebuilding*. Institute for Security Studies, 2010.

Mazurana, Dyan. *Women in Armed Opposition Groups in Africa and the Promotion of International Humanitarian Law and Human Rights: Report of a Workshop Organized in Geneva by Geneva Call and the Program for the Study of International Organization(s) August 26–29, 2004*.

McKay, Susan, and Mazurana, Dyan. *Where Are the Girls? Girls in Fighting Forces in Northern Uganda, Sierra Leone and Mozambique: Their Lives During and After War*. Montreal: Rights & Democracy, 2004.

Melander, Erik, Öberg, Magnus, and Hall, Jonathan. 'Are "New Wars" More Atrocious? Battle Severity, Civilians Killed and Forced Migration Before and After the End of the Cold War'. *European Journal of International Relations* 15, no. 3 (2009): 505–536.

Mitchell, Brian. *Women in the Military: Flirting with Disaster*. Washington, DC; Lanham, MD: Regnery Pub, 1958 (Distributed to the trade by National Book Network, 1998).

Moghadam, Valentine. *Modernising Women: Gender and Social Change in the Middle East*. Boulder, CO: Lynne Rienner, 1993.

Nele, Matz. 'Civilization and the Mandate System Under the League of Nations as Origin of Trusteeship'. *Max Planck Yearbook of United Nations Law* 9, no. 1 (2005): 47–95.

Newman, Edward. 'The "New Wars" Debate: A Historical Perspective Is Needed'. *Security Dialogue* 35, no. 2 (2004): 173–189.

No Standing, Few Prospects: How Peace Is Failing South Sudanese Female Combatants and WAAFG. Human Security Baseline Assessment, Sudan Issue Brief. Small Arms Survey, 2008.

Nuune, Rashid. 'Women on the Frontlines. Gender No Barrier to Carrying an AK47'. *Somalia Report*, 22 August 2011.

'Our Job is to Shoot, Slaughter and Kill': Boko Haram's Reign of Terror in North-East Nigeria. London: Amnesty International, 2015.

Peterson, Spike. ''New Wars' and Gendered Economies'. *Feminist Review* 88 (2008): 7–20.

Piombo, Jessica. *Terrorism and U.S. Counter-Terrorism Programs in Africa: An Overview*. Centre for Contemporary Conflict, 2007.

Rajagopalan, Swarna. 'Gender Violence, Conflict, Internal Displacement and Peacebuilding'. *Peace Prints: South Asian Journal of Peacebuilding* 3, no. 1 (2010): 1–15.

Sajjad, Tazreena. 'Women Guerillas: Marching Toward True Freedom? An Analysis of Women's Experiences in the Frontlines of Guerilla Warfare and in the Post-War Period'. *Agenda: Empowering Women for Gender Equality* no. 59 (2004): 4–16,

Schäfer, Heinrich. 'New Wars and Religious Identity Politics'. In *Religions Today. Their Challenge to the Ecumenical Movement* (2005): 89–104.

Schweitzer, Yoram. *Female Suicide Bombers: Dying for Equality?* Tel Aviv: Jaffee Centre for Strategic Studies, 2006.

Shah, Anup. 'Conflicts in Africa – Introduction'. *Global Issues*, 12 May 2010.

Smith, Dan. 'Women, War and Peace'. *A Briefing Paper for the UNDP Human Development Report Office.* Oslo: International Peace Research Initiative, 1997.

'Somali Women Whipped for Wearing Bras'. *FoxNews.com*, 19 October 2009.

Somalia Al-Shabab Militants Training Women Fighters'. *Alshahid Network*, 2013.

Southern African Women Making Inroads into the Peace and Security Sector. Institute for Security Studies, 2012.

Stern, Orly. 'This Is How Marriage Happens Sometimes'. In Bubenzer, Friederike, and Stern, Orly (eds). *Hope, Pain and Patience: The Lives of Women in South Sudan.* Johannesburg: Jacana Media, 2012.

Stone, Lydia, 'We were all soldiers': Female Combatants in South Sudan's Civil War, in Bubenzer, Friederike, and Stern, Orly (eds). *Hope, Pain & Patience: The Lives of Women in South Sudan.* Johannesburg: Jacana Media, 2012.

Terrorism in the Horn of Africa. United States Institute of Peace, Special Report 113, 2004.

'The Globalisation of Terror: Hezbollah in Africa'. International Centre for the Study of Radicalisation, Department of War Studies, Kings College. http://icsr.info/2012/02/the-globalisation-of-terror-hezbollah-in-africa/.

'The Role of Social Media in the Arab Uprisings – Past and Present'. *Westminster Papers in Communication and Culture* 9, no. 2 (2013).

Titunik, Regina. 'The Myth of the Macho Military', *Polity* 40(2), (2007): 137–163. King, Anthony. 'Women in Combat'. *The RUSI Journal* 158, no. 1 (2013): 4–11.

Turpin, Jennifer. 'Many Faces, Women Confronting War'. In *The Women and War Reader, Lois Ann Lorentzen and Jennifer Turpin.* New York: New York University Press, 1998.

Verhey, Beth. *Reaching the Girls Study on Girls Associated with Armed Forces and Groups in the Democratic Republic of Congo.* London: Save the Children, 2004.

Ward, Jeanne. *If Not Now, When?: Addressing Gender-Based Violence in Refugee, Internally Displaced, and Post-Conflict Settings: A Global Overview.* New York: Reproductive Health for Refugees Consortium, 2002.

West, Harry. 'Girls with Guns: Narrating the Experience of War of Frelimo's "Female Detachment"'. *Anthropological Quarterly* 73, no. 4 (2000): 180–194.

World Development Report 2011: Conflict, Security, and Development. Washington DC: World Bank, 2011.

Wood, Elisabeth. 'Variation in Sexual Violence during War'. *Politics & Society* 34, no. 3 (2006): 307–342.

Cases

Case Concerning the Territorial Dispute, (*Libyan Arab Jamahiriya* v. *Chad*), *ICJ 1994.*
Kasikili/Sedudu Island in Case concerning Kasikili/Sedudu Island (*Botswana* v. *Namibia*), ICJ, 1999.
Land and Maritime Boundary between Cameroon and Nigeria (*Cameroon* v. *Nigeria: Equatorial Guinea intervening*), ICJ 2002.
Situation in the Democratic Republic of the Congo in the case of the Prosecutor v. *Thomas Lubanga Dyilo*, ICC-01/04-01/06, 2012.
The Prosecutor v. *Alex Tamba Brima Bazzy Kamara Santigie Borbor Kanu.* SCSL-04-16-T, 2008.
The Prosecutor v. *Pauline Nyiramasuhuko*, ICTR-98-42-T, 2011.
Western Sahara, Advisory Opinion, ICJ Reports, General List No. 61, 1975.

Treaties

Geneva Convention Relative to the Protection of Civilian Persons in Time of War (Fourth Geneva Convention), 12 August 1949, 75 UNTS 287.
Geneva Convention Relative to the Treatment of Prisoners of War (Third Geneva Convention), 12 August 1949, 75 UNTS 135.
Geneva Convention for the Amelioration of the Condition of Wounded, Sick and Shipwrecked Members of Armed Forces at Sea (Second Geneva Convention), 12 August 1949, 75 UNTS 85.
Geneva Convention for the Amelioration of the Condition of the Wounded and Sick in Armed Forces in the Field (First Geneva Convention), 12 August 1949, 75 UNTS 31.
Optional Protocol to the Convention in the Rights of the Child on the Involvement of Children in Armed Conflict, 25 May, 2000, A/RES/54/263, Article 1.
Rome Statute of the International Criminal Court, 17 July 1998, 92-9227-227-6.
The African Charter on Rights and Welfare of the Child, OAU Doc. CAB/LEG/24.9/49, 1990.
UN General Assembly, *Convention on the Prevention and Punishment of the Crime of Genocide*, 9 December 1948, A/RES/260.
Convention on the Rights of the Child, 20 November, 1989, A/RES/44/25.

Other policy documents

United Nations General Assembly's Resolution on Decolonisation 1514 (1960).

Media articles and websites

Auger, Bridgette. On Location Video: Assaulted in Tahrir, Global Post, 8 February 2013.
Kingsley, Patrick. '80 Sexual Assaults in One Day – The Other Story of Tahrir Square'. *Guardian*, 5 July 2013,
'More Female Soldiers in More Positions in the IDF'. *Website of the Israeli Defence Force*. 2013. www.idf.il/1086-14000-en/Dover.aspx.
'Tunisia's "Sexual Jihad" – Extremist Fatwa or Propaganda?' *BBC*, 27 October 2013.
'Uganda: Bleak Future for Former Female Fighters'. *IRINnews*, 8 March, 2011.
Women in the Military, CBC News Online, 30 May 2006.
Women in Peacekeeping, United Nations Peacekeeping www.un.org/en/peacekeeping/issues/women/womeninpk.shtml

4 Gender and international humanitarian law

Conflicts are gendered spaces. They affect men and women differently. A school of feminist scholars have sought to expose the distinct experiences of women in conflict. They have questioned how IHL responds to conflict's gendered nature and how the law contributes to and perpetuates gendered disparities. Feminist scholars have argued that the – predominantly male – drafters of the IHL conventions held a particular gendered view of conflict, in which certain roles were held by men and women respectively; combatants were perceived to be men, while women were envisaged as civilians or victims of war. Despite the fact that IHL was couched in largely gender-neutral terms, these notions shaped the development of the law and remain pervasive in IHL today.

This chapter reviews some of the literature on feminist theory and its application to both conflict and IHL. Feminist theory frames the discussions in this book, aiming to give coherence to the various topics discussed, while linking this research to a body of work developed by feminist scholars. The chapter begins with an introductory discussion on feminism, defining the central concepts and concerns of this body of thought, before honing in on the ways in which these relate to armed conflict. While this book focuses primarily on women, gender analysis is relational; as such, the chapter describes the role of masculinity and how it underlies militarism and the war-making endeavour. Feminist views on female combatancy are explored, as are the views of others in society about women who fight. The chapter then goes on to examine critiques that feminist scholars have made about IHL, and the principle of distinction specifically, showing what feminist analyses have revealed about the shortcomings and workings of this law. Finally, the chapter considers some approaches that have been used to try improve the gendered state of the law, including international criminal law and the Security Council's Women, Peace and Security Agenda, highlighting the successes and shortcomings of these approaches.

A brief introduction to feminist theory

Feminist theory comprises of both analytical and political claims. Analytically, feminists claim that gender is a key feature of social differentiation operating to shape society.[1] Gender relations are a vital ordering principle pervading society's systems of power, a role that is scarcely acknowledged.[2] Feminists are concerned with the ways that women's experiences are silenced. Hence, they attempt to give voice to these silences, by asking questions about women: Where are the women? What are women going through in various situations? What would different policies, laws and concerns look like if women were properly taken into consideration? In the area of conflict, so long perceived as the quintessential male arena, feminists have sought to portray the unique experiences of women: What do women go through in war? What do they need? In what gender specific ways do women participate in conflict and its aftermath?

Politically, feminists operate from the position that the way that gender shapes the world is unjust. As such, they are dedicated to challenging this. Feminists examine the status of women, with the express purpose of using these understandings to improve women's lives, transforming society and achieving women's empowerment. Feminist writing is grounded in the assumption that women are oppressed and that society, family structures and legal systems support this oppression. They seek to expose relationships of domination and subordination, and to explore the mechanisms through which this dominance occurs and the reasons it persists.[3] In the realm of conflict, feminists seek to understand how the various mechanisms that support, maintain and regulate armed conflict work to subordinate women within these.

A school of feminist thinkers have directed their inquiries towards the law.[4] While there are many different legal feminisms, what they have in common is a view that the way the law treats women is different from the way it treats men, and a contention that the law is instrumental in the continuing subordination of women. Across many branches of law – from employment law, to inheritance, to family law – feminist scholars have demonstrated how laws play a role in perpetuating unfair gendered dynamics.

Feminist legal enquiries have been directed towards international law as a whole, and towards specific parts of international law.[5] Charlesworth and Chinkin explain that a feminist analysis of international law can play two roles. First, it deconstructs the values – explicit and implicit – underlying the international legal system, challenging them for having an incomplete basis; one that excludes women while purporting to represent all. Second, it allows for a reconstruction of international law, recreating the basic concepts in ways that do not facilitate male domination.[6] This dual approach is utilised in the feminist analysis of IHL conducted in this book, enabling a deconstruction of the role of the principle of distinction and its limitations in protecting women, as well as a reconstruction, which casts the role of women differently under IHL.

A number of key concepts form the basis of feminist thought, and are introduced here. Although concepts in this chapter are defined for the purpose of explanation, in reality these terms are more fluid and variable than descriptions suggest. The distinction between 'gender' and 'sex' underpins many feminist ideas. It is arguably the failure by many to understand this difference that is at the route of stereotyping, discrimination and the rigid division of roles according to sex. In 1955, sexologist John Money coined the distinction between sex and gender. 'Sex' he said, referred to the biological differences between men and women, while 'gender' referred to specific qualities or roles filled by each of the sexes, which included the range of characteristics of masculinity and femininity. Money described 'gender roles' as the things people do or say to act out or disclose their identities as men or women.[7] It took some time for this idea to catch on, and it was only in the 1970s when the Western feminist movement took this on that the distinction between sex and gender gained steam. Its value to the feminist discussion, Butler notes, was in moving the discussion away from the "biology is destiny formulation".[8]

Not everyone accepts the clear distinction between sex and gender. Critics argue that the interaction between these is highly complex and that a greater understanding is required about the ways that biological traits interact with the social environment to shape individuals' capacities.[9] Within the realms of both sex and gender, critics argue against a clear binary between men and women, pointing to those who fall between these positions.[10] What is clear is that the way in which people *act out* their sex is important, is learned, is culturally varied and is determined by more than just biological factors. Humans are taught to act as a particular gender, and the ways in which they act as men or women are influenced by social expectations.[11] In societies where the genders are presented and played out more differently from each other, like across Africa, there can be significant negative consequences for those deviating from these norms, consequences that limit the fluidity in both sex and gender.[12] The term gender also refers to other aspects of sexual and gender identities, in addition to male/female identities.[13]

Gender stereotypes are generalisations about the attributes and roles appropriate to the two genders. Stereotypes often incorporate inaccurate assumptions, assumptions that attribute to each of the sexes traits that are not inherent but learned. Stereotypes ignore or are blind to individual traits. As with gendered behaviours, people learn stereotypes from others in their society. Gender stereotypes can be deeply damaging and there can be negative consequences for those failing to act as stereotypes dictate. A key goal of the feminist movement is to challenge stereotypes about female roles, behaviours and positions, exposing them as what they are: learned, socially constructed behaviours that are not innate to women and that can be altered to accommodate differences in choice or circumstance.[14]

Stereotypes about men and women, and socially constructed expectations around gender appropriate behaviour, are glaringly evident in the realm of armed conflict. From time immemorial societies have constructed the ways that men and women should act in war, constructions that have shifted through the years. Largely, throughout history perceptions have existed about women being peaceful and against war, experiencing it predominantly as victims. Men, on the other hand, have been perceived as fighters, being physically stronger and more inclined to such endeavours. Those who have deviated from these expectations have been judged harshly. Men who 'desert' or refuse to fight have been labelled weak, unpatriotic or unchivalrous. As a means of domination, men have been deemed 'feminised', including by rape in war. Female fighters have been labelled as deviants and ostracised during and after conflict. People struggle to accept such deviations from the gendered scripts of conflict. Some people's means of reconciling this is to remove subject's genders, metaphorically speaking. Hogg described the ways in which women who took part in the Rwandan genocide were said not to be women, but rather to be like men or to be likened to monsters.[15] Even Grotius, one of the earliest founders of the laws of war, wrote that women should be spared in war, unless they have committed a crime that ought to be punished in a special manner, or "unless they take the place of men".[16]

Gender stereotypes can be harmful to men and women, exposing them both to risks. While women are subject to specific types of dangers in conflict, men are at a higher risk of being intentionally harmed or killed – in large part due to stereotypes about men being violent and to perceptions that all men are combatants, or at least potential combatants. From World War Two, to Bosnia, to East Timor, sex-selective killings of men have been a common occurrence.[17] Paradoxically, despite the fact that men are at greater risk of being targeted, there tends to be an emphasis on protecting women in conflict. Because they are stereotyped as weak and vulnerable, women are prioritised in evacuation and protection initiatives, consequently putting men at further risk.[18] Gender stereotypes affect compliance with the principle of distinction, ultimately putting both men and women's safety at risk.

Arising from the concept of gender is the concept of 'gender-neutrality', often found in laws or policies. Gender-neutrality is based on the notion that to avoid discrimination, policies should not differentiate on the basis of sex. 'Formally equal' policies therefore do not contain gender distinctions. This notion is problematic, given the unequal starting points for men and women. One cannot create equality in an inherently unequal situation merely by treating everyone alike. Formally equal laws can have highly discriminatory effects for women, when men and women's starting positions are so different. Gardam notes that, "Reform based on the equality model has been convincingly demonstrated to be a singularly blunt instrument to achieve any change for women in a world where they do not live out their lives as the equal of men".[19] While equality between men and women is a central goal of the feminist project, equality as a tool can be unjust when applied in situations where disparities exist, without taking them into account and explicitly addressing these structural inequalities.[20] Many feminist thinkers therefore support having 'substantively equal' laws, that provide for specific differences in treatment and are designed to redress inequalities and solve particular problems.[21] 'Gender specificity' and 'gender neutrality' tend to be presented as binaries; however, the best results might come from identifying a balance or middle ground between them – as this book seeks to do for the principle of distinction.

Much of legal discourse is based on pairs of binaries or opposites, with terms like objective/subjective, protector/protected and active/passive pervading the law.[22] The law, as it is constructed, is reliant on these binaries, with each part of an opposing pair being mutually dependent on the other for meaning and substance. These binaries have become so entrenched in our ways of thinking that they are often perceived of as natural or universal.[23] Binary distinctions are clearly evident in the area of armed conflict. Opposing distinctions like combatant/civilian, military necessity/humanitarianism, victim/perpetrator, protector/protected pervade IHL and the conflict space. Feminists seek to challenge these and the fact that they are perceived as natural. They question whether for each there should be only two positions lying in direct opposition to one another, or rather whether alternatives or middle positions could exist, positions that merge elements of both. Feminist critiques point out how gender informs various binaries and how there tends to be a gendered hierarchical coding in these systems of opposites. Often, one in each pair represents the masculine – consider 'combatants' in relation to 'civilians', or 'military necessity' in relation to 'humanitarianism' – and tends to be prioritised in law and policy.[24]

An important binary discussed extensively in feminist writing is the public/private divide, which sees the world as divided into public and private spaces or issues.[25] State matters and government actions are considered public, while personal lives – including family lives – are private. Traditionally, legislation, policy and international treaties have been seen to pertain to the public sphere, while the private sphere has been seen as outside the realm of regulation. The public/private divide is contested. Feminists argue that a clear line between public and private does not exist, as the impacts of disadvantage in the private sphere spill over and influence the public sphere.[26] For example, women's (private) burden in child rearing affects their ability to participate in public life.[27] Others have accepted a public/private divide yet have pointed their criticisms towards the way the divide has been framed. They argue that this framing creates the false belief that the differences between public and private are givens, rather than social constructions worthy of interrogation.[28]

A public/private divide is strongly evident in conflict and its regulation. Conflict can be seen as the pinnacle of the public sphere, with state agents operating formally in public settings for public goals. Combatants, operating on behalf of the state, represent the public; civilians, the private.[29] However, here too the divide is problematic. MacKinnon argues that there can be no private sphere when women's personal lives have become political and when the degradation of women is part of the public order.[30] Even within the public realm of the military, women are used in more domestic support roles. Sexual violence increases in conflict – private acts, heightened by public conflict. Refugee and IDP camps also marry public and private in manifest ways.

Little thought has apparently been given to whether and how these accepted binaries function in the African context. Conditions in Africa frequently fall somewhere between traditional binary points. In African cultures, individuals are perceived to be responsible for their communities and communities have responsibility over the lives of individuals – with even the African Charter on Human and People's Rights (Banjul Charter) emphasising that the rights of each individual should be exercised with regards to the rights of others.[31] In contexts where community members are enmeshed in each other's lives in this way, are community structures public or private? How does one rule a divide between these spheres? Lewis, who writes about African Islamic feminism, discusses the binary of secular/religion, noting how on the African continent this binary is more rigid in concept than in practice.[32] Looking at conflict, Africa's low-level, sporadically flaring-up conflicts fall in the space between order/anarchy and war/peace.

Focusing on women in Africa, as this work does, risks creating an impression that African women are all the same and are all affected by experiences in similar ways. There is a danger of 'essentialising', or implying that women have a set of common immutable attributes. Discussing women as *a* category risks concealing the many differences between them – such as race, class, religion, socio-economic status and ethnicity – differences that are fundamental to shaping women's experiences.[33] While there may be political, analytical and strategic value in highlighting the common experiences of women, or certain groups of women, it is crucial that this is done in a way that does not disregard their differences. While gender is the primary unit of analysis in feminist research, to properly understand women's experiences requires assessing gender and its interrelationship with other factors of social differentiation. 'Intersectionality' requires examining relationships across multiple dimensions, seeking to understand how different categories operate together and how systems of oppression reflect the intersections between various forms of discrimination.[34] Feminists assess the intersection between gender discrimination and other forms of discrimination, including racism and classism. These factors are critical in considering women in African conflicts, where *racial, religious* and *ethnic* factors are dominant concerns, and where *poor* women are more likely to become involved with armed groups, to be sexually exploited, or to be unable to escape conflict.[35]

There are numerous branches of feminism, each of which provides a different lens though which to understand women's experiences – and which contributes differing insights to the problems posed in this work. Feminists do not speak with one voice. Differing schools of feminism disagree on analysis, interpretation and the appropriate courses of action required to improve women's conditions. The feminist critiques of IHL described later in this chapter integrate arguments from differing schools of feminist thought, making it useful to understand the schools these arguments stem from. Summarised briefly – and recognising that these are not in fact such hard and fast categories – the following is an overview. The 'liberal equality' model of feminism embraces liberal values like equality, arguing that all people are created equal, so women should not be treated unequally on the basis of their gender. The challenge with this paradigm is in ensuring it concerns itself with true equality, not nominal or formal equality.[36] This model locates one of the root causes of women's oppression within legal systems, therefore promoting legal change to remedy this. Some of the core conclusions of this book hold up equality of treatment as a dominant priority, based largely on this school of thought, grappling with what true equality would look like in the context of the principle of distinction. The 'sexual difference' model argues that the law should not conceal gender differences but rather, it should take them into account, as only by recognising and addressing differences can the law improve women's conditions. 'Radical feminism' focuses on patriarchy as the system of power that organises society and dictates male supremacy. It advocates for a radical restructuring of society to defeat patriarchy and male supremacy in all economic, social and political contexts. This school of feminism focuses strongly on opposing the sexual objectification of women and raising consciousness about violence against women in society.[37]

'Postmodern feminism' argues that women's conditions are socially situated, so that there is no such thing as a universal women's experience or voice. Proponents criticise other branches of feminism for their Eurocentrism and for creating the impression that Western women's issues are the same issues that women face the world over, ignoring the unique experiences of 'other' women. They argue that using the term 'women' as a universal group, results in women being defined by only their genders, and not by other factors such as race, class, ethnicity or sexual orientation – factors that are often equally important to women's identities and experiences. Butler notes that,

> The political assumption that there must be a universal basis for feminism, one which must be found in an identity assumed to exist cross-culturally, often accompanies the notion that the oppression of women has some singular form discernible in the universal or hegemonic structure of patriarchy or masculine domination.[38]

Postmodern feminists emphasise that gender presents diverse, local meanings and iterations that are contextually and historically determined. They seek to highlight the ways that race, class and others axes of difference intersect with gender, and the results of these intersections.

'Postcolonial' or 'third world feminists' argue that colonialism and the after-effects of colonialism are intrinsically bound with the gendered experiences of non-white, non-Western women. They argue that colonial policies and institutions played a part in creating patriarchal societies, and that racial, class and sexist ideologies were born from the process of colonial rule. Postcolonial feminists argue that third world women are the world's most exploited people – due in large part to their colonial history.[39] Considering this in relation to Africa, Goredema notes that,

> For African women, feminism is very dependent on a temporal scale shaped by political eras. These eras are pre-colonial, colonial and post-colonial Africa. These eras are dissimilar across African countries because the histories of the liberation struggles are different for each country.[40]

A feminist movement has developed on the African continent, which considers these issues with specific reference to the region. African feminists argue that women's socially determined identities take on different forms in Africa than they do in the West,[41] as do forms of domination and resistance. Due to these differences, they claim, Western feminism's standards are inappropriate to guide the feminist movement on the continent.[42] African scholars point out how African and post-colonial feminisms are perceived as 'other' feminisms by the mainstream feminist movement.[43] Mangena explains that Western feminists see feminism as a science, thereby assuming it must be universal and objective, and applied in the same way to women across the world as the remedy to their problems. She notes, "This in itself is a denial of the possibility of universality with a difference, based on the differentiated material conditions of the various peoples of the world".[44] Western feminism also portrays African women as 'others' – as weak, passive and oppressed.[45]

In their writings, African feminists have questioned who an 'African woman' is, demonstrating the challenges in qualifying this and the dangers of treating African women as a monolithic group. African women live highly diverse lives; some rich and some poor, some educated and some illiterate, some traditional and some modern. These differences, as well as religious and cultural diversities, shape the expectations put onto African women, as well as the way feminism is received in communities. As with post-colonial feminism, African feminism stresses the connections between gender, race and imperialism, emphasising that class differences and the gendered divisions of labour on the continent are intrinsically linked to the historical context.[46] So while recognising the variations in women's experiences, they also seek to locate a shared continental identity, shaped by historical relationships of subordination,[47] demonstrating the differences between those women who were colonised and those who were colonisers.[48]

A key challenge in Africa is in balancing the *equality* of women with the valued right to *culture* – two human rights which sometimes directly conflict. Some feminists and human rights activists argue that certain values, like equality, triumph culture,[49] a view that many in Africa vehemently oppose. Attempt to promote equality by disregarding culture tend to be heavily contested. African feminists therefore emphasise the importance of respecting African culture in feminist efforts. They criticise Western feminism's dismissal of this, which they argue has worked against the movement's success. They promote a strategic approach to the betterment of women's status, arguing that activists must negotiate for change *within* the societal context. If not, they warn, not only will African men reject this – African women will too.[50]

African feminists highlight the centrality of marriage and motherhood to women's lives and identities. They are uncomfortable with the rejection of maternal roles that they perceive to be coming from the West, arguing that in Western feminism's emphasising freedom of choice above marriage and motherhood, it is disregarding African traditions.[51] Bergman explains how,

> … in the west motherhood is respected, but it also can be seen as a sacrifice and an obstacle in women's life. In Africa, the position of the mother is a

> position of authority itself. Motherhood is actually empowering and not disempowering as it is seen in the west.[52]

The feminist movement has faced significant backlash in Africa, with ideas persisting that women's rights are Western constructs that go against the African way of life, with feminism itself being 'un-African'.[53] Of course, this presents an unfair picture of the 'real' African woman, who by this framing must be

> … content with her subordinate position as wife, mother and beast of burden. She is passive in the face of abuse, tolerant of all forms of infidelity; her only real ambition is to retain respectability by laboring for the maintenance of a stable marriage and family and seeing to the satisfaction of her husband's desires.[54]

Masculinity and militarism

Kahssay describes military culture as, "… hyper-masculine, anti-feminine, violence-idealizing and authoritarian…"[55] Masculinity in the military is developed and manipulated, with the military fostering hyper-masculinity to promote military performance by troops. Wood explains that,

> … to persuade men to fight and endure all the terrors and hardships of war, societies need members willing to stand fast under fire. An extremely common way in which that is accomplished relies on the development of sharp distinctions between genders: to become men, boys must become warriors … leaders persuade soldiers that to be a real man is to assert a militaristic masculinity.[56]

The hardships men endure in conflict are tempered by positive feelings evoked by militarised masculinity; men defend their homeland and their women and, in doing so, exercise important parts of citizenship and communal belonging.[57] Masculinity in the military is all encompassing; research has documented how even women in the military see themselves as becoming masculinised.[58]

Militarised masculinity is inherently anti-feminine. It removes femininity from anything having to do with combat. Combat is associated with strength; weakness is seen as feminine.[59] Particular constructions of masculinity and femininity are promoted to facilitate militarisation, entrenching gender identities underpinned by patriarchal attitudes.[60] Militarism therefore helps to sustain patriarchy, while patriarchy in turn sustains militarism.[61] Combat units emphasise the taking of power through violence, and violence is internalised as idealistically masculine, courageous and superior.[62] This sets the tone for harm against women and sexual violence. Brownmiller notes that,

> War provides men with the perfect psychological backdrop to give vent to their contempt for women. The maleness of the military–the brute power of

> weaponry exclusive to their hands, the spiritual bonding of men at arms, the manly discipline of orders given and orders obeyed, the simple logic of the hierarchical combat–confirms for men what they long suspect: that women are peripheral to the world that counts. Men who rape are ordinary Joes, made unordinary by entry into the most exclusive male-only club in the world.[63]

Militarised masculinity leads to women in the military being ostracised and excluded. It makes them vulnerable to gender specific abuses, from both the enemy and those within their own ranks. The perceived link between masculinity and militarism causes militaries to neglect female soldiers' development, thereby becoming self-fulfilling.[64] Labelling the military as masculine also shadows the parts that women – or rather, stereotypically feminine traits – can contribute to effective military operations. Many traits required for military success are in fact traits perceived as 'feminine' – such as camaraderie, discipline and service.[65] Militarised masculinity can actually be harmful for combat effectiveness, leading to discrimination and mistrust of women in the ranks – a problem, given the military's focus on group tasks and effective teamwork.[66]

Uniforms add to the masculinised leaning of the military. Women in militaries are expected to dress like men. Moran notes that,

> As Western observers, we take it for granted that women will take on the clothing and accoutrements of men in times of war. This form of transvestism deemed acceptable and unremarkable in the West, is rarely commented upon. We assume that women entering formerly all-male domains … will dress 'like men'.[67]

As with the way that uniforms are tailored to a masculine norm, military uniforms often centre on Western dress. However, in contrast to mainstream versions of military uniforms, military dress takes on quite different forms and symbolisms in certain regions in Africa – some of which are gendered in wholly different ways. Coulter, who researched combatants in Sierra Leone, notes that,

> … the Sierra Leone war deconstructed any notion of a combat-clad, crew-cut, clean-shaven soldier, as hardly any of the irregular armed combatants conformed with this soldier image. Here, fighters ranged from traditional male hunters, naked or dressed in beads and charms, male rebels sometimes wearing wigs and women's clothes, as well as female and child combatants.… In the 'West', a potent and powerful masculinity needs to shed all feminine attributes and qualities, whereas in this region of West Africa … it is the mixing and transgressing of gender boundaries that increases power.… The rebels were frequently demonized and de-humanized, but they were not feminized.[68]

It is interesting to consider the contrasting messaging behind such symbols of war. Male soldiers in West Africa dressed as women, feminising themselves as a source of added power. In this context, male rape was less common, although not unheard of. In different conflicts where femininity is reviled, men are raped to 'feminise' them – as a means of demonstrating their weakness. This illustrates how malleable gendered symbolism can be. Uniforms play a symbolic part in this, sending out visible gendered messages intended to invoke reactions. Uniforms or distinctive markings, called for by the principle of distinction to distinguish combatants, are both gendered and Westernised, revealing how a purportedly neutral legal requirement conceals underlying ideals – ideals that break down when applied in Africa or when applied to non-traditional actors, such as women taking part in hostilities.

Despite how militarism adversely impacts women, women play a key part in the process of militarisation. Women provide ideological support for this, helping to socialise boys and men to the idea that men are strong and aggressive and helping police that role. A body of literature demonstrates how even 'maternal thinking' (the reasoning and thinking of mothers,[69] arguably the most deeply feminine process), while traditionally seen as resistant to conflict, can in fact be moulded in ways that are congenial to military thinking, making women supportive of war, even encouraging their sons to fight.[70] Women also help make militarism more palatable to society, creating societal impressions of peace and harmony during hostile situations. For example, during South Africa's Apartheid, white women were encouraged to be gentle and ladylike, sustaining the impression of a polite society, thereby concealing the cruel nature of the regime.[71]

Militarism and the related norm of 'military necessity' hold important places in IHL. The basic structure of IHL implicitly justifies and protects that which is required to win in war. Masculinity plays a role in producing armies that can triumph in conflict and hence is promoted by the IHL system. A section later in this chapter will illustrate how masculine interests are prioritised by IHL, further entrenching the place of masculinity in the war-making endeavour.

Views about women in combat

Female combatants deviate from commonly held views about what women should be like. They transgress societal norms about acceptable female behaviour. Female combatants challenge both stereotypes about women as victims and about men as perpetrators.[72] Fighting and violence is men's terrain. Women are regarded as more peaceful, so violent women are perceived of as abnormal. Interestingly, these stereotypes sometimes work in opposite directions; in rural Sierra Leone, women were not understood as peaceful, but rather as being wild, dangerous and in need of control. When women joined rebel groups, it was said that the groups unleashed their *true* nature: that which was unpredictable and wild.[73] Deviations from normal behaviour make people uneasy and this unease is at the root of discrimination against female combatants.[74] Female combatants evoke other prejudices too, including those about sex. As rape is a prevalent aspect of female fighters' experiences, prejudices against those who have sex outside of marital structures overlap with the prejudices around transgressing behavioural norms, leading to overlapping layers of stigma.

People deal with their unease at female fighters in different ways. Some notionally strip female combatants of their feminine status. For example, female terrorists are "… presented as having masculine characteristics, being asexual or failing to correspond biologically or psychologically to their nature".[75] Hogg describes how female genocide perpetrators in Rwanda were seen as 'monsters' rather than women. Some described them as 'non-women', as it was seen as impossible for women to commit such acts.[76] A different approach is that female perpetrators are painted as being victims of men who manipulate them or coerce them into action.[77] For example, much of the discourse on female suicide bombers centres on women having been manipulated or brainwashed,[78] another barrier to women being recognised as true conscious participants in armed processes.

Good or bad, female fighters certainly garner attention. Coulter describes how both during and after the Sierra Leonean war, people loved to recount how brutal rebel women were, how cold blooded, how cruel. People would emphasise at length how fighting women were even tougher than men, a claim not borne out by research.[79] The media, too, is fascinated by female fighters. Kurdish female fighters have been a media favourite in reporting on ISIS.[80] Reporting on African female combatants in the Western media often reveals racist as well as sexist attitudes. A BBC article on female fighters in Liberia describes them as "street-wise girls with attitude but they have the military hardware to back up the look".[81] Another article, describing the head of Liberia's Black Diamond, notes, "She's all sleek muscle and form-fitting clothes, with an AK-47 and red beret. She has a bevy of supporting beauties, equally stylish, who loiter nearby, polished fingernails clutching the cold steel of semi-automatic weapons".[82] Coulter, who sourced these articles, points out that this sexualised language is consistent with the ways Western media depicts black women in other contexts.[83]

For years debates have raged about whether women should be allowed to serve in the military, and in particular, whether they should serve in combat roles. Many arguments have been made about why frontlines are inappropriate for women.[84] Some centre on the fact that women are not physically big and strong enough to fight – arguments that have begun to carry less weight in recent years, as conflicts have become more technologized, often fought remotely using high-tech weaponry that allows significant firepower to be released at the click of a button. Arguments have also been made that women are not psychologically tough or brave enough to handle the hardships of combat. Much of the debate centres on how including women will affect military effectiveness. Some argue that having women in the military stands in the way of male bonding, group cohesion and group morale.[85] Of course, this disregards competing group dynamics that also threaten cohesion, those that are not as societally tolerated today. As an example, Heinecken argues that in the South African National Defence Force, racial, cultural and language differences have far greater negative influences on group cohesion than gender does.[86] A related argument is that including women in combat units will prevent the development of militarised masculinity, crucial to war fighting.[87] Those countering this argument contend that there is no evidence that masculine identities actually improve combat performance; some in fact claim these can harm military effectiveness.[88] Other arguments centre on the fact that if women are allowed in combat, male soldiers will put themselves at risk to protect them, or conversely, that if women go into combat, men will no longer feel the need to protect women in other areas of life, with allowing women to be subject to violence in the military being tantamount to a cultural endorsement of violence against women more generally.

The exclusion of women from combat frontlines must be considered in light of the increasingly ambiguous notion of the 'frontline'. Frontlines today are fluid, with frequent strikes to the 'rear', aimed at destroying supply lines or combat bases. Sophisticated combat technology means that strikes are often made remotely, frequently from locations hundreds of miles away.[89] As conflicts become less linear, women who are not allowed to serve as frontline combatants, yet who are allowed to play support roles in the field, are still put into dangerous and exposed situations. Yet, because they are not permitted to serve in frontline combat, they are sometimes not provided with adequate training on how to protect themselves, making them all the more vulnerable.[90]

Feminist scholars have weighed in on the debate about women's inclusion in combat, often with differing views.[91] Feminist discussions have focussed less on whether women are capable of carrying out military roles – the focus of mainstream discussions – and more on whether women should actually seek to be included in the military.[92] The feminist debate in this area has centred on two political stances. On the one end, liberal feminists argue that equality dictates that women should have the right to military inclusion, as well as the same obligations to serve and defend as men. They therefore argue for the full inclusion of women in the military – including the equal use of women in combat positions, equal conscription and equal treatment of female veterans.[93] Opponents of this view point to the discrimination women face within the military and to the greater efforts required for women to be accepted, as detracting from any notion that women's military participation can ever represent true equality for women.[94]

At the other end are feminists who argue that women are inherently more peaceful and that a commitment to feminism should correlate with a commitment to peace. Proponents claim that women have a tendency towards giving life rather than taking it and that inherently feminine traits are not compatible with militarism. They believe that women should not strive to join the military, but rather, that equality should be achieved by freeing men from this.[95] Critics contest this claim, denying the inherent link between women and peace, arguing that women's tendencies towards peace and passivity are socially conditioned – and that mistaking this confuses sex and gender. A different feminist argument is that women should be included in the military, as their feminine characteristics might affect the way that conflicts play out, thereby changing policy from within.[96] This later sentiment has underscored the UN Security Council's approach in its Women, Peace and Security Agenda.[97] This claim, too, is contested, with arguments made that women will not succeed in bringing institutional change to the military, as they "can only be mere tokens in institutions that are by definition masculinist and violent".[98]

Liberal feminists downplay the inherent differing abilities of men and women. Some argue that the differing physical capabilities of men and women are due to socialisation, and that women can in fact carry as much as men, if given the same training.[99] This approach is criticised by others who argue that in treating male/female differences as entirely socially constructed and not seriously addressing them, feminist activists fail to provide military women with the tools they need to challenge those who raise the physical difference argument.[100] Downplaying the differences between men and women also downplays the ways that women can be of particular value to militaries.[101] Critics also argue that feminist claims based on an individual's rights which fail to consider organisational needs, are not effective for an entity like the military, which is at heart all about subsuming an individual's rights for the greater good. Some point to the paradox in what feminists are claiming for military women. On the one hand, feminists claim that female combatants can be equally fierce fighters, while at the same time they portray them as victims of violence and harassment, in need of special protection.[102] This critique, in fact, reveals the difficult duality inherent in female combatants' experiences, a duality that will be returned to throughout this book.

Feminist critiques of International Humanitarian Law

Feminist scholars assessing IHL have pointed to a range of gendered problems evident in this body of law. Broadly, IHL aims to regulate the actions of those taking part in hostilities, in order to provide protection to those caught up in conflict. Feminist scholars seek to show that IHL would be more successful in meeting its goals if it took better account of gender. The sections below will summarise the central feminist critiques of IHL.[103]

IHL's gendered origins

An examination of IHL's history reveals that the laws were based on certain assumptions about the respective roles of men and women in conflict. The early history of the law provides clues as to the law's gendered origins. One of the main voices who helped shape the laws of war was Hugo Grotius. Writing in the seventeenth century, Grotius noted that in war, "Children should always be spared; women, unless they have been guilty of an extremely serious offense; and old men".[104] Grotius reasoned that women should be spared as they do not have the capacity to devise war. In the same way that children do not deserve to be killed, as they have not yet attained the use of reason, the same holds true for women – unless women commit acts deserving of punishment, which would render them to be like men.[105] Many Enlightenment theorists, to whose writings the origins of modern international law can be traced, argued for the immunity of women based on their innocence or their inherent inability to wage war.[106] An entire chapter of Alberico Gentili's work was dedicated to the immunity of women and children from attack,[107] while Francisco Suarez, writing in the early seventeenth century, noted that, "… it is implicit in natural law that the innocent include children, women and all unable to bear arms".[108]

While women have been viewed as 'innocents', men have been presumed to be the opposite. Throughout the years, men have been seen as presumptive combatants, regardless of whether they participated in armed movements or not.[109] As Vitoria, the Enlightenment theorist, noted, "Everyone able to bear arms should be considered dangerous and must be assumed to be defending the enemy king: they may therefore be killed unless the opposite is clearly true".[110]

Centuries later with the drafting of the GCs and the APs, these ideas remained, albeit presented in more delicate ways. Ideas about strong men and weak women underlie the GCs and their Commentaries and are evident in numerous places. For example, Article 14, GC3, states that, "Women shall be treated with all the regard due to their sex …". The GC Commentaries list points that should be considered in determining what "regard due" to a woman's sex actually means. These include: "weakness" and "pregnancy and child-birth".[111] The inclusion of "weakness" provides insight into the types of consideration the drafters were entertaining when thinking about women.[112] The GCs and their Commentaries are filled with references to "honour" and "modesty", further pointing to a particular view of women on the part of the drafters – drafters who were often male military lawyers and diplomatic representatives.

With the drafting of the 1977 APs, the requirements for distinguishing combatants and civilians moved in the direction of being based on acts, rather than on the 'role status' of the persons in question, allowing for some departure from these gendered ideas. However, the designations of acts retained a gendered quality, with the recognised acts being those typically performed by men. Past notions informed understandings in the APs and have continued to inform the legal developments that have occurred since.[113]

Protective provisions for women of limited use

The IHL conventions set out protections for civilians in war. Female civilians are covered by all the protections aimed at civilians generally.[114] In addition, the conventions also contain protective provisions specifically aimed at women. As examples, Article 27, GC4 states that women are protected against attacks on their honour, including rape, forced prostitution and indecent assault. Article 76, AP1 holds that women should be the objects of special respect and should be protected from rape, forced prostitution and other forms of indecent assault. Article 76, GC4 notes that female civilian internees, or women accused of offences, must be kept in separate quarters to men and placed under the immediate supervision of women, while Article 97, GC4 holds that female internees may only be searched by women. Similar protective provisions for women also apply in NIACs.[115] The conventions also contain protections for women in specific roles, like women who are pregnant or nursing small children. Article 16, GC4 states that, "The wounded and sick, as well as the infirm, and expectant mothers, shall be the object of particular protection and respect". Article 23, GC4 instructs parties to permit the free passage of consignments of essential foods, clothes and tonics intended for children, expectant mothers and maternity cases, and states that in the distribution of relief consignments, priority should be given to expectant mothers, maternity cases and nursing mothers, as well as to children.

Unfortunately, the rules of IHL aimed at protecting civilians tend to be fairly ineffective. The conventions protect civilians from some intentional actions of warring parties, yet they fail to protect them from many of the dangers of military operations.[116] Proportionality and necessity still allow much scope for the unintentional harming of civilians, discussed later in this chapter. Another problem is that the rules for protecting civilians generally tend to take *male* civilians as their starting point, assuming that *all* civilians are the same as men, having the same risks and experiences.[117]

In contrast to the limited protections for civilians in GC4, the other three GCs address different aspects of the protection of combatants. Here too women are included in all the general provisions aimed at all combatants. There are also a number of provisions specifically aimed at female combatants. Most of these relate to female POWs. Female POWs should be accommodated in separate dormitories (Art 25, GC3), under the supervision of women and separate sanitary conveniences should be provided for women (Art 29, GC3). In NIACs too, women deprived of their liberty must be held in separate quarters, under female supervision, except where families are held together (Art 5, AP2). GC1 and GC2, which deal with the wounded and sick in the armed forces at sea and in the field respectively; both state that, "Women shall be treated with all consideration due to their sex".[118] The problem is, as this book argues, the restrictive definitions of combatancy, prevent many women from qualifying as such, meaning they would not be eligible for these protections – one reason that the law's restrictive definitions prejudice women.

There are, therefore, several protections in the conventions specifically aimed at women. But, for the most part, these protections are reserved for women in particular roles: women who are pregnant, rearing children or serving as combatants. However, the lives of women go beyond these roles. Many women affected by conflict do not occupy these specific positions, meaning that most protections will not apply to them. The fact that women are protected *while* they are pregnant, mothering or held as POWs, is not sufficient to conclude that women generally are adequately protected by the law.[119] It is in its general protections that the law fails to provide adequate protection for women in conflict.

Formal equality in inherently unequal situations

On the face of it IHL is gender-neutral, based on a model of formal equality. Throughout the treaties there are reiterations of the fact that the law should be applied without discrimination based on sex, and that "no adverse distinction" should be founded on one of a number of categories, including sex.[120] Only "adverse" distinction is prohibited – differentiation of women is permissible, so long as this is deemed favourable or operates to provide them with specific protection. The limited protective provisions pertaining to women, described above, fall into this category.[121]

Feminist scholars have raised concerns about whether a formally equal system of law can achieve substantively equal results, given existing inequalities and given the vastly different ways in which conflict affects men and women.[122] Conflict exacerbates existing gender disparities and gender discrimination. The Beijing Platform for Action confirms that, "women and girls are particularly affected [by violence in armed conflict] because of their status in society and their sex".[123] Violence against women in conflict should not be understood as something unique – rather, it is the magnification of harmful practices towards women in peacetime. Existing patriarchal ideas and violent practices against women are allowed to flourish in conflict, uncapped and exacerbated by the violent environment.[124] The heightened risks that women face as a result creates the need for targeted protections for women – quite the opposite of what the largely gender-neutral law provides. Formally equal laws ignore the particular vulnerabilities of women in conflict,[125] making no reference to the impact of gender discrimination in worsening acts against women in war – and therefore providing no relief for this.[126]

Of course, there are also dangers in creating too many gender-specific laws. Gender-specific laws run the risks of essentialising and over-emphasising the differences between men and women in ways that are unconstructive – in doing so perpetuating harmful stereotypes. It was in an effort to cater for women's differences that the current female-related provisions of IHL were created, provisions that are themselves subject to criticism, in part because of their heavy concern with biology.[127] A balance is therefore required between having adequate recognition of women's differences and not over-emphasising difference in harmful ways. Both opposing concepts, 'gender specificity' and 'gender neutrality' are problematic in their own ways. Gender neutrality is based on a fiction – the idea that both genders have similar experiences that a uniform law can effectively address. On the other hand, gender specificity often caters to particular types of women, implying that all women fit into these categories. Both approaches to law are therefore founded on false premises.

Tension exists among feminist legal scholars around equality, sameness and difference – and the correct approach to adopt to these.[128] Liberal feminism calls for equality based on similarity of treatment. Others argue that this is not radical enough to address existing inequalities. This book will consider these positions in the context of the principle of distinction – currently an example of largely gender-neutral drafting. If the ways that women participate in conflict are different, should gender-specific combatancy or direct participation requirements be created for women? Or rather, should existing requirements be broadened in a gender-neutral way to further incorporate the types of roles played by women?

Even the latter would be an improvement on the existing position of merely disregarding women and taking men's typical modes of participation as being those that apply to everyone.

IHL's focus on women as victims or mothers; the dangers of perpetuating stereotypes

IHL paints women in two ways: as victims or in terms of their relationships with others.[129] Throughout the law one can detect a reductionist approach to gender; gender is reduced to women, woman are reduced to victims and female victimisation is reduced to sexual violence[130] – reductions that conceal different aspects of women's (and men's) experiences of conflict.

IHL sustains the notion of women as victims in a number of ways. Provisions pertaining to women frequently relate to special protections for women. For example, provisions addressing sexual violence focus on the *protection* of women rather than on the *prohibition* of sexual violence.[131] The failure of IHL to acknowledge that men also experience sexual violence further sustains the female victim/male perpetrator paradigm.[132] Language on sexual violence is framed in terms of women's honour, modesty and chastity. Article 27, GC4 states that, "women shall be especially protected against any attack on their honour, in particular against rape, enforced prostitution, or any form of indecent assault". The reference to honour, rather than to the physical and psychological harms caused by sexual violence is problematic.[133] This implies that women who have been sexually violated are dishonoured – a view already prevalent in many parts of the world, with significant negative repercussions for women, and a view that IHL should not be perpetuating. The inclusion of such provisions lets those who drafted the conventions determine what constructs a women's honour and what deems it removed. Being raped becomes a double assault – first, on a women's body and second, on her honour, in part as a result of IHL deeming this to be the effect of sexual violence. Because IHL deals with protection it has much cause to address women through a victim lens. Yet doing so, however well intentioned, can have the consequence of entrenching perceptions and stereotypes about women as victims.

IHL frequently relates to women in terms of their relationships with others, rather than in their own right. Out of the 42 IHL provisions that deal specifically with women, more than half deal with women *as* child-bearers or *as* mothers – and merely protect women because they are playing these roles.[134] Even the protections against sexual violence seem geared at women *as* men's 'property'. By talking about rape in terms of honour rather than violence, this frames women as 'belonging' to their husbands or families. When women are raped, the men to whom they belong are seen as victims of this harm – their wife/family member's honour – the source of their value – has been infringed.[135] This feeds into a logic behind rape as a weapon of war – a weapon that is used by men against men through the bodies of their women.

While IHL was shaped by gendered norms existing in society – both identified and implicit – the law in turn has influenced the gendered conditions on the ground.[136] These gendered conditions then go on to affect later developments of the law. Recently, this has been evident in the development of international criminal law, where shifts in gendered attitudes have worked their way into the tribunal's jurisprudence, thereby shaping the law. Kinsella describes the mutually reinforcing role of law in shaping society and society in shaping law. She notes that,

> The scholarship that does engage in an analysis of gender and the laws of war focuses primarily on the *protection* of women within the law rather than *the production* of women in the law and, importantly, the production of the laws of war themselves.[137]

With its male-oriented understandings of combatancy and direct participation, the principle of distinction plays a role in perpetuating stereotypes about men and women in conflict. Laws that paint men and women in certain ways entrench expectations of how women should be and should act. Those who stray from these expectations are stigmatised. In these ways the law's framing becomes harmful to women.

A gendered hierarchy implicit in the law

IHL entrenches hierarchies and systems of power: combatants over civilians, public over private, military interests over other concerns. Implicit in these hierarchies is a privileging of male over female concerns.

IHL elevates the interests of men in various ways. First, the IHL rules pertaining to women are portrayed as being less important than other rules.[138] This can be inferred in a number of ways. Rules dealing with women tend to be drafted in a different type of language to other provisions – for example, as mentioned above, provisions are framed in terms of the *protection* of women rather than as express *prohibitions* on offences against them.[139] None of the violations against women, known as 'gender crimes', are designated as 'grave breaches'[140] by the conventions, suggesting that gender crimes were not treated as seriously as many other crimes.[141] In an attempt to address this, the international criminal tribunals have read rape and other violations against women into the grave breaches.[142] However, the need for this additional step of judicial interpretation demonstrates that crimes against women were not originally considered and prioritised. Recently, the 'G8 Declaration 2013' contained an acknowledgement by G8 members that rape in armed conflict is in fact a grave breach of the GCs.[143]

A gendered hierarchy is clearly evident in the principle of distinction. The principle rests on a distinction that is intrinsically gendered. Combatants represent the masculine – the male warriors who defend society – while civilians represent the feminine – those who must be protected.[144] Implicit in this is a privileging of the male, manifested through the privileging of combatants. This book will argue that the masculine nature of 'combatancy' is retained by having a law narrowly defined around the types of roles typically held by men in conflict. One can detect a ranking of the value of lives in the structure of the law: the men of one's own side take priority, followed by the women of one's own side. Next are the men of the enemy, with the enemy's women seen as least important. However, despite being less valuable, women are used to further men's goals. Women's images are manipulated to encourage men to fight. Women at home are portrayed as vulnerable and in need of protection.[145] Alison explains that,

> 'Our women' are chaste, honourable, and to be protected by 'our men'; 'their women' are unchaste and depraved. Wartime propaganda presents the (male) enemy as those who would rape and murder 'our' women and the war effort is directed at saving 'our' women.[146]

A privileging of the male can also be seen in the public/private divide. As with other areas of law, IHL focuses on the public sphere, with its extensive regulation of combatants and the military. By precluding women from 'combatancy' with restrictive definitions, women are removed from the reach of the law. Even when regulating the public space, the law stops short of regulating women's experiences in these spaces. Within militaries, women tend to be utilised in domestic support roles – roles viewed as private and hence unregulated by law. Sexual violence was, until recently, largely shielded by the law's 'public' focus – ignoring the fact that the primary cause of these 'private' harms was in fact the 'public' conflict.

The gendered nature of civilian immunity

The choice of who can and cannot be targeted is laden with value judgements, bringing together considerations of law, military strategy, command hierarchy and public opinion.[147] Determinations of which attacks are permitted or prohibited by the law reflect the values underlying the law and reveal the concerns of those who created and those who maintain the system. There are numerous layers of privileging embedded in targeting rules. These include a privileging of state concerns over non-state ones, a privileging of Western interests over non-Western (including African) concerns, a privileging of military needs over humanitarian considerations, and a privileging of male interests over female ones.

'Civilian immunity' is the central norm underlying the principle of distinction. It holds that civilians should be legally immune from attack. Notions of innocence and guilt underlie the norm. Those who are 'innocent' are seen as deserving protection, while those who are 'guilty' deserve to be targeted. Theorists have offered competing ideas as to how the lines between guilt and innocence should be drawn. One model is act-based, with guilt earned by those who actually *act* guilty.[148] Some classify *fighting* in a war as the only guilty act, while others consider work in war-supporting industries as also constituting guilty acts deserving of targeting. A different model is to interpret innocence as harmlessness and guilt as dangerousness, so those who pose a threat are seen as deserving of attack.[149] No matter which of these models one leans towards, in practice all these calculations of guilt versus innocence lead to the same gendered results: men are guilty; women are innocent and deserving of protection.[150]

The civilian immunity norm is not inherently gendered – rather it has been configured in a gendered way. Carpenter illustrates what this means using the norm of "dressing appropriately". While gender biases might inform what constitutes appropriate dress, appropriate dressing is not intrinsically dependent on gender. Similarly, she argues, civilian immunity is not a 'gender norm' – it is not intrinsically dependent on gender – but rather, it is 'gendered', in that in practice women are more likely to be associated with civilian status than men. While the norm itself is gender-neutral, with *all* civilians held to be protected, in practice gender biases give shape to the norm.[151]

A range of actors operate together to entrench the gendered 'shape' of civilian immunity. Military actors in the field make assumptions based on gender, including assumptions that the men they see are fighters and the women are civilians – assumptions that have led to sex-selective killings of men in numerous contexts. At the level of rhetoric, state actors frequently refer to gender when condemning the killing of civilians or when offering justification for collateral damage.[152] For example, before killing the men at Srebrenica, General Ratko Mladic publically announced that the Army of Republika Srpska had freed women, children and the elderly, thereby demonstrating compliance with civilian immunity. Humanitarian evacuations of women and children further entrench this gendered norm. Perversely, evacuations of women and children legitimise the killing of men by creating the impression that those who remain – the men – must be fighters, or potential fighters, or those more worthy of targeting.[153] Evacuating women and children also removes those whose murders would attract the most negative attention by the international community, further enabling the killing of men. Humanitarian agencies play a role in this too, by using gendered discourse when encouraging the protection of civilians.[154] Attacks against civilians are criticised with reference to the fact that women and children are harmed. Their 'calls to action' often incorporate warnings about 'innocent women and children' being at risk. Even Security Council Resolutions frequently condemn violence against civilians, 'especially women and children' and call for the evacuation of women as a first priority.[155]

Proportionality and military necessity

Some of the protection conferred by the principle of distinction is lost as a result of the other core principles of IHL, proportionality and necessity. The term 'proportionality' is not used in The Hague or Geneva Conventions; rather it is derived from the IHL articles prohibiting indiscriminate attacks. Article 51(5)(b), AP1 includes in those acts considered indiscriminate, attacks, "which may be expected to cause incidental loss of civilian life, injury to civilians, damage to civilian objects, or a combination thereof, which would be excessive in relation to the concrete and direct military advantage anticipated". Proportionality also derives from

Article 57(2), AP1, which deals with precautions in attack and Article 85(3), AP1, which deems violations of proportionality to be grave breaches.

Proportionality can be framed in two ways: as a principle that limits harm to civilians, or, conversely, as a principle that allows for certain numbers of civilians to be targeted. One can use proportionality to argue that an attack is unlawful as a disproportionate number of civilians would be killed by it. Conversely, one can justify the deaths of civilians by arguing that the losses were proportionate to the military advantage gained, thereby rendered lawful by the principle of proportionality. Depending on how it is used, the principle can have protective results or it can diminish the protections conferred by the principle of distinction. Civilian women protected by the principle of distinction might be unintended casualties of attacks on lawful targets.

Proportionality requires a balancing of comparative effects: the anticipated collateral injury to civilians and the anticipated military advantage. One should note that it is 'anticipated' advantages and 'anticipated' losses that are considered, not the 'actual' effects of a strike. What counts is what was foreseen and anticipated at the time an attack was launched. Actual losses may help to infer what actors anticipated before the fact.[156] The clear problem with proportionality is its application. These are notoriously difficult calculations to make as one is balancing unlike things and comparing anticipated events. What is the relative value one gives to each civilian death versus a particular military target? How do you quantify each? Who gets to decide? Is it subjective or objective?

The ways in which these judgements are made are gendered. There is no agreed standard for making these calculations, so these decisions largely fall to the discretion of the actors involved.[157] Decisions tend to be made by military men, reflecting their positioning of interests.[158] Saving the lives of their soldiers is regarded as worth losing civilians for, with military leaders considering lower-risk, higher-casualty methods as legally acceptable. This is justified by the reasoning that male combatant's lives are more valuable as they are working to protect society – or to protect society's women. Military priorities, made by men and reflecting male concerns, are seldom questioned when making proportionality assessments – rather, these are taken as givens.

Proportionality calculations count numbers of casualties, or civilians dead. More men, including male civilians, are killed in conflict. Women tend to be targeted in other ways, such as through sexual violence. Women might also be disproportionately affected by actions other than direct targeting strikes, like those that destroy infrastructure or that lead to population displacement. However, these harms that disproportionately affect women are not factored into proportionality assessments. An attack that is devastating for women – like one that destroys access to healthcare or food supplies[159] – might be considered proportionate, as it does not have a high body count. It is therefore the harms that most strongly affect men that form the basis for determining whether actions have disproportionate effects, discussed further in Chapter 7.

'Military necessity' is the other core principle of IHL. When creating the IHL system, states were concerned with protecting their interests in winning wars.

They wanted to ensure that the IHL conventions would not unduly restrict their actions on the battlefield in ways that would prejudice their national interests. The necessity principle was created to safeguard these interests.[160] While military necessity is seldom referred to in the conventions, it pervades IHL by underlying other rules, with military necessity prioritised, safeguarded and promoted in numerous provisions. Military necessity is a ground of justification for attacks on targets with high civilian costs. 'Direct participation' is, in fact, a military necessity restriction on the principle of distinction – the ability to target civilians who directly participate in hostilities cuts into the blanket protection conferred on all civilians, in the name of military necessity.

As with proportionality, military necessity can operate in opposing directions. Depending on how it is framed, it can be used to elevate military interests or to promote humanitarian concerns. Framed in converse, the principle puts constraints on the military, with rules prohibiting attacks that are not militarily necessary[161] – such as the rules that any attack must be aimed at contributing to the military defeat of an enemy, and that attacks must be directed against military objectives. Military necessity is difficult to measure; its modes of determination are uncertain and subjective. Although necessity is a factor to consider in determining the lawfulness of an attack, this requirement in some ways begs the very question it poses, thereby leaving further discretion to the military actors making these decisions. Military necessity is a binary of humanitarianism, with the IHL system supposedly designed to create a balance between these two positions.[162] The former, which reflects male concerns, tends to be privileged. Rules and actions aimed at humanitarian protection are tolerated in so far as they do not hinder states' ability to win in war.[163]

Feminist challenges to the legal situation

The preceding sections have pointed to the gendered problems apparent in IHL. While there have been no notable moves to amend IHL to tackle these problems, in recent years legal developments in other areas of law have addressed some of the gendered problems pertaining to law and armed conflict. The sections below will describe developments in international criminal law, as well as in the Security Council's 'Women, Peace and Security Agenda'.

International Criminal Law

International criminal law (ICL) is the body of law used to prosecute violations of IHL (war crimes), as well as genocide and crimes against humanity. This law has been applied by the ICC, as well as by the 'ad hoc tribunals' like the ICTR, the ICTY and the Special Court for Sierra Leone (SCSL).

Inclusion of 'gender justice' was one of the most vehemently resisted aspects of ICL.[164] Some of the earlier cases before the ad hoc tribunals refused to hear testimony on or consider sexual violence.[165] The Trial Chamber in the SCSL's *Civil Defence Forces* case determined in the pre-trial phase that counts of sexual violence should not be included in the indictment,[166] with the Trial Chamber later confirming that sexual violence was inadmissible.[167] Women who took to the stands were prohibited from describing the rapes that were perpetrated against them – being asked instead to restrict themselves to describing surrounding events.[168] In time this began to shift, with 'gender crimes' being included in various indictments and judgements, and a body of jurisprudence developing around gender and sexual violence. In the ICTR's *Akeyesu* judgement, rape was characterised as an instrument of genocide.[169] In the ICTY's *Celebici* case, sexual violence was recognised as torture. *Celebici* also considered sexual violence against male detainees.[170] In time, the tribunals gave content to various gender-related crimes and also expanded the definitions of other (non-gender) crimes to incorporate violations against women.

Certain states vigorously opposed the inclusion of 'gender crimes'[171] in the ICC's founding treaty, the Rome Statute. Amongst these were states with strong religious lobbies, which considered their inclusion a threat to religious beliefs. As an example, the crime of 'forced pregnancy' was opposed by those who linked this to legalised abortion.[172] However, despite resistance, as a result of intense lobbying by women's groups (led by the Women's Caucus for Gender Justice), and in response to an increased awareness about the crimes perpetuated against women in Rwanda and Bosnia,[173] gender crimes were included in the Rome Statute. Article 7 includes as 'crimes against humanity'; rape, sexual slavery, enforced sterilisation and other forms of sexual violence of comparable gravity. It also includes these as 'war crimes' in IACs (Article 8(2)(b)(xxii)) and NIACs (Article 8(2)(c)(vi)).

Despite movement in the right direction, ICL's progress on gender has been limited. Beyond examining gender crimes, the tribunals have not conducted any serious level of gender analysis. Feminist efforts have not resulted in structural changes to ICL – rather, just adding women in at certain places. While gendered aspects have been read into crimes, Bennoune notes that, "... creatively patching together interpretations of texts to find space for women's experiences of war may not ultimately be enough".[174] The tribunals' work on gender remains in its early stages, with a way to go before ICL can be said to truly be inclusive of and responsive to women's concerns.

Some might argue that understandings about gender in ICL – imperfect as they are – will trickle down into the interpretation of IHL, helping to integrate gendered notions into this body of law, thereby remedying some of IHL's gendered problems. However, the potential of ICL to 'fix' IHL should not be overstated. Such a process of legal influence is fraught with difficulty and is always influenced by differing agendas, some facilitative and others less so. ICL deals only with specific aspects of IHL; those relating to punishable crimes. The nuts and bolts of IHL are not addressed by ICL's narrow focus, meaning that ICL's interpretations cannot 'fix' problems in those areas. While ICL deals with war crime prosecutions *after* the fact, IHL is important *during* the engagement of conflict. IHL serves an important role in regulating military behaviour on the battlefield, and is used in the creation of national militaries' rules of engagement and military manuals. Ex post facto prosecutions do not assist with the shortcomings of IHL as a regulatory mechanism.[175]

Most women do not have the offences committed against them in war heard at international tribunals. At best these might be tried in domestic courts, which use domestic law and are unlikely to incorporate ICL's complex jurisprudence into their decision-making. Rules of the Rome Statute only become part of domestic law if they have been specifically incorporated by domestic legislation and the ad hoc tribunal's findings are only binding in the specific countries the tribunals address. Domestic courts are therefore more likely to consider IHL than ICL, given that IHL frequently forms the basis of national rules of engagement.

There are many countries where ICL lacks legitimacy. Far fewer countries have ratified the Rome Statute than the GCs.[176] The ICC's perceived biases have eroded the legitimacy of the court in Africa – many African countries oppose its almost exclusive focus on African conflicts and its apparent reluctance to prosecute crimes committed in other parts of the world.[177] The ICC's decision to indict sitting leaders, including Sudan's Omar al-Bashir and Kenya's Uhuru Kenyatta, have led to unified condemnation and resistance by African leaders and the African Union.

It is therefore clear that IHL retains importance in itself and cannot rely on ICL to take care of its inadequate inclusion of gender. This confirms the need for a body of IHL that is functional in itself and is not reliant on other laws to create 'patches' through interpretation. It is implausible to argue that because the tribunals are dealing with gender, there is no need for IHL to improve itself in this regard. If anything, the fact that the tribunals have had to do so much work reading in gender concerns, reveals the extent to which IHL has failed to address these issues sufficiently and the problems caused by this.

Women, peace and security

A series of Security Council (SC) Resolutions form what is known as the Women, Peace and Security Agenda. In October 2000, the SC unanimously passed SC Resolution 1325, the result of years of lobbying by women's organisations.[178] It was the first time the SC had directly addressed the distinct impact of armed conflict on women, giving official recognition to the diverse experiences and roles of women in war.[179] There have been seven related Resolutions since then: SC Resolutions 1820 (2008), 1888 and 1889 (2009), 1960 (2010), 2106 and 2122 (2013) and 2242 (2015). In adopting these Resolutions, directed at all UN member states, the SC has established a normative framework to guide its approach to women in conflict. This provides direction to individual member states, aimed at guiding their actions on women, peace and security.[180] The Resolutions have given political recognition to the fact that gender is relevant to peace and security – a paradigm shift in the way the international community approaches security from a gender perspective.[181]

The Resolutions recognise women as agents: agents of peace and agents for the protection of people's rights. They also recognise women as agents of war –

female combatants are mentioned by reference to DDR for women.[182] The Resolutions emphasise the importance of including women in peacekeeping operations, in civil, military and police functions, encouraging states to provide more female personnel to operations – another endorsement of women in military roles. This marks a move away from the pervasive notion of woman as victims, which has dominated international discourse to date. Disappointingly, despite the recognition of women in alternative roles, the Resolutions repeatedly revert to assumptions that women are peaceful, with numerous references to women taking part in peace-making initiatives – problematic, given the part this can play in entrenching stereotypes.[183]

While improved attitudes and discourse on women at the international political level is important and may in time lead to the political leverage required to improve IHL from a gender perspective, the Resolutions too do not rectify the gendered problems with IHL. They are more helpful in post-conflict reconstruction than they are during conflict, as beyond barring specific acts of sexual violence, they do little to regulate warring parties' actions in hostilities. Article 9, SC Res 1325,

> Calls upon all parties to armed conflict to respect fully international law applicable to the rights and protection of women and girls, especially as civilians, in particular the obligations applicable to them under the Geneva Conventions of 1949 and the Additional Protocols thereto of 1977....[184]

However, given the gendered problems inherent in IHL, will simply mandating the full implementation of this law help women? What version of IHL is the Resolution promoting and mandating? The existing gender-insensitive version or a more gender-evolved version? If it is the latter it hopes to promote, then steps will need to be taken to address the gendered problems within IHL – and the failure to think about these problems in turn becomes a failing with SC Res 1325 and the Women, Peace and Security Agenda.

Although IHL and the principle of distinction are gender-neutral, they were based on a particular gendered view of conflict that envisaged men and women playing particular roles. The problem is that this underlying vision of conflict does not accord with the reality on the ground, in which the effects of conflict, while clearly gendered, are not necessarily gendered in the same ways envisaged by the drafters of the law. The result is gender-neutral law, with particular gendered origins, applied to a quite differently gendered situation on the ground. Later chapters of this book examine the consequences of this discord.

Notes

1 Lacey, Nicola. 'Feminist Legal Theory and the Rights of Women'. In Knop, Karen (ed.), *Gender and Human Rights*. Oxford University Press, 2004.

2 Handrahan, Lori. 'Conflict, Gender, Ethnicity and Post-Conflict Reconstruction'. *Security Dialogue* 35, no. 4 (2004): 429–445.

3 Dalton, Clare. 'Where We Stand: Observations on the Situation of Feminist Legal Thought'. In *Feminist Legal Theory: Foundations and Outlooks*. Vol. 1. London: Dartmouth Publishing Company Limited, 1995.
4 For an overview of feminist legal theories see, Olsen, Frances. *Feminist Legal Theory*. Vol. 1 and 2. The International Library of Essays in Law and Legal Theory. New York: New York University Press, 1995.
5 Buss, Doris and Manji, Ambreena (eds), *International Law: Modern Feminist Approaches*. Oxford: Hart Publishing, 2005. Kouvo, Sari and Zoe Pearson. *Feminist Perspectives on Contemporary International Law*. Oxford: Hart Publishing, 2011.
6 Charlesworth, Hilary and Chinkin, Christine. *The Boundaries of International Law: A Feminist Analysis*. Manchester: Manchester University Press, 2000.
7 Money, John and Coleman, Eli. *John Money: A Tribute*. Abingdon: Routledge, 1991.
8 Butler, Judith. *Gender Trouble: Feminism and the Subversion of Identity*. Abingdon: Routledge, 1990, at 6.
9 Fausto-Sterling, Anne. *Myths of Gender: Biological Theories About Women And Men, Revised Edition*, New York: Basic Books, 1992.
10 Butler, supra note 8, at 6.
11 Schwalbe, Michael. *The Sociologically Examined Life: Pieces of the Conversation*. 4th edition. Columbus, OH: McGraw-Hill Humanities/Social Sciences/Languages, 2007.
12 Hurst, Charles. *Social Inequality: Forms, Causes, and Consequences*. Boston, MA: Pearson, 2012.
13 In General Recommendation 28, the CEDAW Committee notes that, 'The term gender refers to socially constructed identities, attributes and roles for women and men and society's social and cultural meaning for these biological differences resulting in hierarchical relationships between women and men and in the distribution of power and rights favouring men and disadvantaging women.' (General Recommendation No. 28 on the Core Obligations of States Parties under Article 2 of the Convention on the Elimination of All Forms of Discrimination against Women, CEDAW, 2010).
14 Cook, Rebecca. *Gender Stereotyping: Transnational Legal Perspectives*. Pennsylvania Studies in Human Rights. Philadelphia, PA: University of Pennsylvania Press, 2010.
15 Hogg, Nicole. 'Women's Participation in the Rwandan Genocide: Mothers or Monsters?' *International Review of the Red Cross* 92, no. 877 (2010): 69–102.
16 Grotius, Hugo, 'Moderation with Respect to the Right of Killing in a Lawful War, Book 3, Chapter 11, *The Law of War and Peace*, 1625. Re-published by Batoche Books Kitchener, 2001, Ontaria, Canada.
17 Jones, Adam. 'Gendercide and Genocide'. *Journal of Genocide Research* 2, no. 2 (2000): 185–211.
18 Carpenter, Charli. '"Women and Children First": Gender, Norms, and Humanitarian Evacuation in the Balkans 1991–95'. *International Organization* 57, no. 4 (2003): 661–694.
19 Gardam, Judith. 'Women and the Law of Armed Conflict: Why the Silence?' *International and Comparative Law Quarterly* 46, no. (1997): 55–80, at 58–59.
20 Krill, Françoise. 'The Protection of Women in International Humanitarian Law'. *International Review of the Red Cross* 249 (1985). www.icrc.org/eng/resources/documents/article/other/57jmfj.htm
21 MacKinnon, Catharine. 'Substantive Equality: A Perspective'. *Minnesota Law Review* 96, no. 1 (2011): 1–27.
22 Charlesworth, Chinkin, supra note 6.
23 Ibid.

24 Ibid.
25 Pateman, Carole. 'Feminist Critiques of the Public/Private Dichotomy'. *The Disorder of Women. Democracy, Feminism and Political Theory*. Cambridge: Polity Press, 1989.
26 MacKinnon, Catharine. *Toward a Feminist Theory of the State*. 2nd edition. Cambridge: Harvard University Press, 1991.
27 Lacey, supra note 1.
28 See for example, Gavison, Ruth. 'Feminism and the Public/Private Distinction'. *Stanford Law Review* 45, no. 1 (1992): 1–45.
29 Gardam, supra note 19.
30 MacKinnon, supra note 26.
31 Chapter 2: Duties, Article 27–29, African Charter on Human and Peoples' Rights ('Banjul Charter'), 27 June 1981, CAB/LEG/67/3.
32 Lewis, Desiree. 'Introduction: African Feminisms'. *Agenda* no. 50 (2001): 4–10.
33 Charlesworth, Chinkin, supra note 6.
34 Crenshaw, Kimberle. 'Mapping the Margins: Intersectionality, Identity Politics, and Violence against Women of Color'. *Stanford Law Review* 43 (1991): 1241–1299. Carastathis, Anna. 'The Concept of Intersectionality in Feminist Theory'. *Philosophy Compass* 9, no. 5 (2014): 304–314.
35 Lorentzen, Lois and Turpin, Jennifer (eds), *The Women and War Reader*. New York: New York University Press, 1998.
36 Barclay, Claire. 'Toward Substantive Equality: A Feminist Critique of the Notion of Difference in the Canadian and South African Equality Tests'. *International Journal of Discrimination and the Law* 5, no. 2–3 (2001): 167–188.
37 Dworkin, Andrea. *Woman Hating*. New York: Plume, 1991. Mackay, Finn. *Radical Feminism: Feminist Activism in Movement*. Houndsmills, Basingstoke, Hampshire: Palgrave Macmillan, 2015.
38 Butler, supra note 8, at 3.
39 Mohanty, Chandra. 'Under Western Eyes: Feminist Scholarship and Colonial Discourses'. *Feminist Review* 30, no. 1 (1988): 61–88.
40 Goredema, Ruvimbo. 'African Feminism: The African Woman's Struggle for Identity' 1 (2010): 275–241, at 35.
41 Tamale, Sylvia. 'African Feminism: How Should We Change?' *Development* 49, no. 1 (2006): 38–41.
42 Bergman, Mari. 'African Sisterhood –Conceptualizing African Feminist Identity', 2016, at 2. [Online]
43 Ibid.
44 Mangena, Oshadi. 'Feminism (Singular), African Feminisms (Plural) and the African Diaspora'. *Agenda*, no. 58 (1 January 2003): 98–100, at 98.
45 Arnfred, Signe. 'Simone de Beauvoir in Africa: "Woman = the Second Sex?" Issues of African Feminist Thought'. *jenda: A Journal of Culture and African Women Studies* 2, no. 1 (2002): 1–20.
46 Bergman, supra note 42.
47 Lewis, Desiree. 'Discursive Challenges for African Feminism'. *QUEST: An African Journal of Philosophy/Revue Africain E de Philosophie* 20 (2008): 77–96.
48 Goredema, supra note 40.
49 Zechenter, Elizabeth. 'In the Name of Culture: Cultural Relativism and the Abuse of the Individual'. *Journal of Anthropological Research* 53 (1977): 319–347.
50 Tegomoh, Evelyne. 'Experiencing African Feminism'. *Agenda* 54 (2002): 122–128, at 127–128.
51 Bergman, supra note 42.
52 Ibid., at 11.
53 Adichie, Chimamanda Ngozi. *We Should All Be Feminists*. New York: Vintage Books, 2014.

54 Mama, Amina. *Women's Studies and Studies of Women in Africa during the 1990s*. Working Paper Series (Codesria); 96/5. Dakar, Senegal: Codesria, 1996.
55 Kahssay, Jihan. 'Feminist Legal Theory: Challenges Facing Women Combatants'. *Feminist Legal Theory*, 5 October 2012.
56 Wood, Elisabeth. 'Variation in Sexual Violence during War'. *Politics & Society* 34, no. 3 (2006): 307–342, at 326.
57 Handrahan, supra note 2.
58 See for example, Baaz, Maria Eriksson and Stern, Maria. 'Making Sense of Violence: Voices of Soldiers in the Congo (DRC)'. *The Journal of Modern African Studies* 46, no. 01 (2008): 57–86.
59 Kahssay, supra note 55.
60 Cock, Jacklyn. 'Women and the Military: Implications for Demilitarization in the 1990s in South Africa'. *Gender & Society* 8, no. 2 (1994): 152–169.
61 Cockburn, Cynthia. 'Gender Relations as Causal in Militarization and War'. *International Feminist Journal of Politics* 12, no. 2 (2010): 139–157.
62 White, Aaronette. 'Fanon & the African Woman Combatant', in Nhema, Alfred, and Tiyambe Zeleza, Paul (eds), *The Roots of African Conflicts: The Causes and Costs*. 1st edn. Athens, OH: Ohio University Press, 2008.
63 Brownmiller, Susan. *Against Our Will: Men, Women and Rape*. New York: Simon and Schuster, 1975, at 32.
64 Kier, Elizabeth. 'Uniform Justice: Assessing Women in Combat'. *Perspectives on Politics* 1, no. 02 (2003): 343–347.
65 Titunik, Regina. 'The Myth of the Macho Military'. *Polity* 40, no. 2 (2008): 137–163.
66 Kier, supra note 64.
67 Moran, Mary. 'Warriors or Soldiers? Masculinity and Ritual Transvestism in the Liberian Civil War'. In *Feminism, Nationalism, and Militarism*. Arlington, VA: American Anthropological Association, 1995, at 83.
68 Coulter, Chris. 'Female Fighters in the Sierra Leone War: Challenging the Assumptions?' *Feminist Review* 88, no. 1 (2008): 54–73, at 65.
69 Ruddick, Sara. *Maternal Thinking: Toward a Politics of Peace*. Boston, MA: Beacon Press, 1995. Elshtain, Jean. 'On Beautiful Souls, Just Warriors and Feminist Consciousness'. *Women's Studies International Forum* 5, no. 3–4 (1982): 341–348.
70 See for example, Kaplan, Laura. 'Woman as Caretaker: An Archetype That Supports Patriarchal Militarism'. *Hypatia* 9, no. 2 (1994): 123–133. Scheper-Hugher, Nancy. 'Maternal Thinking and the Politics of War'. *Peace Review* 8, no. 3 (1996): 353–358.
71 Cock, supra note 60.
72 Coulter, supra note 68.
73 Ibid.
74 Durham, Helen, and O'Byrne, Katie. 'The Dialogue of Difference: Gender Perspectives on International Humanitarian Law'. *International Review of the Red Cross* 92, no. 877 (2010): 31–52.
75 Hogg, supra note 15, at 101.
76 Ibid.
77 Felices-Luna, Maritza. 'The Involvement of Women in Anti-Establishment Armed Groups: Deviance in the Service of a Citizenship Enterprise'. *Champ Penal/Penal Field* 4 (2007).
78 For example, 'How Islamists Brainwash Female Suicide Bombers'. *CounterJihad*, 8 April 2016. Gentry, Caron E. and Laura Sjoberg. *Beyond Mothers, Monsters, Whores: Thinking about Women's Violence in Global Politics*. London: Zed Books Ltd, 2015.
79 Coulter, supra note 68.
80 For example, Dearden, Lizzie. '"Isis Are Afraid of Girls": Kurdish Female Fighters Believe They Have an Unexpected Advantage Fighting in Syria'. *Independent*, 9 December 2015.

81 'Liberia's Women Killers'. BBC, 26 August 2003. http://news.bbc.co.uk/2/hi/africa/3181529.stm.
82 Itano, Nicole. 'The Sisters-In-Arms of Liberia's War'. *The Christian Science Monitor*, 26 August 2003.
83 Coulter, supra note 68.
84 See for example, Mitchell, Brian. *Women in the Military: Flirting with Disaster*. Washington, DC; Lanham, MD: Regnery Pub, 1958 (Distributed to the trade by National Book Network, 1998). Mitchell, Brian. *Weak Link: The Feminization of the American Military*. Washington DC: Gateway, Regnery. '10 Reasons to Keep Women Out of the Infantry'. *The Patriot Post*. Accessed 16 January 2014.
85 Simons, Anna. 'Women Can Never "Belong" in Combat'. *Orbis* 44, no. 3 (2000): 451–461.
86 Heinecken, Lindy. 'Affirming Gender Equality: The Challenges Facing the South African Armed Forces'. *Current Sociology* 50, no. 5 (2002): 715–728.
87 Goldstein, Joshua. *War and Gender: How Gender Shapes the War System and Vice Versa*. Cambridge: Cambridge University Press, 2003.
88 Kier, supra note 64.
89 Cock, supra note 60.
90 'Former Troops Say Time Has Come for Women in Combat Units'. CNN. 24 January 2013.
91 Carter, April. Should Women Be Soldiers or Pacifists? in Lorentzen, Lois, and Turpin, Jennifer (eds), *The Women and War Reader*. New York: New York University Press, 1998. Chinkin, Christine. 'Women and Peace: Militarism and Oppression'. In Mahoney, Kathleen and Mahoney, Paul (eds), *Human Rights in the Twenty-First Century: A Global Challenge*. Dordrecht, Boston, London: Martinus Nijhoff Publishers, 1993. MacKinnon, Catharine. *Feminism Unmodified*. Cambridge, MA: Harvard University Press, 1987.
92 Duncanson, Claire, and Woodward, Rachel. 'Regendering the Military: Theorizing Women's Military Participation'. *Security Dialogue* 47, no. 1 (1 February 2016): 3–21.
93 Stiehm, Judith (ed.). *It's Our Military Too: Women and the US Military (Women in the Political Economy)*. Philladelphia, PA: Temple University Press, 1996.
94 Duncanson, supra note 92.
95 Cockburn, Cynthia. *From Where We Stand: War, Women's Activism and Feminist Analysis*. London: Zed Books, 2007. Elshtain, Jean. 'On Beautiful Souls, Just Warriors and Feminist Consciousness'. *Women's Studies International Forum*, Special Issue Women and Men's Wars, 5, no. 3 (1 January 1982): 341–348.
96 Heinecken, supra note 86.
97 For example, United Nations Security Council, Security Council Resolution 1325 (2000) [on women and peace and security], 31 October 2000, S/RES/1325.
98 Duncanson, Claire and Woodward, Rachel. 'Regendering the Military: Theorizing Women's Military Participation'. *Security Dialogue* 47, no. 1 (1 February 2016): 3–21, at 5.
99 This argument was made by Representative Patricia Schroeder, 1991, who pointed to famous female athletes as demonstration of the fact that trained females can carry as much and run as fast as some men.
100 Miller, Laura. 'Feminism and the Exclusion of Army Women from Combat'. *Gender Issues* 16, no. 3 (1998): 33–64.
101 Stiehm, Judith. *Arms and the Enlisted Woman*. Philadelphia, PA: Temple University Press, 1989.
102 Ibid.
103 Key writings in this area include Kinsella, Helen. *Securing the Civilian: Sex and Gender in the Laws of War*. Boston, MA: Boston Consortium on Gender, Security and Human Rights, 2004. Gardam, Judith. 'Gender and Non-Combatant Immunity'.

Transnational Law & Contemporary Problems 3 (1993): 345–370. Durham, O'Byrne, supra note 56,

104 Grotius, supra note 16.

105 Ibid.

106 Carpenter, supra note 18.

107 Gentili, Alberico. *De Jure Belli Libri Tres*. Book. 2, Chapter 21, 1612. Republished by Clarendon Press: Oxford, 1877.

108 Suarez, Francisco. *Seleccion de Defensio Fidei y Otras Obras*, Ediciones Desalma, Buenos Aires, 1966, pp. 332–335.

109 Carpenter, supra note 18.

110 Quoted in Carpenter, supra note 18, at 672.

111 Commentary to Article 14, Convention (III) relative to the Treatment of Prisoners of War. Geneva, 12 August 1949, p. 143, paragraph 2, 'The Special Position of Women'.

112 Bennoune, Karima. 'Do We Need New International Law to Protect Women in Armed Conflict?' *Case Western Reserve Journal of International Law* 38 (2006): 363–391.

113 Kinsella, supra note 103.

114 Article 3(1) of GC4.

115 For example, AP2 Art 5(2)(a) and Art 4(2)(e).

116 Gardam, supra note 103.

117 Gardam, supra note 19.

118 Convention (II) for the Amelioration of the Condition of Wounded, Sick and Shipwrecked Members of Armed Forces at Sea. Geneva, 12 August 1949, Article 12, and Convention (I) for the Amelioration of the Condition of the Wounded and Sick in Armed Forces in the Field. Geneva, 12 August 1949, Article 12.

119 Gardam, supra note 19.

120 For example, Articles 12 of GC1 and 2, Art 16 of GC3, Art 27 of GC4, Art 75 of AP1 and Art of AP2 provide for treatment without any adverse distinction founded on sex.

121 Oosterveld, Valerie. 'Feminist Debates on Civilian Women and International Humanitarian Law'. *Windsor Yearbook of Access to Justice* 27 (2009): 385–402.

122 Gardam, Judith, and Charlesworth, Hilary. 'Protection of Women in Armed Conflict'. *Human Rights Quarterly* 9, no. 1991 (2000): 148–66.

123 Article 135 Beijing Platform for Action, The United Nations Fourth World Conference on Women, 1995.

124 Bennoune, supra note 112.

125 Coomaraswamy, Radhika. *Report of the Special Rapporteur on Violence Against Women, Its Causes and Consequences*. United Nations, Commission on Human Rights, Fifty-fourth Session, 1998.

126 Bennoune, supra note 112.

127 Barrow, Amy. 'UN Security Council Resolutions 1325 and 1820: Constructing Gender in Armed Conflict and International Humanitarian Law'. *International Review of the Red Cross* 92, no. 877 (2010): 221–234.

128 See for example Lacey, supra note 1.

129 Bennoune, supra note 112.

130 Sellers, Patricia Viseur. 'Gender Strategy Is Not a Luxury for International Courts'. *American University Journal of Gender, Social Policy & The Law* 17, no. 2 (2009): 301–323.

131 Oosterveld, supra note 121.

132 Barrow, supra note 127.

133 Oosterveld, supra note 121.

134 Durham, O'Byrne, supra note 74.

135 Charlesworth, Chinkin, supra note 6.

136 Kinsella, supra note 103, and Nguyen, Athena, The Influence of Gender Stereotyping on International Humanitarian Law, 2010, available at http://works.bepress.com/athena_nguyen/1.
137 Kinsella, supra note 103, at 2.
138 Gardam, supra note 19. Oosterveld, supra note 121.
139 Oosterveld, supra note 121.
140 Grave breaches are those rules in the Conventions that confer jurisdiction on all state parties to prosecute their violations, and which create a duty for states to seek out perpetrators and to enact legislation designed to prevent these breaches occurring. These are found in GC1, Art 50; GC2, Art 51; GC3, Art 130; GC4, Art 147; GC3, Art 130; and GC4, Art 147.
141 Gardam, supra note 19.
142 Goldstone, Richard, and Dehon, Estelle. 'Engendering Accountability: Gender Crimes Under International Criminal Law'. *New England Journal of Public Policy* 19, no. 1 (2003): 121–145.
143 Declaration on Preventing Sexual Violence in Conflict, G8, 11 April 2013.
144 Gardam, supra note 103.
145 Charlesworth, Chinkin, supra note 6.
146 Alison, Miranda. 'Wartime Sexual Violence: Women's Human Rights and Questions of Masculinity'. *Review of International Studies* 33, no. 1 (2007): 75–90, at 80.
147 Kinsella, supra note 103.
148 Hartigan, Richard. *The Forgotten Victim: A History of the Civilian*. Chicago, IL: Precedent Publishing Inc, 1982.
149 Teichman, Jenny. *Pacifism and the Just War: A Study in Applied Philosophy*. Oxford: Basil Blackwell, 1986.
150 Sjoberg, Laura. *The Paradox of Double Effect: How Feminism Can Save the Immunity Principle*. Boston, MA: Boston Consortium on Gender, Security and Human Rights, 2006.
151 Carpenter, supra note 18.
152 Ibid.
153 Carpenter, Charli. *Innocent Women and Children: Gender, Norms and the Protection of Civilians*. Farnham: Ashgate Publishing Co., 2006.
154 Ibid.
155 Carpender, supra note 18.
156 Estreicher, Samuel. 'Privileging Asymmetric Warfare (Part II)? The 'Proportionality' Principle under International Humanitarian Law'. *Chicago Journal of International Law* 12, no. 1 (2011): 143–157.
157 Fenrick, William. 'Applying IHL Targeting Rules to Practical Situations: Proportionality and Military Objectives'. *Windsor Yearbook of Access to Justice* 27 (2009): 271–283.
158 Gardam, supra note 19.
159 Sjoberg, supra note 150.
160 Schmitt, Michael. 'Military Necessity and Humanity in International Humanitarian Law: Preserving the Delicate Balance'. *Virginia Journal of International Law* 50 (2010): 795–839.
161 Ibid.
162 Adedeji, Lanre. 'Maintaining the Balance Between Military Necessity and Humanity'. *The Lawyers Chronicle*, n.d. http://thelawyerschronicle.com/maintaining-the-balance-between-military-necessity-and-humanity/
163 Gardam, supra note 103.
164 Copelon, Rhonda. 'Gender Crimes as War Crimes: Integrating Crimes against Women into International Criminal Law'. *McGill Law Journal* 46 (2001): 217–240.
165 Kelsall, Michelle Staggs, and Stepakoff, Shanee. ''When We Wanted to Talk About Rape': Silencing Sexual Violence at the Special Court for Sierra Leone'.

The International Journal of Transitional Justice 1 (2007): 355–374. Kendall, Sara, and Staggs, Michelle. *Silencing Sexual Violence: Recent Developments in the CDF Case at the Special Court for Sierra Leone*. Berkeley, CA: UC Berkeley War Crimes Studies Center, 2005.

166 *Decision of Prosecution Request for Leave to Amend Indictment*, SCSL 20 May 2004.

167 *Decision on the Prosecution's Motion for a Ruling on the Admissibility of Evidence*, SCSL, 24 May 2005.

168 Kelsall, Stepakoff, supra note 165.

169 *The Prosecutor versus Jean-Paul Akayesu*, Case No. ICTR-96-4-T, 1998, paras 732–734.

170 *The Prosecutor* v. *Delalic, Mucic, Delic and Landzo (Celebici)*, Trial Chamber Judgement, 16 November 1998, Case No. IT-96–21-T. paras 494–496.

171 The ICC's 2014 Policy Paper on Sexual and Gender-Based Crimes defines gender-based crimes as,

> … those committed against persons, whether male or female, because of their sex and/or socially constructed gender roles. Gender-based crimes are not always manifested as a form of sexual violence. They may include non-sexual attacks on women and girls, and men and boys, because of their gender.

172 Hall Martinez, Katherine. 'Ending Impunity for Gender Crimes under the International Criminal Court'. *The Brown Journal of World Affairs* VI, no. 1 (1999): 65–85.

173 Sadat, Leila. 'Avoiding the Creation of a Gender Ghetto in International Criminal Law'. *International Criminal Law Review* 11 (2011): 655–662.

174 Bennoune, supra note 112, at 387.

175 Ibid.

176 As of April 2012, 121 states have ratified or acceded to the Rome statute, as opposed to 194 countries that have ratified the Geneva Conventions.

177 The ICC's focus on Africa has been criticised as contributing to interventionist, imperialist assumptions. See for example, Jalloh, Charles. 'Regionalizing International Criminal Law'. *International Criminal Law Review* 9 (2009): 445–499.

178 For a history of the adoption of SC Res 1325, Cohn, Carol, Kinsella, Helen, and Gibbings, Sheri. 'Women, Peace and Security Resolution 1325'. *International Feminist Journal of Politics* 6, no. 1 (2004): 130–140.

179 Pratt, Nicola, and Richter-Devroe, Sophie. 'Critically Examining UNSCR 1325 on Women, Peace and Security'. *International Feminist Journal of Politics* 13, no. 4 (2011): 489–503.

180 The Global Network of Women Peacebuilders, In-country and Global Monitoring of UNSC Resolution 1325, *Women Count – Security Council Resolution 1325: Civil Society Monitoring Report*, 2012.

181 Ibid.

182 Article 13 reads, 'Encourages all those involved in the planning for disarmament, demobilization and reintegration to consider the different needs of female and male ex-combatants and to take into account the needs of their dependants', S/RES/1325 (2000).

183 Heathcote, Gina. 'Feminist Politics and the Use of Force: Theorising Feminist Action and Security Council Resolution 1325'. *Socio-Legal Review* 7 (2011): 23–43. Otto, Dianne. 'A Sign of Weakness – Disrupting Gender Certainties in the Implementation of Security Council Resolution 1325'. *Michigan Journal of Gender & Law* 13 (2007): 113–175.

184 S/RES/1325 (2000).

Bibliography

Books and articles

Adedeji, Lanre. 'Maintaining the Balance between Military Necessity and Humanity'. *The Lawyers Chronicle*, n.d. http://thelawyerschronicle.com/maintaining-the-balance-between-military-necessity-and-humanity/

Adichie, Chimamanda Ngozi. *We Should All Be Feminists*. New York: Vintage Books, 2014.

Alison, Miranda. 'Wartime Sexual Violence: Women's Human Rights and Questions of Masculinity'. *Review of International Studies* 33, no. 1 (2007): 75–90.

Arnfred, Signe. 'Simone de Beauvoir in Africa: 'Woman = the Second Sex?' Issues of African Feminist Thought'. *jenda: A Journal of Culture and African Women Studies* 2, no. 1 (2002): 1–20.

Baaz, Maria Eriksson and Stern, Maria. 'Making Sense of Violence: Voices of Soldiers in the Congo (DRC)'. *The Journal of Modern African Studies* 46, no. 01 (2008): 57–86.

Barclay, Claire. 'Toward Substantive Equality: A Feminist Critique of the Notion of Difference in the Canadian and South African Equality Tests'. *International Journal of Discrimination and the Law* 5, no. 2–3 (2001): 167–188.

Barrow, Amy. 'UN Security Council Resolutions 1325 and 1820: Constructing Gender in Armed Conflict and International Humanitarian Law'. *International Review of the Red Cross* 92, no. 877 (2010): 221–234.

Bennoune, Karima. 'Do We Need New International Law to Protect Women in Armed Conflict?' *Case Western Reserve Journal of International Law* 38 (2006): 363–391.

Bergman, Mari. 'African Sisterhood – Conceptualizing African Feminist Identity'. 2016. [Online]

Brownmiller, Susan. *Against Our Will: Men, Women and Rape*. New York: Simon and Schuster, 1975.

Buss, Doris and Manji, Ambreena (eds). *International Law: Modern Feminist Approaches*. Oxford: Hart Publishing, 2005.

Butler, Judith. *Gender Trouble: Feminism and the Subversion of Identity*. Routledge, 1990.

Carastathis, Anna. 'The Concept of Intersectionality in Feminist Theory'. *Philosophy Compass* 9, no. 5 (2014): 304–314.

Carter, April. 'Should Women Be Soldiers or Pacifists?' in Lorentzen, Lois and Turpin, Jennifer (eds), *The Women and War Reader*. New York: New York University Press, 1998.

Carpenter, Charli. *Innocent Women and Children: Gender, Norms and the Protection of Civilians*. Farnham: Ashgate Publishing Co, 2006.

Carpenter, Charli. '"Women and Children First": Gender, Norms, and Humanitarian Evacuation in the Balkans 1991–95'. *International Organization* 57, no. 4 (2003): 661–694.

Charlesworth, Hilary and Chinkin, Christine. *The Boundaries of International Law: A Feminist Analysis*. Manchester: Manchester University Press, 2000.

Chinkin, Christine. 'Women and Peace: Militarism and Oppression'. In Mahoney, Kathleen and Mahoney, Paul (eds), *Human Rights in the Twenty First Century: A Global Challenge*. Dordrecht, Boston, London: Martinus Nijhoff Publishers, 1993.

Cock, Jacklyn. 'Women and the Military: Implications for Demilitarization in the 1990s in South Africa'. *Gender & Society* 8, no. 2 (1994): 152–169.

Cockburn, Cynthia. *From Where We Stand: War, Women's Activism and Feminist Analysis*. London: Zed Books, 2007.

Cockburn, Cynthia. 'Gender Relations as Causal in Militarization and War'. *International Feminist Journal of Politics* 12, no. 2 (2010): 139–157.

Cohn, Carol, Kinsella, Helen and Gibbings, Sheri. 'Women, Peace and Security Resolution 1325'. *International Feminist Journal of Politics* 6, no. 1 (2004): 130–140.

Coomaraswamy, Radhika. *Report of the Special Rapporteur on Violence against Women, Its Causes and Consequences*. United Nations, Commission on Human Rights, Fifty-fourth Session, 1998.

Cook, Rebecca. *Gender Stereotyping: Transnational Legal Perspectives*. Pennsylvania Studies in Human Rights. Philadelphia, PA: University of Pennsylvania Press, 2010.

Copelon, Rhonda. 'Gender Crimes as War Crimes: Integrating Crimes against Women into International Criminal Law'. *McGill Law Journal* 46 (2001): 217–240.

Coulter, Chris. 'Female Fighters in the Sierra Leone War: Challenging the Assumptions?' *Feminist Review* 88, no. 1 (2008): 54–73.

Crenshaw, Kimberle. 'Mapping the Margins: Intersectionality, Identity Politics, and Violence Against Women of Color'. *Stanford Law Review* 43 (1991): 1241–1299.

Dalton, Clare. 'Where We Stand: Observations on the Situation of Feminist Legal Thought'. In *Feminist Legal Theory: Foundations and Outlooks*. Vol. 1. London: Dartmouth Publishing Company Limited, 1995.

Duncanson, Claire and Woodward, Rachel. 'Regendering the Military: Theorizing Women's Military Participation'. *Security Dialogue* 47, no. 1 (1 February 2016): 3–21.

Durham, Helen and O'Byrne, Katie. 'The Dialogue of Difference: Gender Perspectives on International Humanitarian Law'. *International Review of the Red Cross* 92, no. 877 (2010): 31–52.

Dworkin, Andrea. *Woman Hating*. New York: Plume, 1991.

Elshtain, Jean. 'On Beautiful Souls, Just Warriors and Feminist Consciousness'. *Women's Studies International Forum*, Special Issue Women and Men's Wars, 5, no. 3 (1 January 1982): 341–348.

Estreicher, Samuel. 'Privileging Asymmetric Warfare (Part II)? The 'Proportionality' Principle under International Humanitarian Law'. *Chicago Journal of International Law* 12, no. 1 (2011): 143–157.

Fausto-Sterling, Anne. *Myths Of Gender: Biological Theories About Women And Men, Revised Edition*. New York: Basic Books, 1992.

Felices-Luna, Maritza. 'The Involvement of Women in Anti-Establishment Armed Groups: Deviance in the Service of a Citizenship Enterprise'. *Champ Penal/Penal Field* 4 (2007).

Fenrick, William. 'Applying IHL Targeting Rules to Practical Situations: Proportionality and Military Objectives'. *Windsor Yearbook of Access to Justice* 27 (2009): 271–283.

Gardam, Judith. 'Women and the Law of Armed Conflict: Why the Silence?' *International and Comparative Law Quarterly* 46, no. 1 (January 1997): 55–80.

Gardam, Judith. 'Gender and Non-Combatant Immunity'. *Transnational Law & Contemporary Problems* 3 (1993): 345–370.

Gardam, Judith and Charlesworth, Hilary. 'Protection of Women in Armed Conflict'. *Human Rights Quarterly* 22, no. 1 (February 2000): 148–166.

Gateway, Regnery and Fenner, Lorry. *Women in Combat: Civic Duty or Military Liability? (Controversies in Public Policy)*. Georgetown, Washington DC: Georgetown University Press, 2001.

Gavison, Ruth. 'Feminism and the Public/Private Distinction'. *Stanford Law Review* 45, no. 1 (1992): 1–45.

Gentili, Alberico. *De Jure Belli Libri Tres*. Book. 2, Chapter 21, 1612. Republished by Clarendon Press: Oxford, 1877.

Gentry, Caron E. and Laura Sjoberg. *Beyond Mothers, Monsters, Whores: Thinking about Women's Violence in Global Politics*. London: Zed Books Ltd, 2015.

Goldstein, Joshua. *War and Gender: How Gender Shapes the War System and Vice Versa*. Cambridge: Cambridge University Press, 2003.

Goldstone, Richard and Dehon, Estelle. 'Engendering Accountability: Gender Crimes Under International Criminal Law'. *New England Journal of Public Policy* 19, no. 1 (2003): 121–145.

Gordon, Natasha M. '"Tonguing the Body": Placing Female Circumcision within African Feminist Discourse'. *African Issues* 25, no. 2 (January 1997): 24–27.

Goredema, Ruvimbo. 'African Feminism: The African Woman's Struggle for Identity' 1 (2010): 275–241.

Grotius, Hugo, 'Moderation with Respect to the Right of Killing in a Lawful War, Book 3, Chapter 11, *The Law of War and Peace*, 1625. Re-published by Batoche Books Kitchener, 2001, Ontaria, Canada.

Hall Martinez, Katherine. 'Ending Impunity for Gender Crimes under the International Criminal Court'. *The Brown Journal of World Affairs* VI, no. 1 (1999): 65–85.

Handrahan, Lori. 'Conflict, Gender, Ethnicity and Post-Conflict Reconstruction'. *Security Dialogue* 35, no. 4 (2004): 429–445.

Hartigan, Richard. *The Forgotten Victim: A History of the Civilian*. Chicago, IL: Precedent Publishing Inc, 1982.

Heathcote, Gina. 'Feminist Politics and the Use of Force: Theorising Feminist Action and Security Council Resolution 1325'. *Socio-Legal Review* 7 (2011): 23–43.

Heinecken, Lindy. 'Affirming Gender Equality: The Challenges Facing the South African Armed Forces'. *Current Sociology* 50, no. 5 (2002): 715–728.

Hogg, Nicole. 'Women's Participation in the Rwandan Genocide: Mothers or Monsters?' *International Review of the Red Cross* 92, no. 877 (2010): 69–102.

Hurst, Charles. *Social Inequality: Forms, Causes, and Consequences*. Boston, MA: Pearson, 2012.

Itano, Nicole. 'The Sisters-In-Arms of Liberia's War'. *The Christian Science Monitor*, 26 August 2003.

Jalloh, Charles. 'Regionalizing International Criminal Law'. *International Criminal Law Review* 9 (2009): 445–499.

Jones, Adam. 'Gendercide and Genocide'. *Journal of Genocide Research* 2, no. 2 (2000): 185–211.

Kahssay, Jihan. 'Feminist Legal Theory: Challenges Facing Women Combatants'. *Feminist Legal Theory*, 5 October 2012.

Kaplan, Laura. 'Woman as Caretaker: An Archetype that Supports Patriarchal Militarism'. *Hypatia* 9, no. 2 (1994): 123–133.

Kelsall, Michelle Staggs, and Stepakoff, Shanee. '"When We Wanted to Talk About Rape": Silencing Sexual Violence at the Special Court for Sierra Leone'. *The International Journal of Transitional Justice* 1 (2007): 355–374.

Kendall, Sara, and Staggs, Michelle. *Silencing Sexual Violence: Recent Developments in the CDF Case at the Special Court for Sierra Leone*. Berkeley, CA: UC Berkeley War Crimes Studies Center, 2005.

Kier, Elizabeth. 'Uniform Justice: Assessing Women in Combat'. *Perspectives on Politics* 1, no. 02 (2003): 343–347.

King, Anthony. 'Women in Combat'. *The RUSI Journal* 158, no. 1 (2013): 4–11.

Kinsella, Helen. *Securing the Civilian: Sex and Gender in the Laws of War*. Boston, MA: Boston Consortium on Gender, Security and Human Rights, 2004.

Kouvo, Sari, and Zoe Pearson. *Feminist Perspectives on Contemporary International Law*. Oxford: Hart Publishing, 2011.

Krill, Françoise. 'The Protection of Women in International Humanitarian Law'. *International Review of the Red Cross* 249 (1985). www.icrc.org/eng/resources/documents/article/other/57jmfj.htm

Lacey, Nicola. 'Feminist Legal Theory and the Rights of Women'. In *Knop, Karen (ed.), Gender and Human Rights*. Oxford: Oxford University Press, 2004.

Lahiri, Madhumita. 'Crimes and Corrections: Bride Burners, Corrective Rapists, and Other Black Misogynists'. *Feminist Africa, Legal Voice: Special Issue*, no. 15 (December 2011).

Laplante, Lisa J. 'The Domestication of International Criminal Law: A Proposal for Expanding the International Criminal Court's Sphere of Influence'. *The John Marshall Law Review* 43, no. 635 (2010): 635–680.

Lewis, Desiree. 'Discursive Challenges for African Feminism'. *QUEST: An African Journal of Philosophy/Revue Africain E de Philosophie* 20 (2008): 77–96.

Lewis, Desiree. 'Introduction: African Feminisms'. *Agenda* no. 50 (2001): 4–10.

Lorentzen, Lois and Turpin, Jennifer (eds), *The Women and War Reader*. New York: New York University Press, 1998.

Mackay, Finn. *Radical Feminism: Feminist Activism in Movement*. Houndsmills, Basingstoke, Hampshire: Palgrave Macmillan, 2015.

MacKinnon, Catharine. 'Substantive Equality: A Perspective'. *Minnesota Law Review* 96, no. 1 (2011): 1–27.

MacKinnon, Catharine. *Feminism Unmodified*. Cambridge, MA: Harvard University Press, 1987.

MacKinnon, Catharine. *Toward a Feminist Theory of the State*. 2nd edition. Cambridge, MA: Harvard University Press, 1991.

Mama, Amina. *Women's Studies and Studies of Women in Africa during the 1990s*. Working Paper Series (Codesria); 96/5. Dakar, Senegal: Codesria, 1996.

Mangena, Oshadi. 'Feminism (Singular), African Feminisms (Plural) and the African Diaspora'. *Agenda*, no. 58 (1 January 2003): 98–100.

Miller, Laura. 'Feminism and the Exclusion of Army Women from Combat'. *Gender Issues* 16, no. 3 (1998): 33–64.

Mitchell, Brian. *Weak Link: The Feminization of the American Military*. Washington DC: Regnery Gateway, 1989.

Mitchell, Brian. *Women in the Military: Flirting with Disaster*. Washington, DC; Lanham, MD: Regnery Pub, 1958 (Distributed to the trade by National Book Network, 1998).

Mohanty, Chandra. 'Under Western Eyes: Feminist Scholarship and Colonial Discourses'. *Feminist Review*, no. 30 (1988): 61–88.

Money, John and Coleman, Eli. *John Money: A Tribute*. Abingdon: Routledge, 1991.

Moran, Mary. 'Warriors or Soldiers? Masculinity and Ritual Transvestism in the Liberian Civil War'. In *Feminism, Nationalism, and Militarism*. Arlington, VA: American Anthropological Association, 1995.

Nguyen, Athena, The Influence of Gender Stereotyping on International Humanitarian Law, 2010, http://works.bepress.com/athena_nguyen/1.

Olsen, Frances. *Feminist Legal Theory*. Vol. 1 and 2. The International Library of Essays in Law and Legal Theory. New York: New York University Press, 1995.

Oosterveld, Valerie. 'Feminist Debates on Civilian Women and International Humanitarian Law'. *Windsor Yearbook of Access to Justice* 27 (2009): 385–402.

Otto, Dianne. 'A Sign of Weakness – Disrupting Gender Certainties in the Implementation of Security Council Resolution 1325'. *Michigan Journal of Gender & Law* 13 (2007): 113–175.

Pateman, Carole. '"Feminist Critiques of the Public/Private Dichotomy"'. *The Disorder of Women. Democracy, Feminism and Political Theory.* Cambridge: Polity Press, 1989.

Pratt, Nicola, and Richter-Devroe, Sophie. 'Critically Examining UNSCR 1325 on Women, Peace and Security'. *International Feminist Journal of Politics* 13, no. 4 (2011): 489–503.

Ruddick, Sara. *Maternal Thinking: Toward a Politics of Peace.* Beacon Press, 1995. Elshtain, Jean. 'On Beautiful Souls, Just Warriors and Feminist Consciousness'. *Women's Studies International Forum* 5, no. 3–4 (1982): 341–348.

Sadat, Leila. 'Avoiding the Creation of a Gender Ghetto in International Criminal Law'. *International Criminal Law Review* 11 (2011): 655–662.

Scheper-Hugher, Nancy. 'Maternal Thinking and the Politics of War'. *Peace Review* 8, no. 3 (1996): 353–358.

Schmitt, Michael. 'Military Necessity and Humanity in International Humanitarian Law: Preserving the Delicate Balance'. *Virginia Journal of International Law* 50 (2010): 795–839.

Schwalbe, Michael. *The Sociologically Examined Life: Pieces of the Conversation.* 4th edition. Columbus, OH: McGraw-Hill Humanities/Social Sciences/Languages, 2007.

Sellers, Patricia Viseur. 'Gender Strategy Is Not a Luxury for International Courts'. *American University Journal of Gender, Social Policy & the Law* 17, no. 2 (2009): 301–323.

Simons, Anna. 'Women Can Never 'Belong' in Combat'. *Orbis* 44, no. 3 (2000): 451–461.

Sjoberg, Laura. *The Paradox of Double Effect: How Feminism Can Save the Immunity Principle.* Boston, MA: Boston Consortium on Gender, Security and Human Rights, 2006.

Stiehm, Judith (ed.). *It's Our Military Too: Women and the US Military. (Women in the Political Economy).* Philladelphia, PA: Temple University Press, 1996.

Stiehm, Judith. *Arms and the Enlisted Woman.* Philadelphia, PA: Temple University Press, 1989.

Suarez, Francisco. *Seleccion de Defensio Fidei y Otras Obras.* Ediciones Desalma, Buenos Aires, 1966.

Tamale, Sylvia. 'African Feminism: How Should We Change?' *Development* 49, no. 1 (2006): 38–41.

Tegomoh, Evelyne. 'Experiencing African Feminism'. *Agenda* 54 (2002): 122–128.

Teichman, Jenny. *Pacifism and the Just War: A Study in Applied Philosophy.* Oxford: Basil Blackwell, 1986.

The Global Network of Women Peacebuilders, In-country and Global Monitoring of UNSC Resolution 1325, *Women Count – Security Council Resolution 1325: Civil Society Monitoring Report*, 2012.

Titunik, Regina. 'The Myth of the Macho Military'. *Polity* 40, no. 2 (2008): 137–163.

White, Aaronette. 'Fanon & the African Woman Combatant', in Nhema, Alfred and Tiyambe Zeleza, Paul (eds), *The Roots of African Conflicts: The Causes and Costs.* 1st edition. Athens, OH: Ohio University Press, 2008.

'White Women, Black Men & African Feminists'. *MsAfropolitan*, 2013. www.msafropolitan.com/2012/01/white-women-black-men-african-feminists.html.
Wood, Elisabeth. 'Variation in Sexual Violence during War'. *Politics & Society* 34, no. 3 (2006): 307–342, at 326.
Zechenter, Elizabeth. 'In the Name of Culture: Cultural Relativism and the Abuse of the Individual'. *Journal of Anthropological Research* 53 (1977): 319–347.

Cases

Decision of Prosecution Request for Leave to Amend Indictment, SCSL 20 May 2004.
Decision on the Prosecution's Motion for a Ruling on the Admissibility of Evidence, SCSL, 24 May 2005.
The Prosecutor v. *Jean-Paul Akayesu*, Case No. ICTR-96-4-T, 1998, paras 732–734.
The Prosecutor v. *Delalic, Mucic, Delic and Landzo (Celebici)*, Trial Chamber Judgement, 16 November 1998, Case No. IT-96-21-T. paras 494–496.

Treaties

African Charter on Human and Peoples' Rights ('Banjul Charter'), 27 June 1981, CAB/LEG/67/3.
Convention (II) for the Amelioration of the Condition of Wounded, Sick and Shipwrecked Members of Armed Forces at Sea. Geneva, 12 August 1949.
Convention (I) for the Amelioration of the Condition of the Wounded and Sick in Armed Forces in the Field. Geneva, 12 August 1949, Article 12.
Geneva Convention Relative to the Protection of Civilian Persons in Time of War (Fourth Geneva Convention), 12 August 1949, 75 UNTS 287.
Geneva Convention Relative to the Treatment of Prisoners of War (Third Geneva Convention), 12 August 1949, 75 UNTS 135.
Protocol Additional to the Geneva Conventions of 12 August 1949, and relating to the Protection of Victims of International Armed Conflicts (Protocol I), 8 June 1977, 1125 UNTS 3.
Protocol Additional to the Geneva Conventions of 12 August 1949, and relating to the Protection of Victims of Non-International Armed Conflicts (Protocol II), 8 June 1977, 1125 UNTS 609.

Other policy documents

General Recommendation No. 28 on the Core Obligations of States Parties under Article 2 of the Convention on the Elimination of All Forms of Discrimination against Women, CEDAW, 2010.
Commentary to Article 14, Convention (III) relative to the Treatment of Prisoners of War. Geneva, 12 August 1949, p. 143, paragraph 2, 'The Special Position of Women'.
ICC's 2014 Policy Paper on Sexual and Gender-Based Crimes.
United Nations Security Council Resolution 1325 (2000) [on women and peace and security], 31 October 2000, S/RES/1325.
Declaration on Preventing Sexual Violence in Conflict, G8, 11 April 2013.
Beijing Platform for Action, The United Nations Fourth World Conference on Women, 1995.

Media articles

Dearden, Lizzie. '"Isis Are Afraid of Girls": Kurdish Female Fighters Believe They Have an Unexpected Advantage Fighting in Syria'. *Independent*, 9 December 2015.
'Liberia's Women Killers'. BBC, 26 August 2003. http://news.bbc.co.uk/2/hi/africa/3181529.stm.
Former Troops Say Time Has Come for Women in Combat Units'. CNN. 24 January 2013.
'10 Reasons to Keep Women Out of the Infantry'. *The Patriot Post*. Accessed 16 January 2014.

5 The divide between international and non-international armed conflicts

A precursory step to the application of the principle of distinction

It is no longer the norm that conflicts are either IAC or NIAC in character. A defining feature of new wars is the merging of international and internal features. The distinction between IACs and NIACs, one of the central axioms of IHL, has been greatly challenged as a series of complex conflicts have been fought, overflowing across state borders, spanning vast and disparate geographic territories. In many of today's IACs, concurrent internal struggles take place within warring countries. NIACs exhibit unparalleled levels of international involvement: from foreign intervention, to rebel groups coming from or sheltering in neighbouring countries, to the presence of international peacekeepers, humanitarian aid and foreign trade. Africa's porous borders allow for the passing of troops and civilians, including large numbers of women who cross conflict-riddled borders for refuge, subsistence or community.

Despite the fact that so many recent conflicts do not fit neatly into law's IAC and NIAC categories, this divide remains a central axiom of IHL, and the legal consequences of a conflict being labelled IAC or NIAC are significant. Crucially, this divide indicates the legal framework applicable to a conflict, hence determining the status, rights and obligations of parties, as well as the rules to be used post-conflict to prosecute wartime violations. Importantly for this work, the divide determines which version of the principle of distinction is applied. As described in previous chapters, the rules of distinction differ significantly in IACs and NIACs. While those fighting in IACs can be classified 'combatant', granted combatant immunity and protected by POW status, the principle is more limited in NIACs, where fighters have no right to fight, no privileges and no protected status. They also have none of the adjoining incentive for compliance with IHL. As such, one of the key factors affecting the legal status of individual participants to a conflict is the way the conflict they are fighting in is classified. However, with complex facts on the ground, a prevalence of covert operations and political interests at stake, there are often disagreements over appropriate classifications. These disagreements are evident in judicial processes and analyses following conflicts – and are heightened all the more during hostilities, when facts and intentions are concealed by politics, chaos and the 'fog of war'.

It is not just factually that the line between IACs and NIACs is blurring. In recent years, the bodies of law regulating these have also begun to merge to some extent. Developments in ICL and international human rights law (IHRL) have had the effect of shrinking the substantive differences between the laws pertaining to IACs and NIACs. Customary international law (CIL) has also developed to the point that it applies more similarly in IACs and NIACs. The evident merging of the international and non-international, both in fact and in law, the numerous problems arising from this legal divide and the inadequacy of the laws pertaining to NIACs, have led to question about the remaining value of this divide and to calls for a unified body of IHL to be applicable to all armed conflicts.

This chapter discusses the divide between IACs and NIACs, a crucial precursory step to the application of the principle of distinction. This chapter explains how this classification should be made in terms of the law, illustrating the problems inherent in trying to do so and demonstrating how one of the foundational steps for the application of the principle of distinction is a step that often cannot properly be made. The chapter describes how conflicts today, and new wars in particular, factually blur the lines between IACs and NIACs. It points to recent conflicts that have presented particular challenges for this divide – 'internationalised' conflicts, 'transnational' conflicts and those relating to international terrorism – and considers the approaches that have been proposed to allow the law to incorporate these. The chapter then describes the means by which these bodies of law are beginning to merge, considering developments in ICL and IHRL and the part played by CIL in reaching this position. Finally, this chapter will consider the arguments that have been made for the removal of the legal divide between IACs and NIACs, as well as the barriers to its removal – including the part that the principle of distinction plays in preventing a harmonised law.

History of the divide between international and non-international conflicts

Religion was the dominant influence in the early regulation of conflicts. In the Christian world, views about conflict were shaped by a belief in the inequality between Christians and heathens, as well as by the notion that rulers' power was conferred by God. Early canonist writers distinguished 'external wars', fought between Christians and infidels, and 'internal wars', fought among Christians.[1] Followers of Islam also distinguished conflicts among believers from those against non-believers. Early followers of Islam preached that Islam was to be spread until the whole world fell under Islamic rule. As such, they believed that the only relationship that could exist between believers and non-believers was that of 'jihad'. In time, as the Muslim world was divided into separate states, it became necessary to distinguish conflicts fought against non-Islamic states and those fought between Muslims, and from the 12th century onwards, distinct rules and methods of fighting were developed for these differing types of conflicts.[2]

From the 1648 Peace of Westphalia, secular nation-state sovereignty based on territoriality started to emerge, diminishing the influence of religion.[3] International law began to develop around the concept of states, each with its own sovereign. It was understood that to have a 'real' war required having two sovereign states as opponents. A legitimate enemy needed to meet certain requirements. Gentili wrote, "He is an enemy who has a state, a senate, a treasury, united and harmonious citizens, and some basis for a treaty of peace".[4]

Until the twentieth century, internal conflicts, most notably colonial wars, were not considered to be *real* wars, but rather internal matters of domestic security.[5] This was despite the significant levels of militarisation and violence often used by states in dealing with these. However, while this was the formal approach, state practice did not always reflect this position. Abi-Saab explains that,

> This legally radical separation of internal wars from the international level, was not … as rigorously observed in practice as it sounded in theory. One can cite numerous instances, both before, and particularly after the Napoleonic wars, of intervention by major European powers against democratic uprisings.…[6]

Nevertheless, notions of 'real' wars being international – and being the only ones suited to regulation – persisted and shaped the early IHL conventions.

Leading up to the twentieth century, legal regulation of conflict applied only to international conflicts. There was one exception to this – when states recognised non-state fighters as *belligerents*. When this occurred, the laws of war were extended to those conflicts. Internal struggles needed to pass various tiers of severity before they could be said to be *belligerency*. Starting at the most minor, *rebellions* were episodes of violence that were intermittent or that presented merely brief challenges to governments, which they could quell using only police or internal security measures. *Rebels* had no rights or protections under international law, and foreign states could not intervene in support of rebels without this being considered illegal intervention. A step above was *insurgency*, situations of sustained, longer-lasting and more considerable violence. Where states recognised *insurgency*, this revealed that they understood insurgents to be their opposition in fighting and not just criminals. Conflicting parties could choose to apply the laws of war to insurgents. However, recognising an insurgency did not mandate states to apply the law – rather, they had the choice. Finally, *belligerency* was reached when internal fighting was so significant and sustained that it made sense for both sides to be treated equally by law. Once a group was formally recognised as *belligerents*, the laws of war applied to them and they were treated in the same ways that states would be in conflict, subject to the same rights and obligations.[7]

Although recognition of belligerency was discretionary, belligerency could only be recognised on the fulfilment of certain requirements.[8] Both host and third party states could recognise belligerency and this recognition could be express or implied.[9] Recognition of belligerency was significant for the principle of neutrality – a crucial feature in the international relations of the time. The neutrality doctrine allowed states to declare their neutrality towards belligerents, in exchange for which they would receive an internationally recognised protection from involvement.[10] Just as states could not intervene in internal situations, they could also not declare neutrality towards these – with the exception being when belligerency was recognised. In practice, recognition of belligerency was used as a political tool. States recognised belligerency out of self-interest, rather than from a sense of feeling bound by law to do so.[11] Recognition was exercised in an ad hoc manner and there were many situations where it could legally have been granted, yet where states chose not to. By the twentieth century, the doctrine of recognition of belligerency had become obsolete.[12]

In the late nineteenth century began what Moir terms the "age of codification".[13] Francis Lieber attempted to codify the laws of war during the American Civil War, with the 1863 Lieber Code becoming the basis for the IHL treaties that followed. Despite the fact that the Lieber Code was drafted during a civil war, it was geared towards IACs – or at least towards situations where belligerency had been recognised. Lieber was reportedly hesitant to include "section X", entitled "Insurrection – Civil War – Rebellion", for fear of creating the impression that the Code was directed primarily at these sorts of conflicts.[14] Following from the Lieber Code, a number of international conventions codified the laws of war, including the 1864 Geneva Convention, the Hague Conventions of 1899 and 1907 and the 1929 Geneva Conventions. These early conventions applied only to international conflicts.[15]

The push for IHL to be extended to NIACs came from the ICRC, which argued that there was no reason that IHL's protections for victims of war should extend only to those affected by IACs.[16] Since the start of the twentieth century, the ICRC had been trying to assist NIAC victims, yet was prevented from doing this by governments who viewed assistance to victims who sided with insurgents as interference or aiding criminals.[17] In 1912 at the 9th 'International Conference of the Red Cross', the ICRC put forward a draft convention on the role of the Red Cross in civil wars and insurgencies, a proposal that was readily dismissed. In 1921, following World War One, the ICRC was able to include this issue on the agenda of the 10th International Conference and a resolution was passed affirming a right of relief for victims of civil wars and disturbances. In 1938, at the 14th International Conference of the Red Cross, a further resolution was passed, envisaging the application of certain essential principles of the laws of war in civil conflicts.[18] Around this time, the Spanish Civil War (1936–1939) took place, with its intensity and brutality demonstrating to states that NIACs could not simply be ignored by international law.[19] A number of colonial uprisings with high fatalities and devastating effects – including the Iraqi revolt against British rule (1920) and the Syrian revolt against the French (1925–1927) – also illustrated the problems of leaving such situations unregulated.

The ICRC pushed for the 1949 Geneva Conventions to apply fully in NIACs. State parties, however, were resistant to this, fearing international obligations would restrain them in their internal dealings. The 1947 'Conference of Government Experts for the Study of the Conventions for the Protection of War Victims' produced a draft Article that proposed that the principles of the new

Geneva Conventions apply to civil wars, so long as the non-state parties to these conflicts applied the laws too. In 1948, the ICRC submitted a revised version of the Article to the 17th International Conference.[20] The Conference approved this text, with slight modifications,[21] and the modified text was proposed to the 1949 Diplomatic Conference.[22] A number of states there were opposed to the proposed Article, with competing views put forward as to if and when the laws should apply in NIACs. A committee vote revealed that delegations were largely in favour of extending the application of the conventions to NIACs, but were not in favour of the draft Article before them, preferring to delineate more clearly those NIACs to which the conventions would apply. After much debate, a new draft Article was created, adopted as 'Common Article 3' (CA3) by 34 votes to 12.[23]

CA3 has been referred to as a 'treaty in miniature'. This Article, repeated word for word in all four GCs, sets out the basic minimum protections applicable in NIACs.[24] It provides significantly fewer protections than are provided for in IACs. Importantly, while CA3 marked the first time the rules of IHL were explicitly applied to NIACs, this Article also entrenched the legal distinction between IACs and NIACs, with concepts like 'civil war' and 'domestic disturbance' being reconceptualised as 'non-international armed conflict'.[25]

Anti-colonial struggles were often not described as conflicts, as colonial powers did not wish to acknowledge them as anything other than internal unrest. The British characterisation of the Mau Mau uprising in Kenya was a clear example of this. Anti-colonial struggles were often characterised as law-enforcement operations, resulting in large-scale militarised operations that were not regulated as wars. The failure to recognise these as conflicts contributed to Africa's absence from the historic annals of armed conflict and to the Euro-centric leaning of the development of international law. Anti-colonial conflicts were, in fact, critical to the development of international law, serving as the means by which non-European states – previously seen to lack sovereignty – were conferred with sovereignty and included as active members of the international system.[26]

Colonial departures exposed ethnic, religious and tribal rivalries, setting the scenes for the conflicts that followed. Badly placed colonial borders split ethnic or tribal groups, while bringing together hostile groups into the same 'countries'. This provided the basis for national conflicts that would inevitably merge the international and internal, as ethnic groups supported fellow group members across national borders and enemy tribes within countries fought for domination, power or independence. In Sudan, for example, two culturally diverse groups were joined within the same country, under the domination of the Arab population of the North, leading to a 30-year independence-war by the South, followed by inter-ethnic power struggles in South Sudan once independence was gained.

During the latter half of the twentieth century there was a growing recognition of the right to self-determination[27] and of the right to assert this, using force where necessary. It began to be understood that where people *fought* for self-determination, this should be seen as more than just a domestic issue.[28] During the 1960s, the UN General Assembly passed two resolutions recognising the need for certain uniform basic rules to apply to all conflicts, regardless of their nature. Resolution 2444 (1968)[29] talked of the need to respect human rights in all armed conflicts, while Resolution 2675 (1970)[30] laid out basic principles for the protection of civilians in armed conflicts, emphasising that this referred to conflicts of all types. A growing international acceptance of the need for a more inclusive approach to the regulation of conflict became evident.[31]

Between 1974 and 1977, the 'Diplomatic Conference on the Reaffirmation and Development of International Humanitarian Law Applicable in Armed Conflicts' was held, which adopted the 1977 APs.[32] AP1 addressed IACs, expanding their meaning and scope and extending the categories of conflicts considered IAC in nature. Notably, it added to those conflicts considered IAC, conflicts in which people fought against colonial domination, alien occupation or racist regimes in the exercise of their right to self-determination (Art 1(4) AP1). During this process, diplomats tried to negotiate clarifications to CA3, eventually leading to AP2 being adopted, the first international treaty to exclusively address NIACs. The negotiations for AP2 were controversial, centring on two opposing positions: first, that from the point of view of victims of conflict, the distinction between IAC and NIAC was artificial and humanitarian protections should be applicable regardless of the conflict type; and second, that state sovereignty remained an important pillar of international law and hence international law should not regulate internal situations.[33] AP2 was the resulting compromise.

There have been other relevant developments in the years following the APs. New wars began to be fought. Neighbouring countries have fought proxy wars against each other, often supporting rebel groups operating on their neighbour's soil. Another development was the increase in international criminal tribunals, whose jurisprudence began to thresh out the divide between IACs and NIACs, considering how this divide plays out in certain new wars. Further development has occurred since the attacks of September 11th 2001, in the context of the 'war on terror'. Both the actions of international terrorists and the global efforts to counter these have created new types of conflicts, leading to questions about if and when these actions constitute 'armed conflict', and whether these would be IAC or NIAC in nature.[34] Contradictory views have been put forward about this, not least of all by the American government, whose controversial stance has been widely disputed. In recent years the legal spotlight has shifted to focusing on USA, rather than on Europe, as it used to in the past.

This history above has illustrated how understandings about the international and internal character of conflicts have continued to shift, both in society and in law. The law has responded to the circumstances of the time, progressively delineating the divide between IACs and NIACs in response to these.

Problems in the regulation of non-international armed conflicts

Unlike IACs, to which the four GCs and AP1 apply, in NIACs only CA3 and AP2 are applicable. NIACs therefore have less law, the applicable rules are less detailed and they are more limited in terms of the situations they apply to. However, in contrast to the minimal law available, the *need* for coherent regulation of NIACs is great. Today, the bulk of the world's wars are NIAC, or at least primarily so, a pattern that holds true in Africa. To give a sense of numbers, the Department of Peace and Conflict Research at Uppsala University has categorised all armed conflicts taking place since World War Two. Of the 225 conflicts fought between 1946 and 2001, they classified 163 as NIAC. Only 42 conflicts were classified IACs, while the remaining 21 were classified as 'extra-state' – conflicts where a state fights a non-state group operating from the territory of a third country, discussed later in this chapter.[35]

It is not only their prevalence that creates the need for coherent regulation of NIACs. It is also the nature of these conflicts and the evident violations of IHL that characterise them. NIACs frequently exhibit appalling levels of violence: Africa's civil wars have epitomised this – from the butchering of body and limb by rebel groups in Sierra Leone, to the land-scorching policies of Darfur, to the genocidal killings of Rwanda and Burundi. In internal conflicts, close-hand violence, inter-community fighting and a focus on identity politics also leads to high levels of sexual violence and to numerous threats to which women are vulnerable.

As the history above suggested, a main reason for the dearth of law in NIACs was states' reluctance to have international law hinder their ability to address threats within their countries.[36] Governments were also hesitant to grant legal status and rights to those within their countries who were fighting against them and feared that if internal conflicts were regulated, this would grant rebels legitimacy. Counteracting the notion that the application of IHL is always contrary to the interests of states, it can, in fact, be in states' interests to have IHL apply, with IHL in some ways allowing states greater power to act to curtail internal threats.[37] For one thing, where IHL is applicable, the principle of distinction applies, allowing states to kill those directly participating in hostilities. In the normal (non-conflict, non-IHL) course of events, killing is only permitted in exceptional circumstances; human rights law protects the right to life and every time a person is killed specific justification is required as to why that killing was necessary. In contrast, the principle of distinction allows states to kill with no need for justification other than the fact that they were directly participating in hostilities at the time they were targeted.[38] IHL therefore legalises killings that would otherwise be in violation of IHRL.[39] IHL is also advantageous to states when it comes to investigations. Normally, when people are killed by law enforcement actors, states are obliged in terms of IHRL to hold enquiries as to the circumstances of their deaths, with a failure to conduct an independent enquiry being a breach of a state's duty to protect the right to life. Where IHL applies, there is no duty to investigate each killing – rather, investigations are only required where there is evidence the killings were in violation of IHL.[40] A further reason states might want IHL to apply is for the principle of proportionality, which allows for a certain number of civilians to be killed as collateral damage. Outside of IHL no such allowance exists and states are not permitted to target objectives when they know civilians will also be killed.[41]

State interests aside, there are other reasons it is difficult to regulate NIACs. For one thing, NIACs are diverse, with conflicts ranging from those that are highly organised, to those that are scattered, unstructured and hardly discernible from criminal activities. There tend to be a wide range of actors involved in NIACs, who are all differently placed to comply with IHL – from highly organised armed groups with effective hierarchies, to disorganised bands of splintered factions that lack discipline or clear leadership structures. The small rival rebel groups operating locally in north-western Central African Republic (CAR) have little in common with a well-organised mass movement like South Sudan's SPLM, which, during the South Sudan liberation war, had training bases across the borders, international spokespersons and strict codes of conduct – and these groups' capacity and motives to comply with IHL differ significantly. These variances make it challenging to find one law suitable to regulating such diverse actors and situations. Attempts to paint them all with one brush-stroke can result in overly broad and ill-suited laws.[42] This is this same problem that makes the principle of distinction so challenging to formulate in NIACs – as hard as it is to regulate diverse armed actors, it is equally challenging to classify them into clear groupings that can neatly determine who is an appropriate target of attack or not.

There are also challenges around non-state actors' compliance with IHL. IHL was designed to be reciprocal, with parties being restricted in their actions by matching rules aimed at levelling the playing field. Kretzmer explains that,

> Like other branches of international law, LOAC[43] originally rested on assumptions of symmetry and reciprocity. Symmetry demands that the same rules apply to Parties on opposing sides of an armed conflict; reciprocity, that each Party's duty to respect these rules rests on reciprocal respect by the enemy.[44]

However, there is little reciprocity in the law when it comes to non-state actors. Different IHL rules apply to members of state and non-state groups, even where they are performing the same tasks.

In denying non-state actors combatancy privileges, states have created an uneven system of law. Problematically, the privileges they denied them are also the main motivators for compliance with IHL. What is left is a system where non-state actors are expected to comply with this law, yet receive few of the benefits of compliance. It is hardly surprising that they may not wish to abide by rules so clearly disadvantageous to them. Adding to this, the normal compliance mechanisms of international law, including state pressures, sanctions and incentives, do not necessarily function with non-state actors.[45] Compounding the problem is the fact that many non-state actors have little or no training in IHL[46] – often even less than the minimal levels provided to state combatants – and therefore have scant knowledge of the content of IHL. The ICRC has taken some steps towards encouraging IHL compliance by non-state actors; however, this remains a significant challenge.[47]

Women are extremely vulnerable to harm in NIACs, creating a great need for strong protective law. However, at this time when women are most in need of the law's protection, women are forced to rely on the scant law available in NIACs – which has fewer specific protections[48] and which so many parties fail to adhere to. Barrow aptly explains that,

> … the prevalence of non-international armed conflict challenges the foundations of international humanitarian law. Although this is a general dilemma, when considered in the light of gendered understandings of armed conflict, the challenges appear even more acute. Provisions are not sophisticated enough to respond to the complex intersection of gender, ethnicity and other aspects of identity, which may be all the more pertinent in non-international armed conflicts as nationality is not the dominant differentiation between parties.[49]

What are IACs and NIACs in terms of the law?

To apply the principle of distinction, one first needs to ascertain whether a conflict is an IAC or NIAC, as this determines which version of the principle applies. This section sets out how these categories are defined in IHL. Drawing on examples from new wars, it also illustrates the difficulties in applying these definitions in practice.

International armed conflicts

IAC refers to conflicts between states. Article 2, common to all four GCs, defines IACs by setting out the situations to which the GCs apply. It notes that,

> … the present Convention shall apply to all cases of declared war or of any other armed conflict which may arise between two or more of the High Contracting Parties, even if the state of war is not recognized by one of them.

The inclusion of the phrase "or any other armed conflict" in this Article was significant, as it negated the need for a *declaration* of war, or war-making *intention* on the parts of parties. Instead, the determination of whether armed conflict is taking place is a matter of fact, achieved when a threshold of violence has been reached.

AP1 applies in the same circumstances as the GCs (Art 1(3), AP1). However, in AP1, an additional type of conflict was added to those deemed IAC, albeit solely for the purpose of the application of AP1. Article 1(4) AP1 states, "The situations referred to in the preceding paragraph include armed conflicts in which peoples are fighting against colonial domination and alien occupation and against racist regimes in the exercise of their right of self-determination …". The application of this additional category is far from straightforward. Not all conflicts where people fight for self-determination meet the criterion in this clause – only those where they are fighting against the three above-mentioned categories of domination. If a conflict is fought to assert the right to self-determination against a regime that is not colonial, alien occupation or a racist regime, then AP1 will not apply. The tricky question is: how do you distinguish struggles for self-determination that qualify in terms of Art 1(4) from those that do not? The terms in Art 1(4) are broad, they are not defined in legal terms and no clear guidance is provided on their application.[50] Does colonialism refer only to European rule, or does it also refer to domination by African powers? Consider South Sudan – would the SPLA's fight for liberation from Sudan qualify? Was Sudan's rule over South Sudan colonial, alien or racist? Arguments could certainly be made that it was, although these arguments are not obviously convincing.

Things become more complicated when there is more than one 'liberation movement' involved in a struggle. Crawford explains that, "The Protocol contains no system for determining which liberation movement can be considered the 'legitimate' representative of those seeking self-determination".[51] Some argue that for AP1 to apply, those fighting on behalf of a population must be *recognised* as representing a people as their liberation movement – hence requiring a collective recognition by states or regional organisations. There is mixed opinion as to whether this is, in fact, a legal requirement.[52] When different 'liberation movements' fight each other, AP1 does not apply to this.[53] Revisiting the South Sudan example, what should be made of the fact that at one point the SPLA split into competing factions who fought each other? Would this affect their status as a liberation movement for the applicability of AP1? The answers to these questions are unclear. One cannot draw on state practice to clarify the requirements, as the self-determination scenario envisaged in Art 1(4) has never been formally recognised – often because the states concerned in such incidents have not ratified AP1.[54]

Another factor that complicates things is state succession. W*hen* a territory becomes, or declares itself to be, an independent state can affect whether a conflict is IAC or NIAC. If independence was declared before the outbreak of war, this could support the finding that a conflict is IAC. Such was the case in Bosnia, which declared independence from Yugoslavia in 1992 on the eve of the outbreak of war, meaning it was arguably already a separate country when fighting broke out. On the other hand, if a party declares itself an independent state following conflict, the conflict would be NIAC, only taking on a two-state character following the termination of hostilities and the resultant declaration of independence. This was the case in South Sudan, which only declared independence from Sudan in 2011, following a referendum six years after the official ending of hostilities. But this in itself raises further questions; most critically, when does an entity become an independent state? Is the pivotal moment the declaration of independence? Or is recognition of this declaration by other states required? Or is it the achievement of the factual requirements of statehood that is important?[55] In turn, the question of whether a conflict is IAC or NIAC has significance for state succession – whom a conflict was fought between determines who may take power after the conflict and who the parties to a peace agreement might be.

In the ICTY's *Tadić* decision, the Appeals Chamber considered the definition of IACs, elaborating on those situations that would qualify as such. Duško Tadić, a Bosnian Serb former member of the paramilitary forces and a leader of the Serb Democratic Party, was indicted for his participation in attacks on, and murder and mistreatment of Bosnian Muslims and Croats in the Prijedor municipality of Bosnia Herzegovina. In order for ICL's 'grave breaches' regime to apply pursuant to Article 2 of the Rome Statute, the crimes in question needed to have been committed in the context of an IAC, meaning the Chamber needed to determine whether Tadić was acting in an IAC or not. The Appeals Chamber held that a conflict is an IAC if it is fought between two or more states. An internal conflict taking place within the territory of one state can become international if the military forces of another state intervene, or if some of the participants to the internal conflict act 'on behalf of' another state. This refers to NIACs that have been 'internationalised', discussed below. The Chamber held that an IAC can exist concurrently with a NIAC in particular circumstances.[56]

Non-international armed conflicts

NIACs are conflicts in which at least one of the parties is not a state. These can include conflicts between a state and a non-state entity, or conflicts between two non-state entities. GC, CA3 lays down rules that apply in "armed conflict not of an international character occurring in the territory of one of the High Contracting Parties". CA3 does not define "conflict not of an international character", nor does it elaborate on the types of situations it was envisaged this Article would apply to. While some argue that this definitional omission was a mistake, others contend that this was deliberate, to allow future conflicts of types unanticipated by the drafters to fit within a relatively unrestrictive phrase.[57]

There are some clues in the law as to the meaning of the phrase. The use of a negative formulation is notable, revealing that a NIAC is that which does not qualify as IAC. During the various amendment stages leading to the GCs, a list was developed that was included in the Commentaries, which gives indication of the types of situations the drafters anticipated would be covered by CA3. In this list were included factors such as that a non-state party in a covered conflict must have an organised military force, an authority responsible for its acts, must act within a determinate territory and must have the means of respecting IHL. They must also have territory on which they have de facto control as a civil authority. In addition, the government must have recognised the party as insurgents or belligerents.[58] The Commentaries noted that,

> … the conflicts referred to in Article 3 are armed conflicts, with armed forces on either side engaged in hostilities–conflicts, in short, which are in many respects similar to an international war, but take place within the confines of a single country.[59]

AP2, too, does not define NIACs. It does, however, limit the scope of those NIACs that AP2 applies to. Article 1(1), AP2 states that the Protocol shall apply to all armed conflicts *not* covered by AP1,

> … which take place in the territory of a High Contracting Party between its armed forces and dissident armed forces or other organized armed groups which, under responsible command, exercise such control over a part of its territory as to enable them to carry out sustained and concerted military operations and to implement this Protocol.

AP2's application is therefore limited by a number of qualifiers, which also render AP2 only applicable in situations that in many ways resemble IACs.

The satisfaction of these qualifiers can be difficult to ascertain, as these might shift over the course of a conflict. In civil wars, territory is frequently lost and retaken. An armed group might have the ability to apply AP2 at one point, but lose it later for operational reasons if they are weakened and shrunken by fighting. As such, during the course of a single conflict, there might be different conclusions as to whether AP2 applies or not.[60] In new wars, the requirement of territorial control can be particularly limiting, as controlling territory is less central to the conflict endeavour than it was in old wars. Armed groups do not seek to control territory, and when towns are occupied, this is often done temporarily, in order to rest, restock, pillage and move on, rather than with any aim of holding onto control. There are, of course, exceptions to this, with some groups still seeking to control territory – consider Boko Haram's brief occupation of towns in northern Nigeria, declaring them part of its self-declared caliphate – illustrating the inherent inconsistency of new wars.

There are other limitations too; AP2 does not apply to conflicts *between* non-state groups. It requires a state to be one of the parties – a significant excluding factor in African conflicts, where rebel groups frequently fight each other. So too, when there are 'side-conflicts' within a civil war, when armed groups fight each other at the same time as a conflict is fought against a state – common in new wars – these side-conflicts do not count as part of the NIAC to which AP2 applies.[61] Practically, this means that certain parts of fighting activities will be regulated by AP2, while other parts will remain unregulated. Another excluded situation is where there is no recognised government, but rather different groups vying for control of a government, such as in Somalia (at certain times between 1991 and the present) and Angola (1961–1974).[62] It bears repeating that AP2 does not apply to certain wars of national liberation that are rendered IAC for the purposes of applying AP1. AP2 therefore does not apply to a large segment of the internal conflicts taking place today. As well as the numerous substantive limitations, AP2 only applies in countries that have ratified it, further limiting its reach. Importantly, where AP2 does not apply – for substantive or ratification reasons – CA3 might still apply, as its threshold is lower than AP2's.

Both CA3 and AP2 state that a conflict must "take place in the territory of a High Contracting Party". There is some debate about whether NIACs actually need to take place *within* the territory of a single state for CA3 or to AP2 apply. Some contend that NIACs are those conflicts in which at least one of the parties is not a state, regardless of where they occur. This was the position the United States Supreme Court took in *Hamdan* v. *Rumsfeld*,[63] when it accepted as its definition of NIACs, all conflicts *not* fought between two state parties. In this way it included the global 'war on terror' within its understanding of NIAC. This approach has been highly controversial. Dinstein argues that, "… the idea that a NIAC can be global in nature is oxymoronic: an armed conflict can be a NIAC and it can be global, but it cannot be both".[64] The ICRC has taken a pragmatic approach to this, arguing that since the GCs have been almost universally ratified, this makes their territoriality criteria irrelevant, leaving the relevant factor to be the status of the participants rather than the conflict's geographic location.[65] There is no consensus on this point. However, depending on the approach taken, if conflicts not within the territory of a single state are omitted, then many of Africa's new wars would be excluded from the reach of IHL, as these often overflow beyond the territory of a single state. As an example, since the LRA fled Uganda around 2006, the Ugandan government's fight with the LRA spread into South Sudan, CAR and DRC. While this fight is clearly not an IAC, imposing the territoriality requirement would render CA3 and AP2 non-applicable. This is the central issue in the debate on transnational conflicts, discussed later in this chapter.

As the above illustrates, IACs and NIACs can occur simultaneously within the same country, and NIACs regulated by IHL can take place alongside NIACs that are unregulated. This can lead to a complicated web, where different laws apply to different facets of larger conflict situations. All of this is further complicated by the requirement that violence needs to reach a certain threshold in order for IHL to apply.

The threshold of violence

In both IACs and NIACs, the trigger for IHL to apply is the existence of an 'armed conflict'. Violence that does reach this level is not regulated by IHL. The problem is that the term 'armed conflict' is not defined in IHL and there is little clarity as to the level of violence that constitutes the lower threshold of this term. Sassoli explains that,

> As for the lower threshold of an armed conflict, no clear-cut criteria exist, but relevant factors include: intensity; number of active participants; number of victims; duration and protracted character of the violence; organization and discipline of the parties; capability to respect IHL; collective, open, and coordinated character of the hostilities; direct involvement of governmental armed forces (vs. law enforcement agencies); and de facto authority by the non-State actor over potential victims.[66]

Whether a situation constitutes 'armed conflict' is influenced by whether it is IAC or NIAC. Even minor uses of force between states tend to be considered armed conflict for the purposes of rendering IHL applicable. The threshold is higher in internal situations, where fighting must reach a greater level of intensity to constitute armed conflict.[67] In *Tadic*, the ICTY Appeals Chamber held that an armed conflict exists, "whenever there is a resort to armed force between states or protracted armed violence between governmental authorities and organized armed groups or between such groups within a state".[68] Sassoli argues that 'protracted nature' is a problematic requirement as at the outset of hostilities one cannot know how long a conflict will last. It is hard to accept that IHL would not be applicable at the start of a conflict but would only become applicable once a conflict became protracted.[69] A different approach proposed is that for internal violence to become armed conflict depends on the motives of the armed group involved; to qualify, armed groups need to fight for a political cause, hence excluding criminal gangs from being seen as parties to NIACs. Opponents argue that this requirement has no basis in IHL.[70,71]

IHL does not apply to internal tensions, strikes, demonstration, riots, criminal activities, or sporadic or isolated acts of violence – occurrences that do not reach the level of armed conflict. This is even the case where the military is used to deal with these.[72] However, what one often finds in Africa's new wars are long-term, low-level situations, which flare up in sporadic bouts, which taken on their own would not meet the threshold of violence. This means IHL would not be applicable, despite the high levels of inter-personal violence present in these. New wars highlight the tricky continuum between war and peace. They often do not constitute a singular major event leading to defined results, but rather they linger. In fact, keeping them lingering might be exactly what armed actors are working towards. This can make IHL's threshold approach extremely difficult to apply in these cases.

Gender activists mirror the view that conflicts are not events that start and stop once they reach certain thresholds. Cockburn explains that gender organisations,

> … tend to see 'war' not just as spasms of war-fighting, but as part of a continuum leading from militarism (as a persisting mindset, expressed in philosophy, newspaper editorials, political think tanks), through militarization (processes in economy and society that signify preparation for war), to episodes of 'hot' war, and thence to cease fire and stand-off, followed perhaps by an unsteady peace with sustained military investment, beset by sporadic violence that prefigures a further round in the spiral.[73]

The threshold system disregards the fluid nature of conflict, attempting to pinpoint unrealistic start and end moments. Most importantly, this disregards the fact that dangers to civilians, and to women in particular, precede the threshold points and continue well after them – and that IHL's protective laws are needed during those times too.

Determining if and when a situation has passed the threshold and constitutes armed conflict can be difficult in practice. Different indicators often point to contradictory conclusions. The 2011 Egyptian revolution was restricted mainly to violent incidents and protests and did not appear to reach the level of full-blown armed conflict. However, during these incidents, upwards of 846 people were killed in clashes between security forces and protesters.[74] The protest movement was coordinated, attained mass involvement and ultimately led to an overthrow of the country's leadership – features indicative of armed conflict. It is unclear what number of deaths, or what types of events, would have been required to render this an armed conflict. In Libya, similar protests did ignite into armed conflict when, in February 2011 in Benghazi, protesters clashed with security forces who fired into the crowd. The protests grew into a rebellion that soon spread across the country. Johnston points out that in Libya, an internal uprising developed into a NIAC, which was later transformed into an IAC by foreign intervention, before later being 're-internalised' to a NIAC by the international recognition of the National Transitional Council as Libya's legitimate government.[75]

The determination of whether a situation is armed conflict is frequently used as a political tool rather than a legal determination. There are political reasons for states wanting to acknowledge or not acknowledge situations as being armed conflicts. This has been clearly demonstrated by the Security Council's inconsistent referrals to 'armed conflict' in its Resolutions. Sometimes the SC effectively makes a determination that a situation has crossed the threshold, by referring to IHL's applicability in that situation – in effect labelling a situation as armed conflict without expressly saying this. As early as March 2011, SC Resolutions on Libya talked about compliance with IHL – probably because Ghadaffi did not have strong supporters on the SC who could influence it not to do so. In contrast, SC Resolutions on Syria did not mention armed conflict or IHL – rather being restricted to describing 'troop movements', 'military concentrations' and other actions associated with conflict. Resolutions on Syria mentioned violations of human rights, but not of IHL. This was a result of Russia's refusal to allow the situation to be labelled armed conflict. The politicised use of this determination is highly problematic, demonstrating how in this area political considerations are frequently given more value than the wording of the law.

The failure to deem IHL applicable to certain armed situations means civilians in these do not benefit from the protections purposefully created for civilians in hostile situations. Although this book argues that IHL's protections for women are inadequate, these still offer better protection than the alternatives, which are a reliance on domestic law and human rights law to regulate hostile actions – discussed in the conclusion chapter. When disturbances reach the IHL threshold, this also brings increased international scrutiny to the way governments act, which can also have protective effects for civilians.

A converse argument can also be made. A major critique of the new wars theory is that new wars are not real wars. Where politics is absent from armed actor's motives, these wars can more closely resemble banditry or piracy. It bears asking whether it would be preferable to declare new wars as crimes and to deal with them as such, rather than as wars or armed conflicts. It could be argued that their categorisation as 'war' merely serves to legitimate criminal activity.

It is worth mentioning another category, which, while not falling within the threshold of 'armed conflict', frequently overlaps with it. The legal regime pertaining to 'genocide' and the IHL 'armed conflict' regime, anticipate a complete separation between these phenomena. However, this separation is a fiction – in reality armed conflict and genocide often occur together or are intrinsically linked, making this another legal categorisation where the law and the reality do not correlate. Of course, there are reasons for this legal separation; one does not assume that regular armed forces, those whom IHL is directed at regulating, will commit genocide. Genocide can never be justified in *jus ad bello* and as such there is no reason for IHL to regulate it.

The above sections have demonstrated that the legal classifications of IACs and NIACs are far from straightforward. However, despite the difficulties, these demarcations remain critical, determining which law applies and revealing the boundaries at the ends of each category – when a situation is an IAC as opposed to a NIAC, and when it is a NIAC as opposed a more minor disturbance. As complex as this is in theory, it becomes even more difficult when applied to real situations on the ground.

Distinguishing IACs and NIACs in practice

Conflicts in Africa spill over borders. Border crossings happen at all levels – from the 'top' political levels, with the intervention of foreign leaders into neighbouring countries, all the way to the very 'local' level. Cross-border actions at some of these levels are well documented. Charles Taylor, former president of Liberia, was tried by the Special Court for Sierra Leone for actions he committed in Liberia that fuelled Sierra Leone's war.[76] Jean-Pierre Bemba Gombo, a politician from DRC, was tried by the ICC for crimes he committed in CAR. Court records in these cases describe armed groups conducting incursions into neighbouring countries, and travelling across borders to secure weapons and other resources required to fuel their efforts.

Something that garners less international attention is how borders are crossed at the 'local' level during hostilities. Women form an integral part of this, crossing borders as refugees, for trade, for subsistence and for survival – creating a less visible international element to largely internal conflicts. Small-scale cross-border trade can be a key survival mechanism during conflict, one that is largely taken up by women. Women have greater success in wartime cross-border trading, as men struggle to cross borders, more likely to be suspected of rebel involvement. A study in Africa's Great Lakes region found that 74 per cent of traders along four conflict-riddled borders were women.[77] The same was the case along the Sierra Leone/Liberian border during their civil wars.[78] Cross-border trade is difficult work, with women travelling long distances carrying heavy loads. As with many other roles that women play in conflict, the women who take part are stigmatised:

> … the fact that they leave the house early, return home late, are away from their husbands and must speak on friendly terms with the border authorities and

> others (to ensure their goods cross the border at the lowest possible cost) is considered to be morally "bad"; they are often considered as "free women".[79]

Female traders are vulnerable to sexual harassment and exploitation, often by border officials, with common reports of women being made to pay for border crossing favours with sex.[80]

This 'local' level movement – and particularly that of women – is lost in assessments of whether situations are IAC or NIAC, playing no part in influencing how conflicts are classified. When women cross borders in sustaining their day-to-day lives, or even in helping armed groups, there is little talk of this 'internationalising' conflicts. Yet, thinking about the IAC/NIAC divide from the perspective of grassroots behaviour is important. Considering how women behave along borders provides a more accurate picture of the real international or internal nature of a conflict – a view that this divide in the law entirely misses out on. Considering women's cross-border behaviour once again reveals how blunt the law's lines are, and how IHL's IAC/NIAC divide provides an incomplete sense of the nature of a situation.

The sections below will examine some problem categories that exhibit features dominant in new wars, which demonstrate the challenges with labelling conflicts as either IACs or NIACs.

Internationalised conflicts

An 'internationalised' conflict occurs when a foreign state(s) intervenes in what was a NIAC, 'internationalising' it – or rendering it an IAC for the purpose of the application of IHL. Internationalising can take many forms. It can occur when a foreign state sends troops to support one side of a NIAC; it can take the form of a foreign government providing *indirect* support from a distance; and it can take the form of fighting between second and third countries intervening on both sides to a NIAC.[81]

In all domestic conflicts today there tends to be some level of international involvement – even if just at the level of rhetoric, SC Resolutions, or the presence of peacekeepers or humanitarian actors. However a certain level of international involvement must be reached before a conflict can be said to be 'internationalised'.

Different approaches have been put forward as to how the law should deal with internationalised conflicts. The 'fragmented approach' holds that where there are both international and non-international elements to a conflict, depending who the parties are to each particular interaction, different laws will apply. As such, the rules of IAC and NIAC can apply at different times within the same greater conflict.[82] The fragmented approach leads to some practical problems in trying to ascertain what law applies when. Vite illustrates some of the difficult questions that can arise:

> What status needs to be given to civilians taken captive by foreign forces and then handed over to the local group? … does a different set of rules

> need to be applied depending on whether those persons were arrested by the foreign forces or directly by the local group?[83]

Such issues have arisen in Afghanistan's current conflict.[84]

A different approach is that where a foreign state intervenes on behalf of one of the parties to a NIAC, then IAC laws become applicable to the entire conflict. This was the approach proposed by the ICRC in a 1971 report to the 'Conference of Government Experts on the Reaffirmation and Development of International Humanitarian Law Applicable in Armed Conflicts', which read:

> When, in case of non-international armed conflict, one or the other party, or both, benefits from the assistance of operational armed forces afforded by a third State, the parties to the conflict shall apply the whole of the international humanitarian law applicable in international armed conflicts.[85]

This proposal was rejected by the Conference, as governments feared this would encourage civil war parties to seek foreign intervention, in order that IAC rules and protections would apply.[86]

The international criminal tribunals have looked at internationalised conflicts, with the ICTY in particular pondering the question of which body of law to apply to internationalised situations. In the *Tadic* Appeals Chamber, the majority recognised the clashes between Bosnian government forces and Bosnian Serbs and Croatian rebels as being NIAC, unless 'direct involvement' of the Federal Republic of Yugoslavia could be shown. The court held that the Yugoslavian conflict had both international and non-international aspects.[87] In contrast, in the *Mladic* Indictment it was noted that sufficient evidence of direct involvement would render the conflict IAC, and once a conflict was internationalised in this way, IAC laws would apply until the cessation of hostilities.[88] In *Celebici* the Trial Chamber held that if a conflict was found to be international, then "the relevant norms of international humanitarian law apply throughout its territory until the general cessation of hostilities, unless it can be shown that the conflicts in some areas were separate internal conflicts unrelated to the larger international armed conflict".[89]

The ICTY developed a number of tests aimed at determining whether there was sufficient foreign involvement to render a conflict international. The tribunal adopted the test for state responsibility developed by the ICJ in *Nicaragua.*[90] The majority in the *Tadic* Trial Chamber held that in terms of *Nicaragua*, there needed to be a relationship of 'dependence and control' between a foreign state and paramilitaries for them to be considered organs of that state. The relationship needed to be strong enough that the rebel's acts could be imputed to that state. In the *Rajic* Indictment,[91] the court debated the quantum of involvement necessary to render a conflict IAC. The court considered the *Nicaragua* dependence and control test, but held that a more appropriate test was that of "general political and military control". Finally, the *Tadic* Appeals Chamber developed the test of "overall control", recognising that the degree of control required varies according to the circumstances of the case, and differs between private individuals and those in organised groups.

In *The Application of the Convention on the Prevention and Punishment of the Crime of Genocide (Bosnia and Herzegovina* v. *Serbia and Montenegro)*, the ICJ disagreed that the tests for internationalisation and state responsibility need be the same. It held that,

> … logic does not require the same test to be adopted in resolving the two issues, which are very different in nature: the degree and nature of a State's involvement in an armed conflict on another State's territory which is required for the conflict to be characterized as international, can very well, and without logical inconsistency, differ from the degree and nature of involvement required to give rise to that State's responsibility for a specific act committed in the course of the conflict.[92]

The ICJ did not agree with *Tadic*'s 'overall control' test, as it felt it broadened the scope of state responsibility beyond the fundamental principles governing the law of international responsibility. The ICJ would not comment on the test's suitability for establishing internationalising, as this was not in issue in that case.

The dominant view is that a conflict does not become an IAC if a government has invited a foreign army to assist it in fighting a NIAC within its country.[93] However, not all agree with this position. Byron contends that once a civil war is taking place, the argument can be made that a government no longer has competent authority under international law to invite another state to assist, as it is no longer the legitimate authority.[94] This came into issue in 2011 when an intervention force, the Gulf Coordination Council, helped crush protests by Shi'ite Muslims in Bahrain. Bahrain's Sunni government had requested the force to intervene, in line with a defence pact with the Council. The force's largest contingent came from Saudi Arabia, which was worried about the spill-over these protests might have on its own Shi'ite population in the oil-rich eastern part of its country. Opposition groups alleged that this foreign intervention was an international act of war.

International forces or peacekeepers are frequently placed in situations to maintain peace, rather than to fight. Such forces do not have the stated aim of supporting either party to a conflict and do not have a mandate to use force, other than in self-defence or in protection of civilians. As such, the mere *presence* of these forces does not automatically make them *parties* to a conflict – and does not automatically render a situation international.[95] Such international forces can become 'parties' in two situations. The first is if they act in support of one of the parties to a conflict. For example, in 2012, United Nations Organization Stabilization Mission in the Democratic Republic of the Congo (MONUSCO) provided military support to the Congolese government to repel an offense south of Kibumba by rebel group M23, rendering them a party to hostilities. Similarly, the African Union's mission in Somalia has aimed to bolster Somalia's government in its fight against Al-Shabaab. Second, even if a force is not supporting one of the parties, the status of the force will be determined using the criteria normally used to evaluate the existence of NIACs. As such they will be considered 'parties' if their involvement reaches the required level of intensity. Where international forces do qualify as parties to a conflict, most would argue that their involvement renders a conflict IAC, even if the fight in which they become involved is a fight against a non-state armed group. The ICRC take the opposite view, arguing that whether a conflict will be rendered IAC or NIAC depends on who the international force is fighting against.[96]

As IHL only recognises conflicts as IACs or NIACs, 'internationalising' is a way of bringing conflicts that have features of both within IHL's classification. This legal approach does not challenge the categories in the law, but rather, finds a way to frame situations to fit within the law's existing demarcations. In contrast, 'transnational conflicts', discussed in the section that follows, do not fit within IHL's categories, nor do they purport to do so. Transnational conflicts are a non-legal category, or a lens outside of IHL's confines – hence challenging the law's existing categorisations.

Transnational conflicts

Transnational conflicts are not IAC, in that they are not fought between two state parties; yet they are not NIAC, as they take place beyond the boundaries of just one state. Transnational conflicts can take various forms: they can be fought between a state and a non-state armed group, or between different non-state armed groups. The defining feature is that they transcend national borders. As noted above in terms of CA3 and AP2, for the NIAC laws to be applicable, a conflict has to take place "within the territory of a single state". This leads to question about how to classify these situations.

Different types of transnational conflicts bring up distinct legal issues. 'Exported NIACs' (or 'delocalised conflicts' or 'extraterritorial NIACs') occur when parties to a NIAC carry their fighting over onto the territory of a second state with the consent of that second government, be it explicit or tacit. While in terms of the parties involved (government fighting a non-state armed group) this is a standard NIAC, from a territorial perspective there is internationalising.[97] As an example, during the height of Uganda's conflict against the LRA, Ugandan troops went on the offensive, chasing the LRA over the border into South Sudan – from where the LRA continued its attacks into Uganda. A second type is 'cross-border NIACs'. Here state forces conflict with a non-state armed group operating on the territory of another state. This is not a spillover from their own NIAC, but an entirely different conflict.[98] Of course, if that armed group 'belongs to' the state on whose land it is fighting, this would render it IAC. But where this is not the case the legal classification becomes more difficult.

There is disagreement on how the law should deal with transnational conflicts. Some argue that these are an altogether new category of conflict that cannot be accommodated by the IAC/NIAC divide. Some propose that a third legal category should therefore be created, distinct from IACs and NIACs.[99]

Others argue that transnational conflicts are not really armed conflicts, and as such other bodies of law, including IHRL, should be used to regulate them.[100] A different school contends that current laws can, in fact, be interpreted to allow transnational conflicts to fall within existing categorisations. One means (favoured by the ICRC) is to argue that the requirement that NIACs take place *within* the territory of one state is not actually a legal requirement – in which case if a state is engaged in conflict with a non-state armed group, this will qualify as NIAC regardless of the fact that they are operating across an international border.[101]

It is entirely likely that in 1949, with the drafting of the GCs, the territorial rider was not created with the purpose of excluding transnational conflicts. Such conflicts were not common at that point and as such, were not a concern of those negotiating the provisions. However, in the post September 11th 2001 period these conflicts have risen prominently on the international agenda – in part because of international terrorism.

International terrorism

> If the US war on terror is the 'father of all wars', Africa's conflicts are his angry and rebellious offspring, sharing the same disrespect for borders and the close connections to private profiteering. Open conflict is only the surface eruption of much deeper-seated contradictions, vivid ulcers on the skin of an unhealthy body politic governed by a militarist mindset.[102]

Much debate on transnational conflict has taken place around the 'war on terror'. Immediately following the September 11th 2001 World Trade Centre attacks, the US administration asserted that the fight against Al-Qaeda was not an IAC, but was also not covered by CA3 (America is not signatory to AP2, so this law did not apply), hence leaving a gap in regulation – meaning that actions could be taken that were not restricted by IHL (although other bodies of law like IHRL were still arguably applicable). In 2006, the US Supreme Court in *Hamdan* v. *Rumsfeld* took a different approach. It held that the fight against Al-Qaeda was a NIAC, falling under the ambit of CA3, despite the fact that it was not taking place within any one country – with the Court thereby abandoning CA3's territorial rider.[103] Since then, and highly controversially, the US has used the fact that its fight against Al-Qaeda has been categorised NIAC as a means to deny POW status to opponents, who they label 'unlawful combatants', another controversial interpretation. The Obama administration retained this approach, albeit with minor changes. The US approach has been heavily criticised, not only for its questionable legal foundations, but also for the practical problems it presents. Even those within the administration have acknowledged the problems with using the NIAC framework to regulate the 'war on terror'. For example, talking about detention, Bellinger, the former US legal advisor to the Bush administration, conceded that, "Common Article 3, while containing important baseline protections, does not provide a comprehensive set of rules to govern detention of combatants in non-international armed conflict".[104]

The pertinent question is whether either of the categories – IAC or NIAC – are appropriate to regulate the fight against terror, or whether it is appropriate to apply IHL to terrorism at all. Sassoli explains:

> It is uncontroversial to state that international terrorism represents a considerable challenge to the international community and that international law must meet this challenge. What is controversial is whether this challenge must, or at least may, be met by classifying terrorism as 'war' – or, in the terminology of contemporary international law, as 'armed conflict'. … The result – or, for some, the aim – of such a classification as an armed conflict would be the application of the law of armed conflict.…[105]

Merely branding the fight against terror as the 'war on terror' does not render it armed conflict. Individual components of this overall fight would need to qualify as armed conflicts in order for IHL to apply to them. When particular terrorist actions or counterterror measures reach the threshold of violence where they qualify as armed conflict, IHL will apply to these. Terrorism and the 'war on terror' must therefore be divided into different components. To some of these, IAC laws will apply; to some NIAC laws; while to many situations IHL will not be applicable at all.[106]

The problem is that in practice these components are not so easily separable. Terrorism and insurgency today have become entangled, with terrorist acts often part of or linked to broader armed conflicts.[107] It has become more difficult to identify differences between 'organised armed groups', which are regulated by IHL, and 'terror groups'.[108] This speaks to the challenges of determining to which acts respective parts of IHL might apply. Terrorism and counterterror is an area where the blurring lines between IACs, NIACs and 'non-conflicts' become evident. The consequences of such uncertainty can be significant, with confusion in law creating gaps where there is little consensus about what regulation – if any – should apply. Such gaps are used as justification for legally dubious acts, adding further lawlessness to already troubled situations.

The merging of the laws of IAC and NIAC

In recent years there has been a move towards extending the more comprehensive body of law applicable to IACs, to NIACs, or at least towards reducing the substantive differences between the rules applying to each. This move has occurred through a number of means, including through the jurisprudence of the ICL tribunals and developments in IHRL. This move has also been evident in the development of CIL.

When considering this, it is important to acknowledge the institutions that shape international law and to consider their roles and agendas. The ICTY in *Tadic* had an interest in interpreting IACs and NIACs in the way it did, as doing so allowed it to deal with the matters before it. Those working with human rights treaties have an interest in broadening their application to provide the most comprehensive coverage to the most people. Even CIL's developments are interpreted through a particular lens; the ICRC, which compiled a treatise on customary IHL, had an interest in arguing that many of the laws pertaining to IACs also pertained to NIACs, as this furthered its humanitarian goals.

Customary international humanitarian law

In terms of CIL, as demonstrated through state practice and *opinio juris*, many of the laws that in the IHL treaties pertained only to IACs, are now also applicable in NIACs, having attained the status of CIL for NIACs too. If treaty provisions become CIL, they become binding even on parties who are not signatories to the treaties.[109,110]

In 2005, the ICRC produced a study laying out those rules that they believe to be customary IHL.[111] The study concluded that 131 out of the 161 rules identified as customary IHL (almost 81 per cent of the rules) were applicable to both IACs and NIACs. Crawford explains,

> … the study suggests that, where gaps exist in Protocol II … state practice has filled in these gaps, creating rules that are parallel to those contained in Protocol I.… The overarching finding of the ICRC study is that there is a more uniform approach to the regulation of conduct in all armed conflict than had been previously thought.[112]

While many regard this study as being a good indication of the current state of CIL, this has been contested by some – among other things, because it reflects the view of the ICRC but does not reflect reservations of states, commentators and academics.[113]

International courts have also confirmed this development in customary IHL. In 1986, the ICJ affirmed that the provisions of CA3 now reflect CIL.[114] In *Tadic* the ICTY discussed the idea that CIL has extended the law to further cover NIACs, with the tribunal explaining that the emergence of rules governing internal conflict had happened at two levels; treaty law and customary law – with these two bodies mutually supporting and supplementing each other. The tribunal confirmed that as a result of the interplay between these two sets of rules, some treaty rules have gradually become part of CIL.[115]

International criminal law

The international criminal tribunals have played a key role in bringing the IAC and NIAC laws closer together. In the *Tadic* Interlocutory Appeal decision, the ICTY illustrated the means by which these bodies of law were merging, and how the increased regulation of NIACs was occurring through treaties, CIL, state practice, declarations and resolutions. However, the tribunal cautioned that despite this increased merging, the legal distinction between IACs and NIACs remains and there are limits to the extent that the laws governing IACs apply to NIACs. The tribunal noted that,

> Two particular limitations may be noted: (i) only a number of rules and principles governing IACs have gradually been extended to apply to internal conflicts; and (ii) this extension has not taken place in the form of a full and mechanical transplant of those rules to internal conflicts; rather, the general essence of those rules, and not the detailed regulation they may contain, has become applicable to internal conflicts.[116]

Some have been critical of the ICTY's approach. Schmitt notes that,

> Unfortunately, the distinction between "law-finding" and "law-making" has occasionally been blurred … the tribunal's incorporation of such rules neglects the fact that, for reasons outlined above, states, the sole "law-makers in international law" have intentionally crafted a far narrower legal regime for non-international armed conflicts.[117]

The ICC's Rome Statute has also played a role in bringing these bodies of law closer. In Article 8(2)(c) and (e) it explicitly identified those crimes that apply in NIACs. When doing so, it took many of the crimes that had previously only applied to IACs and rendered them applicable to NIACs for the purposes of that law. This being said, the Rome Statute, too, retained the legal divide between IACs and NIACs, still reserving some crimes for IACs and others for NIACs.

International human rights law

IHRL and IHL operate simultaneously in conflicts and are complementary legal regimes. When both apply to a particular matter, IHL is *lex specialis*, meaning that as the more specific body regulating the situation, it takes precedence.[118] IHRL fills in some of the substantive gaps in IHL's regulation of NIACs by guaranteeing at least a certain level of protection to those in NIACs. It guarantees people's human rights and ensures certain safeguards, including procedural safeguards in the case of violations. Some of the protections provided by IHRL are similar to those provided by IHL in IACs.

The two bodies of law developed in parallel following World War Two. Around that time, there began a move, described above, towards some IHL rules being applied in NIACs. The second development was the formation of IHRL, concerned with the ways states treated their citizens. IHRL began to break down the firm shield that state sovereignty had held against international law regulating internal matters.[119] While these developments worked in the same direction,

> they advanced on parallel tracks; different personalities were involved in the projects of IHL and IHRL and represented different State interests. In

> drafting the treaties in the two fields, no serious consideration was given to the relationship between the two branches of law, IHL and IHRL.[120]

Today, there is a great deal of discussion about the interrelationship between these bodies of law,[121] yet there remain numerous unresolved issues about how these bodies work together in practice.[122]

There are problems with relying too heavily on IHRL to regulate NIACs. One problem is that IHRL does not create the same obligations on non-state actors as on states. While IHRL does seem to be moving further in the direction of binding non-state actors, its primary focus remains the regulation of states.[123] Another problem is that certain parts of IHRL can be derogated from in times of conflict.[124] In addition, as Watkin explains,

> … international humanitarian law differs from human rights law in its requirement to interface with "military necessity". At the heart of military necessity is the goal of the submission of the enemy at the earliest possible moment with the least possible expenditure of personnel and resources.… In balancing these two concepts the requirement to distinguish between those who can participate in armed conflict and those who are to be protected from its dangers is perhaps its most fundamental tenet.[125]

With its differing set of priorities IHRL is ill equipped to manage this difficult balance.

Should the IAC/NIAC divide be retained?

The above sections have demonstrated how IACs and NIACs are beginning to merge both factually and in terms of the laws applicable to them. This merging, the many problems with the IAC/NIAC divide, and the evident problems with the regulation of NIACs have led some to question whether the IAC/NIAC divide should be removed and a uniform law applied to all armed conflicts.

There are some who support this divide. Its key value, they argue, derives from the fact that IACs and NIACs are inherently different. For one thing, the relationship between a state and its subjects cannot be compared to a state's international relations. While it is highly exceptional for states to employ force against other states, it is more commonly used against their own citizens – in everyday law enforcement and in quelling riots and disturbances.[126] The relationships between parties to IACs and NIACs are also different; states are regarded as equals on the international playing field, with conflicts between them considered conflicts amongst equals. In contrast, NIACs are seen as fought between non-equals.[127] While one can assume that states are able to fulfil the comprehensive obligations of IAC IHL, non-state armed groups might have less capacity to do this – and IAC rules would be inappropriate in situations where fighters were not actually able to meet these.[128] A different line of argument is that the IAC rules are unsuited to regulating NIACs, as the methods of fighting

NIACs differ to those envisaged by IAC IHL – many NIACs are resisted by states using methods more akin to law enforcement, counter-terrorism or riot control, making the IAC laws inappropriate for regulating this.[129]

A growing voice is calling for the IAC/NIAC divide to be removed. Critics argue that this divide is arbitrary and artificial, and that in many situations it frustrates IHL's humanitarian goals.[130] This divide creates "double standards of conduct" that are unacceptable from a humanitarian perspective. Victims' needs are similar, regardless of whether a conflict is IAC or NIAC.[131] The ICTY in *Tadic* echoed this sentiment, stating that,

> … in the area of armed conflict the distinction between interstate wars and civil wars is losing its value as far as human being are concerned. Why protect civilians from belligerent violence, or ban rape, torture or the wanton destruction of hospitals, churches, museums or private property, as well as proscribe weapons causing unnecessary suffering when two sovereign States are engaged in war, and yet refrain from enacting the same bans or providing the same protection when armed violence has erupted 'only' within the territory of a sovereign State?[132]

It also seems unfair to prosecute those who commit certain acts in IACs, while not prosecuting those who commit the same acts in NIACs.

One of the key arguments for its abolishment relates to how difficult it can be to actually make this distinction in modern conflicts. Particularly at the start of conflict – a point which in itself might be unclear – due to the poor intelligence available or unequal access to information, it may be challenging for parties to make this classification, and hence to know which body of law to apply. The fact that even academics and tribunals struggle with classifying conflicts after the fact, speaks to how difficult this can be for commanders in the heat of battle.[133] It is problematic that important regulatory consequences flow from a classification that is so difficult to make.

Another problem with this distinction is that it creates room for discretion, which can be used politically. States choose interpretations that work best for their needs.[134] Crawford explains: "The promotion of gradations of humanitarian protection will always leave open the possibility of favouring the lowest permissible level of treatment".[135] As an example, states might argue situations are NIACs, in order to not have to provide enemy fighters with POW status – an approach used by the USA in its 'war on terror'. The divide in the law then becomes less about making a legal determination and more about using the law as a tool to achieve political and other objectives. Problems with discretion are compounded by the fact that there is no central organ or arbiter to make authoritative decisions during times of conflict. Finally, having different categories of conflict, with different rules applying, might negatively affect compliance with the law.

While some argue that the divide between IACs and NIACs should be removed, others argue that more categories should be added – for example, adding 'transnational conflicts' as a distinct legal category.[136] It is unclear how this might work in practice; whether a new protocol, treaty or a treaty amendment would be required, and how this might be framed. Of course, if new categories are being created, consideration should also be given to situations that do not meet the threshold for 'armed conflict' – increasingly important given the prevalence of low-level situations with sporadic outbursts in new wars – and to if and how these could be regulated by IHL.

The reasons for abolishing the IAC/NIAC divide are compelling, with a range of humanitarian and practical reasons as to why this division is counter-productive. Among the many evident problems is that the divide results in reduced protections for civilian women – particularly those in NIACs. Be it because women are 'protected' by the problematically weak laws of NIACs, or because the complex IACs/NIACs divide encourages non-compliance, the end result is the same: lesser protection for women caught up in war. Women get lost in IHL's distinctions. Layers of legal complexity conceal their experiences. The IAC/NIAC divide provides yet another layer by which women are hidden, concealed by the technicalities in the law – a clear reason to strive to simplify and remove these complexities. However, despite the reasons for merging these laws, the distinction remains, bringing significant consequences and ultimately affecting the application of the principle of distinction.

IAC/NIAC and the principle of distinction

The IAC/NIAC divide results in a weakened principle of distinction. The version of the principle contained in the NIAC laws is sparse and problematic – with no privileged category of combatant and a reliance on the murky area of direct participation. The fact that a uniform, simple and clear distinction between civilians and combatants does not apply to all conflicts weakens the principle, detracting from its powerful and comprehensive appeal.

However, despite the IAC/NIAC divide working to weaken the principle, the principle is also a key factor standing in the way of a harmonised law. Crawford argues that many of the substantive principles that would make up a uniform law are already in place, through CIL, treaty law and other sources. When viewed together, these provide a 'blanket of protection' in NIACs that is substantively quite similar to protections in IACs. The problem, she argues, comes with the principle of distinction. Those particular rules of CIL that remain applicable *only* in IACs and that have no correlates in NIACs, are those relating to the principle of distinction – and, more specifically, to combatant and POW status and combatant immunity. States have been resistant to granting combatant status to those fighting against them in NIACs, to date refusing to do so. Crawford explains that,

> … if the distinction between types of conflict were ever to be dropped, the matter of how the 'privileged/unprivileged' combatant demarcation could be resolved becomes pivotal. Before a uniform law of armed conflict can be

> created, a uniform approach to participants in armed conflicts will also need to be resolved. The question is how this is to be achieved.[137]

Suggestions have been put forward about how to get around the law's unequal treatment of fighters. Jinks argues that there is an emergent 'protective parity' applicable to all fighters – those who are recognised as combatants and those who are not – that results from the convergence of protections for combatants and civilians.[138] This has arguably created a net of fundamental protections that are nearly as comprehensive as POW status.[139] Another approach is to argue that 'unlawful combatants' – *all* non-state armed actors in NIACs – are protected under GC4, which deals with the protection of civilians. In terms of this approach, a textual reading of the GCs suggests that those who are not protected by GC3 (which protects combatants) would automatically be covered by GC4.[140] This approach feels intuitively problematic, as civilian protections were by their very nature created to protect those *not* fighting or posing a threat to parties to a conflict. Including unlawful combatants in this group may result in weakened protections for true (non-fighting) civilians. Nevertheless, regardless of how one gets to that point, the fact that all fighters are covered by some legal protections helps to get some way around the barrier that the principle of distinction presents to a unified law. If the substantive protections are de facto there anyway, then the differences presented by the principle of distinction may not be as significant a stumbling block as Crawford makes out. The 'blanket of protective schemes' therefore lays the basis for equivalent protections for all – and ultimately for a unified law applicable to IACs and NIACs.[141]

The IAC/NIAC divide affects the principle of distinction and the principle acts as an obstacle for the removal of the IAC/NIAC divide. It is therefore at this juncture that solutions to the problems affecting both distinctions might be found. If the laws pertaining to NIACs were replaced with a unified law, the principle of distinction might function better. In turn, addressing some of the problems with the principle of distinction may remove an obstacle and pave the way for a unified law.

The labelling and classifying of conflicts is political, with classifications often made to support warring parties' goals. It is also gendered in that much of the violence that most affects women does not contribute to determinations of whether situations constitute armed conflict or whether they are IAC or NIAC. Women experience similar violence in war and in peace, and the transition between these states, from women's perspectives, is often no more than a continuum, where the types and intensity of violence vary, yet remain constant in nature.[142]

The divide between IACs and NIACs is problematic. The mix of state interests, politics and simultaneously rigid and ambiguous laws work together to create an area fraught with challenges. New wars have put this divide to the test, clearly exposing its flaws. If the IAC/NIAC divide, such a central axiom in the law, cannot be applied to the dominant conflicts of today without exhibiting such strain, this speaks to another way in which IHL is no longer suitable to regulate modern conflicts.

Notes

1 Bartels, Rogier. 'Timelines, Borderlines and Conflicts, the Historical Evolution of the Legal Divide Between International and Non-international Armed Conflicts'. *International Review of the Red Cross* 91, no. 873 (2009): 35–67.
2 Ibid.
3 Hassan, Daud. 'The Rise of the Territorial State and the Treaty of Westphalia'. *Yearbook of New Zealand Jurisprudence* 9 (2006): 62–70.
4 Gentili, Alberico. 'The Three Books on the Laws of War', in J.B. Scott (ed.), *The Classics of International Law*, Oxford: Clarendon Press, 1933, at 24–25.
5 Moir, Lindsay. 'The Historical Development of the Application of Humanitarian Law in Non-International Armed Conflicts to 1949'. *International & Comparative Law Quarterly* 47, no. 02 (1998): 337–361.
6 Abi-Saab, Georges. 'Non-International Armed Conflicts'. In *International Dimensions of Humanitarian Law*, BRILL (1988): 217–240, at 217–218.
7 Bartels, supra note 1.
8 The requirements were that a group must have taken possession of part of a territory, set up a government of their own and operated in line with IHL. Oppenheim, Lassa. *International Law: A Treatise, Vol. II, War and Neutrality*. London: Longmans, Green and Co., 1906.
9 For example, in the American Civil War, President Lincoln imposed a naval blockade on the whole Southern coast and this was understood to be recognition of the Southern army as belligerents. In the Spanish Civil War, it was argued that some of the government's announcements regarding prisoners and their designating certain areas as zones of war subject to blockades, constituted recognition of the Nationalists as belligerents.
10 'The Law of Neutrality'. In Thomas, A. R. and Duncan, James C. (eds), *Annotated Supplement to The Commander's Handbook on the Law of Naval Operations*, Vol. 73. International Law Studies, Newport, Rhode Island: Naval War College 1999.
11 Moir, supra note 5.
12 See Bartels, supra note 1.
13 Moir, supra note 5.
14 Bartels, supra note 1.
15 Moir, supra note 5.
16 Kretzmer, David. 'Rethinking the Application of IHL in Non-International Armed Conflicts'. *Israel Law Review* 42, no. 1 (2009): 8–45.
17 Bartels, supra note 1.
18 Ibid.
19 Crawford, Emily. 'Unequal before the Law: The Case for the Elimination of the Distinction between International and Non-International Armed Conflict'. *Leiden Journal of International Law* 20, no. 2 (2007): 441–465.
20 According to Pictet's Commentary on the Geneva Convention, this Article read as follows: 'In all cases of armed conflict which are not of an international character, especially cases of civil war, colonial conflicts, or wars of religion, which may occur in the territory of one or more of the High Contracting Parties, the implementing of the principle of the present Convention shall be obligatory on each of the adversaries. The application of the Convention in these circumstances shall in no way depend on the legal status of the Parties to the conflict and shall have no effect on that status.' (Pictet, Jean. *The Geneva Conventions of 12 August 1949: Commentary*. Geneva: International Committee of the Red Cross, 1952, at 42–43).
21 They accepted it with the omission of the words 'especially cases of civil war, colonial conflicts, or wars of religion'.

22 The text of the Final Record shows that the words 'principles of the present Convention' were replaced with 'provisions of the present Convention', promoting a fuller application of the Convention than the original Red Cross draft Article.
23 Bartels, supra note 1.
24 Mack, Michelle. *Increasing Respect for International Humanitarian Law in Non-International Armed Conflicts*. International Committee of the Red Cross, 2008.
25 Crawford, supra note 19.
26 Anghie, Antony. 'The Evolution of International Law: Colonial and Postcolonial Realities'. *Third World Quarterly* 27, no. 5 (2006): 739–753.
27 Batistich, Marija. 'The Right to Self-Determination and International Law'. *Auckland University Law Review* 7, no. 1013 (1995): 1019–1023. McCorquodale, Robert. *Self-Determination in International Law*. Aldershot; Brookfield, Ashgate/Dartmouth, 2000.
28 Crawford, supra note 19.
29 GA Res. 2444, UN Doc. A/7218 (1968).
30 GA Res. 2675, UN Doc. A/8028 (1970).
31 Crawford, supra note 19.
32 Ibid.
33 Levie, Howard. *The Law of Non-International Armed Conflict: Protocol II to the 1949 Geneva Conventions*. Leiden: Martinus Nijhoff Publishers, 1987.
34 Sulmasy, Glenn. 'The Law of Armed Conflict in the Global War on Terror: International Lawyers Fighting the Law War'. *Notre Dame Journal of Law, Ethics & Public Policy* 19, no. 1 (2014): 309–316. Graham, David. 'The Law of Armed Conflict and the War on Terrorism'. In Jacques, Richard (ed.), *Issues in International Law and Military Operations*, 80. Newport, Rhode Island: International Law Studies, 2006.
35 Gleditsch, Nils. 'Armed Conflict 1946–2001: A New Dataset'. *Journal of Peace Research*, 39, no. 5 (2002): 615–637.
36 Murphy, John. 'Will-O'-the-Wisp? The Search for Law in Non-International Armed Conflicts'. In *Non-International Armed Conflict in the Twenty-First Century*, Vol. 88: 15–36. International Law Studies. Newport, Rhode Island: Naval War College Press, 2012.
37 Kretzmer, supra note 16.
38 Ibid.
39 This reasoning was apparent in the Israeli Supreme Court's targeted killings case (*Public Committee Against Torture* v. *Government of Israel*, 13/12/2006, HCJ 769/02), where Israel saw it could only succeed if its arguments were based on IHL, as it was only under IHL that members of armed groups attacking Israel or Israelis could be targeted even while there was no imminent danger.
40 Kretzmer, supra note 16.
41 Ibid.
42 Mack, supra note 24.
43 Law of armed conflict or IHL.
44 Kretzmer, supra note 16, at 11.
45 Mack, supra note 24.
46 For information about non-state groups and IHL, see Ewumbue-Monono, Churchill. 'Respect for International Humanitarian Law by Armed Non-State Actors in Africa'. *International Review of the Red Cross* 88, no. 864 (2006): 905–924. Sassòli, Marco. 'Taking Armed Groups Seriously: Ways to Improve Their Compliance with International Humanitarian Law'. *International Humanitarian Legal Studies* 1 (2010): 5–51.
47 The main methods that are used to get non-state armed groups to adhere with IHL are unilateral declarations, special agreements, ceasefire agreements and Organisation of African Unity Resolutions. Another method is for armed groups to integrate IHL principles into their military doctrines. See, Ewumbue-Monono, supra note 37, or Mack,

supra note 24. Examples of special agreements are a 1962 agreement in Yemen, and a 1967 agreement in Nigeria – both negotiated by the ICRC – containing commitments to abide by the Geneva Conventions.

48 Although AP2 was the first time rape was specifically mentioned in an IHL Convention, the specific protections provided for in NIACs are less.

49 Barrow, Amy. 'UN Security Council Resolutions 1325 and 1820: Constructing Gender in Armed Conflict and International Humanitarian Law'. *International Review of the Red Cross* 92, no. 877 (2010): 221–234, at 223.

50 Vite, Sylvain. 'Typology of Armed Conflicts in International Humanitarian Law: Legal Concepts and Actual Situations'. *International Review of the Red Cross* 91, no. 873 (2009): 69–94.

51 Crawford, supra note 19, at 447.

52 During the negotiations on AP1, a clause was tabled requiring the recognition of regional organisations, however this was not included in the final version of the text. See, Mastorodimos, Konstantinos. 'The Character of the Conflict in Gaza: Another Argument Towards Abolishing the Distinction between International and Non-International Armed Conflicts'. *International Community Law Review* 12, no. 4 (2010): 437–69.

53 Crawford, supra note 19.

54 Vite, supra note 50.

55 The requirements for statehood are set out in the Montevideo Convention on the Rights and Duties of States, 1933.

56 *The Prosecutor* v. *Tadic*, ICTY Appeal Chamber, IT-94–1, 1999, para. 84.

57 Pejic, Jelena. 'Status of Conflict', in Elizabeth Wilmshurst and Susan Breau (eds), *Perspectives on the ICRC Study on Customary International Humanitarian Law*, Cambridge University Press, Cambridge, 2007.

58 Commentary on the Geneva Conventions, supra note 20.

59 Ibid., at 37.

60 Schindler, Dietrich. 'The Different Types of Armed Conflicts According to the Geneva Conventions and Protocols'. In *Recueil Des Cours, Collected Courses, Volume 163*, 117–164. Leiden and Boston: Martinus Nijhoff Publishers, 2007.

61 Crawford, supra note 19.

62 Ibid.

63 *Hamdan* v. *Rumsfeld*, 548 U.S 67, 2006.

64 Dinstein, Yoram. 'Concluding Remarks on Non-International Armed Conflicts'. In *Non-International Armed Conflict in the Twenty-first Century*. Vol. 88. International Law Studies. Newport, Rhode Island: Naval War College Press, 2012, at 400.

65 Mastorodimos, supra note 52.

66 Sassoli, Marco. 'Use and Abuse of the Laws of War in the War on Terrorism'. *Law and Inequality: A Journal of Theory and Practice.* 22 (2004): 195–221, at 201.

67 Odermatt, Jed, 'New Wars and the International/Non-International Armed Conflict Dichotomy', at 7, n.d., www.isisc.org/portal/images/stories/PDF/Paper%20Oder matt.pdf.

68 *The Prosecutor* v. *Tadic*, Decision on the Defence Motion for Interlocutory Appeal on Jurisdiction, 2 October 1995, Case No. IT-94-1-AR72, at para 70.

69 Sassoli, Marco. 'Transnational Armed Groups and International Humanitarian Law'. *Program on Humanitarian Policy and Conflict Research at Harvard University, Occasional Paper Series* 6 (2006).

70 In the *Limaj* case the ICTY considered this issue. The defence had challenged the notion that the fighting was armed conflict, arguing that the actions of the Serbian forces had not been aimed at defeating the enemy's army, but rather at the ethnic cleansing of Kosovo. The tribunal rejected this argument, holding that the intention of the parties is irrelevant to whether there is an armed conflict. They held that there are only two relevant criteria: the intensity of the conflict and the organisation of the

parties. *Prosecutor* v. *Limaj*, Case No. IT-03-66-T, Judgement (Trial Chamber), 30 November 2005, at para 170.

71 Vite, supra note 50.

72 Schmitt, Michael. 'The Principle of Discrimination in 21st Century Warfare'. *Yale Human Rights & Development Law Journal* 2 (1999): 143–182.

73 Cockburn, Cynthia. 'Gender Relations as Causal in Militarization and War'. *International Feminist Journal of Politics* 12, no. 2 (2010): 139–157, at 148.

74 'Egypt Unrest: 846 Killed in Protests – Official Toll'. *BBC*, 19 April 2011.

75 Johnston, Katie. 'Transformations of Conflict Status in Libya'. *Journal of Conflict and Security Law* 17, no. 1 (2012): 81–115.

76 *Prosecutor* v. *Charles Ghankay Taylor*, SCSL-03-1-T, 26 April 2012.

77 Titeca, Kristof, and Kimanuka, Celestin. *Walking in the Dark: Informal Cross-Border Trade in the Great Lakes Region*. International Alert, 2012.

78 *Informal Cross Border Trade Report, Liberia*. New York: UN Women.

79 Kristof, Kimanuka, supra note 77, at 35.

80 Ibid.

81 Vite, supra note 50.

82 Schindler, supra note 60. This fragmented approach was arguably the approach implicitly favoured by the ICJ in the *Nicaragua* decision, when in its analysis of the conflict the Court differentiated between the conflicts between the Nicaraguan government and the Contras, and those between the Nicaraguan government and the USA. Vite, supra note 49. In the *Lubanga* decision, the ICC confirmed that a NIAC could exist alongside an IAC.

83 Vite, supra note 50, at 86.

84 *Detained and Denied in Afghanistan: How to Make U.S. Detention Comply with the Law*. Washington DC: Human Rights First, 2011.

85 Conference of Government Experts on the Reaffirmation and Development of IHL applicable in Armed Conflict, Para 290.

86 Crawford, supra note 19.

87 *The Prosecutor* v. *Tadic*, ICTY Appeal Chamber, IT-94–1, 1999.

88 *The Prosecutor* v. *Karadzic and Mladic*, ICTY, Review of the Indictment Pursuant to Rule 61, IT-95-5-R61 and IT-95-18-R61, 11 July 1996, at para. 88.

89 *The Prosecutor* v. *Delalic, Mucic, Delic and Landzo (Celebici)*, ICTY Trial Chamber, IT-96-21-T, 1998, at para 209.

90 *Case Concerning Military and Paramilitary Activities in and Against Nicaragua (Merits), (Nicaragua* v. *United States)*, ICJ, 1986, 105–115. Here the ICJ looked to determine,

> … whether or not the relationship of the *contras* to the United States Government was so much one of dependence on the one side and control on the other that it would be right to equate the *contras*, for legal purposes, with an organ of the United States Government, or as acting on behalf of that Government.
>
> (para 109)

91 *The Prosecutor* v. *Rajic*, ICTY, Review of the Indictment Pursuant to Rule 61, IT-95-12-R61, 1996.

92 *The Application of the Convention on the Prevention and Punishment of the Crime of Genocide (Bosnia and Herzegovina* v. *Serbia and Montenegro)*, I.C.J. 2007, at para 405.

93 Vite, supra note 50.

94 Byron, Christine. 'Armed Conflicts: International or Non-International'. *Journal of Conflict & Security Law* 6 (2001): 63–90.

95 Vite, supra note 50.

96 Ibid.

97 Schondorf, Roy. 'Extra-State Armed Conflicts: Is There a Need for a New Legal Regime?' *New York University International Law and Politics* 37, no. 1 (2004): 1–78.
98 Vite, supra note 49.
99 Schondorf, supra note 97.
100 Vashakmadze, Mindia. *The Applicability of International Humanitarian Law to 'Transnational' Armed Conflicts*. Working Paper 34. EUI Working Papers, 2009.
101 Vite, supra note 50.
102 Mama, Amina. 'Where We Must Stand: African Women in an Age of War'. *OpenDemocracy, 50.50 Inclusive Democracy*, 28 November 2012.
103 Following from that ruling, the United States has taken steps to ensure that their counterterrorism actions are compliant with CA3. This has included ensuring that the Department of Defence Detainee Directive, the Army Field Manual on Interrogation and the CIA's interrogation and detention programme are compliant with CA3. Bellinger, John. 'Legal Issues in the War on Terrorism – A Reply to Silja N. U. Voneky'. *German Law Journal* 8, no. 9 (2007): 871–878.
104 Ibid., at 878.
105 Sassoli, supra note 66, at 1.
106 Ibid.
107 Gasser, Hans-Peter. 'Acts of Terror, 'Terrorism' and International Humanitarian Law'. *International Review of the Red Cross* 84, no. 847 (2002): 547–570.
108 The definition of terrorism is unsettled in international law. Even the SC Resolutions that address terrorism do not provide a definition of terrorism. For example, SC Res 373 (2001) and SC Res 1624 (2005) talk about combating terrorism and the risks posed by terrorism, but do not define the actions that fall under the term's ambit. Terrorism is understood to be a tactic that certain armed groups adopt, rendering them to be labelled as terrorist groups. However, the label 'terrorism' is frequently assigned because of political considerations – with significant consequences. African governments have labelled certain armed groups as terror groups to get international support in fighting them. Illustrating the erratic way in which these titles are allocated, in 2007 Uganda's LRA made it onto the US State Department terrorist list (as 'other designated organizations'), along with ex-FAR (Forces Armées Rwandaises), the former military of Rwanda – both quintessential 'organised armed groups', rather than the types of groups commonly understood to be terror groups. Piombo, Jessica. *Terrorism and U.S. Counter-Terrorism Programs in Africa: An Overview*. Centre for Contemporary Conflict, 2007.
109 Mack, supra note 24.
110 Treaties are relevant to determining the extent of CIL as they can help ascertain how states view particular international law rules. In the North Sea Continental Shelf case, the ICJ considered the degree of ratification of a treaty relevant in ascertaining whether a law has reached the status of CIL. Drafting treaties is important in focusing international legal opinions. The Continental Shelf case noted that, '… multilateral conventions may have an important role to play in recording and defining rules deriving from custom, or indeed in developing them'. *Continental Shelf Case (Libyan Arab Jamahiriya* v. *Malta), ICJ*, 1985, pp. 29–30, §27.
111 Henckaerts, Jean-Marie. 'Study on Customary International Humanitarian Law: A Contribution to the Understanding and Respect for the Rule of Law in Armed Conflict'. *International Review of the Red Cross* 87, no. 857 (2005): 175–212.
112 Crawford, supra note 19, at 456.
113 Mastorodimos, supra note 52.
114 *Case Concerning Military and Paramilitary Activities in and Against Nicaragua (Merits), (Nicaragua* v. *United States)*, ICJ, 1986.
115 *The Prosecutor* v. *Tadic*, Decision on the Defence Motion for Interlocutory Appeal on Jurisdiction, ICTY, IT-94-1-AR722 1995, para 98.
116 Ibid., para 126.

117 Schmitt, Michael. 'Military Necessity and Humanity in International Humanitarian Law: Preserving the Delicate Balance'. *Virginia Journal of International Law* 50 (2010): 795–839, at 819–820.

118 Para 105, *Legality of the Threat or Use of Nuclear Weapons (Advisory Opinion)* ICJ Rep 226, 1996. Alston, Philip, Academy of European Law, and New York University. Center for Human Rights and Global Justice. *Non-State Actors and Human Rights*. Collected Courses of the Academy of European Law; XIII/3. Oxford; New York: Oxford University Press, 2005.

119 Kretzmer, supra note 16.

120 Ibid., at 10.

121 See for example, Alston, supra note 118, and Doswald-Beck, Louise and Vité, Sylvain. 'International Humanitarian Law and Human Rights Law'. *International Review of the Red Cross* 293 (1993).

122 The ICJ discussed this relationship in the following judgements, *Legality of the Threat or Use of Nuclear Weapons (Advisory Opinion)* [1996] ICJ Rep 226 (§25); *Legal Consequences of the Construction of a Wall in the Occupied Palestinian Territory (Advisory Opinion)* [2004] 43 ILM 1009 at §106–113; and *Armed Activities on the Territory of the Congo (Democratic Republic of Congo* v. *Uganda)* [2006] 45 ILM 271 at §216.

123 Clapham, Andrew. 'Human Rights Obligations of Non-State Actors in Conflict Situations'. *International Review of the Red Cross* 88, no. 863 (2006): 491–523.

124 Derogation clauses can be found in Article 4 of the International Covenant on Civil and Political Rights and Article 15 of the European Convention on Human Rights.

125 Watkin, Kenneth, *Combatants, Unprivileged Belligerents and Conflicts in the 21st Century*, Background Paper prepared for the Informal High-Level Expert Meeting on the Reaffirmation and Development of International Humanitarian Law, Cambridge, 27–29 January 2003, Programme on Humanitarian Policy and Conflict Research at Harvard University, at 2.

126 Moir, Lindsay, *The Law of Internal Armed Conflict*. Cambridge: Cambridge University Press, 2002.

127 Odermatt, supra note 67.

128 Ibid.

129 Ibid.

130 Bartels, supra note 1.

131 Mastorodimos, supra note 52.

132 *The Prosecutor* v. *Tadic*, Decision on the Defence Motion for Interlocutory Appeal on Jurisdiction, ICTY, IT-94-1-AR722 1995, at para. 97.

133 Mastorodimos, supra note 52.

134 Vite, supra note 50.

135 Crawford, supra note 19, at 464.

136 Bartels, supra note 1.

137 Crawford, supra note 19, at 459.

138 Jinks, Derek. 'Protective Parity and the Laws of War'. *Notre Dame Law Review* 79 (2004): 1493–1528.

139 This 'net' of protections comes from GC 4, CA3, Article 75 of AP1, Art 4 and 6 of AP2.

140 Crawford, supra note 19.

141 Ibid.

142 Cockburn, supra note 73.

Bibliography

Books and articles

Abi-Saab, Georges. 'Non-International Armed Conflicts'. In *International Dimensions of Humanitarian Law*. Dordrecht, Boston, London: BRILL (1988): 217–240, at 217–218.

Alston, Philip, Academy of European Law, and New York University. Center for Human Rights and Global Justice. *Non-State Actors and Human Rights*. Collected Courses of the Academy of European Law; XIII/3. Oxford; New York: Oxford University Press, 2005.

Anghie, Antony. 'The Evolution of International Law: Colonial and Postcolonial Realities'. *Third World Quarterly* 27, no. 5 (2006): 739–753.

Bartels, Rogier. 'Timelines, Borderlines and Conflicts, the Historical Evolution of the Legal Divide between International and Non-international Armed Conflicts'. *International Review of the Red Cross* 91, no. 873 (2009): 35–67.

Barrow, Amy. 'UN Security Council Resolutions 1325 and 1820: Constructing Gender in Armed Conflict and International Humanitarian Law'. *International Review of the Red Cross* 92, no. 877 (2010): 221–234.

Batistich, Marija. 'The Right to Self-Determination and International Law'. *Auckland University Law Review* 7, no. 1013 (1995): 1019–1023.

Bellinger, John. 'Legal Issues in the War on Terrorism – A Reply to Silja N. U. Voneky'. *German Law Journal* 8, no. 9 (2007): 871–878.

Byron, Christine. 'Armed Conflicts: International or Non-International'. *Journal of Conflict & Security Law* 6 (2001): 63–90.

Clapham, Andrew. 'Human Rights Obligations of Non-State Actors in Conflict Situations'. *International Review of the Red Cross* 88, no. 863 (2006): 491–523.

Cockburn, Cynthia. 'Gender Relations as Causal in Militarization and War'. *International Feminist Journal of Politics* 12, no. 2 (2010): 139–157.

Crawford, Emily. 'Unequal Before the Law: The Case for the Elimination of the Distinction Between International and Non-International Armed Conflict'. *Leiden Journal of International Law* 20, no. 2 (2007): 441–465.

Detained and Denied in Afghanistan: How to Make U.S. Detention Comply with the Law. New York: Human Rights First, 2011.

Dinstein, Yoram. 'Concluding Remarks on Non-International Armed Conflicts'. In *Non-International Armed Conflict in the Twenty-first Century*. Vol. 88. International Law Studies. Newport, Rhode Island: Naval War College Press, 2012.

Doswald-Beck, Louise and Vité, Sylvain. 'International Humanitarian Law and Human Rights Law'. *International Review of the Red Cross* 293 (1993).

Ewumbue-Monono, Churchill. 'Respect for International Humanitarian Law by Armed Non-State Actors in Africa'. *International Review of the Red Cross* 88, no. 864 (2006): 905–924.

Gasser, Hans-Peter. 'Acts of Terror, 'Terrorism' and International Humanitarian Law'. *International Review of the Red Cross* 84, no. 847 (2002): 547–570.

Gentili, Alberico. 'The Three Books on the Laws of War', in Scott, J. B. (ed.), *The Classics of International Law*. Oxford: Clarendon Press, 1933, at 24–25.

Gleditsch, Nils. 'Armed Conflict 1946–2001: A New Dataset'. *Journal of Peace Research* 29 (2002): 615–637.

Graham, David. 'The Law of Armed Conflict and the War on Terrorism'. In Jacques, Richard (ed.), *Issues in International Law and Military Operations*, 80. Newport, Rhode Island: International Law Studies, 2006.

Hassan, Daud. 'The Rise of the Territorial State and the Treaty of Westphalia'. *Yearbook of New Zealand Jurisprudence* 9 (2006): 62–70.

Henckaerts, Jean-Marie. 'Study on Customary International Humanitarian Law: A Contribution to the Understanding and Respect for the Rule of Law in Armed Conflict'. *International Review of the Red Cross* 87, no. 857 (2005): 175–212.

Informal Cross Border Trade Report, Liberia. New York: UN Women.

Jinks, Derek. 'Protective Parity and the Laws of War'. *Notre Dame Law Review* 79 (2004): 1493–1528.

Johnston, Katie. 'Transformations of Conflict Status in Libya'. *Journal of Conflict and Security Law* 17, no. 1 (2012): 81–115.

Kretzmer, David. 'Rethinking the Application of IHL in Non-International Armed Conflicts'. *Israel Law Review* 42, no. 1 (2009): 8–45.

Levie, Howard. *The Law of Non-International Armed Conflict: Protocol II to the 1949 Geneva Conventions*. Leiden: Martinus Nijhoff Publishers, 1987.

Mama, Amina. 'Where We Must Stand: African Women in an Age of War'. *OpenDemocracy, 50.50 Inclusive Democracy*, 28 November 2012.

Mack, Michelle. *Increasing Respect for International Humanitarian Law in Non-International Armed Conflicts*. Geneva: International Committee of the Red Cross, 2008.

Mastorodimos, Konstantinos. 'The Character of the Conflict in Gaza: Another Argument Towards Abolishing the Distinction between International and Non-International Armed Conflicts'. *International Community Law Review* 12, no. 4 (2010): 437–69.

McCorquodale, Robert. *Self-Determination in International Law*. Aldershot; Brookfield: Ashgate/Dartmouth, 2000.

Moir, Lindsay. 'The Historical Development of the Application of Humanitarian Law in Non-International Armed Conflicts to 1949'. *International & Comparative Law Quarterly* 47, no. 02 (1998): 337–361.

Moir, Lindsay, *The Law of Internal Armed Conflict*. Cambridge: Cambridge University Press, 2002.

Murphy, John. 'Will-O'-the-Wisp? The Search for Law in Non-International Armed Conflicts'. In *Non-International Armed Conflict in the Twenty-First Century*, Vol. 88: 15–36. International Law Studies. Newport, Rhode Island: Naval War College Press, 2012.

Odermatt, Jed, 'New Wars and the International/Non-International Armed Conflict Dichotomy', at 7, n.d., www.isisc.org/portal/images/stories/PDF/Paper%20Odermatt.pdf.

Oppenheim, Lassa. *International Law: A Treatise, Vol. II, War and Neutrality*. London: Longmans, Green and Co., 1906.

Pejic, Jelena. 'Status of Conflict', in Wilmshurst, Elizabeth and Breau, Susan (eds), *Perspectives on the ICRC Study on Customary International Humanitarian Law*. Cambridge: Cambridge University Press, 2007.

Pictet, Jean. *The Geneva Conventions of 12 August 1949: Commentary*. Geneva: International Committee of the Red Cross, 1952.

Piombo, Jessica. *Terrorism and U.S. Counter-Terrorism Programs in Africa: An Overview*. Centre for Contemporary Conflict, 2007.

Prendergast, John. 'The New Face of African Conflict, In Search of a Way Forward'. *Foreign Affairs*, 12 March 2014.

Sassòli, Marco. 'Taking Armed Groups Seriously: Ways to Improve Their Compliance with International Humanitarian Law'. *International Humanitarian Legal Studies* 1 (2010): 5–51.

Sassoli, Marco. 'Transnational Armed Groups and International Humanitarian Law'. *Program on Humanitarian Policy and Conflict Research at Harvard University, Occasional Paper Series* 6 (2006).

Sassoli, Marco. 'Use and Abuse of the Laws of War in the War on Terrorism'. *Law and Inequality: A Journal of Theory and Practice.* 22 (2004): 195–221, at 201.

Schindler, Dietrich. 'The Different Types of Armed Conflicts According to the Geneva Conventions and Protocols'. In *Recueil Des Cours, Collected Courses, Volume 163*, 117–164. Leiden and Boston: Martinus Nijhoff Publishers, 2007.

Schmitt, Michael. 'Military Necessity and Humanity in International Humanitarian Law: Preserving the Delicate Balance'. *Virginia Journal of International Law* 50 (2010): 795–839, at 819–820.

Schmitt, Michael. 'The Principle of Discrimination in 21st Century Warfare'. *Yale Human Rights & Development Law Journal* 2 (1999): 143–82.

Schondorf, Roy. 'Extra-State Armed Conflicts: Is There a Need for a New Legal Regime?' *New York University International Law and Politics* 37, no. 1 (2004): 1–78.

Sulmasy, Glenn. 'The Law of Armed Conflict in the Global War on Terror: International Lawyers Fighting the Law War'. *Notre Dame Journal of Law, Ethics & Public Policy* 19, no. 1 (2014): 309–316.

'The Law of Neutrality'. In Thomas, A. R. and Duncan, James C. (eds), *Annotated Supplement to The Commander's Handbook on the Law of Naval Operations*, Vol. 73. International Law Studies, Newport, Rhode Island: Naval War College 1999.

Titeca, Kristof, and Kimanuka, Celestin. *Walking in the Dark: Informal Cross-Border Trade in the Great Lakes Region*. International Alert, 2012.

Vashakmadze, Mindia. *The Applicability of International Humanitarian Law to 'Transnational' Armed Conflicts*. Working Paper 34. EUI Working Papers, 2009.

Vite, Sylvain. 'Typology of Armed Conflicts in International Humanitarian Law: Legal Concepts and Actual Situations'. *International Review of the Red Cross* 91, no. 873 (2009): 69–94.

Watkin, Kenneth, *Combatants, Unprivileged Belligerents and Conflicts in the 21st Century*, Background Paper prepared for the Informal High-Level Expert Meeting on the Reaffirmation and Development of International Humanitarian Law, Cambridge, 27–29 January 2003, Programme on Humanitarian Policy and Conflict Research at Harvard University.

Cases

Armed Activities on the Territory of the Congo (Democratic Republic of Congo v. *Uganda)* ICJ, 45 ILM 271, 2006.

Case Concerning Military and Paramilitary Activities in and Against Nicaragua (Merits), (Nicaragua v. *United States)*, ICJ, 1986.

Hamdan v. *Rumsfeld*, 548 U.S 67, 2006.

Legal Consequences of the Construction of a Wall in the Occupied Palestinian Territory (Advisory Opinion) [2004] 43 ILM 1009.

Legality of the Threat or Use of Nuclear Weapons (Advisory Opinion) ICJ Rep 226, 1996.

Public Committee Against Torture v. *Government of Israel*, 13/12/2006, HCJ 769/02.

The Application of the Convention on the Prevention and Punishment of the Crime of Genocide (Bosnia and Herzegovina v. *Serbia and Montenegro)*, I.C.J. 2007.

The Prosecutor v. *Charles Ghankay Taylor*, SCSL-03-1-T, 26 April 2012.

The Prosecutor v. *Delalic, Mucic, Delic and Landzo (Celebici)*, ICTY Trial Chamber, IT-96-21-T, 1998.
The Prosecutor v. *Limaj*, Case No. IT-03-66-T, Judgement (Trial Chamber), 30 November 2005.
The Prosecutor v. *Tadic*, ICTY Appeal Chamber, IT-94-1, 1999
The Prosecutor v. *Tadic*, Decision on the Defence Motion for Interlocutory Appeal on Jurisdiction, 2 October 1995, Case No. IT-94-1-AR72.
The Prosecutor v. *Karadzic and Mladic*, ICTY, Review of the Indictment Pursuant to Rule 61, IT-95-5-R61 and IT-95-18-R61, 11 July 1996.
The Prosecutor v. *Rajic*, ICTY, Review of the Indictment Pursuant to Rule 61, IT-95-12-R61, 1996.

Other policy documents

Conference of Government Experts on the Reaffirmation and Development of IHL applicable in Armed Conflict
GA Res. 2444, UN Doc. A/7218 (1968).
GA Res. 2675, UN Doc. A/8028 (1970).

Media articles

'Egypt Unrest: 846 Killed in Protests – Official Toll'. BBC, 19 April 2011.

6 Applying the principle of distinction to women in African war

This chapter examines how the principle of distinction might be applied to women in new wars in Africa. In the sections that follow, the principle is applied to women participating in different ways in African conflicts, going through the various steps to classification and questioning how different women would be categorised; if they'd be combatants or civilians, whether the roles they typically play would constitute direct participation, and what the effects of these classifications would be. The many challenges in making these classifications will be discussed.

For the purposes of this chapter, women are divided into three groups: women in state armed forces, women in non-state armed groups and women contributing to armed movements from within civilian populations. As Chapter 3 described, participation in conflict is fluid, and in practice women often move between these above categories or straddle them. A woman may start off supporting an armed movement as a civilian, before gradually increasing her involvement, becoming a member over time. While recognising this fluidity, these categories have been utilised in this application of the law as they each illustrate certain issues relevant to this discussion.

It is worth noting that there are different reasons that the principle of distinction is applied in practice. The primary reason is to determine who can and cannot be targeted. Another function is to ascertain the status of actors; determining whether they are 'combatants', entitled to the privileges that come with that, whether they are 'civilians', or even 'unlawful combatants'. The principle of distinction is also applied post-conflict by courts and tribunals, in order to assess whether there were violations of the principle that constituted crimes deserving of punishment. These classifications are carried out at different times, in differing circumstances, by different actors. These can yield quite different results; a judge in a tribunal will be provided with more facts and legal analysis than a soldier in combat, and will have the benefit of a holistic view of the conflict and hindsight – not to mention a differing political climate and interests. Recognising how external factors can affect classification results, this chapter will seek to identify the correct legal interpretations – those that might be made were an optimum amount of information available – despite the fact that in practice this is seldom the case. Doing so best allows us to assess the definitions and parameters of the law.

The reality is that the principle of distinction is seldom applied to women. Women largely go unnoticed in legal determinations. Even those women who are actively involved with armed groups are frequently overlooked; their contributions are ignored, or they are looked at as 'wives' rather than 'soldiers'. Academic writing and tribunal judgements seldom categorise female actors. For the most part women are not considered, unless considering them serves a particular agenda. Women are, however, targeted in conflict for strategic reasons. Yet this is seldom done in terms of an application of the principle of distinction – rather, when targeting or not targeting women, the law hardly comes into it at all.

Women in state armed forces

Women in state armed forces can be divided into two groups: those in regular armies and those in irregular state forces.

Women in regular armed forces/armies

Women in regular armed forces are the simplest group to apply the principle of distinction to. In terms of the law, members of state armies are presumed to be combatants.[1] They gain their combatant status from mere membership of armed forces, rather than from the roles that they play within these. This means that even the cook or cleaner in an army is classified combatant. This rule applies to everyone; men, women – even children[2] (although this is qualified by laws prohibiting child recruitment). Membership of armed forces is expressed by formal integration into army units or command structures, as well as by uniforms, insignia and equipment.[3]

Despite the *presumption* of combatancy, armed forces can, in fact, have non-combatant members. Non-combatant status is the exception, occurring in limited circumstances. This is regulated by domestic law, with internal legislation required to render members of state armies as non-combatants. As such it is a legal pronouncement, rather than an individual's role, that renders them non-combatant. States have limited discretion in this regard – such pronouncements must be made in accordance with international law.[4] Importantly, those designated as non-combatants may not be authorised to directly participate in hostilities. So, for example, a person who works with weapon systems cannot be designated non-combatant.[5]

Most state armies still exclude women from active combat. In Africa, only Eritrea allows women into combat. South Africa allows women into 'other military roles' (such as fighter pilots or artillery officers) while other African armies bar women from combat altogether.[6] Depending on the specifics of their domestic laws, (non-combat) women in these national armies might be formally declared as non-combatants. However, where no such legislative declaration exists – which is generally the case – these women would be classified as combatants. As such, they would be entitled to all combatant privileges and obligations, including; POW status, the right to participate in hostilities and the obligation to wear uniforms. They could also be the lawful targets of attack for the duration of their enlistment.

Article 50 of AP1 defines 'civilians' negatively – as those *not* listed within the various categories of combatants. Non-combatant members of armed forces *do* fall within one of categories of combatant (they are members of the armed forces of a party to a conflict – Art 4(1) GC3 and Art 43(1) AP1). Therefore, non-combatant members of armed forces, while not classified as combatants, are also not civilians – and are therefore not covered by the prohibition on attacking civilians. Those attacking state armies need not distinguish between their combatant and non-combatant members, and the fact that there are non-combatant army personnel present at a military base does not mean that those attacking need to take precautionary measures to avoid them – as they would if there were civilians present.[7] In IACs, non-combatant members of state armed forces are entitled to POW status on capture.

An important group to consider in the African context are women who *accompany* state armies but are not actually *members* of the armed forces. In Africa this takes many guises: from sex workers who live and work on or alongside military bases, to the women who follow armies providing services, selling goods and benefitting from the economic opportunities and relative security that being near these forces may bring. Those who *accompany* armed forces have the primary status of civilians.[8] As such, they may not be targets of attack and do not have the right to participate in hostilities. However, if captured in an IAC, they might be entitled to POW status. Article 4(4) GC3, which lists the categories of persons entitled to POW status, includes,

> Persons who accompany the armed forces without actually being members thereof … provided that they have received authorization from the armed forces which they accompany, who shall provide them for that purpose with an identity card similar to the annexed model.[9]

Armies therefore need to decide and act on this. In practice, in Africa the women who accompany armed forces in Africa often do so informally, ignored by armed forces, and not given any authorisation, recognition or identification cards. Hence often they might not be eligible for POW protection.

Determining the status of women in state armies in NIACs is more difficult. The NIAC laws do not provide for combatant status, even for members of state armies. GC3 and AP2 do not mention combatancy or POW status – rather, CA3 and AP2 talk of 'armed forces' – a term not defined in the NIAC laws. Controversy exists about whether members of state armed forces in NIACs are in fact combatants. The ICRC's Interpretive Guidance notes that it is generally accepted that members of state armed forces in NIACs are *not* civilians.[10] According to the ICRC's non-binding customary IHL study, in NIACs members of state armed forces are considered combatants for the purposes of the principle of distinction and can therefore be targeted.[11] As POW status does not exist in NIACs, even members of state armed forces do not receive POW privileges – discussed further in Chapter 7. Therefore in NIACs, army women do not have civilian status, yet they might also not have combatant status. They receive some of the effects of combatant status, yet not all. This illustrates the complicated web that IHL weaves in NIACs.

Women in irregular armed forces, 'belonging to' a state party

In determining the status of *irregular* armed groups in IACs (military groups that are not part of the army), the first consideration is whether an armed group 'belongs to' a state party to a conflict. If it does, it can be considered part of the state armed forces and its members can potentially be classified as combatants.[12] Where an armed group's conduct can be said to be attributable to a state under the international law of state responsibility, then it 'belongs to' that state party. The degree of control required is not settled in international law. The Interpretive Guidance argues that belonging to a state party requires a de facto relationship between the armed group and the state party. This relationship can be officially declared, formed by tacit agreement, or inferred by conduct that makes it clear that a group is fighting for that state party. What is essential is that the group conduct hostilities *on behalf of* and *with agreement of* the state party.[13] As examples, in the ongoing fighting between Rwanda and DRC, rebel groups operating within both countries, have been controlled by – or at least accused of being controlled by – the opposing states.

Where irregular groups fight on behalf of state parties to a conflict, their 'members' – including the women of the group – may be combatants. Therefore, the next thing that must be ascertained is whether the individuals being classified are in fact members. Unlike in regular armies, membership of irregular groups is not governed by domestic law. The Interpretive Guidance suggests that membership of irregular state armed forces must be determined using the same functional criteria used to determine membership in non-state armed groups – namely, "continuous combat function".[14] Women and the continuous combat function standard are discussed in the section that follows, which demonstrates how most women in African armed groups would fail to meet this standard. Membership is a tricky concept; in addition to being a concept in law, this is also a social concept, denoting commonly shared goals. This social concept is in itself gendered, with women often not conceived of as being true active 'members' of groups. This mix of legal and social language goes further towards undermining certainty.

Those women who qualify as 'members' of irregular groups 'belonging to' a state may be combatants if they meet the GC combatancy requirements (Article 4, GC3). In terms of these, they need to be subordinate to responsible command, to have a fixed distinctive emblem, to carry their arms openly, have a certain level of organisation or discipline and to act in accordance with IHL. Where groups do meet these requirements, their members would be entitled to combatant status and to the full set of privileges and obligations that come with that. However, most African irregular groups would fail to meet these stringent combatancy requirements; fighters often do not wear uniforms or emblems, they are ill disciplined, they do not have proper command structures, and they frequently and routinely violate IHL. This being the case, members would not receive combatant status. Of course this conclusion is based on certain premises that underlie our understanding of the law; including about what a proper command structure is, or what would be recognised as a legitimate uniform.

Irregular groups 'belonging to' states also take part in NIACs. As there is no combatant status in NIACs, the relevant issue would not be the classification of these groups, as much as the consequences of individual's actions within these. If a woman was 'directly participating' in such a group, she could be targeted at the time of her participation. An example of female involvement in irregular groups can be seen with the Janjaweed – translated as 'devil on horseback' – the Sudanese militia operating in Darfur with the backing of Omar al-Bashir's government. The 'Hakama', often found alongside the Janjaweed, are Sudanese female traditional singers who praise male fighters with singing and ululating. They have been said to cheer on men during Janjaweed attacks, uttering racial insults as Janjaweed members rape local women. The Hakama also participate in looting.[15] They are therefore 'participating' in alternative ways, which would not constitute direct participation. It feels problematic that the law allows no room to recognise and incorporate such types of participation – with these women being treated by the law just as other civilians would be.

Women in non-state armed groups

In terms of IHL, outside of IACs and state armed forces, there are no combatants. When dealing with non-state groups, the principle of distinction's focus is therefore not placed on status categorisations, but on the actions of individuals and the consequences flowing from these actions. When civilians 'directly participate' in hostilities, they lose their immunity from attack for the duration of their participation. Therefore the critical question when considering non-state armed actors is whether their specific actions constitute direct participation. There are a number of steps involved in determining this.

First, to qualify as direct participation in hostilities, an action must take place in the context of 'hostilities'. This requirement stands in the way of many armed actions in Africa constituting direct participation. The concept of 'hostilities' is linked to 'armed conflict' – meaning that armed actions taken in situations that do not meet the threshold for armed conflict cannot qualify as direct participation. As described in previous chapters, much armed activity in Africa is low-level rebel activity that continues for years, seldom or only sporadically rising to the level of armed conflict. The DRC provides a good example of this. Since the signing of a peace accord and the official ending of conflict in 2003, violence has continued, with numerous rebel groups remaining active in the country. There have been a few flare-ups that could be said to have reached the level of armed conflict, such as the 2012–2013 rebellion of rebel group M23. However, most rebel activity during this time has not reached the armed conflict threshold, meaning that armed actions taken within these could not constitute direct participation.

An evident problem is that situations are fluid, changing with time. It is unclear how parties on the ground are supposed to know the exact moment that a situation passes the threshold into hostilities, rendering actions to be direct participation. It is widely recognised that direct participation assessments take into consideration an individual's movements. However, it is seldom acknowledged how the fluidity in a broader situation can also effect direct participation determinations, as can the political pressures that might influence armed conflict threshold determinations.

Even during armed conflict, not all violent conduct is considered 'part of' hostilities. Actions can only qualify as direct participation if those acts are part of the conduct of war – or put differently, if they are carried out by a party to a conflict in the furtherance of conflict goals.[16] In practice, it is often hard to tell who the parties to a conflict are and which of their acts are in furtherance of conflict goals. In new wars, a range of actors operate with diverse motivations, blending criminality and hostilities in ways that make it difficult to decipher which acts are part of the conflict and which are not. Sudan's Janjaweed and Murahaleen militias conducted violent slave raids during the conflicts in South Sudan and Darfur, where thousands were abducted and sold as slaves. Were these acts of conflict that would render them direct participation? The militias made money from the sale of slaves, suggesting that these were criminal enterprises. Yet, on the other hand the raids in which abductions took place were integral components of the armed conflict and were politically driven. Effectively, the raids served dual goals.

Taking this further, if the kidnapping raids could be classified as direct participation, could the same be said of the other tasks involved in selling the slave victims? What of those who fed the victims, or transported and sold the slaves – actions without which the trading of slaves would not be possible? Which of the different component actions that make up a criminal enterprise can constitute direct participation when carried out by armed groups? If the goal of criminal activity is to earn funds to keep an armed struggle going, does that render the crime part of the conduct of war? Is the determining factor what the money is needed for? A similar question can be asked about pillaging of mineral fields by armed groups: must one distinguish when rebels are doing this to pay for the continuation of a rebellion, or when they are doing it purely for the purposes of profit? The reality is that crime by armed groups is often committed for both reasons – and even where it is done to keep rebellion going, this in itself is often done to extend the time during which pillaging for profit can occur. There are no clear answers to these questions – yet these reveal some of the problems in trying to apply this legal standard in new wars.

If this hurdle is passed and it is found that actions are taken in the context of hostilities, one must then determine whether individual actions constitute direct participation. Chapter 2 described the various conflicting interpretations of direct participation. The ICRC has attempted to clarify these in its Interpretive

Guidance – although its suggested requirements are by no means accepted by all.[17] Going with the Interpretive Guidance's requirements for the sake of this discussion, three requirements must be met for an act to constitute direct participation. First, the act must be likely to adversely affect the military operations or capacity of a party to the conflict, or alternatively to inflict death, injury or destruction on persons or objects protected against direct attack (threshold of harm); second, there must be a direct causal link between the act and the harm likely to result from that act, or from a coordinated military operation of which that act constitutes an integral part (direct causation); and third, the act must be specifically designed to cause the harm, in support of one party to the conflict to the detriment of another (belligerent nexus).[18] In practice, these three requirements are interlinked and blend into one another. While these requirements might make sense in theory, when applied to new wars, problems quickly become evident.

> Our only motive to exist was killing. That is the only thing that we thought about … I burned houses, captured people, I carried looted properties. I was responsible for tying people, and killing. I was not too good at shooting, but I was an expert in burning houses. This was less risky.
>
> (Girl soldier, Sierra Leone)[19]

In some conflicts in Africa women have been actively involved in fighting. They have taken part in attacks, shooting, killing and military raids – acts that clearly constitute direct participation. Women have been involved in perpetrating attacks directed at civilians; killing, maiming, facilitating rapes and amputating civilian limbs. According to the Interpretive Guidance, while not directed at a party to a conflict, attacks levelled (direct causation) against civilians that reach a certain gravity (threshold of harm), can constitute direct participation. However, the belligerent nexus requirement poses a problem here. Many acts of harm against civilians are not designed to cause harm in support of one party to the conflict to the detriment of another. The Interpretive Guidance is silent on how to deal with this. But this is an important question in new wars, where harming civilians is frequently a central strategy, yet not one designed to harm warring parties in the traditional sense. This problem reveals how the Interpretive Guidance's requirements are geared at certain types of military objectives, while new wars operate in wholly different ways.

Consider an example; in 2014 Islamist Group Boko Haram kidnapped over 200 girls from the city of Chibuk in northeastern Nigeria, many of whom were reportedly sold or trafficked into marriages. In March 2015, 506 women and children were reportedly abducted from the town of Damasak. Boko Haram have also committed numerous other violent acts against civilians, as well as other large-scale abductions. Would these actions constitute direct participation in hostilities? The preliminary questions are whether Boko Haram is involved in an armed conflict, of what type and against whom? Boko Haram seems to be fighting the Nigerian government – in addition to all Nigerian civilians who do not hold the extreme Islamist beliefs that they do. Boko Haram have conducted recent attacks in Cameroon, Chad and Niger, suggesting they are also fighting neighbouring governments and populations, adding an international element to what was formerly an internal war. Boko Haram's declaration of an Islamic caliphate raises interesting questions about internationalising – a topic beyond the scope of this chapter. In looking at Boko Haram's actions, it seems the threshold of harm and direct causation elements are easily met. However, in considering the belligerent nexus requirement, the abduction of the schoolgirls did not seem to be aimed at supporting one party to the conflict to the detriment of the other – this was not an overtly military task, it was not targeted at a fighting enemy, and could therefore not have had the effect of weakening government or any other parties' capacity to fight. However, the actions did seem to be intrinsically connected to the 'goals' of the conflict. 'Boko Haram' in Hausa means 'Western education is a sin'. Abducting girls from school could be said to be central to the group's message and mandate. Their general conflict seems to be less about defeating an enemy than about defeating an idea or way of life – in which case, kidnapping girls could be argued to be highly relevant to this.

This raises the related issue of military necessity – a problematic concept in new wars. Historically, where tactics have been shown to be militarily effective or central to achieving warring parties' goals, the law has tended to be more permissive of them, justified by IHL's 'necessity' principle.[20] But, this concept, too, is challenged by the differing goals of new wars. In these, the *aims* of conflict might not be to *defeat* an enemy and *win* a war, but rather to harm, kill or displace civilians or, even, to keep girls out of school. If a conflicting party's goal is to harm civilians, or if harming civilians does truly facilitate a group's aims in terms of the new war's strategy, does this make targeting civilians acceptable in terms of military necessity? If the *enemy* in new wars is a particular ethnic group – rather than a group of fighters – can members of that civilian group be considered military objectives? These questions again demonstrate how the traditional notions underpinning the IHL system – those supporting a specific military notion of conflict goals – make little sense in light of the aims and tactics of new wars.

Many women in African conflicts are involved in roles that do not require the perpetration of violence. Describing the lives of women in South Sudan's conflict, Stone explains that,

> In many respects, women's daily routines during the war mirrored those of peacetime; they collected water and firewood, prepared food, cared for children and sustained the daily necessities of life. However, in addition, they also carried food, ammunition and medication to the frontlines, and would return with wounded combatants who they cared for, or had to bury if they did not survive. One of the most important roles for women was to clear up after a battle, and gather resources for their comrades. Ammunition stocks took priority, and several women interviewed claimed to have carried up to 50 kilograms of ammunition from the scenes of raids.[21]

Tasks like collecting firewood and water, preparing food and looking after armed group bases would not constitute direct participation – despite how important these might be to the subsistence of a group. These are not designed to cause harm (threshold of harm) to the opposing side's military capacity (belligerent nexus) and there is no direct causal link (direct causation) between their roles and the harm caused to the other side.

Harder to classify are those tasks performed by women that are more closely related to the waging of war, like carrying supplies and ammunition to the frontlines. Women often play roles in preparation for, or following from an attack – with the actual attacks carried out by men. Chapter 2 explained how acts 'in preparation for' attacks can constitute direct participation if they have a 'military nature'. The narrow notion of military nature seems problematic if one considers what it actually takes to carry off successful military operations today – 'non-military' preparatory components, or rather, those actions that are not physical, violent or kinetic, can be much more critical to the success of an attack and can render it far more deadly. Understandings of the military versus non-military nature of acts derive from an establishment view of conflict, one that is ill suited to the realities of modern warfare. The Commentaries excluded preparatory acts like recruiting and training from being considered as direct participation[22] – also problematic, in that providing in-depth training on how to use particular weapons systems in preparation for a strike, seems like a quintessentially military task, and one that is certainly within the ambit of combatants in state armies.

The ICRC's Interpretive Guidance weighs in on preparatory acts, stating that such acts – for example, carrying or preparing ammunition – would not constitute direct participation unless they were being specifically prepared for a precise attack, so that the tailored preparation formed an integral part of that specific attack.[23] So if women were carrying ammunition to the frontline in order that it would be available there for general use, this would not qualify as direct participation, but if they were carrying ammunition to a specified location, in order that it would be used in a particular attack, this might quality. In terms of the Interpretive Guidance's approach, if training was conducted for a specific attack and formed an integral part of that planned attack, it could be argued to be direct participation after all.

> She received military training and was selected to be a bodyguard of the senior commander and his captive "wife". She was trained in the use of and carried a two-pistol grip machine gun. The commander would move under her cover when he went out into the field and during fighting. She was also responsible for watching over the commander and his captive "wife" when back at the compound. Additionally, she served as a night security guard in the compound on alert for any attacks....
>
> (RUF, Sierra Leone)[24]

Women acting as guards generally; guarding group's bases or guarding specific individuals, would not be directly participating. However, they might be directly participating if they were keeping guard as part of a specific attack, and the guarding formed an integral part thereof. If a woman were guarding a specific individual – as in the quote above – and he was directly participating in an attack, an argument could be made that she was directly participating too. Of course, a counter-argument could also be made that a bodyguard does not become a direct participant just because the person being guarded takes part in an attack. There is no clarity on which of these positions is legally correct. Acts like caring for the wounded and carrying wounded from the fighting front, often performed by women, do not constitute direct participation – although, notably, it is actually an IHL obligation to care for war wounded.[25] Clearing up battle-grounds and burying the dead also do not qualify, despite the fact that these might be standard armed group functions – although in limited cases one could conceivably argue that clearing up is a part of a coordinated military operation of which that specific act constitutes an integral part.

While these nuances are somewhat helpful in theory, it is difficult to see how armed actors in Africa could be expected to make these distinctions in practice. As an example, if enemies see women in opposing armed groups carrying bundles of ammunition, how could they be expected to know whether these bundles were being carried generally to or from an area of fighting, or if the ammunition was being carried to a specific planned attack?

What becomes clear in applying the law to women in African non-state groups is that most of the tasks that women typically play in these groups do not meet accepted understandings of direct participation. Women's participation takes different forms to those of men, forms that tend to be removed from the military focused, kinetic notions underlying current understanding of direct participation. This application of the law demonstrates the male bias underlying the concept, a concept that was primarily crafted to encompass those roles held by men.

Those women who are classified as directly participating can be targeted for the duration of their direct participation. Again, this is simpler in theory than practice. Women in armed groups might be allocated a range of assignments, some of which constitute direct participation and some of which do not. It is hard to see how those in opposing groups could be expected to know who is en route to what task and when different assignments begin and end. Consider members of armed groups living on a secluded base in 'the bush', where all individuals work on a range of tasks, both combat and non-combat. It would be nearly impossible for enemy fighters to determine the starts and ends of specific activities. It is not clear that the precise distinctions IHL expects one to make even exist in the planning and execution of actions. There is evident fluidity in new wars fighting, with attacks frequently not planned and organised in the way IHL anticipates – and not having formal starting and ending points, which demarcate the boundaries of these actions.

To deal with these problems, the Interpretive Guidance proposes focusing on group membership rather than on specific individual action. In terms of its approach, to determine whether women can be targeted, one must determine if they hold a 'continuous combat function'. To establish this, one must determine whether a women's direct participation is *occasional*, in which case she would be a civilian and would lose her protection from attack for just the duration of her direct participation, or continuous, in which case she would lose her protection for the duration of her membership in the armed group. Applying this standard to women in African armed groups raises many questions. What percentage of a woman's time would need to be spent fighting to achieve continuous combat function? Could women whose normal tasks include a mix of both duties relating to battle and other support and domestic duties ever have continuous combat functions? The answers to these questions are not clear. In framing its continuous combat function approach, the Interpretive Guidance foresees a clear separation between a movement and its armed wing.[26] However, this, too, does not make sense in all African contexts. While this might work with certain liberation parties, like Apartheid South Africa's African National Congress and its separate armed wing, Umkhonto we Sizwe, it does not hold true with more integrated political secessionist movements. In its fight against Sudan, the SPLA/M's 'Army' and 'Movement' were one and the same, with all in the population getting involved in any ways that they could.

Adding to the problems with continuous combat function is that when it comes to gender, this gets us no further than a direct participation assessment. Continuous combat function uses the same standard as direct participation, which is blind to gender roles and insensitive to the ways in which women participate in conflict. African armed groups rely heavily on traditional gender roles in the functioning of their groups. Merely enquiring about individuals' functions, while ignoring the ways that gender roles play out in these groups, is a blunt mechanism for separating women into targetable and non-targetable units. In applying IHL, one is trying to manipulate African roles into technical Western classifications, with results that are unsatisfactory in practice.

Participation by those within the civilian population

Many armed groups are reliant on support from civilians, who provide them with food, resources and shelter, as well as ad hoc labour. Sometimes this support is provided voluntarily, while at other times civilians are forced to provide this. Here, individuals are not absorbed into armed groups, but rather play roles on a more ad hoc or isolated basis – although as has been explained, the line with armed group 'membership' tends to blur. For the most part this civilian support would not constitute direct participation.

There are, however, times when contributions by civilians could be said to constitute direct participation. A civilian woman might be forced to carry ammunition to a specific site for an armed group to use in a particular planned attack, with the moving of the ammunition being a critical component of that attack. As with participation within armed groups, the voluntary or coerced nature of the action would not affect its classification – discussed in the next chapter.

The problem is that while most civilian actions do *not* constitute direct participation, those in opposing groups may be unwilling to ignore those contributions.

In particular, lesser-resourced groups in asymmetrical conflicts may feel they do not have the luxury of ignoring those contributing to their enemies' efforts. They may also wish to discourage further support for their enemies by civilian populations by targeting civilians who support their opponents, regardless of the fact that this is disallowed by the law. The fact that IHL does not provide armed groups a means to lawfully deal with support provided by civilian populations, might encourage violations of the law. Conversely, the narrow interpretation of direct participation, which excludes participating civilians from being targeted, might encourage armed groups to use civilians in certain roles knowing they will be immune from attack,[27] creating a perverse incentive for armed groups to involve more civilians in conflict. While a narrow interpretation of direct participation might appear to be protective of women, in putting many outside the realm of lawful targeting this may ultimately lead to a more dangerous situation for women more generally. Of course, this is not to say that the clear solution is to broaden the law allowing a wider group to be targeted – clearly that comes with its own set of problems, problems that are deliberated in the chapters that follow.

World-over, civilian women have been targeted for their participation in conflict – participation that often does not meet the level of direct participation. 'Women Under Siege' collates information about women in the Syrian conflict. It tells of one woman detained, raped and tortured at a checkpoint, charged with "being from a neighborhood which had rebelled against the regime".[28] Another Syrian women was imprisoned, tortured and sexually abused for eight months for putting up revolutionary posters,[29] while another was detained for nursing wounded rebels.[30] Just because women are not "directly participating" does not mean they are left alone. Men, too, are targeted for actions that do not meet the standard of direct participation. For example, the Pentagon has included on its "target list" Afghani drug traffickers with ties to the Taliban, as they argue the drug money helps to finance Taliban's operations.[31] The legality of this is dubious, demonstrating a set of rules that are not consistently followed in practice – even by those in dominant government regimes.

There is currently much academic discussion about how IHL should deal with increased civilians on the battle space. As with much IHL literature, this tends to focus on particular types of civilian involvement, in particular types of conflict – most notably male private civilian contractors in the conflicts the USA are involved in in Iraq and Afghanistan.[32] The IHL literature scarcely considers different types of civilian involvement, like that of African women contributing to new wars. Conclusions about private civilian contractors do not necessarily translate to the disempowered, exploited and coerced civilian women embroiled in African conflicts.

Conclusions from applying the law

In applying the law to these groups in this chapter, I was struck by how difficult it was to make these classifications. Often, it is altogether unclear how the law should be applied to a given group. In many situations, convincing arguments could be made that actions are direct participation or that they are not, leaving little in the way of legal clarity – problematic given the grave consequences of a direct participation label. The law is complex, often vague, with competing interpretations that sometimes lead to wholly different results. The law is also highly nuanced, with minor differences in actions or circumstances changing legal classifications completely.

The facts to which the law is applied are also unclear. IHL is applied in the 'fog of war'. The conflict arena is messy, often characterised by a lack of clear ascertainable information. Those applying IHL in battle do so in moments of stress and danger. In addition to obscuring facts, conflicts also distort perceptions. People in war hate their enemies. Enemies become dehumanised. Soldiers feel this too, perhaps even more acutely.[33] It is incorrect to assume that soldiers *can* make wholly rational decisions in conflict, unaffected by the sentiments and circumstances surrounding them.

Distinction is not a science. While the principle of distinction is inherently legalistic, reality is not legalistic at all. Events, people and actions rarely break down into the neat categories proposed by the law. As such, applications of IHL require manipulating facts to fit within rigid legal categories. Judgment calls need to be made and lines need to be drawn in cases where people could reasonably fit into more than one category. What is evident is that in many cases the distinctions the law requires are not ones that can actually be made in practice. In new wars, the rules of IHL are often unworkable or highly impractical.

Difficulties in applying this law are particularly acute in Africa, where armed actors often still rely on relatively unsophisticated intelligence methods. Conflicts currently fought by Western powers in other regions tend to utilise sophisticated surveillance and intelligence technology, such as unmanned combat aerial vehicles (drones), which allow them to ascertain precise details about an enemy, and hence facilitate their making the distinctions required by the law. Of course, these technologies bring a host of different problems.[34] In contrast, in many African conflicts assessments are still made in crude ways, relying on what actors can personally see or ascertain in a curtailed environment. This means it is seldom possible for those outside of armed groups to ascertain with any level of clarity, what different individuals within groups are doing and when. The interpretations of direct participation seem better suited to counterterror or targeted killing type situations, where a good deal of specific intelligence is collected about each individual target – rather than to the types of fighting found in Africa's new wars, where armed groups clash with other groups with little intelligence collected about specific participants.

Adding to the problem is that those who are subject to IHL are generally fighters who often have little, if any, understanding of IHL.[35] While resource-rich armies might have legal advisors providing on-the-moment legal advice, for other armed actors this is not the case. The problem is amplified in Africa, where fighters are likely to be uneducated, often illiterate and therefore little versed in the nuances of this highly complex law. If academics, judges and specialised experts can hardly work out how people should be classified in difficult cases, how can we expect scarcely educated and trained fighters to? It seems a failing that the law does not properly cater for use by those it is intended for – fighters whose actions are to be regulated by it in conflict.

Another evident problem is that the factors leading to women being perceived as combatants on the ground in Africa, often differ to those laid out by the principle of distinction. In some African groups, women are considered combatants even where they do not fight, while in others women are not seen as combatants even when actively involved in fighting.[36] South Sudan's SPLA recruited females throughout the war. However, quite early on in the war an SPLA decision was made to keep women away from frontline combat and to restrict them to support duties. Despite this, thousands of women continued to be recruited, and at times were promoted to high ranks within the movement. They were considered by others within the SPLA to be combatants and they considered themselves as such – and importantly, they were considered by the enemy to be combatants and targeted as such.[37] In contrast, the LRA's abducted girls took part in active fighting. Despite this they were seen as 'abductees' or 'wives', not as 'combatants'. Even the Ugandan government and the militaries fighting the LRA recognised these women were not normal combatants, making efforts to rescue them rather than to target them. One of the often-stated difficulties in fighting the LRA was the known presence of so many children and women, who, despite fighting, were understood to not be true combatants.

The labelling of female fighters on the ground takes many variations – most of which veer from the notions found in IHL. This disjuncture between legal classifications and local perceptions is problematic. For one thing, those conducting targeting are expected to use criteria that differ from the ways in which they understand the facts on the ground. Fighters might be legally prohibited from targeting those who they see to be combatants participating actively against them. This is likely to negatively impact on adherence with the law.

The question of how local perceptions can or should be utilised in distinction classifications is difficult. It is clearly important to have universal rules that apply in the same way to people in all conflicts. Allowing for too much regional or circumstantial variation would make for an unpredictable, unworkable law. Perhaps the real problem is that IHL's definitions and classifications are so removed from the realities of today's conflicts – in Africa and more broadly – that they fail to provide a workably broad regulation. Perhaps, rather than the answer being that local specifications should be taken into account, a generalised law is required – but one that is more reflective of real participation in conflict, and better suited to accommodating new and alternative modes of participation, including those of women.

When drafted, the principle of distinction was anticipated to be applied to particular contexts and to particular types of actors. When one applies the law to 'atypical' examples (like conflicts in Africa) and 'atypical' actors (like female participants) – all of which are in fact highly typical today – this reveals the fault lines and inconsistencies in the law, shedding light on the law's inadequacy for use in these contexts. The next chapter answers the central questions posed in this book; given these problems, does the principle of distinction actually operate to protect and serve women in the context of new wars? And if not, what is it actually achieving?

Notes

1 Medical and religious personnel are the exceptions to the rule that grants combatant status to members of state armed forces, because they are understood to enjoy the right to neutrality.
2 Fleck, Dieter. *The Handbook of Humanitarian Law in Armed Conflicts*. 2nd edition. Oxford: Oxford University Press, 2008, at 87.
3 'Interpretive Guidance on the Notion of Direct Participation in Hostilities Under International Humanitarian Law'. *International Review of the Red Cross* 90, no. 872 (2009): 991–1047.
4 Fleck, supra note 3.
5 Ibid.
6 Fisher, Max. 'Map: Which Countries Allow Women in Front-Line Combat Roles?' *Washington Post*, 25 January 2013.
7 Fleck, supra note 3.
8 Ibid.
9 Article 4(4) GC3.
10 Interpretive Guidance, supra note 4.
11 Rule 1 and 3, Henckaerts, Jean-Marie. 'Study on Customary International Humanitarian Law: A Contribution to the Understanding and Respect for the Rule of Law in Armed Conflict'. *International Review of the Red Cross* 87, no. 857 (2005): 175–212.
12 If a non-state armed group in an IAC does not 'belong to' a state party to the conflict, then in terms of the Geneva Conventions, its members would be classified as civilians. One should, however, note that that such an armed group might still be regarded as a party to a separate NIAC occurring concurrently. Were that the case, the NIAC laws would be used to determine their status.
13 Interpretive Guidance, supra note 4.
14 Part 2, A ii 3b, Interpretive Guidance, supra note 4.
15 *Sudan: Darfur: Rape as a Weapon of War: Sexual Violence and Its Consequences*. London: Amnesty International, 18 July 2004.
16 Interpretive Guidance, supra note 4.
17 Schmitt, Michael. 'Deconstructing Direct Participation in Hostilities: The Constitutive Elements'. *New York University International Law and Politics* 42, no. 3 (2010): 697–740.
18 Interpretive Guidance, supra note 4.
19 Denov, Myriam. *Child Soldiers: Sierra Leone's Revolutionary United Front*. Cambridge: Cambridge University Press, 2010, at 111.
20 For example, IHL has historically tolerated methods of warfare that states found useful, while banning weapons when no influential state wanted them anymore, such as blinding weapons.
21 Stone, Lydia, 'We Were all Soldiers': Female Combatants in South Sudan's Civil War, in Bubenzer, Friederike, and Stern, Orly (eds), *Hope, Pain & Patience: The Lives of Women in South Sudan*. Johannesburg: Jacana Media, 2012, at 34.
22 Queguiner, Francois. 'Direct Participation in Hostilities under International Humanitarian Law'. *Program on Humanitarian Policy and Conflict Research at Harvard University*, 2003.
23 Part 2 V 2 a, Interpretive Guidance, supra note 4.
24 McKay, Susan, and Mazurana, Dyan. *Where Are the Girls? Girls in Fighting Forces in Northern Uganda, Sierra Leone and Mozambique: Their Lives During and After War*. Montreal: Rights & Democracy, 2004, at 92.

25 Art 12 and 15, GC1, Art 12 and Art 18 GC2, Art 16 GC4, Art 10 AP 1.
26 Part 2, II, 3 a, Interpretive Guidance, supra note 4.
27 Schmitt, Michael. '"Direct Participation in Hostilities" and 21st Century Armed Conflict'. In Fischer, Horst (ed.), *Crisis Management and Humanitarian Protection: Festschrift Fur*, 505–29. Berlin: BWV, 2004.
28 'Women under Siege, Documenting Sexualized Violence in Syria, Woman Describes Multiple Rapes at Idlib Checkpoint'. *Crowdmap*. https://womenundersiegesyria.crowdmap.com/reports/view/254.
29 'Women under Siege, Woman, 25, Tells Vanity Fair of Sexual Abuse in Multiple Detention Centers'. *Crowdmap*. https://womenundersiegesyria.crowdmap.com/reports/view/237.
30 'Women under Siege, Former Prisoner Gives Account of Torture and Rape in Hama Detention Center'. *Crowdmap*. https://womenundersiegesyria.crowdmap.com/reports/view/150.
31 Risen, James. 'U.S. to Hunt Down Afghan Drug Lords Tied to Taliban'. *New York Times*, 10 August 2009.
32 See, Carmola, Kateri. *Private Security Contractors and New Wars: Risk, Law, and Ethics*. Contemporary Security Studies. Abingdon: Routledge, 2010. Cameron, Lindsey. 'Private Military Companies: Their Status under International Humanitarian Law and its Impact on their Regulation'. *International Review of the Red Cross* 88, no. 863 (2006): 573–98. Faite, Alexandre. 'Involvement of Private Contractors in Armed Conflict: Implications under International Humanitarian Law'. *Defence Studies*, 4, no. 2 (2004): 166–183.
33 Brough, Michael. 'Dehumanization of the Enemy and the Moral Equality of Soldiers'. In Brough, M. W., Lango. J. W. and van der Linden, H. (eds), *Rethinking the Just War Tradition*, 149–170. Albany, NY: State University of New York Press, 2007.
34 For a discussion about the types of issues that the principle of distinction confronts in more technologically sophisticated settings, see Schmitt, supra note 24. Wagner, Markus. 'Autonomy in the Battlespace: Independently Operating Weapon Systems and the Law of Armed Conflict'. In *International Humanitarian Law and the Changing Technology of War*. Leiden: Nijhoff, 2013, 99–122.
35 For information about training of armed forces on IHL see, Roberts, David. 'Training the Armed Forces to Respect International Humanitarian Law: The Perspective of the ICRC Delegate to the Armed and Security Forces of South Asia'. *International Review of the Red Cross* 319 (1997): 433–446.
36 Verhey, Beth, 'Reaching the Girls, Study on Girls Associated with Armed Forces and Groups in the Democratic Republic of Congo'. London: Save the Children UK, CARE, IFESH and IRC, 2004.
37 Stone, supra note 23.

Bibliography

Books and articles

Baaz, Maria Eriksson, and Stern, Maria. 'Making Sense of Violence: Voices of Soldiers in the Congo (DRC)'. *The Journal of Modern African Studies* 46, no. 01 (2008): 57–86.

Brough, Michael. 'Dehumanization of the Enemy and the Moral Equality of Soldiers'. In Brough, M. W., Lango. J. W. and van der Linden, H. (eds), *Rethinking the Just War Tradition*, 149–170. Albany, NY: State University of New York Press, 2007. Cameron, Lindsey. 'Private Military Companies: Their Status under International Humanitarian Law and its Impact on their Regulation'. *International Review of the Red Cross* 88, no. 863 (2006): 573–598.

Carmola, Kateri. *Private Security Contractors and New Wars: Risk, Law, and Ethics*. Contemporary Security Studies. Abingdon: Routledge, 2010.

Denov, Myriam. *Child Soldiers: Sierra Leone's Revolutionary United Front*. Cambridge: Cambridge University Press, 2010.

Faite, Alexandre. 'Involvement of Private Contractors in Armed Conflict: Implications under International Humanitarian Law'. *Defence Studies*, 4, no. 2 (2004): 166–183.

Fisher, Max. 'Map: Which Countries Allow Women in Front-Line Combat Roles?' *Washington Post*, 25 January 2013.

Fleck, Dieter. *The Handbook of Humanitarian Law in Armed Conflicts*. 2nd edition. Oxford: Oxford University Press, 2008.

Henckaerts, Jean-Marie. 'Study on Customary International Humanitarian Law: A Contribution to the Understanding and Respect for the Rule of Law in Armed Conflict'. *International Review of the Red Cross* 87, no. 857 (2005): 175–212.

McKay, Susan and Mazurana, Dyan. *Where Are the Girls? Girls in Fighting Forces in Northern Uganda, Sierra Leone and Mozambique: Their Lives during and After War*. Montreal: Rights & Democracy, 2004.

Queguiner, Francois. 'Direct Participation in Hostilities Under International Humanitarian Law'. *Program on Humanitarian Policy and Conflict Research at Harvard University* (2003).

Risen, James. 'U.S. to Hunt Down Afghan Drug Lords Tied to Taliban'. *New York Times*, 10 August 2009.

Roberts, David. 'Training the Armed Forces to Respect International Humanitarian Law: The Perspective of the ICRC'. *International Review of the Red Cross* 319 (1997): 433–446.

Schmitt, Michael. 'Deconstructing Direct Participation in Hostilities: The Constitutive Elements'. *New York University International Law and Politics* 42, no. 3 (2010): 697–740.

Schmitt, Michael. ''Direct Participation in Hostilities' and 21st Century Armed Conflict'. In Fischer, Horst (ed.), *Crisis Management and Humanitarian Protection: Festschrift Fur*, 505–529. Berlin: BWV, 2004.

Stone, Lydia, 'We Were all Soldiers': Female Combatants in South Sudan's Civil War, in Bubenzer, Friederike, and Stern, Orly. *Hope, Pain & Patience: The Lives of Women in South Sudan*. Johannesburg: Jacana Media, 2012.

Verhey, Beth, 'Reaching the Girls, Study on Girls Associated with Armed Forces and Groups in the Democratic Republic of Congo', London: Save the Children UK, CARE, IFESH and IRC, 2004.

Wagner, Markus. 'Autonomy in the Battlespace: Independently Operating Weapon Systems and the Law of Armed Conflict'. In *International Humanitarian Law and the Changing Technology of War*, Leiden: Nijhoff, 2013, 99–122.

Cases

The Prosecutor v. *Alex Tamba Brima Bazzy Kamara Santigie Borbor Kanu*. SCSL-04-16-T, 2008.

Treaties

Geneva Convention Relative to the Protection of Civilian Persons in Time of War (Fourth Geneva Convention), 12 August 1949, 75 UNTS 287.

Geneva Convention Relative to the Treatment of Prisoners of War (Third Geneva Convention), 12 August 1949, 75 UNTS 135.

Geneva Convention for the Amelioration of the Condition of Wounded, Sick and Shipwrecked Members of Armed Forces at Sea (Second Geneva Convention), 12 August 1949, 75 UNTS 85.

Geneva Convention for the Amelioration of the Condition of the Wounded and Sick in Armed Forces in the Field (First Geneva Convention), 12 August 1949, 75 UNTS 31.

Protocol Additional to the Geneva Conventions of 12 August 1949, and relating to the Protection of Victims of International Armed Conflicts (Protocol I), 8 June 1977, 1125 UNTS 3.

Other policy documents

'Interpretive Guidance on the Notion of Direct Participation in Hostilities Under International Humanitarian Law'. *International Review of the Red Cross* 90, no. 872 (2009): 991–1047.

Media articles and websites

Sudan: Darfur: Rape as a Weapon of War: Sexual Violence and Its Consequences. Amnesty International, 18 July 2004.

Sengupta, Kim. 'Girl Soldiers: The Forgotten Victims of War'. *Independent*, 25 April 2005.

'Women under Siege, Documenting Sexualized Violence in Syria, Woman Describes Multiple Rapes at Idlib Checkpoint'. *Crowdmap.* https://womenundersiegesyria.crowdmap.com/reports/view/254.

'Women Under Siege, Woman, 25, Tells Vanity Fair of Sexual Abuse in Multiple Detention Centers'. *Crowdmap.* https://womenundersiegesyria.crowdmap.com/reports/view/237.

'Women Under Siege, Former Prisoner Gives Account of Torture and Rape in Hama Detention Center'. *Crowdmap.* https://womenundersiegesyria.crowdmap.com/reports/view/150.

7 Does the principle of distinction serve women in modern conflict?

Does the principle of distinction in its current formulation serve women in conflict, or does it fail to do so, even putting women at increased risk? This chapter draws together the findings and discussions from earlier chapters, looking to see what they reveal about the principle of distinction and its application to women in Africa's new wars.

The previous chapter demonstrated how few women fit into the legal fold as 'combatants' or 'direct participants' in hostilities. The narrow wording of the laws and their accepted interpretations effectively exclude many women from being recognised as combatants or direct participants, even where women are actively engaged in armed movements. The results for women are mixed. One the one hand, this operates to provide many women with legal protection from attack; if women are not classified as combatants or direct participants, then they may not be targeted in attack. However, this chapter will argue that there are also negative consequences for women that stem from this – effects that are indirect and more difficult to identify.

The chapter examines these effects, considering the many ways in which the principle of distinction impacts on women: positive and negative, direct and indirect, evident and implied. It considers the principle's effects in a range of areas; the way it perpetuates stereotypes, how it governs targeting, its relationship with voluntariness, its failure to protect women from those within their own armed groups, the treatment of female prisoners, and the principle's effects post-conflict. Finally, the chapter considers the broader questions this book raises: Does the principle of distinction serve and protect women? If it fails women, what does this tell us about the principle's adequacy to perform its role in regulating Africa's new wars?

The principle of distinction's varied impacts on women

The principle of distinction perpetuates stereotypes about women and victimhood

The law's failure to adequately incorporate female participation affects the ways in which society understands the contributions of women to armed struggles.

The law plays a part in shaping perceptions of reality, while societal perceptions in turn influence how things are regulated, in mutually reinforcing processes.[1] Where laws portray women in certain ways, this entrenches expectations about how women should be and should act, reinforcing gender roles rather than challenging them.

A framing of the principle that prevents women from being recognised as combatants or direct participants, perpetuates the view that women are not active participants in conflict – instead, promoting the notion that most women are victims. This portrayal of women as victims in turn works to conceal the active roles that women play in conflict. Even when the facts on the ground lie in stark contrast to these notions – even when women are actively participating in armed movements – this law creates an additional barrier to this participation being seen and recognised. Of course, stereotypes about women do not stem solely from the law. These are already prevalent in society, derived from patriarchal norms and deeply entrenched societal beliefs. However, the law plays a part in furthering existing stereotypes, normalising them, formalising them, justifying them, and providing them with a perceived legal 'stamp of approval'.

There are negative consequences to the law's entrenching perceptions about women as victims of conflict. For one thing, this promotes further victimisation of women – both from within and without armed groups. Conceptualisations that paint women as victims of war tacitly allow for, or normalise, the further victimisation of women. A perception that women are not 'real' combatants can contribute to women being discriminated against and mistreated by their male armed group peers. This also contributes to women being seen as 'spoils of war', to be used and abused at victors' wills.

Of course, painting women as victims, as the law does, can also be beneficial to them. Chapter 4 described the humanitarian world's preference for protecting 'women and children', the perceived victims of war. Women are frequently encouraged to present themselves as victims, as doing so can work to their benefit. Arguing for the removal of this 'victim' label should be done with caution, as this can also be harmful to the women one is trying to protect. This being said, the benefits of being framed as victims are not consistently conferred. Often, at the exact moments when women most need to be recognised as victims and protected as such, the opposite occurs. As an example, families and communities of abducted women returning home from armed groups frequently do not treat them as victims, instead blaming them, rejecting them and further victimising them.[2]

Most women embroiled in conflict are in some ways 'victims' of war. Even those who are actively involved in waging war often have stories of immense suffering, coercive circumstances and exploitation – stories that could certainly be portrayed using a victim lens. However, this lens serves to obscure other facets of women's experiences. While it is important to highlight the victimising aspects of women's experiences, solely doing so runs the risk of relegating women to "... voiceless victims, often devoid of agency, moral conscience, and economic potential".[3] Coulter points out how few writers manage to move away from notions of female combatants as victims, in part because of the sexual victimisation they face. In her work, she attempts to present a more layered account of Sierra Leone's female fighters. She notes,

> Whatever their personal circumstances, they grew from girls to women during a period of intense and sometimes extreme social change. While many definitely did what they could to flee the war zone, some took the opportunity to loot and fight in the destructive trail of the various fighting forces. During the decade-long war, most of them also fell in love, some married, others divorced, and most had children.[4]

Providing a more nuanced account of women in war lies at the heart of the SC's Women, Peace and Security Agenda. In addition to considering women as victims of war and exploring the protections they require, the SC Resolutions – particularly the later ones – also include other representations of women, as actors and agents.[5] Otto explains that,

> This shift from victim to valued contributor disturbs not only the traditional narrative of women's weakness and vulnerability, and their need for (male/state/military) protection, but is also disruptive of the gendered ways of thinking that have served to legitimate armed conflict (as 'manly') and silence alternative ways of thinking (as feminine or 'wimpish').[6]

However, while taking important steps in this direction, the Resolutions have been inconsistent in this regard and ultimately have not gone far enough. For example, they fail to deal with the structural factors, such as poverty, that prevent women from truly being agents with transformational capacity.[7]

Humanitarian discourse seems to have an inability to hold on to the fact that victim, agent and perpetrator can co-exist within the same person. The field is laden with ideas about the dichotomy between victim and perpetrator – and the adjunct lack of agency for victims. However, this polarised binary position is inadequate to describe the lived experiences of female combatants.[8] Female combatants provide a striking illustration of the duality of victim and perpetrator. To get any real sense of the experiences of women participating in African conflicts, notions of victimhood, perpetration and agency must be considered together. For one thing, where one finds violence *by* women, one often finds violence *against* women. The two go hand in hand. Women perpetrate violence, yet are themselves subject to violence. Some women assert their power by becoming involved in hostilities. By becoming a perpetrator, a woman can escape being, or feeling like, a victim, providing some perceived sense of control over her life. Carrying a gun can provide some security and can prevent women becoming victims of further violence. Sometimes women exercise their agency by being cruel towards others. Female combatants' violence against civilians can be perceived as a form of revenge – only redirected, as they have no scope to level revenge against those who have actually harmed them.[9]

Being a victim is often portrayed as synonymous with a lack of agency. However, even within situations of immense victimisation, women retain agency. In the most constrained circumstances, women have some choice about how to act and some space for negotiation. Of course, one should not overstate this; their choices are constrained due to their circumstances, due to poverty and due to the fact that they are women. The choice between dying, experiencing continuous violence, or fighting is not much of a choice. Coulter acknowledges that, "… even with a gun in hand, my informants' choices were circumscribed – by convention, tradition, morality, religion, family, or fear – in ways that were different from men's".[10] However, even within these constrained spaces, women can still navigate how they wish to act, employing a range of strategies. Denov explains,

> Girls in fighting forces made conscious attempts to protect themselves and negotiate their security during their time with the armed group.… Such attempts to negotiate their safety were done through a variety of means including the use of small arms, through 'marriages' to powerful commanders, through the perpetration of severe acts of violence, through subtle and bold acts of resistance.[11]

Female combatants blend elements of victimhood and perpetration in striking and complex ways. This nuanced picture is far removed from that which underlies the principle of distinction – where the dichotomy between combatant/civilian or those directly participating/not leaves no room for complex combinations. The principle of distinction assumes a single identity – fighter or not fighter. In contrast, women assume numerous identities, identities for which the law's binaries leave little room.

Voluntariness

Voluntariness and consent are central themes of feminist thought. Voluntariness is not addressed by the principle of distinction. There is no requirement that to qualify as a combatant or direct participant one needs to be acting voluntarily. In fact, many state armies have compulsory enlistment, something that has never been framed as problematic in IHL. Those forcibly recruited into armies and armed groups are classified in the same ways as those who act voluntarily.

The threat of state military conscription is a real fear for many – and there can be terrible consequences for those who refuse to enlist, including death and imprisonment. State conscription can be as violent and harmful as that by non-state actors – sometimes made worse because recruits cannot seek state protection. Eritrea has mandatory national service, including for women. Although by decree this should be limited to 18 months, in practice this is often prolonged indefinitely, keeping youth in perpetual bondage. Conscripts are paid under $30 a month, are poorly fed, often to the point of emaciation, and female conscripts have reportedly been sexually abused by commanders. Human Rights Watch estimates that an average 1,500 Eritreans flee the country each month to escape conscription, with border guards having orders to shoot-to-kill escapees.[12]

There are, however, differentiating factors between state conscription and involuntary recruitment by armed groups. In both the international system and domestically, states are perceived as having authority to demand conscription. State authority legitimises military command.[13] Non-state groups do not have state-sanctioned authority, giving their recruitment a different position in law. While voluntariness may not be a factor for the application of the principle of distinction, this does not mean that forced recruitment by non-state actors is legally permitted. Abducting women into armed groups violates various laws, including international law prohibitions on recruiting children (when abductees are underage) and domestic laws against kidnapping, rape and violence. It is therefore not that forced recruitment is ignored by law – rather, questions of voluntariness are disregarded by the principle of distinction. However, as the principle is the law's primary legal mechanism for protection in conflict, this seems to be a problem.

Something feels troubling about withholding the principle of distinction's protections from those acting entirely against their will, often in such extreme cruel circumstances. In IHL, failing to make any provision for even extreme degrees of compulsion and for the possibility of differential treatment for those in these situations, it shows itself to be blind to the nuances of participation and consent in new wars. Of course, distinction is not only there to protect – rather, the law aims to strike a balance between the needs of military actors and humanitarian concerns. That those who are forced to participate can still be lawful targets is understood to be a necessary consequence of this balance. However, it feels like an unsuitable balance has been struck. As Sjoberg notes, the distinction between civilian and combatant does,

> not take into account the complexities of consent, human interdependence, and political choice in a way that allows true distinction between 'those who ought to be held liable for the war' and 'those who ought not be liable for the war'.[14]

While the law is clear on the fact that voluntariness is not a factor in determining combatancy or direct participation, there have been some recent inroads in this area, suggesting that this area of law might be developing. Voluntariness comes up in discussions about human shields – those who stand in the way of legitimate targets in order to prevent attacks on them. In the literature on human shields[15] a distinction is made between 'voluntary' and 'involuntary' human shields. Schmitt argues that if people wilfully put themselves in the way of military targets to avert attacks, their actions might constitute direct participation.[16] As voluntary shields take positive steps to frustrate actions that would contribute to military goals, they are affecting them in a direct causal way. Intent is therefore key; one is only a voluntary shield if it is one's explicit *intent* to *frustrate* a military operation – those merely electing to remain in dangerous places are not voluntary human shields.[17] A different view is that human shields are not directly participating, as their actions do not meet a qualitative threshold – they are not *doing* enough. Merely getting in the way by creating moral pause on the part of an attacker is not enough to constitute an action.[18]

Those used as shields tend to be those seen as dispensable, generally those with subordinate positions in society, like women. On the Women Under Siege website, a woman recounts that,

> I saw maybe 100 women stripped naked and used as human shields, forced to walk on all sides of the army tanks during the fighting. When their tanks rolled back into the Alawite neighborhood, the women disappeared with them.[19]

Another woman she said she saw, "a column of 10 to 15 women walking in front of Assad's tanks",

> They made the women walk in front of the tanks first to use them as shields. They passed a resistance area and then stripped them and raped them and killed them … the girls being raped were screaming 'God, we have nobody but you'. No one could help them.[20]

The framing of some people as 'shields' underscores the importance of recognition of participants in conflict. Those whose contributions are recognised and valued are labelled direct participants or combatants. Those who are undervalued and perceived as dispensable are labelled as shields. The law's labelling reveals what its system values – and with its labelling, the law entrenches these values. This speaks to why it is important that women also be recognised as combatants and direct participants by IHL; the alternative to recognising women's participation, is having them seen as dispensable. Gender inequality plays out both in the differing roles, as well as in the different framing of these roles.

The Interpretive Guidance briefly touches on voluntariness in the context of direct participation. When discussing the 'belligerent nexus' requirement for direct participation, the Interpretive Guidance confirms that,

> … belligerent nexus is generally not influenced by factors such as personal distress or preference, or by the mental ability or willingness of persons to assume responsibility for their conduct. Accordingly, even civilians forced to directly participate in hostilities or children below the lawful recruitment age may lose protection against attack.[21]

However, it goes on to say that in exceptional circumstances, such as where persons are "completely deprived of their physical freedom of action (e.g. when they are involuntary human shields physically coerced into providing cover in close combat)", the person's mental state *could* affect the belligerent nexus. It notes,

> Civilians in such extreme circumstances cannot be regarded as performing an action (i.e. doing something) in any meaningful sense and, therefore, remain protected against direct attack despite the belligerent nexus of the military operation in which they are being instrumentalized.[22]

By bringing up such extreme circumstances, one could argue that a door is being opened for further development in this direction.

Voluntariness comes up in the literature on child soldiers. The ICC's Lubanga decision considers voluntariness in relation to child (boy and girl) combatants in the DRC. Coomaraswamy, the UN Special Representative for Children and Armed Conflict, testified to the ICC that when it comes to children, it can be difficult to distinguish enlistment (voluntary recruitment) and conscription (recruitment with elements of compulsion). Children often join groups 'voluntarily' as they are orphans seeking a means of survival, lacking any other viable options, support or role models. She noted that, "... the line between voluntary and forced recruitment is therefore not only legally irrelevant but practically superficial in the context of children in armed conflict".[23] When considering the vulnerable positions of women in African societies and their lack of alternative options, especially when left without the societally sanctioned protection of men, many of the arguments made in relation to children could apply to them just as well. Of course, saying this risks infantilising women by categorising them with children, something already done all too often. However, thinking about child combatants opens up room for possible differential treatment of certain fighters, which takes into consideration their circumstances – an idea that could prove useful for women.

Sinha proposes an interesting approach to dealing with child combatants.[24] He proposes a category of "victimised combatants" or "super-privileged combatants" who are entitled to special treatment. This concept, he claims, is implicitly located in IHL.

> The conventions treat combatants as participants in armed conflict who deserve special treatment when they suffer harm. The first two conventions concern wounded or sick armed forces (in the field and at sea, respectively), while the third addresses captured combatants.... These conventions effectively outline rules for treating combatants with additional care when they are especially vulnerable – once they have become victims of illness, injury or capture. It seems, however, that if there is a class of combatants who are victims in virtue of being combatants in the first place, they might be entitled to special consideration above and beyond what is guaranteed to the standard soldier.[25]

According to Sinha's model, certain vulnerable combatants – in the case of his discussion, child combatants – would be *presumed* to be victimised, and as such would be entitled to 'super-privileges'. These super-privileges could be as follows: first, these combatants would need to be subdued using minimal force and be given the opportunity to surrender in cases where other combatants might not be. Second, when captured, different rules would apply to their detention. They should not be detained for the entire duration of the conflict, but rather, should have an option of early repatriation and unification with their family, or if held, should be held in a manner more akin to being a ward of the state. Effectively, they should be treated as victims rather than POWs. Whereas regular combatants must meet certain requirements for POW status, victimised combatants would receive privileges regardless of their actions.[26]

While Sinha's proposal was formulated for child soldiers, this idea could prove useful for other fighters – including forcibly recruited women. Sinha notes that, "If coercion into service is the morally relevant criterion for earning super privileges, then some adults will warrant such privileges too".[27] Of course, there would be challenges in applying this to adults – even more so than for children. For one thing, children, merely by virtue of being under 18, are understood to be unable to consent and therefore to be victimised. At least with younger children, one can tell they are children just by looking at them (although this might be less certain with teenagers). In contrast, when dealing with adult women, it is harder to tell on sight if they are coerced, necessitating more of an examination into their actions and narratives, making it harder to rely on a presumption of victimisation. A further problem is that a system like this could further entrench stereotypes about women as victims. Furthermore, integrating deviations such as these into the law would further complicate an already over-complex legal situation and would introduce solutions which are far from practical.

It seems as though a door is opening narrowly around the issue of voluntariness, with the idea being raised – albeit in very limited circumstances – that this could be a relevant factor for the principle of distinction. It is hard to know what part voluntariness *should* play. While it feels problematic for the principle to ignore consent altogether, locating an appropriate role is fraught with difficulty. It would seem unfair to propose that mandatory army conscripts may be targeted, while those forcibly recruited by non-state armed groups many not be. The means by which voluntariness could be taken into account in the principle of distinction could be an interesting area of future research.

Complicating any moves to integrate voluntariness into the law is the fact that the distinction between *voluntary* and *involuntary* recruitment or action is often far from clear. Coercive circumstances and curtailed choices can prevent genuine consent. Women who *voluntarily* enter armed groups often do so as they have few viable alternative – life outside the group in a war-riddled country might be the more dangerous and onerous option. Women might *choose* to be armed group 'wives', as the alternative is to be sexually available to all armed group men. The SCSL's Brima Appeals Chamber reflected this, stating that,

> … the relative benefits that victims of forced marriage received from the perpetrators neither signifies consent to the forced conjugal association, nor does it vitiate the criminal nature of the perpetrator's conduct given the environment of violence and coercion in which these events took place.[28]

The ICC's definition of rape[29] also acknowledges that coercive circumstance may remove consent. In Akeyesu, the ICTR explained that, "... coercive circumstances need not be evidenced by a show of physical force. ... coercion may be inherent in certain circumstances, such as armed conflict ...".[30]

There exist degrees and nuances of consent. Some women wholeheartedly wish to participate in conflict; others are forced using extreme brutality – and then there are grey areas in between. Some join armed groups thinking they are signing up for particular experiences, which then turn out to be very different – not unlike victims of human trafficking. A complex picture emerges; while women's choices are constrained by circumstances, these remain choices nevertheless. Where women have choices, these tend to still be constrained. Coercion and voluntariness present as binaries – however, in practice these blur. The principle of distinction's approach of focusing purely on individual action misses out on all of this.

Voluntary and involuntary participation in conflict are intrinsically tied in with sexual activity. This connection is at times so clear that it is formalised, with female combatants being labelled 'wives' instead of soldiers, denoting the centrality of their sexual roles to their armed group mandate. The experiences of female 'combatants' or armed group 'wives' are not wholly dissimilar to the experiences of those held in 'sexual slavery' in other contexts. If one looks at descriptions of 'rape camps' in Bosnia, described in ICTY cases like Kunarac, Kovac and Vukovic[31] (the 'rape camp case'), the experiences of women held in sexual slavery overlap with accounts of female combatancy in Africa. Across the conflict literature one finds the labels: 'female combatants'; 'women associated with armed groups'; 'sex slaves'; 'forced wives' or 'rape victims'. Yet, these are not clear distinct categories and there is much evident overlap between them. Legal analysis separates them, dealing with each discretely, disregarding the overlaps. Most women involved with armed groups fall somewhere along a continuum, once again speaking to legal categorisations that do not operate effectively in practice. These categories are challenged further in Africa. For example, the concept of 'forced marriage' can be tricky in the context of traditional societies, where marriages are never selected by individuals alone. The SCSL Appeals Chamber in the AFRC case, was the first court to recognise forced marriage as a separate crime – distinct from sexual slavery.[32] However, this distinction is criticised because the crime of forced marriage is largely indistinguishable from sexual slavery, other than by a declarative act (actors declaring the relationship to be marriage). The 'distinct elements' of forced marriage provided by the Appeals Chamber resorted to stereotypical tasks attached to marriage. However, for the crimes of sexual slavery and enslavement these same acts were characterised as proof of forced labour.[33]

It is worth noting that it is not only women who experience involuntary exploitation in conflict. Sexual exploitation and abuse of men has been recorded in numerous cases, including the ICTY's *Tadic* decision. The forms by which men are sexually exploited sometimes differ, yet the underlying presence of a lack of voluntariness and of circumstances of coercion remain. These factors are not unique to women in war.

One cannot separate women's participation in conflict, sex and a lack of consent. However, as with other aspects of women's participation, IHL overlooks these connections, disregarding considerations of voluntariness and never addressing the coercive, victimising and abusive circumstances surrounding women's participation in hostilities. The laws of distinction are purportedly premised on a distinction between those who pose a threat and are deserving of targeting and those who do not. This premise falls flat when considering women in African conflicts; embroiled involuntarily and abusively, and little deserving of being targets of attack.

Women, targeting and the principle of distinction

> In March 1994, a faction called the Armed Islamic Group issued a statement classifying all unveiled women who appear in public as potential military targets. To punctuate this threat, gunmen on a motorbike shot and killed two unveiled high school female students who were standing at the bus station waiting to go home.[34]
>
> (Algeria)

Gender can have lethal consequences. Women and men are targeted differently in conflict – and often for different reasons. More men in conflict are killed, both in battle where greater numbers of men tend to be active fighters, as well as off the battlefield.[35] Jones notes,

> That the gender-selective mass killing and "disappearance" of males, especially "battle-age" males, remains a pervasive feature of contemporary conflict is not open to dispute. Indeed, its frequency across cultures and conflict types marks it as a possibly *definitional* element of contemporary warfare, state terrorism, mob violence, and paramilitary brigandage.[36]

There are institutional, political and cultural reasons for targeting men. Killing men can give an enemy a more secure hold over an area – once the men are lost, women and children have fewer means of returning or revolting. Sometimes men are killed for revenge.[37] Men are also targeted due to a perception that all men are fighters, potential fighters, or even the fighters of future generations.[38] Notably, those doing the targeting are also primarily men.

There are other forms of targeting more commonly directed at women.[39] A number of new wars have seen extreme levels of sexual violence used systematically as a 'weapon of war'. This varies in type – from rape, to sexual slavery, to forced marriage, to rape as an instrument of genocide. It also varies in intensity, scale and motive.[40] Related ways that women are attacked include; deliberate infection with HIV, recording acts of sexual violence for the production of pornography, sexual mutilation, medical experimentation on reproductive organs, forced cohabitation, forced impregnation, forced abortion, enforced sterilisation, strip-searching, forced public nudity, sexual humiliation, trafficking in women and enforced prostitution.[41]

There are other types of attacks that, while not specifically targeted at women – or even at civilian populations – have particularly harsh effects on women, or gender-specific consequences. Military strikes that lead to population displacement, the destruction or expropriation of homes, and the destruction of property can bear particular tolls on women, who are vulnerable to certain dangers when without shelter. Actions leading to food shortages or the withholding of humanitarian assistance, acutely affect women, as women tend to be the ones primarily responsible for feeding children.[42] The destruction of the environment also affects women greatly, as in Africa women tend to be tasked with growing or gathering food[43] – with 80 per cent of food on the continent cultivated by women.[44]

Women are targeted for different reasons to men. Attacking women is a cheap and effective way of destabilising entire populations. Although most victims of wartime rape are women, the wider social impact is experienced by both genders.[45] Women's bodies are tied up with the identity and prestige of a community.[46] Attacks on women are carried out to undermine family structures and hence to destabilise whole communities.[47] Sometimes women are targeted as a means of communicating with and punishing men. In cultures where men are seen to be the protectors, targeting women can be a deep blow to them. Brownmiller notes that, "The act that is played out upon [the rape victim] is a message passed between men – vivid proof of victory for one and loss and defeat for the other".[48] Rape is also used to achieve military aims, including terrorising populations or encouraging them to comply. Rape might be used as part of an advance military offensive to clear civilians from an area before an attack. It is also used as retribution for the actions or intentions of relatives and community members. Sometimes women are targeted because they themselves are participating in or supporting armed movements. Rape is a cheap weapon – always affordable for resource-pushed groups.[49] The reasons and methods of targeting women vary, yet what is clear is that specific calculations lead to women being targeted in attack. IHL makes no provision for this, treating all targeting in the same way, assuming that the targeting of women plays out in the same way that the targeting of men does.

In terms of the principle of distinction, belligerents are prohibited from *attacking* civilians. Slightly different wording for this is used in the various conventions. Article 48, AP 1 states that parties, "... *shall direct their operations* only against military objectives". Article 13(2), AP2 states that, "The civilian population as such, as well as individual civilians, *shall not be the object of attack*". The question is, what actions are actually barred by this prohibition? Is it just the killing of civilians that is prohibited, or does this also incorporate the causing of other forms of harm against civilians? Does the principle of distinction adequately incorporate and prohibit the distinct forms of targeting that tend to be geared towards women in conflict?

To determine what actions are included in the principle's prohibition, the first port of call is the concept of 'attack' – mentioned above in AP2. 'Attack' is an important threshold term in international law, with various restrictions and prohibitions triggered when something qualifies as such.[50] The term 'attack' is used in both *jus ad bellum* and *jus in bello*, functioning differently in these two bodies, having distinct purposes and meanings in each.[51] In IHL, Article 49(1), AP1 defines 'attacks' as "acts of violence against the adversary, whether in offence or in defence". While attacks are often framed as negative, they can also have a positive bent, like attacks made in terms of the Responsibility To Protect doctrine.

In AP1 the principle of distinction is framed in terms of 'military operations' rather than 'attacks'. However, not all military operations directed at civilians are included in the prohibition. The principle of distinction does not prohibit military operations that have no physical consequences for civilians. Schmitt explains that,

> … longstanding State practice demonstrates that non-destructive psychological operations directed at the civilian population, such as dropping leaflets, broadcasting to the enemy population, or even jamming enemy public broadcasts, are lawful as long as no physical consequences attend them.[52]

Others emphasise the *physical nature* of prohibited actions. Bothe and Solf note that, "… the term 'acts of violence' denotes physical force. Thus, the concept of 'attacks' does not include dissemination of propaganda, embargoes, or other non-physical means of psychological or economic warfare".[53]

While the above reveals that not *all* military operations against civilians are prohibited by the principle, there is authority for the fact that more is prohibited than just killing of civilians. The 2013 Tallinn Manual on the International Law Applicable to Cyber Warfare, in defining cyber-attacks, notes that, "… it is, in light of the law of armed conflict's underlying humanitarian purpose, reasonable to extend the definition to serious illness and severe mental suffering that are tantamount to injury …".[54] Also in the cyber warfare context, Schmitt notes that,

> Attacks can be redefined as operations that result in, or if unsuccessful were originally expected to result in, death or injury of individuals or destruction or damage of objects. The notion of injury includes illness that might result from a cyber operation, as in the case of attacking a water treatment plant in order to contaminate drinking water. It is also sensible, based for example on the prohibition of terror attacks and starvation, to extend the concept to acts producing serious suffering not otherwise justified by the notion of military necessity.[55]

Schmitt therefore includes a psychological element – one confirmed by the ICRC's study on customary IHL, which in Rule 2, describing the principle of distinction, states that, "Acts or threats of violence the primary purpose of which is to spread terror among the civilian population are prohibited".[56]

When considering women, one pertinent question is, does the principle of distinction's prohibition on attacking civilians incorporate a prohibition on using sexual violence against them? If rape is used as a 'weapon' in war, does the principle of distinction extend to prohibiting the use of that 'weapon' against civilians? Sexual violence is prohibited by other parts of IHL,[57] giving this question more academic than practical importance. But it still merits asking; is raping civilian women a violation of the principle of distinction?

From a humanitarian perspective, it seems unfair to exclude sexual violence from the prohibition on attack, given the physical and psychological harm it causes women. Sexual violence can result in the death of its victims; violent rapes can lead to fatality through injury or infection. Many conflicts where rape has been systematically used, particularly in Africa, have occurred in countries with high HIV rates and critical shortages in health and treatment facilities.[58] HIV levels are particularly high amongst combatants,[59] the ones using the 'weapon' of rape. In certain conflicts there has been documented evidence of rapes being committed with the express purpose of spreading HIV to victims. In Rwanda, HIV positive Hutus purposely tried to infect Tutsi women with HIV as a tool of genocide,[60] resulting in staggering numbers of infections and deaths following the genocide. It would seem incongruous to exclude this potentially deadly act from the principle of distinction's prohibition, while other acts that lead to death are included. It would also make little sense that acts that may not be committed against lawful targets (combatants) would be permitted against civilians; in terms of IHL there are clear limitations on the types of attacks permitted against lawful targets – one can kill combatants, but cannot subject them to unnecessary suffering,[61] with raping combatants seen as violating this rule.

However, despite the logical and humanitarian appeal of reading a prohibition against sexual violence into the ambit of the principle of distinction, there is no consensus that this is actually included.[62] Gardam argues that it is difficult to find evidence that civilian immunity, at any part of its development, was supposed to include protection from rape – simply put, women were of peripheral concern in the process of devising protections for non-combatants.[63] However, Gardam also notes that the rationale usually provided for the law not including certain actions within its ambit, are the demands of military necessity. Military necessity, she argues, should be wholly irrelevant to outlawing rape in conflict.[64]

Troublingly, it is not clear that military necessity is wholly irrelevant in the context of rape. There is ample documentation of the fact that sexual violence can, in fact, be an effective tool for armed groups to use to achieve their aims, such as forcing compliance or encouraging populations to flee.[65] One could argue that for poorly resourced groups, like many of those found in African new wars, who lack other viable means of attaining their objectives, it is *militarily necessary* for them to utilise sexual violence as a tool, given how cheap and readily available this is and how effective it can be in achieving certain goals. Does the demonstrated utility of sexual violence open up room for military necessity to be used as a justification for it? Or conversely, is the outright prohibition of rape in IHL, despite its effectiveness, a sign that military necessity is being given less weight? The military necessity problem is not particular to rape – there are many other harmful actions that are central to the strategies used by fighters in new wars. Where these are shown to be effective and necessary for this type of warfare, should these be justified in terms of military necessity?

What of the indirect harms that effect women in particularly acute ways? Are the actions that cause these harms adequately encompassed by the principle of distinction? Sjoberg explains that,

> A precision-guided missile targeted to hit a power-producing plant will not immediately kill very many civilians, but those who depend on that power source will experience long-term effects … precision-targeting industries in an enemy territory may have long-term economic or health effects which amount to or surpass the harm that could be caused by the direct targeting of civilians in war.[66]

A reading of the law suggests that it is unlikely that *indirect* attacks such as these are incorporated in distinction's prohibition on attacking civilians. The principle does not prohibit strikes that *only* result in longer-term consequences – effects that women really suffer from. Rather, the principle's focus is on immediate injury and death – harms more likely to be suffered by men. Unless attacks also have short-term consequences, these would not be covered by the principle's prohibition, even where the scale of the long-term harm is more significant.[67] That only physical attacks with immediate kinetic effects are prohibited by the principle is problematic, revealing how the principle ignores the real nature of harm caused to civilians in conflict. This also reveals how the principle ignores those harms more strongly affecting women, while centring on those that are suffered by men.

What would be preferable is a principle that takes cognisance of the real effects of actions – short and long term, direct and indirect – prohibiting all of those which have harmful effects for civilians, not just those that fill technical requirements. One approach might be to rely more heavily on the concept of *harm* in establishing whether actions are prohibited by the principle.[68] However, harm itself is a difficult concept and identifying 'harmful effects' can lead to further challenges. Lieblich notes that,

> … while positive IHL is unequivocal about the need prevent or at least minimize civilian harm, it does not tell us – beyond the obvious – what this harm is. How far, temporally, is harm measured? Where does the causal chain of harm end? To what extent does harm transcend the purely physical into the economical and emotional?[69]

Feminists discuss harm in the context of reparations, arguing that reparations programmes – like the principle of distinction – do not adequately encompass the types of harms women actually suffer.[70] As an example, the South African reparations programme was criticised for,

> exclusion of the structural social and economic violence which imperiled day-to-day subsistence under apartheid. As women have traditionally been

responsible for subsistence (food, care, and shelter), the exclusion of these harms rendered women's experiences of apartheid less visible.[71]

The principle of distinction fails to protect women from those in their own groups

> They taught us the history of our country, starting from colonial slavery, and they told us we should hate whites. We slept in large rooms, the men and women together. We were raped by the boys. I can't even count how many times by how many different men. If we complained to the camp commander, we were beaten and they would call us sell-outs to the MDC.[72]
>
> (Zimbabwe)

Threats to women in new wars do not only come from the enemy. Women in armed groups are vulnerable to attacks by those within their own groups. Discussing child combatants in the ICC's Lubanga decision, Judge Odio Benito acknowledged these risks:

> Children are protected from child recruitment not only because they can be at risk for being a potential target to the "enemy" but also because they will be at risk from their "own" armed group who has recruited them and will subject these children to brutal trainings, torture and ill-treatment, sexual violence and other activities and living conditions that are incompatible and in violation to these children's fundamental rights.[73]

The same holds true for adult women in armed groups. Women complaining about this might be deemed traitorous or unpatriotic and said to be undermining war efforts and unit cohesion.

The principle of distinction is outward looking, concerned with how people treat their enemies. It seeks to protect from threats deriving from enemies in war. The principle does not look inwards. It does not acknowledge that women face dangers from their own sides and does not protect women from these threats – or from any other threats that do not derive from enemy fighters. The principle is therefore partially blind, ignoring the fact that women require protection within their own groups. It provides only partial legal protection, failing to protect women from *all* sources of danger they face in conflict.

One can respond that it is not IHL or the principle of distinction's place to protect women from internal threats. IHL was explicitly created to protect people from *enemy* actions in hostilities, with its narrow focus being one of its strengths. Accordingly, there should be more appropriate legal mechanisms by which women are protected from those on their own sides.

The problem is that there are no legal mechanisms that can properly protect women from those in their own groups. Human rights law, while possibly applicable, cannot fulfil this role, as it is targeted primarily at states and is difficult to enforce against non-state armed actors.[74] Human rights law's application is also limited in armed conflicts and IHL, as the *lex specialis*, would take precedence in the regulation of armed group behaviour. Domestic law systems that regulate crime and public safety tend to break down in conflict and are almost impossible to enforce against those in non-state armed groups. There is therefore no law that adequately fills this gap in the principle of distinction's reach.

Prisoner of war status and women

One of the key combatant privileges is POW status. POW status was designed to play an incentivising role in the IHL system; in exchange for abiding by IHL and physically distinguishing themselves as combatants, fighters would be rewarded with protection and a prescribed level of treatment on capture. The continued relevance of POW status in new wars – as both a fact and an incentive for compliance with IHL – is questionable. POW status pertains only to IACs, which many new wars are not. So too, POW status only accrues to fighters 'belonging to' state parties to a conflict, while in new wars a high proportion of fighters fight for non-state armed groups.

Just because the NIAC conventions do not provide for POW status, does not mean that prisoners are not taken in these conflicts. Tuck explains that,

> Detention by armed groups is neither infrequent nor, necessarily, small-scale.... Just as 'armed groups are characterised by their great diversity', so too are their dealings with detainees. The extent, frequency, and location of detention differ, as do the infrastructure, expertise, and financial resources available for the administration of detention. Some armed groups expressly recognize the humanitarian entitlements of detainees and regulate the conduct of their members accordingly, while others do not.[75]

There are certain features that are particular to detention by non-state armed groups, arising from the clandestine, informal and hidden nature of detention in these conflicts. Tuck explains further,

> Perhaps most peculiar to armed groups is a tendency to detain persons in undisclosed, remote locales, without standard detention infrastructure. This is a logical consequence of waging war against better-resourced states, in which the armed group's survival is dependent upon clandestine operations. For the detainees, the implications are a dearth of essential items/services, an absence of family contact, frequent transfers, exposure to harsh climatic variables, and so forth.[76]

Notably, detention by non-state groups is often labelled differently, being framed as taking hostages or as detention as a form of targeting.

The laws governing detention *by* non-state groups are inadequate. The minimal standards in the NIAC laws do not provide adequate regulation, with rules about detention conditions, transfers and procedural safeguards either absent or lacking any level of specificity.[77] Human rights law can provide some guidance, guaranteeing the rights of detainees to certain standards of treatment. However, human rights law is not satisfactory as a regulating mechanism for non-state armed actors. Effectively, at this point we are left with no one body of law that can adequately regulate detention in NIACs.

The status of detainees *from* non-state armed groups and the question of the law applicable to them, has been the topic of much controversy in recent years. Most prominently, this has come up in the context of Guantanamo Bay and the detention of Taliban and other fighters in Afghanistan and Iraq.[78] Detention in new wars has become tangled up with questions about detention of terrorists.[79] In *Serdar Mohammed* v. *Ministry of Defence*, considering the detention of Taliban commanders in Afghanistan, the United Kingdom's High Court of Justice confirmed that IHL does not *authorise* detention in NIACs, as neither CA3 nor AP2 contain provisions empowering parties to detain prisoners. The court explained that CA3 and AP2 are purely humanitarian in purpose, aimed at securing fundamental guarantees. They therefore guarantee minimum standards of treatment to those detained, while not actually providing legal authority for actors to detain. Detention *may* be lawful under the law of the state on whose territory the conflict is being fought, or it may be wholly unlawful, yet regardless, the NIAC conventions set out minimum standards of treatment to be provided to those held.[80] The lack of clear law guiding detention in NIACs has allowed for differing and often contradictory interpretations. Goodman points to the problems with the USA's approach to this:

> … policymakers and advocates of U.S. practices improperly conflated two classes of individuals subject to detention: civilians who directly participate in hostilities ('unlawful combatants') and civilians who have not directly participated but nevertheless pose a security threat. … commentators on both sides have also improperly equated rules governing two coercive measures: administrative detention and military tribunals.[81]

It is interesting to consider who prisoners in new wars might be. In new wars, entire population groups are seen to be 'enemies'. Fighters and non-fighters might be detained together, with little distinction made between those participating and those not participating. In conflicts from Bosnia to Rwanda, civilians have been interned merely for belonging to certain ethnic or other groups. This is not permitted by IHL. GC4 (Article 5, 27, 41–43, and 78) permits the detention or internment of civilians *if* they pose a security threat, even where there is no evidence that they have directly participated in hostilities – a principle that also applies in NIACs. For each detainee a specific determination is required that they pose a threat to that state's security,[82] otherwise they may not be lawfully detained. However, this rule is challenged by the differing notion of 'enemy' in new wars, and is frequently disregarded in these conflicts.

POW protection presents itself as gender-neutral – a protective status applicable to men and women alike.[83] It is, in fact, highly gendered. Despite the recognition in IHL that there can be female POWs, vastly more men are detained in conflict. Of course, if one blurs the distinction between internment of POWs and the detention of 'enemy' civilians in conflict, then the numbers of women get higher. This again illustrates how the ways people are labelled or categorised affects our perceptions of their numbers. The punishments doled out to prisoners also take gendered forms. Male prisoners are more often beaten, tortured or killed.[84]

Female prisoners are more likely to be sexually violated. Sexual assaults of female prisoners in conflict have been documented around the world.[85] In Zimbabwe, from 2,000, women who were known to be opponents of Mugabe's Zanu PF party were held in camps run by the youth militia, the Green Bombers, where they were subjected to sexual violence.[86] The Women Under Siege website contains numerous documented reports of women involved with, or accused of being involved with, the Syrian opposition being detained and subjected to sexualised violence.[87] Forced prostitution has been another punishment for women detained in war. Asia's 'comfort women' are the best-known example, with up to 200,000 women forced into sexual slavery by the Japanese military in World War Two. The Nazis, too, made female prisoners work in brothels to service forced labourers in the concentration camps, out of a notion that this would increase labourers' productivity. Brothels were opened in Nazi camps (staffed by non-Jewish inmates, for non-Jewish prisoners).[88] Here again, the line between those imprisoned for their participation in conflict and those imprisoned for their group membership blurs, with sexual exploitation happening across the spectrum. In the Bosnian war, Muslim women were detained and repeatedly raped in detention facilities dubbed as 'rape camps'. So, too, in Rwanda, Tutsi women were cordoned off at selected detention sites to be raped, as part of the commission of genocide.

There are, of course, exceptions to the gender particular forms of punishments described above. Female prisoners are also beaten, tortured and killed, and male detainees are raped. Storr notes that,

> Twenty-one per cent of Sri Lankan males who were seen at a London torture treatment centre reported sexual abuse while in detention. In El Salvador, 76% of male political prisoners surveyed in the 1980s described at least one incidence of sexual torture. A study of 6,000 concentration-camp inmates in Sarajevo found that 80% of men reported having been raped.[89]

More recently, and subject to much international attention, in Iraq's Abu Ghraib prison, American officials were accused of sexually assaulting male prisoners, raping and sexually violating them with objects including truncheons, wire and phosphorescent tubes. Female prisoners were raped in Abu Ghraib, too. Of course, none of these 'punishments' are permitted by IHL. POW status was designed to prevent combatants from continuing fighting – not to punish them for their acts.[90]

This book has argued that women are less likely to qualify as combatants and hence to receive protective POW status. As women are less likely to have POW protection, they are at increased risk of violence on capture, as enemies might be more willing to harm those who have not been conferred protected status. Interestingly, arguments about the treatment of female detainees are often used to try keep women out of combat roles. Debates about women in combat often centre on concerns about women being mistreated by enemies on capture, with arguments made that these risks are too high to justify allowing women into combat. This concern is questionable. Is there something inherently worse or less acceptable about *female* prisoners being mistreated? If there is, this almost certainly centres on sexual violence and on the concern that capturers cannot be trusted not to rape. This appears to rest on an assumption that enemies will respect rights of male prisoners more and will not rape them – an assumption not borne out by the facts. A reverse discrimination is at play here. Such arguments condone sending men into situations where they may be captured and tortured, while not sending women into the same situations. However, these arguments are also unfair towards women. Rhonda Cornum, an American soldier captured and sexually assaulted by Iraqi forces during the Gulf war, argues that,

> Every 15 seconds in America, some woman is assaulted. Why are they worried about a woman getting assaulted once every 10 years in a war overseas? It's ridiculous ... clearly it's an emotional argument they use (to argue that women should be kept away from the frontlines) because they can't think of a rational one.[91]

At their essence, concerns about female prisoners are based on the notion that POWs – much like combatants – should be male, with women not fitting into this picture.

Distinction and the post-conflict period

> Regardless of what a female non-combatant may have survived and whatever heroic acts of courage she may have committed, a woman is expected to devote her attention to the returning male 'war hero', and there is a tendency to minimize, if not outright deny, her war experience. The woman was not a fighter, and hence is not a hero.[92]

Although IHL and the principle of distinction were created to regulate *during* conflict, they continue to have an effect once conflicts end. Here, too, the principle of distinction fails women. IHL focuses on periods of formal fighting and once the state of 'armed conflict' terminates, IHL ceases to apply. This cessation of the operation of the law is based on the notion that threats of violence cease with the ending of conflict. Feminist analyses of post-conflict periods have shown this to be untrue.[93] Chapter 3 described how security remains a real concern for women following from conflict. Ceasefires and peace treaties may officially terminate hostilities, yet insecurity lingers. Violence against civilians remains a constant feature post-conflict – and a significant feature in women's lives.[94] The termination of IHL's application also rests on the assumption that post-conflict, domestic laws operate properly and can serve to protect people. This, too, is not the case, with it often taking years before legal systems and enforcement mechanisms are up and running. IHL therefore stops in its application at a time when women still require this law's protection.

Much of the violence committed against women post-conflict is domestic violence, committed by husbands and others, often traumatised by the war's events. One could argue that this type of violence would not fall under IHL's rubric anyway. However, this argument fails to take into account the fact that domestic violence is exacerbated by conflict, with the heightened levels of domestic violence being intrinsically liked to the war. Treating 'private' violence as wholly separate to conflict-related activities is misleading. Arguing that separate laws must regulate these separate spheres fails to acknowledge the interconnections between them.

The principle of distinction affects female fighters post-conflict. This book has argued that IHL's restrictive definitions shape the ways women's contributions to armed struggles are perceived by society, by perpetuating the view that women are not actively involved in combat. This has a number of effects in the post-conflict period.

For one thing, where women are not labelled as combatants they are more likely to be excluded from disarmament, demobilisation and reintegration programmes. DDR programs are implemented as part of peace-making initiatives, and aim to demobilise combatants and facilitate their reintegration into civilian life. In exchange for giving up their weapons and leaving armed group structures, former combatants are given 'reintegration packages' consisting of money, goods, skills training and other assistance. This support can be critical for former combatants, who often leave armed groups with no homes, no skills and nowhere to go. DDR programmes have traditionally focused on male combatants. Women have been excluded from several programmes and, where included, their specific needs have not been well addressed. The numbers of women going through DDR have been far lower than men. In Sierra Leone, between 1998 and 2002, 60,769 men went through DDR, while only 4,876 women took part. Put differently, women constituted 7.4 per cent of adults going through DDR, despite the fact that this percentage was significantly lower than the percentage of women serving in Sierra Leone's armed groups[95] – estimated by some as being up to 30 per cent. In the DRC, from December 2003 to September 2004, 1,718 boy soldiers went through DDR, while only 23 girls went through the program, despite the fact that those interviewed said between 30 and 40 per cent of those in the units were girls.[96]

Before starting a DDR program, planners decide who their 'target group' is and develop selection criteria for determining who belongs to this group. Women are frequently excluded because of the chosen criteria.[97] Some programs, like the one in Sierra Leone, determined that people needed to hand in weapons in order to be admitted to the programme. As many women held non-fighting roles in the armed groups, for which they were not allocated weapons, they could not gain access to the programme.[98] In CAR unit commanders were asked to list and name those in their units who would be admitted to the DDR programme. Often commanders did not list the women in their units – sometimes out of blatant discrimination, but often because they considered them 'wives' rather than 'combatants', and therefore felt they were not worthy of the programme.[99] In CAR, towards the last phase of DDR, women were removed from the programme altogether. The explanation provided by a former employee was that the authorities did not find it 'normal' for women to be combatants and therefore assumed the women must have been given their weapons by family members, rather than being real combatants.[100] These examples illustrate the problems that can arise from entrenching views that women are not *real* combatants. In recent years some DDR programmes have included women who performed support roles in armed groups – known in humanitarian circles as 'women associated with armed forces' – within their programme.[101] This has marked a shift from approaching DDR from a purely security lens (focused on removing armed fighters from fighting life), to a lens that recognises a broader group to be both deserving of and in need of support. This latter view would align with a move towards a less security-bound principle of distinction, one that takes into account who is deserving of protection.

The failure to acknowledge women's roles in conflict also contributes to women being excluded from peace negotiations, with negotiating positions awarded to those seen to have contributed to the fight. Over the past 25 years, only one out of every 40 signatories to peace treaties has been female.[102] Castillo Diaz notes that,

> … women represent a strikingly low number of negotiators.… Women's participation in negotiating delegations averaged less than 8 per cent in the 14 cases for which such information was available. Fewer than 3 per cent of signatories in the peace processes included in this sample were women, and women were absent from chief mediating roles in UN-brokered talks.[103]

Problematically, when women are excluded from peace processes, the resultant treaties tend to ignore women's concerns. A UNIFEM study that reviewed the substantive provisions of 585 peace agreements from 102 peace processes since 1990 found that only 16 per cent of treaties (92 treaties) contained any reference to gender or women. This increased from 11 to 27 per cent following SC Res 1325. In only seven treaties were the needs of female combatants in DDR mentioned and in only four was sexual violence recognised as a violation of ceasefire.[104] CEDAW General Recommendation 30 emphasises the importance of including women in peace processes, recommending that women and civil society organisations addressing women's issues should be included in all peace negotiations.[105] SC Res 1325 and the other Resolutions of the Women, Peace and Security Agenda also refer to the importance of including women in these processes.

Disregarding women's roles in conflicts also leads to women being denied political positions post-conflict, as these are frequently offered as 'rewards' to those who have contributed best to armed struggles. Globally, women still only hold one in five political positions[106] and these numbers are often particularly low in post-conflict states. The exception is when quotas are put in place. Following its genocide, Rwanda pushed for female equality and inclusion, putting in place a strict quota for women in politics. As a result, Rwanda now has the highest percentage of female parliamentarians in the world – as of 2014, there were 63.8 per cent women in the lower house and 38.5 per cent in the upper house. However, often even when women are placed in political positions following conflict, they are not given *real* power to exercise their roles, rather being placed as figureheads and not given space to voice their positions.[107] However, from an equality perspective, women's inclusion is imperative and the narrative of women's participation in conflict, influenced by IHL, plays a part in influencing this.

It seems that for women, both being branded combatant *and* not being branded combatant are problematic. If women are not recognised as combatants, they are excluded from benefits. On the other hand, where women are seen as combatants, they are stigmatised and marginalised. The principle of distinction sits in the centre of this, tacitly shaping the way in which women's contributions to conflicts are recognised and perceived – and therefore complicit in bringing this range of consequences.

Does the principle of distinction serve women?

The above subsections have pointed to the many effects and failings the principle of distinction exhibits in relation to women. What is left is to question whether overall the principle in its current formulation is beneficial to and protective of women or, rather, whether it fails them.

The answer is mixed. The fact that IHL excludes many of the roles that women play in conflict from qualifying as combatancy or direct participation keeps many women from being lawful targets of attack. Stereotypes about women as victims can have protective effects for them, leading to women being evacuated first and prioritised in protection initiatives. In terms of pure legal protection, women certainly gain from being classified civilians.

However, there are also negative effects arising from this. The preceding sections described some of the harmful effects for women flowing from the principle – effects that are indirect, frequently hidden and largely unacknowledged. Paradoxically, in providing larger numbers of women with legal protection from attack, the current application of the principle compromises women's social and political standing, exposing them to other sorts of disadvantages and dangers.

Of course one must question the extent to which the negative effects described in the sections above can, in fact, be attributed to the principle of distinction. To what extent is it really the legal classification of women as civilians in IHL that results in women being stereotyped, victimised or barred from partaking in negotiations and political positions? Can one really attribute these to the principle of distinction? Many of these effects have nothing at all to do with the conduct of hostilities – that which IHL was created to regulate. Discrimination and stereotyping of women is deeply rooted in society and would persist even if the legal labels in IHL were framed differently.

While it is true that the principle is not solely responsible for these effects, it is important to take note of the part that the law does play. Even if it is just in subtle, cumulative ways, all of the influences that create, entrench or legitimise particular views of women play a part in perpetuating these. While IHL may not be solely to blame, and in fact may not even be a dominant cause of these consequences, to the extent that the law contributes at all, this bears noting, highlighting and addressing. While not seeking to overstate the role that the principle of distinction plays in entrenching societal norms and discrimination, this work seeks to illuminate the contributory role it plays. Only by doing this in each of the many forums where patriarchal views are given a voice will these norms begin to shift. The negative consequences flowing from the principle of distinction may not even be bad enough to merit suggesting the law be changed; it might be that the protective benefits to women flowing from the principle outweigh the harmful ones. However, even where the effects are minor and indirect, these are still important to recognise.

The problems with the principle of distinction are not restricted to gendered problems. There are numerous ways in which the principle is failing everyone. At its most basic, the principle of distinction fails to serve women simply by failing to operate effectively. With up to 90 per cent of conflict casualties today being civilians, many of these women, one can see a principle in crisis. However, the broader problems with the principle have gendered dimensions that are important to recognise.

Having a law that is framed inappropriately has the potential to encourage non-compliance. Framing the law too narrowly, categorising women who are clearly taking part in war efforts as not being targetable participants, might contribute to a disregard for the law. Those fighting on the ground are frequently aware of the essential roles that women play in opposing armed groups, and of the fact that groups are reliant on these contributions to keep their efforts going. Fighters might be unwilling to ignore this – particularly those in weaker groups who may feel they do not have the luxury of not striking those who are integral to the maintenance of their enemies' forces. If the law does not allow fighters to lawfully target those whom they know to be acting against them, this can be a disincentive to abiding by IHL. Schmitt makes the argument that narrowly interpreting 'direct participation', while expanding protection from attack to more people, actually increases the risk to the rest of civilians by encouraging non-compliance.[108] This argument applies well to women; not incorporating women who are actually participating into the law's fold can put greater numbers of civilian women at risk.

One of the reasons for the principle's failings is the practical difficulty in applying this law, demonstrated in the previous chapter. Women get lost under the many layers of legal complication. In making a distinction assessment, actors must first decide whether a situation is IAC or NIAC, a choice laden with problems. They must also determine whether actors are under the control of a party to a conflict. Following that, they must determine if fighters are combatants, civilians, non-combatants or even unlawful combatants. If it is resolved that they are technically civilians, it then needs to be determined whether their actions constitute direct participation, again no simple feat. Under all of these layers of complication are women, who are already rendered invisible by society and stereotypes that conceal the ways in which they participate. These work hand in hand with the confusing, ambiguous law, to ensure that women remain hidden, hardly classified at all, and not adequately protected by the principle of distinction.

Even where the principle does apply its protective reach, the types of harm prohibited by it are too narrow to properly protect women. It is questionable whether the principle incorporates in its prohibitions sexual attacks or non-lethal attacks with long-term indirect consequences of which women often bear the brunt. In terms of substantive protection, the principle fails to extend far enough to protect women from the distinct types of harm they actually face in conflict.

The gendered problems with the principle of distinction provide a lens with which to view broader problems with the principle – those that apply to everyone. In the principle not standing up to gender analysis, this reveals deeper problems. For one thing, the fact that the principle cannot adequately regulate women participating in conflict, suggests it might not function well for other 'challenging' groups – or groups of fighters that veer from those imagined or anticipated by the law's drafters. Considering African women reveals how poorly the law functions when applied to those who are not European-uniformed-men. The gendered failings of the principle of distinction expose the biases in the law. They reveal the hierarchies and privileging implicit in IHL and way the law rests on these. This privileging reduces the effectiveness of the system. For one thing, it removes incentive for certain parties – those the law places in disadvantaged positions – to comply. If the law is privileging the stronger, then it is failing in what it purports to be doing – protecting the weaker.

The gendered problems expose how the principle contains categorisations that are not reflective of real conditions of conflict or of the actual ways in which people participate in hostilities. Regulation that is premised on inaccurate categories cannot optimally regulate. The effects of this can be significant. If the principle contains incoherent categories, this can be confusing for military actors. Given unworkable definitions of civilians and combatants, military actors may feel bound to conclude that more people are protected civilians, a conclusion they might be unwilling to accept as this hampers their ability to achieve their goals. Alternatively, they might determine that larger numbers are combatants, in which case they would target them. Both of these lead to negative results, working against the goals of compliance and protection. The principle of distinction is legally incoherent; even assuming that fighters did wish to apply the law in new wars, the principle is too uncertain for them to properly use to regulate their actions.

IHL is based on categories and binaries that underlie its norms and trigger the application of different rules. The law is applied differently in 'IACs' and 'NIACs', to 'civilians' and 'combatants', to 'military objects' and 'civilian objects'. The very structure of the law rests on these binaries, with them being the basis for determining what actions are allowed or disallowed. Shany argues that IHL's problem is that its binary categorisations lack precision. They tend to be open-ended rather than clear categories. Ambiguous phrases like 'direct participation in hostilities' or making an 'effective contribution to military action' are common application triggers. This can lead to conflicting interpretations and uncertainty about if and when certain IHL rules apply – uncertainty that can have serious ramifications in practice.[109] Exacerbating the problem is the fact that there are no independent decision-making bodies or procedures that can, in real-time, provide interpretations or adjudications of the law, meaning that conflicting interpretations are acted out and perpetuated.[110] The law's binaries are challenged by new wars, conflicts that inherently break down many of the distinctions the law is based on. Kaldor notes that in the context of new wars,

> … the distinction between state and non-state, public and private, external and internal, economic and political, and even war and peace are breaking down. Moreover the breakdown of these binary distinctions is both a cause and a consequence of violence.[111]

Women get lost in IHL's binary categorisations, which are reflective of reality and which ignore women's experiences. The principle of distinction rests on gendered distinctions, such as male-fighter/female-civilian, assuming clear-cut gender roles, when the roles played out in conflict are, in fact, quite mixed and fluid. Gender critiques expose further problematic binaries too. Voluntary/involuntary is shown to be too simplistic – both in the context of armed group recruitment and in the complexities of sexual consent. Women in conflict demonstrate the difficulties with the public/private divide; IHL regulates the public space, focusing on the military and those recognised as combatants, while largely ignoring participants who do not qualify as combatants and ignoring 'private' violence, despite the fact that this might be caused or exacerbated by 'public' conflict.

When considering women in African conflicts, we see that new wars break down the binaries, at the same time that gender distinctions put them under pressure. Despite the problems with these binaries, the IHL system as it stands rests on these. Challenging these distinctions tests the very foundations the law rests on. Without the law's triggering binaries, there is no way of determining what rules apply when. We are therefore left with a body of law that is reliant on distinctions that are often not viable in modern conflict. The very structure of IHL is dependent on classifications that are sometimes impossible, sometimes invisible and often harmful.

While in form the principle of distinction is gender-neutral, in practice it is highly gendered, with the principle's gendered nature protecting men more than women. The principle of distinction is faulty for all and faulty particularly for women. It lets down both genders equally in certain ways, and women specifically in other ways. Of course, many of the failings of the principle were not intentionally created to harm or prejudice women. Many were borne of a failure to consider women altogether. What we are left with is a law drafted without women in mind, which has some protective effects for women, as well as a range of negative side effects. The question that remains is what should be done about this.

Notes

1 Kinsella, Helen. *Securing the Civilian: Sex and Gender in the Laws of War*. Boston, MA: Boston Consortium on Gender, Security and Human Rights, 2004. Nguyen, Athena. The Influence of Gender Stereotyping on International Humanitarian Law, 2010. http://works.bepress.com/athena_nguyen/1.
2 Coulter, Chris. 'Female Fighters in the Sierra Leone War: Challenging the Assumptions?' *Feminist Review* 88, no. 1 (2008): 54–73.
3 Denov, Myriam. *Girls in Fighting Forces: Moving Beyond Victimhood*. A Summary of the Research Findings on Girls and Armed Conflict from CIDA's Child Protection Research Fund, 2007, at 2.
4 Coulter, supra note 2, at 55.
5 Pratt, Nicola and Richter-Devroe, Sophie. 'Critically Examining UNSCR 1325 on Women, Peace and Security'. *International Feminist Journal of Politics* 13, no. 4 (2011): 489–503.
6 Otto, Dianne. 'The Exile of Inclusion: Reflections on Gender Issues in International Law over the Last Decade'. *The Melbourne Journal of International Law* 10 (2009): 11–26.
7 Shepherd, Laura. 'Sex, Security and Superhero(in)es: From 1325 to 1820 and Beyond'. *International Feminist Journal of Politics* 13, no. 4 (2011): 504–21.
8 Coulter, supra note 2,
9 Ibid.
10 Ibid., at 68.
11 Denov, supra note 3, at 12.
12 *World Report 2013: Eritrea*. Human Rights Watch. www.hrw.org/world-report/2013/country-chapters/eritrea.
13 Britt, Jason. 'Unwilling Warriors: An Examination of the Power to Conscript in Peacetime'. *Northwestern Journal of Law and Social Policy* 4, no. 3 (2009): 400–423.
14 Sjoberg, Laura. *The Paradox of Double Effect: How Feminism Can Save the Immunity Principle*. Boston, MA: Boston Consortium on Gender, Security and Human Rights, 2006.
15 See for example, Lyall, Rewi. 'Voluntary Human Shields, Direct Participation in Hostilities and the International Humanitarian Law Obligations of States'. *Melbourne Journal of International Law* 9 (2008): 313–333. De Belle, Stéphanie Bouchié. 'Chained to Cannons or Wearing Targets on Their T-Shirts: Human Shields in International Humanitarian Law'. *International Review of the Red Cross* 90, no. 872 (2008): 883–906.
16 Schmitt, Michael. 'Human Shields in International Humanitarian Law'. *Columbia Journal of Transnational Law* 47 (2009): 292–338. Lyall, Rewi. Ibid.
17 Ibid.
18 Queguiner, Jean-François. 'Precautions under the Law Governing the Conduct of Hostilities'. *International Review of the Red Cross* 88, no. 864 (2006): 793–821.

19 'Women Under Siege, Woman Says She Witnessed Women Stripped and Used as Human Shields'. *Crowdmap*. https://womenundersiegesyria.crowdmap.com/reports/view/235.
20 'Women Under Siege, Woman Tells Toronto Star Women Were Raped and Used as Human Shields in Homs'. *Crowdmap*. https://womenundersiegesyria.crowdmap.com/reports/view/182.
21 Part 2 V 3 b, 'Interpretive Guidance on the Notion of Direct Participation in Hostilities Under International Humanitarian Law'. *International Review of the Red Cross* 90, no. 872 (2009): 991–1047.
22 Ibid.
23 Written Submissions of the United Nations Special Representative of the Secretary-General on Children and Armed Conflict Submitted in application of Rule 103 of the Rules of Procedure and Evidence, Annex A, para 14. *Situation in the Democratic Republic of the Congo in the case of the Prosecutor* v. *Thomas Lubanga Dyilo*, No: ICC-01/04-01/06, at 280.
24 Sinha, Alex. 'Child Soldiers as Super-Privileged Combatants'. *The International Journal of Human Rights* 17, no. 4 (2013): 584–603.
25 Ibid., at 587.
26 Ibid.
27 Ibid., at 587–588.
28 *The Prosecutor* v. *Brima*, Case No. SCSL-2004-16-T, Appeals Judgment, 2008, at para 190.
29 Contained in the Elements of Crime Annex of the Rome Statute.
30 *The Prosecutor* v. *Brima*, supra note 28, at para 688.
31 *The Prosecutor* v. *Dragoljub Kunarac Radomir Kovac and Zoran Vukovic*, ICTY, IT-96-23-T & IT-96-23/1-T, 2001.
32 *The Prosecutor* v. *Alex Tamba Brima Bazzy Kamara Santigie Borbor Kanu*. SCSL-04-16-T, Appeals Judgement, 2008.
33 Gong-Gershowitz, Jennifer. 'Forced Marriage: A 'New' Crime against Humanity?' *Northwestern Journal of International Human Rights* 8, no. 1, Article 3 (2009): 53–76.
34 Coomaraswamy, Radhika. *Report of the Special Rapporteur on Violence Against Women, Its Causes and Consequences*. United Nations, Commission on Human Rights, Fifty-fourth Session, 1998.
35 For example, there is evidence from countries ranging from Bosnia, East Timor and Kosovo of men being rounded up and executed. Daniel Vangroenweghe, an anthropologist in Congo in the 1970s found demographic evidence that many men had been killed in punitive raids, or worked to death as rubber slaves. Even the Rwandan genocide, where all Tutsis were targeted, saw far more men killed. It is estimated that 70 per cent of the Rwandan population today are women.
36 Jones, Adam. 'Gendercide and Genocide'. *Journal of Genocide Research* 2, no. 2 (2000): 185–211, at 189.
37 Ibid.
38 Carpenter. Charli. '"Women and Children First": Gender, Norms, and Humanitarian Evacuation in the Balkans 1991–95'. *International Organization* 57, no. 4 (2003): 661–694.
39 There have been few documented cases of women being cordoned off and killed while men were kept alive. Where women are killed in conflict, this tends to be in situations where the whole population is targeted to be killed. Jones, supra note 36.
40 Bastick, Megan, Grimm, Karin and Kunz, Rahel. *Sexual Violence in Armed Conflict, Global Overview and Implications for the Security Sector*. Geneva: Geneva Centre for the Democratic Control of Armed Forces, 2007.
41 Bennoune, Karima. 'Do We Need New International Law to Protect Women in Armed Conflict?' *Case Western Reserve Journal of International Law* 38 (2006): 363–391.

42 Ibid.
43 Turpin, Jennifer. 'Many Faces, Women Confronting War'. In *The Women and War Reader, Lois Ann Lorentzen and Jennifer Turpin*. New York: New York University Press, 1998.
44 Vickers 1991, in Ibid.
45 Bastick, supra note 40.
46 Rajagopalan, Swarna. 'Gender Violence, Conflict, Internal Displacement and Peacebuilding'. *Peace Prints: South Asian Journal of Peacebuilding* 3, no. 1 (2010): 1–15.
47 Barrow, Amy. 'UN Security Council Resolutions 1325 and 1820: Constructing Gender in Armed Conflict and International Humanitarian Law'. *International Review of the Red Cross* 92, no. 877 (2010): 221–234.
48 Brownmiller, Susan. *Against Our Will: Men, Women and Rape*. New York: Simon and Schuster, 1975.
49 See, Wood, Elisabeth. 'Variation in Sexual Violence during War'. *Politics & Society* 34, no. 3 (2006): 307–342. Bastick et al., supra note 40.
50 For more information about the differing uses of these terms in the different bodies of law, see Schmitt, Michael. '"Attack" as a Term of Art in International Law: The Cyber Operations Context'. In *2012 4th International Conference on Cyber Conflict*. Tallinn, 2012.
51 Ibid.
52 Ibid., at 289.
53 Bothe, Michael, Partsch, Karl and Solf, Waldemar. *New Rules for Victims of Armed Conflicts: Commentary on the Two 1977 Protocols Additional to the Geneva Conventions of 1949*. Leiden: Martinus Nijhoff Publishers, 1982, at 289.
54 Schmitt, Michael, and NATO Cooperative Cyber Defence Centre of Excellence. *Tallinn Manual on the International Law Applicable to Cyber Warfare: Prepared by the International Group of Experts at the Invitation of the NATO Cooperative Cyber Defence Centre of Excellence*. Cambridge: Cambridge University Press, 2013, at 108.
55 Ibid., at 291.
56 Henckaerts, Jean-Marie. 'Study on Customary International Humanitarian Law: A Contribution to the Understanding and Respect for the Rule of Law in Armed Conflict'. *International Review of the Red Cross* 87, no. 857 (2005): 175–212.
57 Art 75(2)(b) AP1, Article 4(2)(e) AP2, Article 27 GC4. In addition, ICTR Statute Article 4(e) and Statute of the Special Court for Sierra Leone, Article 3(e).
58 There is data to support the fact that there is a link between sexual violence and HIV infection at the individual level. El-Bushra, Judy. *How Should We Understand Sexual Violence and HIV/AIDS in Conflict Contexts?* AIDS, Security and Conflict Initiative (ACSI) Report no. 17, 2008.
59 HIV prevalence rates in militaries are estimated to be two to five times higher than in general populations. McInnes, Colin, 'HIV, AIDS and Conflict in Africa: Why Isn't It (Even) Worse?' Paper for Annual Conference of the International Studies Associate, 2009.
60 Rehn, Elisabeth and Sirleaf, Ellen Johnson. 'Women, War and Peace: The Independent Experts' Assessment on the Impact of Armed Conflict on Women and Women's Role in Peace-building', New York: UNIFEM, 2002.
61 The Interpretive Guidance, in Recommendation IX, which deals with 'restraints on the use of force in direct attack', writes that even where people may be attacked, there are restrictions. '... the kind and degree of forces which is permissible against persons not entitled to protection against direct attack must not exceed what is actually necessary to accomplish a legitimate military purpose in the prevailing circumstances'. Interpretive Guidance supra note 21, at 996.
62 Benshoof, Janet. 'The Other Red Line: The Use of Rape as an Unlawful Tactic of Warfare'. *Global Policy* 5, no. 2 (2014): 146–158.

63 Gardam, Judith. 'Gender and Non-Combatant Immunity'. *Transnational Law & Contemporary Problems* 3 (1993): 345–370.

64 Ibid.

65 See, for example, Enloe, Cynthia. *Manoeuvres the International Politics of Militarizing Women's Lives*. Berkeley, CA: University of California Press, 2000. Wood, supra note 49. Trabucchi, Eugenia. 'Rape Warfare and International Humanitarian Law'. *Human Architecture: Journal of the Sociology of Self-Knowledge* 6, no. 4 (2008): 39–48.

66 Sjoberg, supra note 14, at 4.

67 Ibid.

68 There is precedent in international law for relying heavily on the idea of harm. The concept of harm is found in a number of international conventions, including the 1948 Genocide Convention, the Declaration for the Elimination of Violence Against Women, the 1948 Convention Against Torture, among others.

69 Lieblich, Eliav. *Beyond Life and Limb: Exploring Incidental Mental Harm Under International Humanitarian Law*. SSRN Scholarly Paper. Rochester, NY: Social Science Research Network, 10 June 2013, at 3.

70 Renard Painter, Genevieve. 'Thinking Past Rights: Towards Feminist Theories of Reparations'. *Windsor Yearbook of Access to Justice* 2 (2011). King, Jamesina. 'Gender and Reparations in Sierra Leone: The Wounds of War Remain Open'. In *What Happened To the Women? Gender and Reparations for Human Rights Violations*, 247–83. New York: International Centre for Transitional Justice, 2006.

71 Renard Painter, Ibid., at 10.

72 Meldrum, Andrew. 'Mugabe's Youth Militias 'Raping Women Held Captive in Camps'. *Guardian*, 18 March 2003.

73 *Situation in the Democratic Republic of the Congo in the case of the Prosecutor* v. *Thomas Lubanga Dyilo*, No: ICC-01/04-01/06, Dissenting judgement (2012), at para 19.

74 Alston, Philip, Academy of European Law, and New York University. Center for Human Rights and Global Justice. *Non-State Actors and Human Rights*. Collected Courses of the Academy of European Law; XIII/3. Oxford; New York: Oxford University Press, 2005.

75 Tuck, David. 'Detention by Armed Groups: Overcoming Challenges to Humanitarian Action'. *International Review of the Red Cross* 93, no. 888 (2011): 759–782, at 761.

76 Ibid., at 764.

77 Ibid.

78 Moore, Catherine. 'The United States, International Humanitarian Law and the Prisoners at Guantanamo Bay'. *The International Journal of Human Rights* 7, no. 2 (2003): 1–27. Arai-Takahashi, Yutaka. 'Disentangling Legal Quagmires: The Legal Characterisation of the Armed Conflicts in Afghanistan since 6/7 October 2001 and the Question of Prisoner of War Status'. *Yearbook of International Humanitarian Law* 5 (2002): 61–105.

79 Macken, Claire. *Counter-Terrorism and the Detention of Suspected Terrorists: Preventive Detention and International Human Rights Law*. Routledge Research in Terrorism and Law. Abingdon: Routledge, 2011. Cassel, Douglass. 'Pretrial and Preventive Detention of Suspected Terrorists: Options and Constraints under International Law'. *The Journal of Criminal Law and Criminology*, no. 3 (2008): 811–852.

80 *Serdar Mohammed* v. *Ministry of Defence*, EWHC 1369 (QB), 2014.

81 Goodman, Ryan. 'The Detention of Civilians in Armed Conflict'. *The American Journal of International Law* 103, no. 1 (2009): 48–74, at 49.

82 Ibid.

83 The IHL conventions expressly provide for female POWs by including a number of special protections for female prisoners. For example, Article 25, GC3 provides for separate quarters for female POWs. Article 88 GC3 states that,

> In no case may a woman prisoner of war be awarded or sentenced to a punishment more severe, or treated whilst undergoing punishment more severely, than a male member of the armed forces of the Detaining Power dealt with for a similar offence.

84 Jones, supra note 36.
85 See for example, 'The Dark and Secret Dungeons of Iraq. Horror Stories of Female Prisoners'. *Global Research.* Accessed 10 December 2013.
86 Clifford, Cassandra. 'Rape Camps in Zimbabwe'. *Foreign Policy Association*, 9 July 2008. Wines, Michael. 'Reports of Rape and Torture Inside Zimbabwean Militia'. *New York Times*, 28 December 2003.
87 'Women Under Siege'. *Crowdmap.* https://womenundersiegesyria.crowdmap.com/.
88 Sommer, Robert. *Das KZ-Bordell: sexuelle Zwangsarbeit in nationalsozialistischen Konzentrationslagern* (The Concentration Camp Brothel), Paderborn: Schöningh, 2009.
89 Storr, Will. 'The Rape of Men: The Darkest Secret of War'. *Guardian*, 17 July 2011.
90 Dinstein, Yoram. *The Conduct of Hostilities under the Law of International Armed Conflict.* Cambridge: Cambridge University Press, 2004.
91 'A Woman's Burden', *Time*, 28 March 2003.
92 Handrahan, Lori. 'Conflict, Gender, Ethnicity and Post-Conflict Reconstruction'. *Security Dialogue* 35, no. 4 (2004): 429–445, at 433.
93 Ibid.
94 Manjoo, Rashida and McRaith, Calleigh. 'Gender-Based Violence and Justice in Conflict and Post-Conflict Areas'. *Cornell International Law Journal* 44 (2011): 11–31.
95 Lowiki, Jane and Pilsbury, Allison, *Disarmament, Demobilisation and Reintegration, and Gender-based Violence in Sierra Leone*, excerpts from Precious Resources, Adolescents in the Reconstruction of Sierra Leone, Women's Commission for Refugee Women and Children, 1–19, (2002).
96 Verhey, Beth. *Reaching the Girls, Study on Girls Associated with Armed Forces and Groups in the Democratic Republic of Congo.* London: Save the Children UK, CARE, IFESH and IRC (2004).
97 Schroeder, Emily, *A Window of Opportunity in the Democratic Republic of the Congo: Incorporating a Gender Perspective in the Disarmament, Demobilization and Reintegration Process*, Centre for Security Sector Management, Peace Conflict & Development Issue, (2004).
98 Lowiki, Pilsbury, supra note 95.
99 Ibid.
100 Lamb, Guy, and Stern, Orly. *Assessing the Reintegration of Ex-Combatants in the Context of Instability and Informal Economies, The Cases of the Central African Republic, the Democratic Republic of Congo and South Sudan.* World Bank, Transitional Demobilization and Reintegration Program, 2011.
101 Children and Women Associated with Armed Forces and Groups, Issue Paper, Second International Conference on DDR and Stability in Africa Kinshasa, Democratic Republic of Congo, 12–14 June 2007.
102 Castillo Diaz, Pablo. 'Women's Participation in Peace Negotiations: Connections between Presence and Influence'. New York: UNIFEM, 2010.
103 Ibid., at 1.
104 Ibid.
105 General Recommendation No. 30 on Women in Conflict Prevention, Conflict and Post-Conflict Situations. CEDAW/C/GC/30, 2013.
106 Lukatela, Ana. *Gender and Post-Conflict Governance: Understanding the Challenges.* New York: UN Women, 2012.

107 Arabi, Asha. '"In Power Without Power": Women in Politics and Leadership Positions in South Sudan'. In Bubenzer, Friederike and Stern, Orly (eds), *Hope, Pain & Patience: The Lives of Women in South Sudan.* Johannesburg: Jacana Media, 2012.
108 Schmitt, Michael. '"Direct Participation in Hostilities" and 21st Century Armed Conflict'. In Fischer, Horst (ed.), *Crisis Management and Humanitarian Protection: Festschrift Fur*, 505–529. Berlin: BWV, 2004.
109 Shany, Yuval. 'Binary Law Meets Complex Reality: The Occupation of Gaza Debate'. *Israel Law Review* 41 (2008): 68–86.
110 Ibid.
111 Kaldor, Mary. 'In Defence of New Wars'. *Stability* 2, no. 1 (2013), at 2.

Bibliography

Books and articles

Alston, Philip, Academy of European Law, and New York University. Center for Human Rights and Global Justice. *Non-State Actors and Human Rights.* Collected Courses of the Academy of European Law; XIII/3. Oxford; New York: Oxford University Press, 2005.

Arabi, Asha. '"In Power Without Power": Women in Politics and Leadership Positions in South Sudan'. In Bubenzer, Friederike, and Stern, Orly (eds), *Hope, Pain & Patience: The Lives of Women in South Sudan.* Johannesburg: Jacana Media, 2012.

Arai-Takahashi, Yutaka. 'Disentangling Legal Quagmires: The Legal Characterisation of the Armed Conflicts in Afghanistan since 6/7 October 2001 and the Question of Prisoner of War Status'. *Yearbook of International Humanitarian Law* 5 (2002): 61–105.

Bangura, Barbara. *Returning the Girls Home: Reintegration and Resocialisation of Abducted and Ex-Girl Soldiers. A Case Study from Sierra Leone, West Africa.* West Africa Network for Peace Building, 2002.

Bastick, Megan, Grimm, Karin and Kunz, Rahel. 'Sexual Violence in Armed Conflict, Global Overview and Implications for the Security Sector'. Geneva: Geneva Centre for the Democratic Control of Armed Forces, 2007.

Barrow, Amy. 'UN Security Council Resolutions 1325 and 1820: Constructing Gender in Armed Conflict and International Humanitarian Law'. *International Review of the Red Cross* 92, no. 877 (2010): 221–234.

Bennoune, Karima. '"Do We Need New International Law to Protect Women in Armed Conflict?"' *Case Western Reserve Journal of International Law* 38 (2006): 363–391.

Benshoof, Janet. 'The Other Red Line: The Use of Rape as an Unlawful Tactic of Warfare'. *Global Policy* 5, no. 2 (2014): 146–158.

Bothe, Michael, Partsch, Karl and Solf, Waldemar. *New Rules for Victims of Armed Conflicts: Commentary on the Two 1977 Protocols Additional to the Geneva Conventions of 1949.* Leiden: Martinus Nijhoff Publishers, 1982.

Brownmiller, Susan. *Against Our Will: Men, Women and Rape.* New York: Simon and Schuster, 1975.

Britt, Jason. 'Unwilling Warriors: An Examination of the Power to Conscript in Peacetime'. *Northwestern Journal of Law and Social Policy* 4, no. 3 (2009): 400–423.

Carpenter. Charli. '"Women and Children First": Gender, Norms, and Humanitarian Evacuation in the Balkans 1991–95'. *International Organization* 57, no. 4 (2003): 661–694.

Cassel, Douglass. 'Pretrial and Preventive Detention of Suspected Terrorists: Options and Constraints under International Law'. *The Journal of Criminal Law and Criminology*, no. 3 (2008): 811–852.

Castillo Diaz, Pablo. 'Women's Participation in Peace Negotiations: Connections between Presence and Influence'. New York: UNIFEM, 2010.

Children and Women Associated with Armed Forces and Groups, Issue Paper, Second International Conference on DDR and Stability in Africa Kinshasa, Democratic Republic of Congo, 12–14 June 2007.

Coomaraswamy, Radhika. *Report of the Special Rapporteur on Violence Against Women, Its Causes and Consequences*. United Nations, Commission on Human Rights, Fifty-fourth Session, 1998.

Coulter, Chris. 'Female Fighters in the Sierra Leone War: Challenging the Assumptions?' *Feminist Review* 88, no. 1 (2008): 54–73.

De Belle, Stéphanie Bouchié. 'Chained to Cannons or Wearing Targets on Their T-Shirts: Human Shields in International Humanitarian Law'. *International Review of the Red Cross* 90, no. 872 (2008): 883–906.

Denov, Myriam. *Girls in Fighting Forces: Moving Beyond Victimhood*. A Summary of the Research Findings on Girls and Armed Conflict from CIDA's Child Protection Research Fund, 2007.

Dinstein, Yoram. *The Conduct of Hostilities under the Law of International Armed Conflict*. Cambridge: Cambridge University Press, 2004.

El-Bushra, Judy. *How Should We Understand Sexual Violence and HIV/AIDS in Conflict Contexts?* AIDS, Security and Conflict Initiative (ACSI) Report no. 17, 2008.

Enloe, Cynthia. *Manoeuvres the International Politics of Militarizing Women's Lives*. Berkeley, CA: University of California Press, 2000.

Gardam, Judith. 'Gender and Non-Combatant Immunity'. *Transnational Law & Contemporary Problems* 3 (1993): 345–370.

Gong-Gershowitz, Jennifer. 'Forced Marriage: A "New" Crime against Humanity?' *Northwestern Journal of International Human Rights* 8, no. 1, Article 3 (2009): 53–76.

Goodman, Ryan. 'The Detention of Civilians in Armed Conflict'. *The American Journal of International Law* 103, no. 1 (2009): 48–74.

Handrahan, Lori. 'Conflict, Gender, Ethnicity and Post-Conflict Reconstruction'. *Security Dialogue* 35, no. 4 (2004): 429–445.

Henckaerts, Jean-Marie. 'Study on Customary International Humanitarian Law: A Contribution to the Understanding and Respect for the Rule of Law in Armed Conflict'. *International Review of the Red Cross* 87, no. 857 (2005): 175–212.

Jones, Adam. 'Gendercide and Genocide'. *Journal of Genocide Research* 2, no. 2 (2000): 185–211.

Kaldor, Mary. 'In Defence of New Wars'. *Stability* 2, no. 1 (2013).

King, Jamesina. 'Gender and Reparations in Sierra Leone: The Wounds of War Remain Open'. In *What Happened To the Women? Gender and Reparations for Human Rights Violations*, 247–283. New York: International Centre for Transitional Justice, 2006.

Kinsella, Helen. *Securing the Civilian: Sex and Gender in the Laws of War*. Boston, MA: Boston Consortium on Gender, Security and Human Rights, 2004.

Lamb, Guy, and Stern, Orly. *Assessing the Reintegration of Ex-Combatants in the Context of Instability and Informal Economies, the Cases of the Central African Republic, the Democratic Republic of Congo and South Sudan*. Washington DC: World Bank, Transitional Demobilization and Reintegration Program, 2011.

Lieblich, Eliav. *Beyond Life and Limb: Exploring Incidental Mental Harm Under International Humanitarian Law*. SSRN Scholarly Paper. Rochester, NY: Social Science Research Network, 10 June 2013.

Lowiki, Jane, and Pilsbury, Allison, *Disarmament, Demobilisation and Reintegration, and Gender-based Violence in Sierra Leone*, excerpts from Precious Resources, Adolescents in the Reconstruction of Sierra Leone, Women's Commission for Refugee Women and Children, 1–19 (2002).

Lukatela, Ana. *Gender and Post-Conflict Governance: Understanding the Challenges*. UN Women, 2012.

Lyall, Rewi. 'Voluntary Human Shields, Direct Participation in Hostilities and the International Humanitarian Law Obligations of States'. *Melbourne Journal of International Law* 9 (2008): 313–333.

Macken, Claire. *Counter-Terrorism and the Detention of Suspected Terrorists: Preventive Detention and International Human Rights Law*. Routledge Research in Terrorism and Law. Abingdon: Routledge, 2011.

Manjoo, Rashida, and McRaith, Calleigh. 'Gender-Based Violence and Justice in Conflict and Post-Conflict Areas'. *Cornell International Law Journal* 44 (2011): 11–31.

McInnes, Colin, 'HIV, AIDS and Conflict in Africa: Why Isn't It (Even) Worse?' Paper for Annual Conference of the International Studies Associate, 2009.

Moore, Catherine. 'The United States, International Humanitarian Law and the Prisoners at Guantanamo Bay'. *The International Journal of Human Rights* 7, no. 2 (2003): 1–27.

Nguyen, Athena. 'The Influence of Gender Stereotyping on International Humanitarian Law'. 2010. http://works.bepress.com/athena_nguyen/1.

Otto, Dianne. 'The Exile of Inclusion: Reflections on Gender Issues in International Law Over the Last Decade'. *The Melbourne Journal of International Law* 10 (2009): 11–26.

Pratt, Nicola and Richter-Devroe, Sophie. 'Critically Examining UNSCR 1325 on Women, Peace and Security'. *International Feminist Journal of Politics* 13, no. 4 (2011): 489–503.

Queguiner, Jean-François. 'Precautions under the Law Governing the Conduct of Hostilities'. *International Review of the Red Cross* 88, no. 864 (2006): 793–821.

Rajagopalan, Swarna. 'Gender Violence, Conflict, Internal Displacement and Peacebuilding'. *Peace Prints: South Asian Journal of Peacebuilding* 3, no. 1 (2010): 1–15.

Rehn Elisabeth, and Sirleaf, Ellen Johnson, 'Women, War and Peace: The Independent Experts' Assessment on the Impact of Armed Conflict on Women and Women's Role in Peace-building'. UNIFEM, 2002.

Renard Painter, Genevieve. 'Thinking Past Rights: Towards Feminist Theories of Reparations'. *Windsor Yearbook of Access to Justice* 2 (2011).

Schmitt, Michael. ''Attack' as a Term of Art in International Law: The Cyber Operations Context'. In *2012 4th International Conference on Cyber Conflict*. Tallinn, 2012.

Schmitt, Michael. ''Direct Participation in Hostilities' and 21st Century Armed Conflict'. In Fischer, Horst (ed.), *Crisis Management and Humanitarian Protection: Festschrift Fur*, 505–529. Berlin: BWV, 2004.

Schmitt, Michael. 'Human Shields in International Humanitarian Law'. *Columbia Journal of Transnational Law* 47 (2009): 292–338.

Schmitt, Michael, and NATO Cooperative Cyber Defence Centre of Excellence. *Tallinn Manual on the International Law Applicable to Cyber Warfare: Prepared by the International Group of Experts at the Invitation of the NATO Cooperative Cyber Defence Centre of Excellence*. Cambridge: Cambridge University Press, 2013.

Schroeder, Emily, *A Window of Opportunity in the Democratic Republic of the Congo: Incorporating a Gender Perspective in the Disarmament, Demobilization and Reintegration Process*. Centre for Security Sector Management, Peace Conflict & Development Issue (2004).
Shany, Yuval. 'Binary Law Meets Complex Reality: The Occupation of Gaza Debate'. *Israel Law Review* 41 (2008): 68–86.
Shepherd, Laura. 'Sex, Security and Superhero(in)es: From 1325 to 1820 and Beyond'. *International Feminist Journal of Politics* 13, no. 4 (2011): 504–21.
Sinha, Alex. 'Child Soldiers as Super-Privileged Combatants'. *The International Journal of Human Rights* 17, no. 4 (2013): 584–603.
Sjoberg, Laura. *The Paradox of Double Effect: How Feminism Can Save the Immunity Principle*. Boston Consortium on Gender, Security and Human Rights, 2006.
Sommer, Robert. *Das KZ-Bordell: sexuelle Zwangsarbeit in nationalsozialistischen Konzentrationslagern* (The Concentration Camp Brothel), Paderborn: Schöningh, 2009.
Turpin, Jennifer. 'Many Faces, Women Confronting War'. In *The Women and War Reader, Lois Ann Lorentzen and Jennifer Turpin*. New York: New York University Press, 1998.
'The Dark and Secret Dungeons of Iraq. Horror Stories of Female Prisoners'. *Global Research*. Accessed 10 December 2013.
Trabucchi, Eugenia. 'Rape Warfare and International Humanitarian Law'. *Human Architecture: Journal of the Sociology of Self-Knowledge* 6, no. 4 (2008): 39–48.
Tuck, David. 'Detention by Armed Groups: Overcoming Challenges to Humanitarian Action'. *International Review of the Red Cross* 93, no. 888 (2011): 759–782.
Verhey, Beth. *Reaching the Girls, Study on Girls Associated with Armed Forces and Groups in the Democratic Republic of Congo*. London: Save the Children UK, CARE, IFESH and IRC (2004).
Wood, Elisabeth. 'Variation in Sexual Violence during War'. *Politics & Society* 34, no. 3 (2006): 307–342.

Cases

Situation in the Democratic Republic of the Congo in the case of the Prosecutor v. *Thomas Lubanga Dyilo*, No: ICC-01/04-01/06.
Serdar Mohammed v. *Ministry of Defence*, EWHC 1369 (QB), 2014.
The Prosecutor v. *Brima*, Case No. SCSL-2004-16-T, Appeals Judgment, 2008.
The Prosecutor v. *Dragoljub Kunarac Radomir Kovac and Zoran Vukovic*, ICTY, IT-96-23-T & IT-96-23/1-T, 2001.

Treaties

Rome Statute
Protocol Additional to the Geneva Conventions of 12 August 1949, and relating to the Protection of Victims of International Armed Conflicts (Protocol I), 8 June 1977, 1125 UNTS 3.
Protocol Additional to the Geneva Conventions of 12 August 1949, and relating to the Protection of Victims of Non-International Armed Conflicts (Protocol II), 8 June 1977, 1125 UNTS 609.

Geneva Convention Relative to the Protection of Civilian Persons in Time of War (Fourth Geneva Convention), 12 August 1949, 75 UNTS 287.
ICTR Statute
Statute of the Special Court for Sierra Leone

Other policy documents

General Recommendation No. 30 on Women in Conflict Prevention, Conflict and Post-Conflict Situations. CEDAW/C/GC/30, 2013.
'Interpretive Guidance on the Notion of Direct Participation in Hostilities Under International Humanitarian Law'. *International Review of the Red Cross* 90, no. 872 (2009): 991–1047.
Written Submissions of the United Nations Special Representative of the Secretary-General on Children and Armed Conflict Submitted in application of Rule 103 of the Rules of Procedure and Evidence, Annex A, para 14. *Situation in the Democratic Republic of the Congo in the case of the Prosecutor* v. *Thomas Lubanga Dyilo*, No: ICC-01/04-01/06.

Media and websites

'A Woman's Burden', *Time*, 28 March 2003.
Clifford, Cassandra. 'Rape Camps in Zimbabwe'. *Foreign Policy Association*, 9 July 2008.
Meldrum, Andrew. 'Mugabe's Youth Militias "Raping Women Held Captive in Camps" '. *Guardian*, 18 March 2003.
Storr, Will. 'The Rape of Men: The Darkest Secret of War'. *Guardian*, 17 July 2011.
Wines, Michael. 'Reports of Rape and Torture inside Zimbabwean Militia'. *New York Times*, 28 December 2003.
'Women Under Siege, Woman Says She Witnessed Women Stripped and Used as Human Shields'. *Crowdmap*. https://womenundersiegesyria.crowdmap.com/reports/view/235.
'Women Under Siege, Woman Tells Toronto Star Women Were Raped and Used as Human Shields in Homs'. *Crowdmap*. https://womenundersiegesyria.crowdmap.com/reports/view/182.
World Report 2013: Eritrea. Human Rights Watch. www.hrw.org/world-report/2013/country-chapters/eritrea.
'Women Under Siege'. *Crowdmap*. https://womenundersiegesyria.crowdmap.com/.

8 Conclusions

This book has conducted a feminist critique of the principle of distinction both broadly, as well as in the specific context of African conflicts. Much has changed since the drafting of the IHL conventions. Conflicts have transformed; in the ways they are fought, in their inter/intra-state character, in the nature of the parties fighting and in the targeting of civilians. New wars – complex, chaotic and multifaceted – have become the norm. Among the many changes seen, have been shifts in the ways that women participate, shifts that have often mirrored the changes in women's status in society more generally. What we are left with is a set of laws too narrow to adequately encompass these changes in conflict and the differing ways in which women participate.

This book has demonstrated the ways in which IHL prejudices women, neglecting their specific needs, concealing their experiences and painting them in particular stereotypical ways. However, the principle of distinction's failings are not restricted to gendered ones. The principle is in a state of crisis, tragically evidenced by the staggering number of civilians killed in modern conflicts. Armed groups disregard IHL for a range of reasons – many of which have nothing to do with the wording and framing of the law. Some of the core tactics by which new wars are waged – ethnic cleansing, terrorising of civilians and targeted sexual violence – lie in direct conflict with IHL's rules, making it impossible for armed groups to fight this type of warfare within the bounds of the law. Given these chosen strategies, it seems unlikely that any law, no matter how it was framed, could curb these behaviours.

However, one does need to consider the role that IHL plays in this. States have created a regulatory system in which the majority of actors in today's conflicts – non-state armed actors – are in no ways incentivised to comply. They are disadvantaged by this system at every step of the way, giving them every reason to flout this body of law. Adding to the problem is that this outdated regulatory body has largely been reduced to a fiction – a law laden with categorisations that scarcely resemble what is found on the ground. Legal descriptions of combatants and direct participants look little like the actors seen in today's conflicts. The criteria aimed at distinguishing IACs and NIACs scarcely resemble the part internal, part transnational and part internationalised struggles we see raging across the globe. Even where armed actors have the will to adhere to the law, these problems make it confusing, difficult and sometimes outright impossible to follow and adhere to. IHL was designed for a different type of conflict, the type that was dominant when drafting the GCs and APs, a time where states fought states using armed, uniformed men. The principle of distinction strains at the seams when applied to these new wars. The many evident problems with the principle, both gendered and more general, reveal an untenable legal situation, and a law that is in every way failing to fulfil its goals. There seems to be a need for change.

This concluding chapter summarises the key arguments made in this work. It considers whether the problems with the principle speak to the need for legal change, and what such change might look like. It describes some of the potential means by which the legal status quo could be shifted, highlighting risks and pitfalls inherent in these approaches. It discusses the implications of this research, as well as potential avenues for future research.

The central themes of this work

This research has questioned the principle of distinction's capacity to regulate and protect in new wars. A few themes have run through the research, working together to shed light on different aspects of this broader question. The first was that of women in armed conflict; the research sought to highlight the different ways in which women participate in conflict, their diverse needs and experiences, as well as the gendered effects of IHL. The second theme related to new wars and to problems in regulating these, including the paucity of laws regulating NIACs, the problems created by the merging of IACs and NIACs, and challenges of compliance and incentives in these conflicts. The third theme related to Africa, a region where the bulk of the world's conflicts are taking place, yet which is underexplored in terms of legal analysis and which has historically contributed little to IHL's development. Through an exploration of these themes, this research has shone a spotlight on the principle of distinction and its application in modern conflicts, with particular respect to women.

This book questioned whether the principle of distinction serves women in modern day conflict, or whether it fails them, even putting women at greater risk or disadvantage. It questioned whether the principle is suitable to be applied to women participating in conflict, containing provisions that adequately encompass the roles played by women in new wars, or rather whether the laws are based on out-dated and incorrect perceptions of women's roles, failing to reflect the gendered reality in these conflicts, and thereby failing to adequately regulate women's involvement and protection during hostilities.

The book argued that the narrow definitions in the principle of distinction effectively exclude women who participate in conflicts from falling within its ambit. Women in African conflicts participate differently to men – much as in other parts of the world. The principle of distinction's terms were drafted with typical male participation in mind. The result is that few women fall within the legal definitions of combatancy and direct participation, even when women are actively involved in hostilities.

This has a range of effects for women – beneficial and harmful, direct and indirect, during conflict and post-conflict. The framing of the law can work to the benefit of some women, while prejudicing others. If women are excluded from definitions of combatancy and direct participation, then they are legally protected from being targets of attack, clearly advantageous to the women in question. However, less beneficial are some of indirect effects that stem from this. The narrowly framed law entrenches the view that men are fighters and women are not. This view is already prevalent in society, derived from patriarchal norms and societal stereotypes about female behaviour. Even when the facts on the ground lie in stark contrast to these notions – like where women are actively and visibly taking part in armed movements – the law plays a role in concealing this, creating an additional barrier to women's contributions being recognised. The narrow framing of the law entrenches ideas about women perpetually being civilians and victims in war, in need of protection, lacking agency – and never actors, participants or agents. Conceptualisations that paint women as victims in turn tacitly allow for, or normalise, the further victimisation of women – by those within armed groups and those outside of them; by those on their own 'side' and by those from the enemy. Reinforcing stereotypes about male fighters also entrenches views about it being acceptable for men to fight, views that are highly problematic for society.

The effects of the principle extend post-conflict too. Fighters are honoured in post-conflict states, pedestalled and rewarded with positions of influence and authority. Where women's contributions are not recognised, then women are not awarded these positions. They then tend to be excluded from peace negotiations, political positions, reparations programmes and demobilisation and reintegration assistance conferred on former combatants. Understandings derived in part from the principle of distinction therefore affect the post-conflict setting and shape post-war reconstruction in ways that are prejudicial to women. Male contributions are rewarded, so male interests are prioritised. Women's concerns are left off of the agenda, as those who did not truly participate are not deemed worthy of war's rewards.

As well as being prejudicial to women, the gendered problems with the law detract from the efficiency of the principle more generally, and reveal deeper problems that diminish the law's effectiveness. Laws that fail to take account of the diverse experiences of women miss the complexity of the situations they were designed to regulate. The fact that the law's categorisations do not make sense for women, is revealing of the ways in which IHL fails to properly categorise and demarcate other aspects of conflict. Laws that are premised on inaccurate, outdated or unworkable categorisations cannot hope to properly regulate.

The law's relationship with gender also exposes the stereotypes implicit in the law, revealing how the law rests on these and how the law in turn perpetuates them. IHL's underlying assumption that women are innocent, passive or victims, leads to it ignoring those women who are not, failing to consider or properly regulate them, with assumptions making the law blind to those in alternative roles. Similar 'blind spots' can be found elsewhere in IHL – this law is blind to alternative types of conflicts, to conflicts that merge the law's categorisations, to conflicts that do not look like those envisaged by the drafters. These blind spots reveal that the principle is not a robust one that can be applied generally. Gender analysis reveals the hierarchies implicit in the law – of which gender is only one. These hierarchies benefit some at the expense of others: men over women, combatants over civilians, state actors over non-state actors. Problematically, these hierarchies affect people's willingness to abide by the law. Armed actors are unlikely to be motivated by a system that is consistently and systemically prejudicial towards them.

This book has endeavoured to reveal what conflict *should* look like in terms of the vision underlying IHL. Without admitting to it, IHL provides a normative vision of conflict; one that is masculine and Eurocentric. Looking at *women* fighting in *African* conflicts puts the margins in the centre, providing a double challenge to the underlying normative visions of conflict and, in doing so, disrupting the layers of assumptions underlying IHL. 'Africa', 'women' and 'new wars' are all atypical according to the constructions underlying IHL – despite the fact that these are quite typical in conflict today. These lenses collapse the traditional pictures implicit in IHL, challenging the notions of what 'normal' war and 'typical' fighters should be. But, if atypical examples push the regulatory system to the point of non-functioning, what is the continued use of this system?

IHL was created for classic old wars. It strains at the seams when applied to new wars. New wars challenge IHL in a range of ways. For one thing, targeting civilians tends to be a key strategy in new wars. The fact that the principle of distinction prohibits the targeting of civilians means it is prohibiting a central tactic of hostilities. IHL was designed to strike a balance between military necessity and humanitarian concerns, prohibiting those actions of cruelty not necessary for the goal of military victory. However, where the law prohibits a central strategy of conflict, as it does in new wars, then it takes on an altogether different relationship with war fighting – one that actors are less likely to accept. This is further complicated by the fact that 'military victory' is frequently not a goal in new wars – often the goal is just to keep hostilities going so that armed actors can continue to exploit the situation. New wars are often not true IACs or NIACs, the fighters neither civilians nor combatants. So much of what is seen in these fails to correspond with what IHL envisages.

More specifically than just new wars, this book has sought to illustrate how the laws do not make sense in Africa. People participate differently in African conflicts to the ways anticipated and required by IHL. There are stark differences in the ways men and women participate, influenced by the traditional gender roles prevalent across the continent. Africa has seen a prevalence of long-term, low-level armed situations, which do not meet the definitions of 'armed conflict', IACs or NIACs. Adding to the problem is that many African conflicts remain technologically unsophisticated, using little in the way of high-tech military intelligence, making the determinations required by IHL more difficult to make. These conflicts tend to be fought by little-educated fighters who are unlikely to be trained in the nuances of IHL. Even if fighters were trained in the nuances of the law, and had the military intelligence available, it would still be difficult to determine who is fighter and non-fighter, because of the ways these roles blend in practice. The situation is made more difficult by the fact that most African conflicts involve non-state armed groups, meaning one is dealing with the murky area of 'direct participation'. In Africa we are left with little-educated fighters with poor intelligence technology applying the murkiest part of the law in a context where the classifications are the most unclear – one can hardly be surprised the law does not function optimally in this context.

The problems with the principle of distinction must be looked at in the context of IHL more broadly. Distinction sits at the core of IHL and problems with distinction expose problems with the broader body of law. IHL's principles are interrelated, meaning that problems with distinction affect the other core principles and vice versa. One cannot determine if acts violate proportionality if one cannot first ascertain who is a lawful target. So too, if it is unclear whether a conflict is IAC or NIAC, then it is not clear what version of the principle of distinction to apply. If distinction, IHL's central protection mechanism, is failing, this brings not only the principle of distinction into question, but also IHL's capacity to fulfil its broader mandate – that of providing constraints and protection in conflict.

There are therefore numerous problems with this law that are separate but interrelated. The law fails women in new wars, first and foremost because it is not functioning properly. However, in addition to the ways it fails everyone, it also fails women in specific ways. Those failings pertaining to everyone and those pertaining to women are interrelated. The organising principle of IHL assumes males as the primary actors. Bringing in women as actors destabilises the entire construct of IHL. We are left with a destabilised law, operating in conflicts that by their very nature push IHL beyond its field of comfortable operation.

Rethinking the principle of distinction

The many failings described above suggest that the overall regulation of conflict – as well as many of the concepts within and underlying the law – need to be reconsidered. This section will highlight some of the specific areas of law that merit reconsideration, before moving on to the question of how such changes might actually be achieved.

First, we need to challenge our outright acceptance of the principle of distinction. Is the principle of distinction really the best legal mechanism to apply in conflict? For years there has been blind acceptance of this principle and its central role in IHL, an acceptance that has made the international community complacent about the principle's failings. We should interrogate our assumption that the principle is capable of doing what it purports to do. As this book has demonstrated, the principle is impractical, complex, often out of touch with local realities, and, in many contexts, all but impossible to apply. How can we argue for the application of a principle that cannot be workably applied? In NIACs, where there is no civilian/combatant divide and all we are left with is 'direct participation', does this concept even constitute an operational principle of distinction? We need to question if the principle is serving any function in new wars. If it is not meeting its stated goals, what is it actually doing? Given how little it is achieving in these conflicts, would anything be different if we removed this principle altogether? Perhaps protection in conflict might be better served by replacing distinction with something else, or altering it in significant ways. If distinction is to continue being held up as the foundational core of IHL, then we need to continuously analyse it – and where it is failing, address these failures. The situation we have at the moment, of large-scale recognition of the principle's failings, yet what seems to be a despondent acceptance of these, is unacceptable given the grave consequences of having a body of law with a dysfunctional central protection mechanism regulating violent conflict.

IHL and the principle of distinction operate *during* armed conflict. This too needs to be challenged. The notion that IHL should apply only during active armed conflict, and that its importance and effects simply cease the moment a peace treaty is signed, is flawed. Both the effects of violence, and the effects of the law, seep over into non-conflict times. The idea of a set period of 'armed conflict', with specific dangers that a narrowly tailored body of regulation can address, clearly does not work in new wars. In these, there might not be a single intense period of 'armed conflict' but, rather, long-term, low-level situations with sporadic flare-ups that temporarily reach the level of armed conflict before receding again. Even during the quiet gaps, violence continues to some extent, including through targeted sexual violence against women. The 'armed conflict' model means that in those 'quiet times', armed actors will not be regulated by IHL. Post conflict too, instability persists and the dangers to women continue. CEDAW's General Comment 30 expressly recognises that, "… the transition from conflict to post-conflict is often not linear and can involve cessations of conflict and then slippages back into conflict – a cycle that can continue for long periods of time".[1] This threshold for the application of IHL therefore needs to be reconsidered. There is a need to find a mechanism to ensure that longer-term conflicts are regulated in their entirety, not just during flare-ups, ensuring there are no gaps in protection. Chosen legal triggers must ensure the law is operational at all times when civilians require protection, and not just when technical requirements are met.

The other threshold too, the IAC/NIAC distinction, also needs to be interrogated. Chapter 5 argued for the eradication of this distinction – in part because it is often unworkable in new wars. There is already an evident movement towards merging these categories in law and practice. However, as Chapter 5 explained, removing the IAC/NIAC divide would necessitate rethinking the principle of distinction in NIACs. Until states are willing to concede that non-state fighters should have the recognition and privileges that come with combatancy, the two bodies of law cannot properly align. The principle of distinction therefore lies at the core of the IAC/NIAC problem, illustrating the inter-connected nature of IHL's many problems.

Within the principle of distinction there are also concepts that need to be interrogated. Among these is the binary distinction between 'civilian' and 'combatant'. Is this a valuable distinction to retain, or might there be an alternative indicator better suited to demarcating participation in modern conflicts? If we believe this distinction retains merit, should the parameters of what is a civilian and a combatant be shifted? Perhaps most pressingly, thought needs to be given to if and how non-state actors can be better incorporated within this. What are the costs to the efficacy of the principle in failing to include them, given the dominance of non-state actors in new wars? In determining how narrowly or widely combatancy should be framed, a calculation must be made. If combatancy is framed too widely and un-uniformed, undisciplined, unorganised fighters are allowed to qualify, this leads to a blurring of combatant and civilian that can erode the principle and its stark, simple appeal. On the other hand, if combatancy is framed too narrowly, as in its current formulation, then many fighters are excluded from the fold, removing their incentive to comply with IHL, ultimately detracting from the law's effectiveness. AP1 marked the start of a shift towards encouraging irregular participants to abide by the law by offering them combatant status. The principle needs to shift further in this direction. As irregular fighters are today the norm, a law that does not properly incorporate them risks sliding into irrelevance.

Understandings of 'direct participation' also need to be challenged. The problem is clear: if the term is framed narrowly, with fewer activities qualifying as direct participation, then more people are legally protected from attack. But, while a narrow interpretation appears to provide protection to a larger number, this can actually increase the risk to civilian populations, creating confusion and encouraging disrespect for the law – particularly by those threatened by the actions of those said to not be 'directly participating'. Wide definitions that allow more people to be targeted may ultimately increase the protection of civilians by promoting compliance.[2] Conversely, the exclusion of women by the narrow understandings of direct participation may ultimately be harmful for women, leading to more civilian women being attacked. As such, there might be greater benefit in working towards a wider, more inclusive notion that better reflects the true ways in which people – including women – participate in new wars, and which incorporates more participating women into the fold.

The treatment of non-state armed groups in IHL also needs to be addressed. The ICRC's 'continuous combat function' is a positive first step towards aligning the regulation of armed groups with the realities of modern conflict. However, continuous combat function has its limitations. Of particular relevance to this works is that it does not get one around the gendered problems inherent in the concept of 'direct participation'. Only those who 'continuously directly participate in hostilities' have a continuous combat function. Reliance on the direct participation standard here once again leads to the effective exclusion of women. The 'continuous' part of the approach is promising, with continuous action being a useful way to determine membership – and one that is more likely to be inclusive of women than other methods might be, such as those that require that formal criteria to be met or recognition by group leaders. However, the action standard, 'direction participation', might be replaced with one that is more gender inclusive. There are other evident problems with the continuous combat function standard. When considering clashes between African armed groups, it seems unlikely that enemies would have access to the sort of detailed information required to know which members directly participate, when, and for whom this participation reaches the level of continuous combat function. Particularly given low levels of military intelligence technology in this context, this seems to be a largely unrealistic standard.

Another area where attention is required is the relationship between IHL and Africa. IHL was drafted with the European context in mind, with conflicts in the rest of the world – and particularly in Africa – scarcely being considered in the formation and development of the law. Many of IHL's rules make little sense in the African context. Given that today a sizeable number of the world's conflicts take place in Africa, this situation is untenable. Thought needs to be given to making IHL more workable on and inclusive of the African continent. Legal developments should not assume that people throughout the world participate in conflict in 'Western' ways. They should not assume that all people have access to similar technology – be this for intelligence purposes or for targeting – or similar levels of training, or legal capacity that would allow them to deal with highly complex regulation. In any future processes to amend or develop the laws, attention must be paid to ensuring African voices and concerns are included on a substantial level. Be they interpretive processes – like those conducted by the ICRC – or judicial processes at the international tribunals, attention needs to be paid to ensuring developments are applicable in Africa. Furthermore, attention should be directed not only to the punitive aspects of African conflicts, as we see with the ICC, but also to its regulatory aspects. Including African actors in law-making processes would go a long way towards promoting goodwill towards the system, rather than alienating African actors, as the ICC has done. Failing to do this creates a danger of Africa effectively removing itself from the system.

The way forward

Deciding on the best direction for legal change is fraught with challenges. What should be done to further incorporate women into the principle of distinction? If women participate differently in conflict, should gender specific combatancy or direct participation requirements be created for women? Alternatively, should existing requirements be broadened in a gender-neutral way to further incorporate the types of roles played by women? In the narrow principle of distinction excluding women from definitions of combatancy and direct participation, this provides many with legal protection from attack, putting them outside the bounds of those who can be lawfully targeted. Despite the fact that the law may be unjust, prejudicial and indirectly harmful, there are clear legal benefits to women that stem from this. Attempts to make the principle's definitions wider, to further incorporate women into the fold, would also make more women eligible for targeting.

My view is that equality is paramount – even where this may lead to disadvantages for some women. The overall long-term harm to women of allowing inequality to persist merely because it is beneficial to women in some situations is great. A commitment to gender equality demands and justifies certain short-terms harms. True gender equality will only arise when all situations of unfairness are tackled – even those that benefit women. In my view, what is therefore required is a broadening of the understandings of combatancy and direct participation, so that these better incorporate the ways in which women participate in hostilities – and do not centre only on men's participation. Gender specific requirements are not needed, rather a gender-neutral law is preferable, yet one that incorporates everyone's participation – even if the result is that more women become legally eligible for attack. Many will disagree with this conclusion – it is clearly counter-intuitive from a protection perspective.

Although most feminist scholars working in this area agree that there are problems with this body of law, not all agree that it merits amendment. A debate exists amongst feminist scholars about whether the provisions of IHL are inadequate – needing to be reconceptualised and revised (the 'revisionist school') – or whether there are in fact sufficient protections for women in the law, with the main problems resulting from the lack of adherence and enforcement (the 'enforcement school').[3] The ICRC's position aligns with the enforcement school,[4] with proponents arguing that women have demonstrated resilience in conflict, showing they do not require further tailored legal protections.[5] The revisionist school points to the limited capacity of gender-neutral law to achieve substantive equality given the inherently unequal conditions in conflict that are fuelled by gender inequality. They argue that if IHL does not recognise and address these inequalities, it reinforces discrimination against women.[6] The enforcement school responds by arguing that IHL is restricted in its goals, operating to serve a specific purpose under extreme circumstances – with its narrow focus being one of the reasons for its ability to operate. They claim that IHL was not designed to deal with systemic societal problems like gender inequality and that such criticisms of IHL are unfair as they disregard IHL's mandate and limits.[7]

Even those who support the revisionist approach are aware of the dangers of reopening discussions on IHL's texts. Legal amendment brings the risk of new law that is worse from a gender and protection perspective, a danger feminist lawyers are acutely aware of. If legal amendment processes were set in motion today, these would likely once again be dominated by men and male concerns, as IHL and international security remains a heavily male dominated field. The current political climate, with its fixation on state security, might lead to new laws being codified that work to the detriment of individual protection.[8] Such a process might also open to question issues that are currently considered resolved. In addition, trying to amend the IHL conventions could undermine their legitimacy, at a time where IHL's legitimacy is already greatly challenged. Interfering with the well-established rules of IHL today might therefore be counter-productive

There are significant obstacles to changing international law. Processes of legal amendment are slow, political, context-driven and challenging in terms of achieving consensus. Developments in the law tend to be influenced by the powerful – normally male military actors from politically dominant countries. Negotiating treaties tends to be a long, difficult and highly political process. The drafting of the GCs took years of work – including a 'Preliminary Conference of National Red Cross Societies' in 1945, a 'Conference of Government Experts in 1947, and finally, the International Conference of the Red Cross' in Stockholm in 1948. The Diplomatic Conference itself, where the treaty text was finally agreed, took almost four months. Leading to the creation of the APs, the ICRC held consultations and conducted studies throughout the 1960s and 1970s. Four separate conferences of government experts and Red Cross representatives were held in 1971 and 1972 before the draft APs were finally drafted. These were presented to the Diplomatic Conference in 1974, which then held four sessions between 1974 and 1977, before finally accepting the APs.

Obtaining the state support required for adoption and ratification of treaties can be a tremendous challenge. Historically, states have been less willing to accept changes to the 'means and methods of warfare' rules (Hague rules) than to humanitarian rules (Geneva rules). This is one reason that the GCs were easier to negotiate than the APs, which focused more on means and methods. MacKinnon highlights the swift developments that can occur where there is political will. She points to the changes in IHL's interpretation evident since September 11th 2001 (including the increased willingness to treat non-state actors as states in order to invoke IHL and justify actions of self-defence) as examples of the rapid legal developments that can occur where there is international support for this.[9] It is extremely challenging to come up with changes that are workable and acceptable to all law-making parties. For legal changes to be accepted, they need to not skew the balance between military necessity and humanitarianism in a way that is unacceptable to states.[10] Proposals that veer too far in the humanitarian direction tend to be labelled naïve and pacifist and rejected by military personnel, who tend to be powerful voices within states. The consequences of having only some countries signing onto treaties is that this creates complex issues around successive treaties, with differing states having different legal obligations[11] – a far from optimal situation. Treaty changes also need to allow for future changes in the nature of conflicts, a task fraught with difficulty.

Given that so many actors in new wars are non-state actors, creating a law with increased legitimacy requires bringing non-state actors into the fold. In terms of process, this could mean including more non-state armed actors as negotiating parties in law making processes.[12] Their views might be useful in addressing some problems described in this work, determining ways to incentivise non-state actors to abide by IHL and better incorporating their interests into treaties. It would clearly be impossible to attain participation and consent from all non-state armed actors, as new armed groups are formed and dissolved all the time. However, bringing some larger, longer-term groups into a process might be helpful and strategically prudent. The barrier to involving non-state groups is that states would likely be resistant to legitimating them by bringing them into such processes. However, working towards a less state-centric approach is critical if a new law is to be effective in regulating new wars.

An alternative to trying to alter existing IHL treaties or creating a new general IHL treaty, would be creating a new Optional Protocol to the GCs, which deals with women in conflict. Such a protocol could address all aspects of the treatment of women and could deal with women in their various roles – as civilians, combatants and the various shades in between. It might prove more acceptable to states – less risky and less politically fraught – to accept obligations specifically relating to women, rather than going into broader aspects of the means and methods of warfare.[13] The current international political climate might also be more supportive of this. There is clearly political traction on combatting sexual violence in conflict, evidenced by the British Foreign and Commonwealth Office's hosting the 2014 'Global Summit to End Sexual Violence in Conflict' in London and other high-profile initiatives aimed at this. This traction could be utilised to address some of the broader issues facing women in war and to address some of the gendered problems relating to the principle of distinction.

Achieving treaty change – even a focused protocol for women – is difficult. As such, this is also not a particularly promising route for remedying the problems raised in this book. Given the difficulties described above, most legal development is achieved through 'soft law' measures, with changes made through shifting legal interpretations rather than by altering the word of the law.[14] Of course, as with treaty processes, soft law processes are also influenced by decision-makers, political dispositions and aligning circumstances. In addition, the results of these processes are often controversial and lack consensus and legitimacy, doing little to achieve legal clarity and certainty.

Soft law change was what the ICRC was attempting with its Interpretive Guidance. The Interpretive Guidance aimed to propose new interpretations of the principle of distinction – and in particular, of direct participation – that would make the principle better suitable to regulating modern conflicts. However, there were problems with the ICRC's approach. For one thing, the Interpretive Guidance deals primarily with certain types of modern conflicts, those relating to counter-terrorism and those that Western countries have been involved with in the Middle East. It does this while purporting to present solutions that would be applicable to *all* modern conflicts. The conflicts addressed in the Interpretive Guidance look little like new wars in Africa, and, as this book has argued, many of its provisions make little sense when applied in this context. The Interpretive Guidance therefore perpetuates a problem already seen in previous treaties – it extends its coverage to limited types of new conflicts, yet does not get around the problem of making the law applicable to *all* modern conflict. This is not to say that the Interpretive Guidance falls squarely back on 'old wars' assumptions; in some ways it moves away from these, focusing, for example, on non-state actors as dominant players. Yet, it does not go far enough towards creating a system capable of regulating new wars. Another problem is that the Interpretive Guidance's interpretations seem more suited to dealing with terrorism than classic armed groups. Its proposed means of determining who is directly participating seem better suited to counter-terrorism or 'targeted killings' operations – where a good deal of intelligence is collected about each target, who is carefully studied, tracked and surgically struck – rather than to disorganised groups violently clashing with each other in Africa. In these latter conflicts it is often near impossible to determine the detailed facts the Interpretive Guidance requires to make its distinctions. A further problem is how controversial the Interpretive Guidance's interpretations have been. The cascade of criticism by leading scholars[15] reveals that it did not represent consensus on how IHL should be interpreted. This has detracted from the role it might have played in shifting the field.

The Interpretive Guidance disregards women in much the same way as the existing IHL conventions do.[16] As with the conventions, the Interpretive Guidance's definitions exclude the roles that women typically play from its reach. This can be seen in the narrow, highly military-focused definitions proposed for 'direct participation' and 'continuous combat function'. The Interpretive Guidance is yet another example of gender-neutral regulation that fails to adequately encompass the roles women play. As such, the Interpretive Guidance does not help women any more than the IHL treaties did, rather perpetuating the gendered problems we saw before.

Instead of relying on IHL to assist women in conflict, other options lie in downplaying IHL and leaning more heavily on others areas of law and policy, including IHRL and ICL. Much of the interpretive work on IHL has been done through ICL, with the tribunals debating, interpreting and developing IHL's terms and phrases. Practitioners and scholars in the ICL field place great reliance on the part ICL can play in remedying IHL's shortcomings. However, there are limits to the role ICL can play in remedying IHL and on the extent to which it should be relied on in this regard. ICL operates ex post facto, focusing on crime and punishment. It is not regulatory in its focus. While ICL may help to clarify concepts, it does not provide clear, binding provisions, capable of being used for regulation and able to achieve regulatory certainty. In addition ICL provides judicial interpretation and is therefore subject to fluctuation – problematic if armed actors are to rely on its meanings. In fact, tasking courts briefed with interpreting ICL with defining IHL has the potential to create layers of confusion. ICL's work around gender has been piecemeal and has only taken us so far; while demonstrating the importance of integrating gender considerations, the tribunals have not shown how these considerations can be practically integrated into IHL.

IHRL provides some protection for those who do not fall within protected IHL categories, guaranteeing at least some minimal protections to those who are not eligible for IHL's more rigorous cover. IHRL can therefore be useful in filling protection gaps for those who 'fall through the cracks' of IHL's categorisations. In recent years there has been increased attention given to the interrelationship between IHRL and IHL, particularly in NIACs where the gaps are greater.[17] However, there are also problems with relying too heavily on IHRL.

This body of law is largely geared towards states. While there have been some inroads in this regard and increased recognition of the fact that non-state actors can be bound by human rights norms,[18] IHRL is still not optimally suited to nor designed for the regulation of non-state actors. IHRL also has gendered problems of its own – for example, it excludes men from women's rights instruments and tends to entrench the binary distinction between the sexes.

While both IHRL and ICL do offer some promise for the development of IHL, there are also problems with the way these work together. The three bodies of law – IHL, IHRL and ICL – operate and have developed in silos. At the same time they interact, bleeding into, affecting and shaping each other. This separation and mixing are inconsistent, ad hoc and little understood – even by those working in these respective fields. Legal practitioners tend to specialise in an area, frequently having limited understanding of the others.

The final remaining approach is to rely on policy documents explaining IHL, targeted at practitioners and actors in the field, including humanitarian and military actors. Military manuals are key in the domestic application of IHL. Others policy areas have also made some inroads with regards to gender and can provide models for how IHL policy documents could incorporate gendered understandings. As an example, in the area of refugee law, the 2002 UNHCR guidelines on gender-related persecution explicitly recognise nuances relating to female participation in conflict. Paragraph 33 reads:

> The image of a political refugee as someone who is fleeing persecution for his or her direct involvement in political activity does not always correspond to the reality of the experiences of women in some societies. Women are less likely than their male counterparts to engage in high profile political activity and are more often involved in 'low level' political activities that reflect dominant gender roles. For example, a woman may work in nursing sick rebel soldiers, in the recruitment of sympathisers, or in the preparation and dissemination of leaflets. Women are also frequently attributed with political opinions of their family or male relatives, and subjected to persecution because of the activities of their male relatives.[19]

IHL policy documents could try to incorporate understandings such as these, helping to a limited extent to get around the problems caused by IHL's blindness to gendered nuances.

Implications of this research

Exploring the gendered aspects of the principle of distinction and its application in new wars in Africa is important. It is important for women; for years the experiences of women in conflict have been silenced, lost to a male-dominated narrative. Women make up half of all people in conflict, making findings about women, law and war enormously important, particularly where these can be harnessed towards improving women's conditions.

This work is also important more broadly. The principle of distinction is the law's central mechanism for the protection of civilians in conflict. The practical consequences of a failing mechanism are grim – escalating civilian deaths and a law unable to prevent it. Issues with the principle need to be continuously interrogated and problems addressed. By understanding the ways in which the law treats and fails women, we can better understand the true workings of this law. If the principle of distinction fails such a significant portion of the population, this gives insight as to how it fails others. Conversely, strategies to improve the law will be bettered by seeing that these adequately cover women in conflict; ensuring these are inclusive, relevant to real situations on the ground and capable of regulating 'different' groups. As conflicts change further and more unconventional groups become involved in waging war, this will become increasingly important.

Despite this research focusing on one core principle of IHL, its reach is wider. Many of the challenges to the principle of distinction described above are common across IHL more broadly. The act of honing in on one core principle allows us to focus in greater detail than would have been possible had we been assessing the entire body of IHL. When examined through a gendered lens, the principle of distinction reveals issues that are relevant to the other core principles – proportionality and necessity – and to IHL as a whole. A study of the principle of distinction also reveals problems pertaining to other bodies of laws. One does not only find the civilian/combatant distinction in IHL. It also comes into play in the 'crimes against humanity' regime. If the civilian/combatant divide does not function in IHL, this speaks to how it might function when applied in that context too. ICL is inherently affected by problems in IHL, while at the same time working to rectify these, and as such this study can also provide insights useful for ICL.

This research can serve as an entry point for further potential research. This concluding chapter sets out some elements of the law that would benefit from rethinking. Each of these are important avenues for future research. This book has focused on the gendered aspects of distinction. Further research is also needed on the gendered workings of the other core principles; proportionality and necessity, and on how their gendered aspects play out in new wars and in Africa. Such research might also examine the ways the core principles of IHL operate together in a gendered fashion, demonstrating the consequences for women of the interplay between these.

There is a need for further research about the role that IHL actually plays in new wars and the extent to which belligerents in these conflicts consider and have their actions shaped by IHL. Only by understanding why the law is followed or ignored and what factors affect adherence, can we begin to work towards increased compliance. If the protection of women is one's ultimate goal, addressing the gendered problems can only take you so far – ultimately IHL can only protect if belligerents adhere to it. Work around IHL compliance in new wars is therefore critically required.

This conclusion chapter has described the difficulties in changing the legal status quo. Given the many demonstrable failings with the application of IHL in modern conflicts, it seems likely that at some point there will be a concerted effort to rework this law. This process is unlikely to come from feminist activists or scholars, but rather, from IHL and military practitioners more generally, those who on a daily basis witness the broader failings of this system. When such a process happens, it is hoped that the gendered insights provided in this book might be considered and that this might play a part in illuminating the roles, experiences and needs of women, ensuring that these are incorporated into a new law. It is hoped that the content and analysis in this work may some day help to achieve a more inclusive, more realistic and ultimately more effective body of law regulating armed conflict.

Reality informs law and law informs reality. The principle of distinction and its relationship to women provides an illustration of this at work. However, stronger than the influence of law, is the pull of the gradually changing positions of women in society. As women begin to play more dominant roles in all walks of life, this progression is mirrored in the fighting of wars. If the laws of war do not adapt to reflect this reality, they will be rendered irrelevant. Reassessing the principle of distinction through a gendered lens is therefore a crucial step required to bring IHL in line with the new realities of modern conflict and the realities of life for African women.

Notes

1 Para 4, General Recommendation No. 30 on Women in Conflict Prevention, Conflict and Post-Conflict Situations. CEDAW/C/GC/30, 2013.

2 Schmitt, Michael. '"Direct Participation in Hostilities" and 21st Century Armed Conflict'. In Fischer, Horst (ed.), *Crisis Management and Humanitarian Protection: Festschrift Fur*, 505–529. Berlin: BWV, 2004.

3 See for example, Oosterveld, Valerie. 'Feminist Debates on Civilian Women and International Humanitarian Law'. *Windsor Yearbook of Access to Justice* 27 (2009): 385–402.

4 Bennoune, Karima. 'Do We Need New International Law to Protect Women in Armed Conflict?' *Case Western Reserve Journal of International Law* 38 (2006): 363–391.

5 Lindsey, Charlotte. *Women Facing War*. Geneva: International Committee of the Red Cross, 2001.

6 Krill, Françoise. 'The Protection of Women in International Humanitarian Law'. *International Review of the Red Cross* 249 (1985). www.icrc.org/eng/resources/documents/article/other/57jmfj.htm

7 Oosterveld, supra note 3.

8 MacLaren, Malcolm and Schwendimann, Felix. 'An Exercise in the Development of International Law: The New ICRC Study on Customary International Humanitarian Law'. *German Law Journal* 6, no. 9 (2005): 1217–1242.

9 MacKinnon, Catharine. 'Women's September 11th: Rethinking the International Law of Conflict'. *Harvard International Law Journal* 47 (2006): 1–31.

10 Schmitt, Michael. 'Military Necessity and Humanity in International Humanitarian Law: Preserving the Delicate Balance'. *Virginia Journal of International Law* 50 (2010): 795–839.

11 Article 30 – Application of Successive Treaties Relating to the Same Subject-Matter, United Nations Convention on the Law of Treaties, 23 May 1969, Entry into Force: 27 January 1980.

12 Rondeau, Sophie. 'Participation of Armed Groups in the Development of the Law Applicable to Armed Conflicts'. *International Review of the Red Cross* 93, no. 883 (2011): 649–672. Herr, Stefanie. *Binding Non-State Armed Groups to International Humanitarian Law – Geneva Call and the Ban of Anti-Personnel Mines: Lessons from Sudan*. Peace Research Institute Frankfurt, 2010.

13 Gardam, Judith. 'Women and the Law of Armed Conflict: Why the Silence?' *The International and Comparative Law Quarterly* 46, no. 1 (January 1997): 55–80.

14 Shaffer, Gregory, and Pollack, Mark. 'Hard Versus Soft Law in International Security'. *Boston College Law Review* 52, no. 4 (2011): 1147–1241. Cubie, Dug. 'An Analysis of Soft Law Applicable to Humanitarian Assistance: Relative Normativity in Action?' *Journal of International Humanitarian Legal Studies* 2 (2011): 177–215.

15 Goodman, Ryan and Jinks, Derek. 'The ICRC Interpretive Guidance on the Notion of Direct Participation in Hostilities under International Humanitarian Law: An Introduction to the Forum'. *New York University International Law and Politics* 42 (2010): 637–640.

16 There are only two specific mentions of women in the Interpretive Guidance. These are both found in the footnotes, and refer to concrete illustrative examples that were provided during the expert meetings. The one example, provided during discussions on voluntary human shields, was of a woman 'who shielded two fighters with her billowing robe, allowing them to shoot at their adversary from behind her' (p. 1024). The other, which came up in discussions about transmitting tactical information about an attack as a means of adversely affecting the military operations or capacity of a party to a conflict, was of a 'civilian woman who repeatedly peeked into a building where troops had taken cover in order to indicate their position to the attacking enemy forces' (p. 1018).

17 Sasoli, Marco, and Olson, Laura. 'The Relationship between International Humanitarian and Human Rights Law Where It Matters: Admissible Killing and Internment of Fighters in Non-International Armed Conflicts'. *International Review of the Red Cross* 90, 871 (2008): 599–627. *International Humanitarian Law and International Human Rights Law: Pas de Deux*. The Collected Courses of the Academy of European Law, v. 19/1. Oxford: Oxford University Press, 2011. Matthews, Hannah. 'The Interaction Between International Human Rights Law and International Humanitarian Law: Seeking the Most Effective Protection for Civilians in Non-International Armed Conflicts'. *The International Journal of Human Rights* 17, no. 5 (2013): 633–645.

18 Alston, Philip, Academy of European Law, and New York University. Center for Human Rights and Global Justice. *Non-State Actors and Human Rights*. Collected Courses of the Academy of European Law; XIII/3. Oxford; New York: Oxford University Press, 2005.

19 Article 22, 'Guidelines on International Protection No. 1: Gender-Related Persecution Within the Context of Article 1A(2) of the 1951 Convention And/or Its 1967 Protocol Relating to the Status of Refugees (HCR/GIP/02/01)'. *UNHCR*.

Bibliography

Books and articles

Alston, Philip, Academy of European Law, and New York University. Center for Human Rights and Global Justice. *Non-State Actors and Human Rights*. Collected Courses of the Academy of European Law; XIII/3. Oxford; New York: Oxford University Press, 2005.

Bennoune, Karima. 'Do We Need New International Law to Protect Women in Armed Conflict?' *Case Western Reserve Journal of International Law* 38 (2006): 363–391.

Cubie, Dug. 'An Analysis of Soft Law Applicable to Humanitarian Assistance: Relative Normativity in Action?' *Journal of International Humanitarian Legal Studies* 2 (2011): 177–215.

Dreyfus, Tom. 'The 'Half-Invention' of Gender Identity in International Human Rights Law: From CEDAW to the Yogyakarta Principles'. *Australian Feminist Law Journal* 37, no. 1 (2012): 33–50.

Gardam, Judith. 'Women and the Law of Armed Conflict: Why the Silence?' *The International and Comparative Law Quarterly* 46, no. 1 (January 1997): 55–80.

Goodman, Ryan, and Jinks, Derek. 'The ICRC Interpretive Guidance on the Notion of Direct Participation in Hostilities under International Humanitarian Law: An Introduction to the Forum'. *New York University International Law and Politics* 42 (2010): 637–640.

Herr, Stefanie. *Binding Non-State Armed Groups to International Humanitarian Law – Geneva Call and the Ban of Anti-Personnel Mines: Lessons from Sudan*. Peace Research Institute Frankfurt, 2010.

Krill, Françoise. 'The Protection of Women in International Humanitarian Law'. *International Review of the Red Cross* 249 (1985). www.icrc.org/eng/resources/documents/article/other/57jmfj.htm

Lindsey, Charlotte. *Women Facing War*. Geneva: International Committee of the Red Cross, 2001.

MacLaren, Malcolm, and Schwendimann, Felix. 'An Exercise in the Development of International Law: The New ICRC Study on Customary International Humanitarian Law'. *German Law Journal* 6, no. 9 (2005): 1217–1242.

MacKinnon, Catharine. 'Women's September 11th: Rethinking the International Law of Conflict'. *Harvard International Law Journal* 47 (2006): 1–31.

Matthews, Hannah. 'The Interaction between International Human Rights Law and International Humanitarian Law: Seeking the Most Effective Protection for Civilians in Non-International Armed Conflicts'. *The International Journal of Human Rights* 17, no. 5 (2013): 633–645.

Oosterveld, Valerie. 'Feminist Debates on Civilian Women and International Humanitarian Law'. *Windsor Yearbook of Access to Justice* 27 (2009): 385–402.

Rondeau, Sophie. 'Participation of Armed Groups in the Development of the Law Applicable to Armed Conflicts'. *International Review of the Red Cross* 93, no. 883 (2011): 649–672.

Rosenblum, Darren. 'Unsex CEDAW, or What's Wrong With Women's Rights'. *Pace Law Faculty Publications*, 1 January 2011.

Sasoli, Marco, and Olson, Laura. 'The Relationship between International Humanitarian and Human Rights Law Where It Matters: Admissible Killing and Internment of Fighters in Non-International Armed Conflicts'. *International Review of the Red Cross* 90, 871 (2008): 599–627. *International Humanitarian Law and International Human Rights Law: Pas de Deux*. The Collected Courses of the Academy of European Law, v. 19/1. Oxford: Oxford University Press, 2011.

Schmitt, Michael. ''Direct Participation in Hostilities' and 21st Century Armed Conflict'. In Fischer, Horst (ed.) *Crisis Management and Humanitarian Protection: Festschrift Fur*, 505–529. Berlin: BWV, 2004.

Schmitt, Michael. 'Military Necessity and Humanity in International Humanitarian Law: Preserving the Delicate Balance'. *Virginia Journal of International Law* 50 (2010): 795–839.

Shaffer, Gregory, and Pollack, Mark. 'Hard Versus Soft Law in International Security'. *Boston College Law Review* 52, no. 4 (2011): 1147–1241.

Treaties

Application of Successive Treaties Relating to the Same Subject-Matter, United Nations Convention on the Law of Treaties, 23 May 1969, Entry into Force: 27 January 1980.

Policy documents

General Recommendation No. 30 on Women in Conflict Prevention, Conflict and Post-Conflict Situations. CEDAW/C/GC/30, 2013.

Guidelines on International Protection No. 1: Gender-Related Persecution Within the Context of Article 1A(2) of the 1951 Convention And/or Its 1967 Protocol Relating to the Status of Refugees (HCR/GIP/02/01). *UNHCR*.

Index

For Product Safety Concerns and Information please contact our EU representative GPSR@taylorandfrancis.com
Taylor & Francis Verlag GmbH, Kaufingerstraße 24, 80331 München, Germany

www.ingramcontent.com/pod-product-compliance
Ingram Content Group UK Ltd.
Pitfield, Milton Keynes, MK11 3LW, UK
UKHW011002180926
475701UK00004B/511
* 9 7 8 0 3 6 7 4 8 0 5 1 6 *